CELTS AND THE CLASSICAL WORLD

CELTS
and
the Classical World

H.D. RANKIN

CROOM HELM
London & Sydney

AREOPAGITICA PRESS

© 1987 H.D. Rankin
Croom Helm Ltd, Provident House,
Burrell Row, Beckenham, Kent BR3 1AT

Croom Helm Australia, 44–50 Waterloo Road,
North Ryde, 2113, New South Wales

British Library Cataloguing in Publication Data

Rankin, H.D.
  Celts and the classical world.
  1. Civilization, Celtic
  I. Title
  936.4'004916   CB206

  ISBN 0–7099–2295–7

Published in North America in 1987 by
Timber Press,
9999 S.W. Wilshire,
Portland, OR 97225,
USA

Library of Congress Cataloging-in-Publication Data

Rankin, H.D.
  Celts and the Classical World.

  Bibliography: p.
  Includes index.
  1. Celts. 2. Celts – Public opinion. 3. Public
opinion – Greece. 4. Public opinion – Rome. 5. Celts –
Cross-cultural studies. I. Title.
D70.R36 1987 306'.089916038 87-19141
ISBN 0-918400-06-6

Filmset by Mayhew Typesetting, Bristol, England
Printed and bound in Great Britain by Mackays of Chatham Ltd, Kent

Contents

For Anne and Aidan

1

Origins, Languages and Associations

To observe the Celts through the eyes of the Greeks and Romans
is the first aim of this book. We shall scrutinise their perceptions
of this powerful and numerous group of peoples, who lived to the
north of their Mediterranean world, and who had the inconvenient habit of coming south. In this chapter we shall consider what
may be the earliest Classical references to the Celts. We shall try
to identify and describe as far as we can within the evidence who
and what the Celts were, and what was their origin. Most of our
evidence in this and the following chapters comes from the
literature of Greece and Rome. The Celts themselves had a lasting
prejudice against putting important matters in writing. Not until
we reach the eighth century AD, about three centuries after the
end of the period which mainly concerns us, do we find insular
Celts, not Romanised, but influenced by Rome through Christianity, beginning to set down in writing a literature which was not
predominantly Classical in form and content.

Specifically we have to discuss from Greek and Roman points
of view some late Bronze Age and Iron Age peoples of Europe
who, as far as we may conjecture, spoke dialects of Indo-European
origin which are close to what we would now describe as Celtic,
and who had a distinctive, but not unique mode of Iron Age
culture. Like ourselves, when we talk about the Celtic-descended
societies of Wales, Brittany, Cornwall, Man, Scotland and
Ireland, the Greeks and Romans had a broad and generally
coherent understanding of what they meant by Celtae (Keltoi),
Galli and Galatai, even though they occasionally were mistaken
about the ethnic affiliations of more remote tribes with whom they
had not yet made contact. The word 'Celt' as an ethnic attribute
was first used by Greeks to refer to people living to the north of

the Greek colony of Massalia (Marseilles) in Southern France. The meaning of the name is obscure. Possible roots are kel 'exalt' or kel 'strike', as in Latin *percello*. Another suggestion is k^wel 'turn', Latin *incola* 'settler'. There are other suggestions. 'Galli' was the name the Romans gave to the tumult of warriors who wrecked their city in 390 BC; it may be connected with other IE words for 'stranger' or 'enemy' such as Latin *hostis*, Gothic *gasts* (Stokes 1894: 108). The Romans habitually used 'Galli' for all peoples of Celtic language and culture, and it is not known whether it was originally the name of an individual tribe, or a description given by a wandering tribe or tribes to themselves (Whatmough 1970: 15). The invaders of Greece and Asia Minor in the third century BC were known to the Greeks as 'Galatai', which may perhaps have a parallel in Old Irish *galdae* 'warlike' and *galgart* a 'champion'. Julius Caesar divides his Gaul into three ethnic regions, by no means culturally or linguistically identical: Celtae, Aquitani, and Belgae (*BG* I.1), and he mentions many tribal names within these sections which have their individual meanings. Classical writers did not describe the inhabitants of Ireland and Britain as Celts. Nor did the Anglo-Normans or English in later centuries. The name was first used as an embracing ethnic and cultural term in the sixteenth century AD by George Buchanan, and taken up in the seventeenth century AD by Edward Lhuyd (T.G.E. Powell 1958: 15). We shall use Celt as a general term, but Gaul, Galli, Galatai, Goidelic, Brythonic, Britanni, Picti (Cruithni), Érainn and other specific names will occur from time to time.

Our earliest Greek literary source which mentions Celts is embedded in the text of a late imperial Latin author. Rufus Festus Avienus was proconsul of Africa in 366 AD. He claimed descent from Musonius Rufus, the distinguished and eccentric Stoic philosopher exiled by Nero in 65 AD. Like his famous antecedent, he came from Volsinii in Etruria. His burial inscription proclaims him a successful man, happy in his career, wife and children; proud of his poems, and a worshipper of the Etruscan goddess, Nortia, who not inappropriately was concerned with fortune.

The poem which interests us is his *Ora Maritima*, a description of the shores of the known world. The first part of this incompletely extant work describes the Atlantic coastline and the coast of the Mediterranean from the Pillars of Hercules to Massalia (Latin: Massilia).

Avienus dedicated his poem to Probus, a consul who may have

2

held office in 406 AD. The work is written in iambic verse, and it shows self-conscious, but no doubt, sincere learning. Avienus was a man of education and ability, and we should not be too dismayed by his habit of dropping into his text the names both of famous and of obscure authorities. Amongst others, he mentions Hecataeus, Himilco the Carthaginian, Hellanicus, Scylax of Caryanda, Herodotus, Thucydides, Sallust; also Damastes, Bacorus of Rhodes, and Euctemon of Attica. We cannot tell how deeply read he was in all of these authors. Some of the less distinguished must by this time have been hard to obtain in the original, but he claims (41) to have consulted a great number of writers and to communicate information that has not been available at large. He was a competent writer of verse, but we should be rash to call him a talented poet, even within the restrictions of the didactic genre.

We shall not be incautious, I suggest, if we accept that Avienus is the carrier of some very early information about the Celts in the Classical world. I say this not so much in spite of his pompous and pawky style, as because of it: in concentrating on his own erudite image of himself and grappling with the technical problems of versification, he probably left himself less time for the pure distortion of facts, though we may possibly have to fear some parallax effect inherited from the translators who in some instances came between the Greek originals and his staid iambics.

Avienus' description in the second part of his poem of the coastal voyage from the neighbourhood of Tartessus (probably near Cadiz) to Massalia, makes no mention of the Massaliote settlement of Emporiai (Ampurias). From the evidence of pottery which has been found on its site, Emporiai was in being as early as the middle of the sixth century BC (Tierney 1960: 193–4). It can be argued that if the town had already been founded at the time of the early sailing instructions on which Avienus' source is based, it would have been mentioned, and the information would have been conveyed to us by Avienus. The omission, however, may be merely apparent. John Hind has suggested (1972) that Emporiai, which means 'markets', was the popular name for the place referred to as Pyrene by Avienus, and that this could be the 'Portus Pyrenaei' mentioned by Livy (38.8). However this particular matter stands, it is clear that Avienus had access to a range of ancient materials which themselves embodied information from a very early date.

The seafaring inhabitants of Phocaea in Ionia investigated the

Western Mediterranean and Iberian littorals long before they established what was to become the great city of Massalia in 600 BC. Many of their trading stations and settlements on the shore of the Iberian peninsula were eliminated after their excessively expensive victory over the Carthaginians in the sea battle at Alalia in 540 BC. Since Avienus refers to a number of these outposts, it is not unlikely that his earliest source antedates that battle (Savory 1968: 239). Somewhat later accretions adhere to this early account. He also used information from the *Periplus of the Northern Sea* by Himilco, the Carthaginian admiral who explored the waters of Northern Europe. This would represent current knowledge at the end of the sixth century BC.

Avienus seems almost to be looking down on a tidal model of the region:

80　The circle of the outspread earth lies before us
　　　　panoramic;
　　and in turn the waters flow around this circle;
　　but where a deep salt bay projects itself
　　into the land just as the waters of our own
　　　　[Mediterranean]
　　sea stretch for a long distance [into the land mass],
　　this is the Atlantic Gulf.
85　Here is the town of Gaddir, earlier known as
　　　　Tartessus;
　　here are the pillars of enduring Hercules: Abyla and
　　　　Calpe:
　　Calpe is on the left (as you sail into the straits from
　　　　the Atlantic);
　　Abyla is next to Libya (on the African side of the
　　　　straits).
　　They are racked by the North wind, but still
　　　　remain in place.

The layout is being contemplated from outside the straits, from the Atlantic side. The poet identifies Gaddir with Tartessus (Biblical Tarshish). However, this city's site has never been identified. It is said to have been powerful and rich, but its people remain unknown.

90　And here the peak of an eminent ridge rises up;
　　an earlier age called it Oestrymnis:

a high bulk of lofty (pediment) slopes down steeply
to the warm South wind. Underneath the peak of
  this high eminence
the gulf Oestrymnicus yawns on the inhabitants.
In this arise the islands, the Oestrymnides,
placed at their ease, rich in the mining of tin and
  lead.
A vigorous tribe lives here, proud-spirited,
  energetic, skilful.
On all the ridges trade is carried on:
the sea froths far and wide with their famous ships,
and they cut through the swell of the beast-haunted
  ocean.
104 These people do not build their boats with pine
    wood —

nor, says Avienus redundantly, do they use any other kind of
wood; instead they do something quite astonishing: they make
their ships out of skins joined together:

and run the vast salt sea on leather hides.

The reference is to curraghs, still used in this century by the
people of the Aran Islands. Pliny mentions the use of these by the
British (*NH* 7.56). According to Strabo (3.155), the Lusitani of
Spain also had them. The places which are mentioned here may
have been thought to be in the Bay of Biscay (the Oestrymnic
gulf?). The Oestrymnides may be the Cassiterides, possibly
Cornwall, the peninsular status of which was not necessarily
understood by the earliest writers.

From line 130 onwards, Avienus moves towards the only
explicit reference to the Celts in the poem:

If anybody has the courage to urge his boat
into the waves away from the Oestrymnides
under the pole of Lycaon (in the Northern sky)
where the air is freezing, he comes to the Ligurian
  land, deserted
by its people: for it has been emptied by the power
  of the Celts
a long time since in many battles. The Ligurians,
  displaced, as fate often

does to people, have come to these regions. Here
     they hold on in rough country
with frequent thickets and harsh cliffs, where
     mountains threaten the sky.
For a long time they lived a timid life in narrow
     confines,
far from the sea; for they were frightened of the sea
because of their previous danger.
Afterwards, when safety renewed their confidence,
     quiet peace persuaded them —

and we are told by the poet that they moved down to Ophiussa, probably in northern Spain, and then to the Mediterranean shores and Sardinia.

We seem to have here a shadowy ancient account of the arrival in Spain of a pre-Celtic people who came into the peninsula from the North. This may be a dim reflection of a population that spoke an IE dialect which was not Celtic. In the conglomerate of Iberian linguistic remains, traces of this kind of dialect have been found. It is suggested that they came by ship, and that the Celts who expelled them also used ships. Perhaps the northern zone from which they were displaced was in the area of Jutland where the Cimbri lived in later historical times. The old compiler and source whom Avienus is using seems to be explaining the presence of Ligurians in the neighbourhood of Massalia together with the presence of Celts in the region to the north of them, as well as the presence of 'Ligurians' in Spain.

Avienus tells us that from the Oestrymnides it is two days' sailing to

107 the Sacred Island — the ancient authorities call it
       this —
     rich in its land it lies amid the waves,
     and widely the race of Hiberni inhabit it.
     On the other hand is situated the island of the
       Albions nearby.

Since Britain and Ireland are designated as islands, this part of the story may be based on an ancient *Periplus* or 'Circumnavigation'. We need not regard this item as being of significantly high antiquity. The same can be said of Avienus' use of the Greek interpretation of the name for Ireland as 'sacred island'. The name 'Ierne' seemed to the Greeks to be connected with their word for 'sacred', *hieros*. He refers to the larger island as 'Albion' rather than using any name involving /Brett/ or /Prett/, but there is very little to be deduced from this, or from the fact that neither Ierne nor Albion seem to be words of Celtic origin.

Avienus says (111ff) that Tartessus engaged in trade with the region of the Oestrymnides. Carthaginian merchants also came to it. In this connection he mentions Himilco, who from his own experience said that the journey took four months. There follows a description of a sea heavy with weed, which must be the Sargasso Sea.

In the lower Guadalquivir valley there are traces of what could be a Celtic style of living combined with influences from the Eastern Mediterranean. This culture, which has been dated to the sixth century BC, may be a blend of Celtic culture with that of Tartessus. This has been confirmed by the investigation of tumuli in the district which could have been the graves of Celtic chiefs (Arribas 1981: 46).

Avienus does not mention Celts as inhabitants of Spain. One interpretation of his words might allow us to suppose that his source regarded them as resident in Southern France. We do not know how far north he intends us to place the land under the constellation of Lycaon. He mentions the Saefi and the Cempses: they live near the Ligurians. They are mentioned once in this poem, and nowhere else. We need not believe that they are Celts pushing against Ligurians. Nor are the Cynetes, who also occur in other authors, proven Celts; though we note that they are said to be neighbours of Tartessus. Perhaps we should resist the temptation to infer that Avienus' sources are telling us about a time when Ligurians were settled on the Mediterranean coasts of France and Spain; when Celts were to the north of Ligurians in France, but not yet an identifiable presence in Spain. This would be a time earlier than the sixth century BC. The luxurious contents of the burial at Vix in the Côte d'Or proves the existence in the sixth century BC of a flourishing community engaged in trade with the Greek world, no doubt through Massalia. Probably it was a Celtic community, and no mere weed-like growth, but the product of lengthy settlement. We cannot exclude the possibility that the supposed Celtic neighbours of Tartessus represent a comparable development. They were not near enough to a major Greek settlement to attract literary attention.

Avienus' information has an atmosphere of the archaic, and I do not think that the impression is entirely false. We discern darkly ancient movements of tribes, supported rather than disproved by later and modern evidence. It is possible that some of the sources of Avienus may have carried information older than anything we have in other writers. If this should be the case, then the next most ancient author to whom we have access on this topic is the geographer Hecataeus of Miletus, who was active at the end of the sixth century BC. In one of his fragments, he refers to Narbo as a Celtic city and trade centre (*FGH* 54); he says that Massalia (*FGH* 55) is a city in Ligurian territory near Celtic territory. He is quoted by Strabo as having said this in his work on *Europe*. The distinction he makes between Ligurian and Celtic areas probably shows that he is aware of cultural and linguistic differences between them. Of known ancient geographers, Hecataeus seems to be the first to lay stress upon the influence of physical environment on biological and cultural development.

In his *Europe*, he also refers to 'Nyrax, a Celtic city' (*FGH* 56). There is no certainty about the location of this city: one candidate has been Noreia in a generally accepted heartland of the early Celtic tribes in Austria. This area is the old habitation of the Bronze Age Urnfield (from the thirteenth to the seventh centuries BC) and Bronze/Iron Hallstatt (from the eighth century BC) cultures, whose members were, if the widely held view is correct, speakers of a kind of Celtic. Certainly there are many placenames of almost certain Celtic derivation in these areas of habitation.

Herodotus of Halicarnassus (5th century BC) is traditionally the father of History, but essentially he was an epic poet in prose, as his uncle Panyassis was in verse. Nevertheless he was a highly intelligent gatherer and assimilator of information, and we should pay attention to what he says about the Celts in the second book of his *Historiai* or 'Researches'.

In a passage which compares the Nile with the Danube, he says that the Danube rises amongst the Celts and the city of Pyrene and flows through Europe, splitting it in the middle. The Celts, he says, live outside the pillars of Heracles, and have common boundaries with the Cynesioi who live to the West of all the other inhabitants of Europe (2.33).

We can elicit from these remarks that in Herodotus' time the Celts were settled in Iberia and lived close to the Cynetoi (or Cynetes). Herodotus has no notion of the source of the Danube, but he is aware that it rises in Celtic territory, and that much we can regard as being based on some reliable and well-informed source. He seems to have blended two streams of information: one which tells of Celts living near the upper reaches of the Danube; the other referring to the presence of Celts in Spain, and their penetration into its South-West. Separately these stories are credible enough. The fact that there were Celtic peoples in Spain next to the Cynesioi and also in Central Europe made it seem reasonable enough to him, or his informants, that the Danube rose far in the West in the Celtic lands of the Iberian peninsula.

Herodotus has nothing to say about the cultural characteristics or language of the Celts. Are we in a significantly more favourable position than he was, when we talk about Celts at this early stage of their infringement of the European consciousness? Though we have no linguistic evidence, we usually suppose that we are talking about groups of IE speakers who achieved a recognisable cultural consistency in archaeological terms in the areas associated with the Urnfield Bronze Age cemeteries and the Hallstatt Iron Age culture in western Central Europe. These cultures are represented in many parts of Europe. Both occur in the Iberian peninsula as well as in the Danube valley.

Placenames of apparent Celtic derivation occur in the Northern Alpine areas of these archaeological provinces. This may suggest that in this part of Europe the Celtic peoples had their original home, in the sense that it may have been the region in which they developed their individual character as distinct from other presumable IE groups. Placenames cannot be the basis for certainty in this matter. There are other areas of Urnfield and Hallstatt culture and even of familiarly 'Celtic' La Tène type of culture (5th century BC onwards) which are not considered to be in fact of Celtic habitation. It is not easy to assume the monolingual uniformity of any inhabited area in ancient times. Even if we accept the testimony of placenames, it can only point to the relative predominance of speakers of the dialect in question at a time hardly to be defined within a couple of centuries. In modern Ireland and Scotland, Celtic placenames are certainly prominent. This would not help a future archaeologist to discern that he was not dealing with a uniform linguistic province, but with one in which the language which had provided the placenames had become marginal and remote. At the same time he would have grasped, without being aware, that the culture which still spoke the language and that which did not still had many features in common. However, it is reasonable to accept that in the fourth and third centuries BC the Celtic peoples dominated northern and central Europe from the Black Sea to Spain (Momigliano 1975: 51). This is the message of the Greek and Roman authors, who, together with the archaeologists of the present time, are convincing on this point.

The Celts, like other IE societies, had social strata: kings, warrior-aristocrats and at least two grades of clienthood, one more respectable than the other (Strabo 4.4.24 (Pos.), Caesar *BG* 6.13). Insular literature of later centuries gives us a picture of a relatively complex social system composed not only of noble warriors and druids, but of various groups devoted to particular skills and professions, or agricultural and service functions. The learned classes consisted of druids and various grades of poets. There is archaeological evidence for the emergence in the Halstatt culture of a social pattern which differed from that of the Urnfield in constructing, undoubtedly for a minority, elaborate and richly furnished tombs. The Hallstatt grave at Vix (6th century BC), the burial of a young woman, illustrates this by its store of magnificent Greek bronze and ceramic ware, its interred four-wheeled chariot, and other valuable articles (Piggott 1983: 138ff). The construction of hill-forts at this period may also indicate the emergence of a class within society which had conspicuous power and prestige. We need not assume that the holders of these forts or the deceased in these luxurious graves represent an intrusive wave of foreign heroes alien to the greater part of the local population. At the same time we must avoid any assumption of cultural or racial homogeneity in the populations we are considering. The technology of ancient killing did not develop to the point where it could easily eliminate whole populations.

The occurrence of chariots in elaborate burials may be evidence that they were princely status symbols rather than vehicles actively useful in Western European terrain (Neustupny and Neustupny 1961: 143). The chariots found in burials of the Iron Age often were elegant and delicate vehicles, consisting of a multitude of carefully wrought components. They must have been extremely expensive to make. There is evidence that chariots were buried with their owners as early as the third millennium BC (Piggott ibid.). As an instrument of war they fell out of general use in the European Iron Age. This had more to do with changes in the science of war than their unsuitability in the contemporary European landscape. The chariot continued to be used in war by the British in their wars with the Romans, when its use on the continent was merely an ancient memory. The Galatians employed the chariot to intimidate and soften the resistance of opposing armies in Asia. In spite of frequent references to chariots in the Irish sagas, there is no tangible evidence that the chariot was ever used as a war-machine in Ireland. The placename 'Carpat' (OIr., 'chariot') may arouse speculation. Wheeled vehicles were no doubt used for civil purposes in Ireland, as they were in the rest of the European Iron Age province.

Like the Greeks and Romans, the Continental Celts of histor-ical times had substantially moved away from kingly rule, though they preserved the name of king in designating their great over-lords in war, such as Dumno*rix* ('world-king') and Vercingeto*rix* ('great king of those who march to attack': cf. Ir. *cingim*: D.E. Evans 1967: 177–8, 279). Some of these names may have been declarative titles assumed for the purposes of leadership like the modern 'Stalin'. Kings survived in Ireland well into the medieval period. The title *rí* designated local kings of districts rather than the rulers of agglomerations of tribes. The *rí* retained many of the attributes of the IE sacral ruler (Wagner 1971, MacCana 1979).

It is only when we have Greek and Latin literary evidence that we find our first definitive indications of those cultural themes which are characteristic of the Celts, namely: the druidic priesthood, head-hunting, the cult of the severed head, human sacrifice, distinctive laws of hospitality, a heroic warrior class, and orders of bards and poets.

Some of these are by no means uniquely characteristic of the Celts, and not all of them can be proved to coexist in any given Celtic tribe. The Celtic custom of sacrificing prisoners to the gods was noted by Hieronymus of Cardia in the third century BC; Phylarchus, another writer of the same century, mentions their banqueting customs, the competitive and perilous nature of which is also described by Poseidonius, and may be recaptured graphic-ally in the much later Irish stories of the *Fled Bricrend* (*Bricriu's feast*) and *Scél Muice Meic Dathó* (*The story of Mac Datho's pig*). Aristotle's school, and just possibly the philosopher himself, had some awareness of druids. Polybius certainly knew about them. He knew also of their intense interest in the dead, whom they would praise after death in battle as much as the victorious living. The praise of dead heroes has been a lasting strain in Celtic poetry and eloquence. Even in this century we have Padraig Pearse's memorable utterance over the grave of O'Donovan Rossa, 'the fools, the fools, they have left us our glorious dead' (Dudley Edwards 1977: 236).

In the sixth century BC the Greeks of Massalia could distinguish Celts from Ligures, another IE-speaking people, who were the native residents they had met when they first arrived. The Romans also correctly identified the people whom they called Galli, who attacked their city in 390 BC: the individual tribes were known by name, and the tribal names were Celtic. The Romans were to have ample opportunity of improving their acquaintance with them: having wrecked Etruscan power, they stayed in Northern Italy, parts of which became so Celtic or Gallic in character that the region became known as Cisalpine Gaul. They only ceased to be an acute menace to Italy after their defeat in the battle of Telamon in 225 BC. In 192 BC, the tribes of Northern Italy finally submitted to Rome, but the Celtic menace was never forgotten.

By the fifth century BC Celts had settled in substantial numbers in the Eastern Alpine zone. Some of them made moves towards the East in the fourth and third centuries BC. These migrations threatened Greece, damaged Thrace, and led to large settlements of Celts in Asia Minor. Their travels eventually took them as far as the south of Russia, and put them in a position to threaten the old Greek colony of Olbia (Borysthenes) in the Crimea. This outflow of population and energy did not necessarily involve huge hostings of warriors in every area. The numbers must in some cases have been modest, though formidable in the field at the first onset. The collapse of Celtic domination in the whole region from the North Sea to the Pontus in the centuries following this expansion is partly due to their relative fewness. The expansion of the third century BC had become almost a dispersal in the second century BC. Migration carried in it the seeds of the decline of Celtic power. But the vast army which accumulated from a succession of war-parties to menace Greece in the third century BC can hardly have seemed to exhibit any such encouraging symptoms to Greece's inhabitants as they awaited invasion.

It is difficult to determine when Celtic-speaking people arrived in Britain. They were dominant in the island at the time of Caesar's invasion in 55–54 BC. Pytheas of Massilia (4th century BC) calls the country *Brettanike*, a Celtic name, which itself suggests that the Celts were long established there in his time. If we base our view on the incidence of La Tène artefacts, we should be sure that Celtic people were in Britain at least in the third century BC. That an incursion of people of Hallstatt 'C' culture took place in the seventh century BC bringing Iron Age techniques with them (and possibly Celtic speech) now seems less likely than it used to be, for there is evidence of a gradual blend and overlap between Urnfield and HaC cultural forms in Britain, rather than a sudden change resulting from an invasion (Champion 1975). We have noted that Celtic placenames are found in areas associated with Urnfield culture both in Central Europe and Spain. Although the argument from placenames should be deployed with some caution and bearing in mind that not all Urnfield remains can securely be connected with Celtic habitation, the British evidence might suggest that Celtic people, in the sense of speakers of Celtic, were in residence even before Hallstatt characteristics began to be prominent in the British style of living. There may also have been an earlier level of IE-speaking people in Britain before the Celts.

In Ireland the La Tène Iron Age continued unbroken by Roman interference, though modified by Christianity and its carrier-waves of Greco-Roman classicism. It survived until the Middle Ages, and arguably to the threshold of the modern period. We have the testimony of a native literature which is of the utmost interest, not only artistically, but for the historical light it can throw upon an essentially protohistoric way of life, which Roman influence had elsewhere in the Celtic world transformed into a partial imitation of Classical civilisation. La Tène styles and artistic themes may give us an indication of Celtic presence in third century BC Ireland. As in the case of Britain, we should be rash to suppose that this attested with certainty the earliest time of Celtic habitation. It may be that Celtic people were living in the country at a much earlier date. Irish, that is, Goidelic (Gaelic), tradition, records several invasions of Ireland in the remote past by tribes, all of whom were regarded as Celtic — though we cannot discount the likelihood that they were assimilated to the Celtic tradition by the historians in the course of centuries. The list contains the Cruithni (Priteni) or Picts; the Fir Bolg who were also called Érainn (Iverni); the Lagin, together with the Domnainn and the Gálioin, whose efficiency provoked Gaelic jealousy in the saga; then the Goidels or Gaels themselves, who were supposed to be the last of the immigrants. Although T.F. O'Rahilly's strong emphasis (1946) on the Pretannic (Brythonic, Gaulish) p-Celtic character of the earlier invasions has been challenged, there are no overwhelming arguments against the view that some portions of the ancient Irish population spoke this species of Celtic, nor can it be proved that some such speakers were not in residence when the Goidels arrived, either from Gaul or Spain — or indeed Britain, bringing their q-Celtic form of speech. Nor can it be disproved that the first century BC was the probable time of their arrival, though equally, a somewhat earlier date for the beginning of their immigration could be argued.

These later arrivals spoke a language which may be regarded as more archaic than the p-Celtic and other IE and non-IE languages which they probably found in places in Ireland. There is enough evidence for q-Celtic in Spain to urge the view that the Irish Goidels originated in that country. This idea certainly would be in agreement with the myth of the sons of Míl. Gaul also has its claims: not only in some of its tribal names, but in the element of q-Celtic which is to be seen in the Coligny Calendar's inscription. This may suggest religious archaism involving the use of an older form of speech. It could also represent local speech habits. The tradition of four invasions of Ireland in *LGE* (*Lebor Gabála Érenn*) and elsewhere supports the view that Celtic people were resident in Ireland for several centuries before the Roman conquest of Gaul. That the three earlier layers were substantially Pretannic or Gaulish in speech cannot be disproved, though we may note O'Rahilly's point that Ptolemy's (1st century AD) account of Ireland, in which several placenames are certainly p-Celtic, is based on earlier sources, such as Marinus (1st century BC) or Pytheas (4th century BC), who wrote centuries before Ptolemy's time (1946: 41ff).

Let us now consider the advance of Celtic migrations in the East. The large number of Macedonian coins found in Celtic sites along the Danube may be taken to indicate that the relationship between the Macedon of Philip II and these tribes involved something more than brisk commerce (Hubert 1934: 35). The Macedonian king may have found it expedient to bribe them in order to facilitate his campaign against the Illyrians: it would be helpful if they agreed either to harrass the Illyrians or, at least, not to help them against Philip. When Alexander the Great encountered Celtic ambassadors in his expedition across the Danube in 335 BC (Diod. 17.113.2; Arrian *Anab.* 7.15.4) he arranged with them that they should keep the Illyrians in play during his war against the Thracians. These Celts are supposed to have been in residence along the shores of the Ionic Gulf, and they may have been an offshoot of the Celtic influx into Italy.

The death of Lysimachus, one of Alexander's powerful

successors, enabled the Celts to penetrate Greece. With this king of Thrace and part of the north of Asia Minor removed from their path, they could foresee lucrative depredations in the peninsula of Greece (see Chapter 5). They reached Delphi in 278 BC. Their defeat by combined Greek forces in the neighbourhood of Thermopylae brought their ambitions in this area to an end, and as they withdrew, they settled in the Balkans, where their presence is attested not only by LT artefacts, but in placenames, such as Singidunum, the Romanised version of the Celtic name of what was to become Belgrade. Some settled in south-eastern Thrace, where Tylis became their capital. In 278 BC a combined expedition of three tribes entered Asia Minor, where they ultimately founded the kingdom of Galatia (see Chapter 9), which was to retain its Celtic character for centuries. These tribes, the Tectosages, Tolistobogii and Trocmi (or Trocmes), seem to have had an important cult centre in Drunemeton, a 'nemed' sanctuary. The Tectosages settled in a place which later became Ancyra (Ankara).

The aims of the Celts were far-reaching and imaginative rather than clearly defined. From Asia Minor, a group of them took service in the army of Antigonus Gonatas, who lent several thousand of these mercenaries to Ptolemy Philadelphus to enable him to prosecute an internal war against his brother (Hubert 1934: 51). They helped him to win, and then revolted. Even the disastrous consequences of their attack on Delphi, which was the high point of their military achievement in Greece, did not blunt their capacity for enterprising hope. Pausanias (1.7.2) says that they contemplated a great attack on Egypt. Probably in the first instance they wanted to acquire plunder from its legendary resources of wealth, rather than to settle. In their great migrations, settlement was a secondary, but in the event, an important objective. Hubert compares them with the Franks and Mongols of later times (ibid. 52). There is evidence of Celtic presence in Upper Egypt in 185 BC: an inscription in Greek tells joyfully how several mercenaries (some with Greek names) caught a fox, presumably in a period of rest and recreation. Probably it was a jackal, but there is no doubt from the inscription that its captors were Celts.

The route that the Celts followed along the Danube is marked by the remains of destroyed Hallstatt sites. Fortified townships (*oppida*) along the south bank of the Danube have distinctly Celtic names in antiquity: Vindobona, Carnuntum, Brigetio and

Arrabona are clear examples. These *oppida* may be taken to be a line of defence against northern tribes here and elsewhere in Europe where they occur.

The part of Central Europe which is now Czechoslovakia has traces of LT culture, which more than likely was Celtic (Neustupny and Neustupny 1961: 146). In the *oppida* of Slovakia, the craft of the smith was well developed, and this might suggest that it was closely connected with the needs of a warrior class of the kind we find evidenced in Celtic societies elsewhere. Torques are found imprinted on Celtic coinage: there are coins imitating those of Philip II which may have been the currency of the Boii. Distinctly Celtic motives, such as the boar, appear on coinage of the second century BC. Names, Celtic beyond reasonable doubt, occur on coins of this region — for example the names of leaders such as Nonnos and Biatec constitute the earliest written inscriptions of the area (Neustupny and Neustupny 1961: 152).

Celts seem first to have appeared in Hungary in the LT period (Szabo 1971: 10). They probably arrived in Pannonia about the same time as their kinsmen invaded Italy in the first decade of the fourth century BC. We shall mention later the story of Ambigatus, king of the Bituriges in Gaul, who sent his nephews Bellovesus and Segovesus to conquer Italy and the Hercynian Forest: it also has some relevance here. We know that in the eastern part of Hungary there were speakers of an Iranic dialect who were of Cimmerian descent and had become assimilated to the Scythians who had defeated them and settled in their territory. These were the Sigynnae (Herodotus 5.9). Their name may have the meaning 'merchant' in an IE dialect spoken in Pannonia before the arrival of the Celts.

The region which in modern times became Poland was also touched by Celtic migration. These Celts came from Bohemia (which bears the name of the Boii) through the Ktodzko valley and impinged on an already established Lusatian/Hallstatt culture. They seem to have come as a full community, with farmers and craftsmen as well as warriors. Celtic burials of the type which consisted of a flat grave, *oppida* and coin hordes point to a palpable Celtic presence in Silesia in the second century BC (Jazdzewski 1965: 137). We need not suppose that Celts were ever numerically predominant in the areas of Poland where traces of their occupation have been found.

In the region where the Danube flows into the Pontus, a Thracian or Getic culture flourished in the third century BC with

typical LT material and artistic standards (Berciu 1967: 150).
Traces of Celtic presence begin to be seen after 300 BC, representing the great efflux of Celts into the Balkans and Greece. The
Thracian-Getic people had an efficient technology and a political
system capable of appointing a war-leader, and consequently were
not easily invaded or dominated by the Celts (Berciu 1967: 147–
50). In the same part of Eastern Europe, however, the city of
Tomis (Costanza), which was originally colonised from Miletus,
came under Celtic occupation in the third and second centuries
BC. There is evidence of a Celtic component in its population for
some time. Its Hellenistic cemetery has produced several brooches
of LT B2 or LT C style; these were found in company with
contemporary Greek pottery. Callatis, a Dorian foundation dating
from the sixth century BC, also shows evidence of Celts in
residence or passing through towards the south-west of Russia
where they co-operated with the Scythians in menacing Olbia.

In noting Olbia's problem, we may point out that there is
nothing to suggest that the Tauri, in spite of their name and their
legendary predilection for human sacrifice to a sinister version of
Artemis, were Celtic. These inhabitants of the Crimea, in the
terms of the myth which Euripides has made so famous in his
Iphigeneia in Tauris, were simply following old and respectable IE
traditions, as were the Celts themselves. The old trading city of
Olbia, also called Borysthenes, was originally founded by Miletus.
In this wave of Celtic expansion it was oppressed by Skiroi and
Galatai. The so-called 'Protogenes' inscription of Olbia, which
mentions Galatai, probably belongs to a period considerably later
than the fourth century BC to which it has been attributed; it may
be of early second century BC (Minns 1913: 125).

Celtic tribes remained a strong and disruptive influence in this
eastern zone for generations, but their local enemies never disappeared, and lived on to seize their opportunity of recovery and
revenge. In 88 BC such an occasion arose when the Celtic Scordisci were defeated by a Roman army which was under the
command of a member of the Scipio family, and the Pannones
were able to get back their lost lands. In turn, the Dacians, led by
their king Bouribistes, defeated the Scordisci, Boii, and Taurisci
in 60 BC. Vast tracts of land previously occupied by Boii were
desolated and formed what Strabo called the Boian desert. Finally,
in 35 BC, Octavian, seeking a defensible boundary for the Roman
imperium, pushed into Illyricum and crushed the Pannones. He
destroyed their inter-tribal organisation but shrewdly left the

residual Celtic area intact and in alliance with Rome as an insurance against future awkwardness on the part of the Pannones. Celts continued to live in this country and may be identified by personal names even in the third century AD, though as time passed they became increasingly assimilated with other inhabitants. On the other bank of the Danube, the vacuum created by Octavian's campaign was filled by Iranian-speaking peoples, the Jasygs, a splinter conglomerate of Scythians and Dacians, together with the Dacians proper, who took over lands which the Celts and Pannones could no longer hold. The surviving Celts in these districts began to live after the Dacian style and even to take Dacian names. Old, complex, ceremonial names, such as Dumnorix, 'world-king', which imply concentrations of power between allied tribes, no longer occur in the inscriptions of this Eastern area. Argument from silence though it may be, this may be taken to indicate that Celtic capacity to coordinate military power on a large scale had been broken (Szabo 1971: 26).

We have mentioned the long frontier of Celtic forts and *oppida* stretching across Europe which separated the Celts from another group of predominantly IE peoples, the Germans, who are identified by Poseidonius in the thirteenth book of his *Histories* (Ath. 153e). He seems to have located them beyond the Rhine and towards the east, and to have remarked that in physical type, way of life and customs, they were very similar to Celts, exceeding them somewhat in ferocity, size and fairness of head (Str. 7.1.2). This would seem to be a reasonable estimate of the ancient Germans, who in many places blended with the Celts: their language shows notable borrowings from Celtic, and their social organisation present similarities to that of the Celts and other IE-speaking nations such as Scythians, Thracians, and Dacians. The Germans were to become in time the most formidable enemies ever faced by Rome. In the early days of their development, towards the end of the second millennium BC, they are estimated to have occupied extensive tracts of the western Baltic, Jutland and parts of Sweden. A few centuries later they seem to have reached the Harz mountains and the Teutoburger Wald (Anderson 1938: xi) the probable scene of a severe Roman defeat at their hands in 9 AD, when they destroyed the three legions of Quinctilius Varus. By the end of the sixth century BC, the Germans had expanded into Belgium and the southern part of Holland. They occupied both banks of the lower Rhine, and they reached as far south as the Ardennes.

Across Europe the long line of Celtic hill-forts may be said to have restrained German expansion for centuries, though, as we have said, there was considerable intermingling. Certain tribes of Gaul, such as the Aedui, boasted Germanic descent. The Belgae also were a mixture of German and Celt. There is no reason to suppose that it was specifically German pressure that detonated the great Celtic invasions of Italy and Bohemia at the end of the fifth century BC. There is no evidence that the line of Celtic fortifications did not hold good at that time. On the other hand, Celtic pressure seems to have caused Eastern Germanic tribes, such as the Bastarnae, to move eastwards. These appear as raiders and mercenaries in the Danube valley at the end of the third century BC. They seem to have made contact with the Bodini (Hdt. 4.21), whose name is connected with the Slavonic word for 'water': 'boda' (Minns 1913: 103). The Bodini may have been a Slavic tribe. That Slavs made the acquaintance of Celtic peoples through the medium of German may be suggested by the name they gave them in Old Slavonic, which was Vlachs, and this seems to correspond with Gothic Walkhoz (cf. Welsh, Volcae etc.). The Slavs continued to call Celtic and Latin speakers 'Vlachs'.

The widely travelled and powerful Boii were prominent in the Celtic expansion of the fourth and third centuries BC. Many places bear their name: Bononia in Moesia and in Italy exemplify the range of their spread through Europe. To the south of their sphere of influence the Scordisci were dominant, and to the west, the Taurisci. They were a composite tribe of many scattered sections whose relationships are not precisely known. It was the Boii of the Hercynian Forest who repelled the Cimbri in 114 BC, when, in company with the Teutones and Ambrones, this tribe from the region of Jutland made its way through Europe in search of new lands to the south. These wanderers did not move at random: they used the Elbe valley to avoid the Celtic hill-forts. When they were repulsed by the Scordisci who lived in what is now the northern part of Yugoslavia, they made their way westwards through Austria into Gaul. They had already defeated a Roman army in 113 BC, and they were to continue undefeated by Roman arms for a number of years. Their activities in southern Gaul and Spain made them a clear menace to Roman security. They devastated a Roman army at Arausio (Orange) in 105 BC, and they were crushed only by the strategic genius and new model army of Caius Marius in 102 BC and 101 BC. They were harbingers of Germanic dangers which were to be realised in later centuries: they were no mere rabble, but a well organised movement involving a whole population of men, families and their transport (Champion 1980).

In time, the Boii of the Hercynian Forest found themselves being displaced from their territory by the Germanic Marcomani. The Boii were edged towards the east into Austria and Pannonia where they came eventually into disastrous contact with the Dacians.

Poseidonius (Str. 7.29.3) mentions the Boii as resident in the 'Hercynian Forest'. According to Julius Caesar (*BG* 6.24) the Volcae and Tectosages were also settled in this region. The term seems earlier to have included the western mountain ranges of Germany, but later it was confined to the Sudetes and Carpathians.

We begin to learn of significantly insistent Germanic penetration into Celtic lands in the first century BC. The Celtic Helvetii moved out of western Switzerland in 58 BC: their migration was caused by Germanic pressure. Their attempt to move down the valley of the Rhone was blocked, and when they tried to go towards the west into Gaul, Julius Caesar defeated them and sent the remnant of the migration back to their homeland. In 71 BC, the Arverni and Sequani had invited a German tribe, the Suebi, into Celtic territory to help them against the Aedui. When they had given the help that was asked of them, the Suebi were unwilling to return home. The consequences of this attitude have been described by Julius Caesar in his *Bellum Gallicum* (*BG*): more foreign interference in Gallic affairs was one of them — this time on the part of Rome. Caesar's success against the Helvetii encouraged the chief men of the tribes to think that they might conveniently use him against the Germans. We find in the *Agricola* of Tacitus (24) that an exiled Irish prince tried to persuade the Romans to help him to be reinstated. Later, a well-known princely quarrel in Ireland would cause the Anglo-Normans to be invited to intrude in Irish affairs. There seems to have been no cultural or racial prejudice amongst the Celts which rendered such a course of action emotionally distasteful.

In the next portion of this chapter we shall consider two connected themes: the language or languages of the Celts, and the relationship of their language and culture with those of Eastern IE peoples and others; for example, between Celtic, Italic and Hittite (together with its related dialects), an obvious point in common is the medio-passive verbal ending in /r/, which is more probably to be regarded as an archaic feature rather than a secondary characteristic independently achieved. We shall see that there are other points of correspondence.

We do not know in what part of the IE province between the Altai and the Alps the language of the Celts developed. Some arguments favour an Eastern origin. It seems less unlikely that Celtic achieved its historically recognisable form in the region north of the Alps in which Celts first appear to have emerged as a formidable concentration of peoples.

Celtic still survives in two varieties, conveniently separable by their respective treatment of IE/k^w/. This becomes /q/ or /c/ in Goidelic, which includes Irish (Old, Middle and Modern), Scots Gaelic and Manx; whereas it becomes /p/ in Brythonic, which is represented by Welsh (in its older and more recent forms), Breton, Cornish, probably most of Continental Gaulish, Galatian (Asia Minor) and one of the languages associated with the Picts. The Celtic languages of Gaul and the rest of the European mainland in ancient times are represented by inscriptions, personal names and placenames: in Irish and Welsh there is copious literature.

Differences in the historic Celtic languages could suggest an ancient distinction between Proto-Celtic tribes which relates to their different times of arrival in the parts of Europe in which it is supposed that the Celts developed their strengths; but it is difficult to make firm statements as to whether the Celts of history were formed by layers of arriving population who already spoke some form of Celtic which they imposed on previous Celtic-speaking as distinct from other IE-speaking residents. We have met the suggestion in the case of Ireland that a small conquering caste of Goidelic-speaking warriors imposed their dialect on a mass of Brythonic-speaking natives.

We have no knowledge of historical events in the ontogeny of either species of Celtic. We can, however, entertain reasonable speculations about their early evolution. Insular Celtic languages retain old or archaic linguistic features: at the same time, since they have subsisted on the outer edge of the IE domain, they have been more subject to influence from contact with non-IE languages in their environment than have those at its centre. The evolutionary changes in the Celtic languages of Britain and Ireland may show the effects of their contact with languages of the 'Atlantic' area which are very different from IE (Wagner 1971: 208). But in antiquity, in the times which concern us, Celtic was a main European language, and in no respect marginal. This would not give it immunity from the effects of local and pre-Celtic influences, but at the time which concerns us, it might be supposed that their effects would not necessarily be so marked. Conjugated prepositions, such as Irish 'dom' 'to me', 'dot' 'to you' etc., developed in Insular Celtic, but not, so far as we know, in that of the Continent. The presence of a relatival form of the verb in Insular Celtic may be another peculiarity of this kind.

The distribution of important kinship terms provides some grounds for supposing that Goidelic was more marginal, and 'Brythonic' more central in the IE domain. The word for 'father' which is found in languages such as Goidelic (q-Celtic), Latin, Greek, Osco-Umbrian, Germanic, Armenian and Indic is of the 'pater' type, whereas in p-Celtic, Baltic, Slavic, Albanian, Luwian and Hittite (both Cuneiform and Hieroglyphic), it is of the childlike 'atta' type (Bonfante 1946). This type seems to be deeply rooted in Slavic, and its association with uniquely different denominations for wife's parents may suggest a special differentiation of social organisation amongst Slavic speakers (Friedrich 1966: 8–9). The remains of Illyrian show personal names such as 'Atto', 'Tatto'. This could suggest that Illyrian usage was adopted by p-Celtic speakers for this particular kinship term. Illyrian, or Veneto-Illyrian, was no doubt in contact with Celtic in Central Europe and the Danubian area (MacWhite 1957: 15). There is also the view that 'Illyrian' was the IE language spoken in vast tracts of Europe before the advent of Celtic.

Traces of q-Celtic are discernible in Gaul, in tribal names such as 'Sequani' and 'Quariates' (*EIHM* 147). The Coligny Calendar, the oldest Celtic written work of significance that survives, has q-Celtic forms such as 'equos' instead of Brythonic or Gaulish 'epos' which we might expect. If we supposed that this was evidence of sacral archaism in the language of the Calendar (MacWhite 1957: 16), we should only be agreeing to the priority of q-Celtic in a particular region. Its general seniority would not be established.

The argument has been put forward that the q/p difference is merely allophonic, and does not indicate a categorical division of radical significance in the early stages of the language (Hamp 1962). Yet it is hard not to regard the difference as being both old and important, though we must avoid being influenced excessively by the manifest and profound differences between the descendant languages Irish and Welsh. Both Celtic tongues agree in their loss of /*p/ in initial position (Ir. *iasc*, Lat. *piscis*, Ger. *fisk*). This seems to have taken place later than the assimilation of /p/ — /k^w/ to /k^w/ — /k^w/ whereby /penk^{w}e/, 'five', became *coic* in q-Celtic, and *pimp* in p-Celtic (Schmidt 1974: 334). We cannot say when this assimilation took place. It may not have been until the fifth century AD that loss of inflections and other changes in the two kinds of Celtic rendered them mutually unintelligible. A certain theoretical assumption about the uniform evolution of language suggests that the two representative forms, Irish and Welsh, would originally have been the same language in the eighth century BC. Uniformity, however, has as little applicability to the history of languages as to any other branch of history.

Evidence from Gaul and Spain suggests in both countries the coexistence of the two forms of Celtic. There is little doubt that they were also contemporaries in La Tène Ireland (MacWhite 1957: 19–20; *EIHM* 205–6). Remaining as cautious as we can in our approach to the various arguments which surround, but cannot directly meet the problems of the two kinds of Celtic, we may say that p-Celtic seems to have been quantitatively predominant in most of the Celtic realm in the period of antiquity that concerns us.

This would not preclude the political or ceremonial overlordship of q-Celtic speakers at some times and in some places during this period. Nor can we determine the evolutionary seniority of one over the other, though if we accept that both were derived from 'Common Celtic' or some 'Proto-Celtic' we are committed to some assumption of priority, since it is hardly likely that they both evolved from their predecessor (the singular itself begs questions) at precisely the same time. These terms, 'Indo-European' and 'Proto-Indo-European', tend to promote an unprovable model of linear evolution; the emergence of a known from an unknown. More usefully, they can describe communities of linguistic features.

We have mentioned the view that both q- and p- forms of Celtic are to be found amongst the ancient languages of Spain (Tovar 1958). The evidence in Spain for q-Celtic is not so certain as it is in Gaul. It may be that some other IE language is represented by apparently q-material. The Spanish peninsula of antiquity has left behind a mixed and difficult linguistic fossil-bed. There are traces of Iberian, which apparently was a non-IE language; there is Celtiberian, which in some classifications is regarded as Celtic but may not have been entirely so; there is also Basque, still surviving; and Celtic itself, which is considered by some to have been the

speech of the historic Celtiberians (Tovar 1961: 115). Some placenames have affinities with those of North Africa: for example,
Baesippo, Basilipo, offer comparison with Hippo in Africa. This
may represent the influence of Tartessus. These names are spread
throughout the south-west of the peninsula: other names ending
in -issa, and -essa, may be relics of another layer of language
which occurs in placenames all over the Mediterranean area.
Basque has been thought to have features in common with Caucasian, Finno-Ugrian, and Palaeo-Siberian languages. The word
'ezher' in Basque means 'left hand'; in the idiom, it really means
'half-hand': this way of referring to paired objects occurs in
Finno-Ugrian and also in Irish, which has the same idiom in such
expressions as 'leathlámh' which means 'half-hand' literally, but
idiomatically means 'one hand'. In this kind of expression which
involves 'leath-', 'half' or 'side', Irish may show the influence of
some lost Pre-Celtic language of Ireland. We do not know the
order in which the various IE and non-IE languages came into
Spain. Perhaps a blend of IE and non-IE speakers came in association (Tovar 1961: 118), in the way that the Alani accompanied
Germanic invaders of the Iberian peninsula in the fifth century
AD.

There is doubt whether the linguistic remains which have been
designated Celtiberian represent one or more IE languages
(Schmoll 1958; Tovar 1961). These remnants preserve /p/, which
is lost in Celtic; also, unlike known Celtic dialects, they show a
genitive singular of o- stems ending in 'o', instead of 'i'. It has
been suggested that the 'o' genitive is an adoption of the /od/
ablatival morpheme for service as a genitive. This has parallels in
Lithuanian and Slavic (Schmidt 1974: 335). It could be a variant
in a particular dialect of early Celtic, or residual evidence of a non-
Celtic IE language. Celtic itself is attested by Spanish placenames
such as Segobriga (Segovia) (Meid 1972: 1191).

It used to be more fashionable than it is now to call non-Celtic
IE languages 'Illyrian'. As a portmanteau term it still has a certain
utility, when used without doctrinal commitment. Illyrian proper
was an ancient IE language of the Central European plain and the
Balkan peninsula. Its sphere was bounded in the South by Epirus,
where the Greek-speaking province begins, and by the mountains
of Macedonia, beyond which Macedonian predominated. It was
spoken in Pannonia, where it sometimes coexisted with Celtic and
sometimes was displaced by it. To the east of the Central European plain it gave way to Thracian, and north of the Danube to

Dacian, a variant of Thracian. When we speak of non-Celtic IE languages of Western Europe, Britain and Ireland, we might be better advised to use the term 'European'. Ligurian, a language upon which Celtic impinged in Southern France, has also been promoted at times to a general 'European' status, after the fashion of Illyrian.

In the Celtiberian dialect /kʷ/ is not changed to /p/: this is a point in common with q-Celtic. In the inscriptions from Lusitania in the north-west of the peninsula, initial /p/ is preserved: this, as we have seen, disappears from Celtic. There is also evidence of p-Celtic, which may characterise a layer of population that came into Spain from Southern Gaul. In the Spain of Classical antiquity, p-Celtic was not dominant. Dialects were widely spoken which had characteristics strongly suggestive of q-Celtic, albeit with features which were individual, though not necessarily primitive. These coexisted with language of an IE character which was not Celtic, as well as with non-IE speech.

For a long time it has been recognised that Italic and Celtic dialects of the ancient world had characteristics in common. There are also points of correspondence between both groups and Indo-Iranian. The similarities between Italic and Celtic are insufficient to substantiate the old theory of Italo-Celtic unity. The differences between them are too marked for this view to be credible in an undiluted form. Latin retains a full set of vowels; the IE vocalic inheritance of Celtic has been subject to distortions and fusions of almost geological violence. Older insular Celtic has complexes of preverbs and infixed pronouns which do not appear in Italic, but which have some representation in Hittite. In Celtic adjectives, there is an equative degree, in addition to comparative and superlative: this does not occur in Italic. Italic, but not Celtic, makes its interrogative pronouns serve also as relative pronouns. Hittite also uses interrogatives for this purpose. Celtic has a relatival form of the verb, a feature which may indicate some non-IE influence (Watkins 1966).

The Celtic and Italic words for 'king', *rix* (modern Irish *rí*) and *rex*, have an equivalent in Indic *rāj*. The use of this word in distantly separated parts of the IE domain might suggest that it is a surviving archaism, referring to the ancient sacral function of the king (Benveniste 1973: 307). It may signify the ritual demarcation of sacral boundaries in a straight line: consider the Latin verb 'rego' and the Greek, 'oregō', both of which carry the meaning of 'stretching forth'. The name of the *rex sacrorum*, the Roman functionary with the residual duties of the priest-king in a city which gloried in its abolition of kings, may give some general support for this view. Both Celtic and Italic have an 'a' subjunctive (it may also be identified in Tocharian): both have passive/deponent verbal endings in 'r'. So also has Hittite and some related dialects. There is the suggestion that the 'r' forms developed independently in the languages in which they occur by the suffixation of a particle to the verb-ending, but the coincidence would be so striking as to require very substantial demonstration. As in Celtic, so also in Italic, /p/ — /kʷ/ becomes /kʷ/ — /kʷ/ and /p/ — /p/ according to dialect, as in '*quinque*' and '*Pompeius*'. The 'b' future, which is found in Latin and other Italic dialects, occurs also in Celtic: both Celtic and Italic retain the /samo/ suffix for the superlative degree of adjectives. These are some of the obvious points of resemblance. There are considerably more.

In the range of correspondences, Latin seems to have points markedly in common with q-Celtic, whereas Oscan and Sabellian seem to be closer to p-Celtic. These and other factors could suggest an earlier geographical continuity between the ancestors of Italic and Celtic speakers. If so, there is, I fear, no means whereby we can say where this region was situated, how large it was or when various groups found themselves dwelling in it or passing through it. There are no grounds for postulating a primeval cultural and linguistic conglomerate of peoples from which Celts and Italics split off, the former to populate Central Europe, France, Spain, Britain, and Ireland; the latter to settle in the peninsula of Italy. On the other hand, it is feasible enough to suppose that groups of peoples spoke varieties of IE which became more closely related through neighbourhood and contact: that these people lived to the north of the Alps, and that speakers of Italic and Celtic ultimately derived their languages from them. There would seem to be nothing primarily objectionable about agreeing with Dillon (1944: 129), that the various peoples might have begun to make their moves in the latter part of the second millennium BC.

The theory that Celts originated in the East goes back to an early period of inspired intuition in Celtic studies. Sir William Betham attempted to prove in his *Etruria Celtica* (1842) that the Celts were of Phoenician origin. The early Irish, under Classical influence, repeatedly connected their ancestry with the Scythians. There does not seem to be any single source for their view that the ancestral Scota was of Scythian origin (*LGE* 2.52.14). There is no need to pursue the search: the similarity of the words is argument enough, especially when we consider the case-form: 'Scuith'.

An interpolated comment at *LGE* 2.52.141 makes the point that Scota could be a place in Scythia, Petraea: also that Fenius Farsaid, the father of Gaedil Glas, instituted poetry and the profession of bards to keep the early records of the race. Fenius was a prince of Scythia.

A variant of the story (*LGE* 2.41.129) makes Scota the wife of Míl, and says that she was so named because it was the custom of the country to call women after the tribe of their husband; so she was called 'Scota' because she was married to a 'Scot'. In another version she is the wife of the Nel who came to the tower of Nimrud from Scythia in order to separate out the Gaelic language from all the others that were to be found at this Babel. In *LGE* 2.44, we find that:

> Baath mac Magoc mac Iathfed, it is from him come
> the Gael
> and the men of Scythia. And he had a son, the
> glorious
> distinguished leader, who was called Fenius
> Farsaich. He was
> one of the seventy-two chiefs who went to build the
> tower of
> Nimrud from which the languages were scattered.

The tradition, which has an account of the adventures of the Scythian-derived people on their way from Scythia to Spain, may well have been invented in order to give the ancestors of the Irish Gael a connection with the ancient Classical world by means of the numerous contacts with the Greeks which are mentioned in the course of the story. On the margin of that great world in which the Classical theme still predominated and was the essential mark of civilisation, the Gael of the early medieval period felt the need to acquire Classical connections as the proof of the antique respectability which he was sure he possessed, but was unable to document. These myths are flavoured by the wanderings of Odysseus, Aeneas, and the Children of Israel: Moses is one of the cast of ancient heroes who makes a brief appearance in the story. These stories were in circulation when Nennius wrote his *Historia Britonum* about the end of the ninth century AD. It is scarcely possible that the story retains a dim memory of the old Greek view that northern Europe and Asia were occupied by Celts in the west and Scythians in the east. Yet we might almost suspect such a continuity, much attenuated, when we hear that Gaedil Glas, the son of Scota, Pharaoh's daughter, composed the Gaelic language from seventy-two languages (*LGE* 2.13.5), and find a list of the languages in a poem (*LGE* 2.86). The list is apparently derived from the list of languages in Isidore of Seville (7th century AD). The list is as much a list of places as of tongues:

> the word's tongues, scrutinise them yourselves:
> Bithynian, Scythian, Cilician, Hyrcanian —

and so on in a long verse list, which, we may reasonably conclude, has more part in the old Celtic custom of oral mnemonic than it has in Classical didactic poetry. We may suppose that Isidore's punning etymologies have been an influence in the argument of the myth.

Our modern story is that the Proto-Indo-European dialects (PIE) originated in the fourth millennium BC, and were of an Indo-Hittite character. In the postulated Indo-European domain, between the Danube and the Oxus, and the Altai and Northern Europe, PIE dialects developed, one (or more than one) of which was to become Celtic, as others were to become Greek, Germanic, Indic, and Italic. Wagner (1971: 220) is the most cogent contemporary advocate of the view that Celtic had its origins towards the east of the European portion of this IE linguistic province. He draws attention to isoglosses between Celtic and more easterly varieties of IE dialects such as Thracian and Scythian (Ossetic). Amongst 'centum' IE dialects, those which retain /k/, Celtic has many points in common with the 'satem' or more easterly group, in which this phoneme becomes /s/. Thracian has been argued to hold a middle position between 'satem' and 'centum' types of dialect (Wagner 1971: 212).

It is true that in historical times, Celts and Thracians sometimes found themselves with common boundaries, but the isoglosses would seem to suggest contact more ancient than the fourth and third centuries BC, when the Celts were moving eastwards. But we cannot be sure; Wagner (1971: 212) points out that the Irish word for 'hen', which is 'cearc', has no equivalent in western IE languages, but is parallel by 'kark' in Ossetic, and by similar words in other Iranian dialects of IE (ibid. 226). We might also mention 'kerkos' in Greek. Ossetic is thought to have been the language of the Scythians, specifically of the Alani, a Scythic tribe, who, with the Sarmatae, followed other Scythic peoples in their wanderings towards the west. It survives in two dialects spoken by several hundred thousand people in the USSR (Comrie 1981: 164). Once it was spoken in Hungary, and the historic Yas may have been its western representatives in this region (Wagner 1971: 205). 'Cearc' is an interesting correspondence, but it may be a relatively late borrowing. The names of domestic animals are often borrowings from those who have kept them earlier than the borrowers — witness our own names for breeds of cattle such as 'Frisian' or 'Pinzgauer' which have been adopted from foreign countries. And the borrowing may not imply direct contact or mixing of peoples, merely some kind of communication. If 'cearc' is a borrowing from, let us say, the fifth or fourth century BC, there is still the interesting question of how it got into Irish. Who introduced it or brought it with them to the island, and when? We bear in mind that the animal in question is not one of man's oldest companions and that it has an eastern origin, as well as a voice that lends itself readily to crude onomatopoeia.

Of more general significance, perhaps, is a word designating a social relationship: Ogam Irish 'muccoi' seems to mean that the person whose name the word follows in the inscription belongs to the clan of whatever name follows it. It may be connected with the Old Irish 'macc' meaning 'surety' (Wagner 1971: 248), and it invites comparison with Thracian 'mukkag', 'kindred'. Personal names have been found in Thracian which have a similar element, and there is the Roman gentile name 'Mucius' (Wagner 1971: 226).

In this context a relationship might be suggested between 'Rhesus', the Thracian 'horse-king' of the *Iliad*, and the /regs/, *rex*, *rix*, *rí* of Italic and Celtic (Wagner 1971: 225). That the Celts and the ancient Thracians are said to have been specially religious proves nothing: Greek authors are frequently impressed by the piety of distant tribes, such as the Aithiopes in Homer. The Agathyrsoi may have resembled the Celts in handing on their laws in the form of verse and songs (Wagner ibid.), but this is by no means an unusual method of archival conservation amongst primitive peoples. Nor is it uncommon to find that drinking has a ritual importance: the fact that it had amongst the Celts and Thracians is worthy of note, but it does not endorse the view that these peoples were close in origins or that they enjoyed a prolonged symbiosis in early or prehistory.

The most notable cultural resemblances between western insular Celts and Thracian, Phrygian, and Scythic tribes are as follows (Wagner 1971: 247ff):

1 Rider-god: Eochaidh (Dagde), Rhesus, and the Thracian Rider-god.
2 Hermes the oath-god of the Thracians and Scythians; Lugh in the Irish tradition.
3 Ceremonial use of drink in religious and quasi-religious group bonding.
4 Raiding habits: Homeric *boelasiai*, *Taín Bó Cúalgne*.
5 Wakes, funeral games: rejoicing at death as the inception of a better afterlife.
6 River and well worship amongst Thracians, Irish, and Brythonic Celts.
7 The three-headed rider-god (specimen found at Philip-popolis); Celtic tricephalic statues.
8 Pastoral emphasis: small respect for agriculture.

These similarities may be the relics of some primeval association from IE times in which speakers of the ancestral dialects of Thracian and Celtic (and Greek) were in process of moving towards the west. Yet there would not seem to be conclusive arguments in these points of similarity for the idea that the Celts were of specifically eastern origin. The parallels may simply be IE in character. They may represent the ways of life of an aristo-cratic, warlike, semi-pastoral social system which could in prehistory have been found anywhere between the Rhine and the Caucasus. The balance of likely arguments from language and other evidence would suggest that IE peoples originated in the Caucasian region. Where individual IE peoples and their languages grew up to their recognisable identities is a different matter.

Points of likeness between the hypothesised reconstruction of Proto-Caucasian and PIE tend to suggest an eastern origin for the latter. PIE, which also can only have the status of a retrospective theoretical construct, seems to share with Proto-Caucasian a coinciding range of glottal and velar sounds. The vocabulary of PIE which refers to animals, domestic or merely familiar, corn grains, wagon parts, and the use of metal (copper or bronze), could easily relate to the Kurgan culture of the third millennium BC in the Caucasian, Caspian area. This was characterised by the construction of small settlements like the primitive Greek *polis*, Indic *puras*, or Celtic *dún* or *oppidum*. Also there was the custom of burying leaders in mounds (*kurgany*). This custom, is of course, typical of a certain stage of cultural development in many different peoples, including the S'hang dynasts of China (Lloyd 1967: 3). It has implications for their views of the afterlife. Possibly it was about the middle of the third millennium BC when various groups speaking IE dialects spread out towards Asia Minor and Greece: others may have reached the Baltic and the Rhine at much the same time (Friedrich 1966: 3).

Speakers of IE dialects seem to have formed a dominating and culturally defined group everywhere they went from India to western Europe. Most groups had a royal or aristocratic social structure, and were divided into distinct, but not always rigid classes. Aggressive leadership in war probably evolved from the need for firm guidance of communities on the move, either seasonally, or in more distant migrations. The possession of wheeled transport and a relatively developed metal technology enhanced their social organisation and enabled these restless and adaptable tribes to become dominant in most of the places where they settled. Perhaps the latest phase of this IE restlessness is to be seen in the expansion of the American frontier in the nineteenth century AD.

We have noted features shared by Italic and Celtic, and also that both have elements in common with Indo-Iranic languages. Not only general vocabulary and certain morphological features are involved, but more specialised lexical items concerning personal qualities and relationships, functions within the respective societies, names of commonly used tools and instruments. Corresponding with Latin *erus* (*esus*), 'master', and the Gaulish divinity 'Esus', we find the Sanskrit 'asura' used of a person with magical powers, and Old Persian, 'ahura-mazdah'. The Irish 'aire', 'freeman', matches Sanskrit 'arya'; Irish 'bodor', 'deaf', corresponds with Sanskrit 'badhara' and 'cecht', 'power'; with Sanskrit 'śakti' (Vendryes 1908: 266–70). There are also parallels in custom between Celtic and Indic cultures. Myles Dillon (1947 and 1975) has discussed these fully and we need only mention the more obvious likenesses.

Ancient Celts and Indians both seem to have attributed to kings a truth peculiar to their sacral and kingly function and continuous with the truth that supports the whole cosmos. We have an outline of this in the Irish *Audacht Morainn*, 'Morann's Testament', which was compiled not later than the eighth century AD and is attributed to the teaching of Morann, a legendary lawgiver of the first century BC and the teacher of the great king Cormac Mac Airt who himself is supposed to have composed the 'Tecosa' or 'Instructions' which traditionally carry his name. There are also evidences of truth-ordeals and ceremonies concerning oaths in both societies (Wagner 1971: 2; Dillon 1947: 139). Ancient Irish and Indians followed a custom sanctioned by law in which the offended person fasted against the person who had done him injury; both societies had several grades of marriage. The Irish 'derbfine' type of family structure and the Indian 'sapinda' both embrace in their circuits of membership three past generations and three forward generations. An individual's ritual obligations stretched back to his great-grandfather and forward to his great-grandchildren: there were other designations for relationship outside the four-generation cycle in which the individual was at the same time a member of the final generation of the ascending group and the first of the descending. In Irish terms this was the 'derbfine' or 'true family'. The system is not confined to Indic and Celtic family structures, but is clearly represented in them (Dillon 1975: 95).

Giraldus Cambrensis (12th century AD) was scandalised by a ritual inauguration of kings practised in a remote part of Ulster. In this ceremony, the inaugurand had sexual intercourse with a white mare in the presence of his assembled people (Wagner 1971: 42). The mare was subsequently killed and the king drank the soup that was made from her. This evident invocation of fertility is in keeping with the Irish idea that a ruler should mate with the goddess who represents the country or impersonates it. The dilute vestiges of this ancient theme may be seen in the patriotic Irish and Hiberno-English songs in which from the seventeenth century AD, Ireland is addressed as a beloved woman in distress (Dillon 1975: 106–7). The white mare may be another identity of the Celtic horse-goddess of the Continent, Epona. This Ulster celebration has been compared with the Indian sacrifice of 'aśvamedha' in which a stallion was sacrificed, and the queen had intercourse with it after its death by suffocation. There might seem to be no obvious parallel between two ceremonies except that they both involved human sexual use of a horse. It has, however, been pointed out that the Irish mythical queen or goddess, Medb, had among her numerous consorts a certain Eochaidh, and this name is clearly connected with 'ech', 'horse'. Medb may be connected with /medhu/, 'mead', which might produce a possible Proto-Celtic /medua/. The theme of ritual drunkenness in connection with the sacrifice of horses may be indicated by the Gaulish name Epomeduos, which is the equivalent of the Vedic kingly name 'Aśvamedha. Thus Medb's name may be a shortened form of the compound /ekʷomedua/, just as the Irish war-goddess Badb corresponds to the Gaulish Cathubodua. These considerations bring the Irish and the Indian rites into clearer perspective in relation to each other (Puhvel 1970b: 166–7).

Such archaic survivals in the customs of outer areas of the IE domain may only indicate the conservatism of marginal zones rather than an ancient close association between peoples. We have no incontrovertible assurance that Celtic peoples owe their origin to a specifically eastern warrior culture imposing itself upon an Eastern European culture of the Urnfield, Lausatian type, and introducing the lordly habit of tumulus burial (Meid 1972: 1197). Certainly the Celts belonged to the old IE world of Homeric archaism, rather than to the more complex and developed world of Mediterranean IE speakers of the Classical and later periods. Throughout the history of their relationship with the Greeks and Romans, it was their archaism that made them most terrifying and which rendered them always eventually vincible. However we estimate their culture in comparison with that of Greece, we should find it difficult to assert that they were less civilised than the Romans.

2

Massilia, an Early Contact

The Phocaeans who founded Massalia (Latin: Massilia) in 600 BC were probably the first Greek settlers of any consequence in the Western Mediterranean. There is a doubtful tradition that the Rhodians were an earlier thalassocracy in the region after the Trojan War (Euseb. 225). The placename Rhode, modern Rosas, scarcely gives a sufficient proof of their active presence. The traditional date of their activity is the tenth century BC, but there is no evidence that the Greeks were present in the area in any significant strength before the seventh century BC (Morel 1967: 380). Before the arrival of the Greeks, Phoenicians colonised the coasts of Spain and Southern France, and these areas were within the Carthaginian sphere of influence. By the time the Phocaean Greeks settled at Massilia, other places of settlement had effectively been closed to them by hostility of the Carthaginians and the Etruscans (Morel 1967: 399). The people of Phocaea abandoned the home city in Ionia to the Persians in 545 BC, and decided to find a new home in the west. At this point, the patience of Carthaginians and Etruscans wore out, and hostilities began which were eventually to result in the doubtful Greek victory of Alalia in 540 BC, which so damaged Greek power that the Greeks had to abandon the colony of Alalia in Corsica from which their remnants only escaped with great difficulty.

The story that the king of Tartessus gave the Phocaeans funds to build the walls of Massilia is not convincing in the form in which it has been handed down. A more plausible explanation is that the new western trade route was brilliantly profitable to the earliest Greek adventurers (Clerc 1929: 84). Herodotus tells (4.152) how Colaeus of Samos set sail from home for Egypt, but an adverse wind took him to Tartessus where he sold his cargo at an immense profit, and came back to make a magnificent dedication in the temple of Hera. A similar piece of commercial virtuosity may underly the walls of Massalia. On the other hand, we can imagine that the king of Tartessus might find it expedient to encourage new trading partners in that part of the Mediterranean in order to counterbalance the influence of existing powers who were too well established for his comfort.

Pompeius Trogus and Livy believe that Massalia was settled in the reign of the elder Tarquin at Rome (658–578 BC). Timaeus' view was that the foundation took place one hundred and twenty years before the Battle of Salamis. This gives the date 600 BC on which the suspicion falls that it is four standard generations before Salamis. However, this apparent neatness may not be an insuperable barrier to accepting that there were colonising activities around this date. There may have been several phases in the settlement of the city, and at least two of them could have been major migrations. A substantial infusion of new inhabitants may have followed the surrender of Ionian Phocaea to the forces of Harpagus in 545 BC, though they would have had to face determined opposition from the alliance of Carthage and the Etruscans, both of which powers thought it in their interest to keep this movement of Greeks from the East to a minimum. After the battle of Alalia the whole region would have been too dangerous for large-scale migration to be an attractive proposition (Clerc 1929: 130), though we may suppose that there were numerous refugees on the move in small groups in search of a secure home in Massalia or elsewhere. Most of those who were displaced from Alalia settled first in Rhegium: Herodotus reports (1.116) that they subsequently moved to Elea (Velia) on the south-west coast of Italy, a city later to become famous in the history of philosophy as the home of that great intellectual innovator, Parmenides.

Massalia (I shall use the Greek form of this name in predominantly Greek contexts) was strongly influenced in much of the course of its history by local Celtic culture (Livy 38.17). In Classical times, the languages spoken in the city remained three: Latin, Greek and Celtic. This is attested by the polymath Varro quoted by Isidore of Seville (*Orig.* 15.1.63), and may be taken to reflect the situation at the end of the Roman Republic. But at the time of the city's foundation the local tribes with whom the Greeks had to deal were no doubt Ligurian. The Celts were just over the geographical and historical horizon. Though there is some reason to suppose that they were making their way into Spain quite early in the sixth century BC (Arribas 1981: 46), they had not yet reached the southern coast of France in the foundation years of Massalia. Aristotle is said to have written a *Constitution of Massalia* (Ath. 576ab) in which he told the story of its foundation as follows:

> The Phocaeans of Ionia in the course of their trading founded Massalia. Euxenus of Phocaea was the guest-friend of Nanos, for this was the name of their king. Nanos was arranging his daughter's marriage, and by chance Euxenus arrived and was invited to the feast. Now the marriage (selection of bridegroom) was conducted in the following fashion: the girl had to come in after the dinner and to give a bowl of wine mixed with water to the one amongst the suitors she wanted. The one she gave it to, this would be her bridegroom. The girl came in, and through chance, or for some other cause, she gave it to Euxenus. The girl's name was Petta. When this happened, and with the father asking him to accept her on the grounds that the choice was inspired by the god, Euxenus took her as his wife, changing her name to Aristoxene. And there is a family in Massalia to this day descended from this girl, called the Protiadai: Protos was the name of the son of Euxenus and Aristoxene.

We need not doubt that this version has its roots in Aristotle, and some of his words may indeed be preserved in the text. The *mythos* may have some earlier underlying source which he used. It certainly justifies, as such a *mythos* must, the presence of its principals' descendants and their social importance in the region (Dottin 1915: 140, Clerc 1929: 118). The attribution of the unexpected choice of spouse to the will of a god is a likely enough practice in a primitive community. The divine factor in the girl's choice would be assumed no matter on which of the assembled eligibles her choice fell. In the Greek world we encounter choice of bridegroom for the daughter from a list of supposedly suitable candidates, as in the famous sixth century BC courting party held by Cleisthenes of Sicyon for his daughter Agariste, in which Hippocleides of Athens, having been short-listed, danced away his chances, upside down and on a table, at the concluding symposium of the selection board (Hdt. 6.126–9). On this occasion the choice was that of Cleisthenes, not Agariste. Other patrilineal and patriarchal methods of selecting mates for children included brideshows, like that held by the Byzantine empress Eirene for her son;

or in an early, mythologised form, the choice of Paris. In societies which were not Greek, or in the earlier stages of Greek society, in which women enjoyed higher status, the girl could choose, or have a definite say in the choice: witness in the *Odyssey* Nausicaa's encouragement of Odysseus, and her initial comments — polite and frank — about the desirability of having such a man as her husband, are not trifling (*Od.* 6.244). In the Homeric *epos* traces of matrilineal custom became embedded in an early layer of oral poetic stratification. We see that Menelaus became ruler of Sparta through marrying Helen. There seems to be no question of her brothers, Castor and Pollux, ruling the state. According to the ancient tradition, Helen was allowed to choose her husband from an array of candidates (Eur. *IA* 68–9). Euripides rationalises the event for fifth-century BC Athens by saying that her father decided to allow her freedom of choice in order to relieve himself of the pressure and odium involved in making the decision himself. Fear of provoking jealous anger in powerful neighbours whose sons have been rejected must even in the most ancient times have been an additional incentive to maintaining the gods' prerogative of choice.

At the presumed death of Odysseus, Penelope was expected to choose one of the suitors, all of whom belonged to an eligible category of men. She seems to have had the right to make her choice independently: her son, as titular head of the family, would have had the formal duty of giving her to her new husband.

Perhaps the Massaliote foundation-myth is influenced by this kind of epic exoticism. On the other hand, it could be that the local tribe of the Segobrigai, like the Picts of Northern Britain, expected their princesses to be exogamic (*FF* 2.114ff; Chadwick 1949: 84–9). The changing of Petta's name could suggest a ritual, rather than the Hellenisation of barbaric royalty. That she made her choice 'by chance or for some other cause' may reveal to us Aristotle's (or some earlier writer's) suspicion that the whole business was arranged in advance.

From Pompeius Trogus we have a slightly different version of the story (Justin 43.3.4). We hear that merchant adventurers from Phocaea in Ionia, called Simois and Protis, arrived in the region and encountered Nanos, a king of the Segobrigai. The king introduced his daughter Petta, or Gyptis, to the strangers, telling her to offer drink to the one she would choose as husband. She seems to have offered it to Protis, who married her, and took the name, auspicious in the circumstances, of 'Euxenus' ('Good Guest'): she took the name Aristoxene, which has the same meaning in a more intensive form as that of her husband.

We have no evidence that the Segobrigai had any Celtic connections at this time. They seem to have been Ligurian, belonging to a branch of IE-speaking people who have already been settled for a considerable time in the region. The name 'Nanos' and its feminine 'Nanna' occur in Celtic areas where there is a Ligurian element in the population. 'Petta' actually does seem to have in its root meaning of 'pet' something small and affectionate, and its kindred may survive in the French 'petit'. Etymological argument cannot establish the tribe's identity, but the tradition that they were Ligures seems reasonable. Word-endings of the 'briga' type are common in Spain in territory not specifically associated with Celtic settlement: the form is relatively rare in Gaul (Clerc 1929: 147). Nanos, or Nannos, was succeeded by Cananos, who disliked the new city. He entered into a plot to infiltrate his warriors into it, on a festival day in harmless-looking wagons, but the device failed.

It is reasonable to suppose that the Celts had arrived in the region of Southern France some considerable time before their irruption into Northern Italy. By the fifth century BC they had established themselves firmly in what was to become Cisalpine Gaul, and at the end of that century they were strong enough to threaten the safety of Rome. Aristotle says that:

> around the Ligurian land a river as large as the Rhone is absorbed and emerges in another place.
>
> (*Meteor*. 351.a16)

This river is most likely to be the Po, which Pliny incorrectly describes as plunging underground (*HN* 3.6). Aristotle may be using an old-fashioned source which knew of Ligurians but not Celts in the river-valley, though it is to be noted that nothing in his text specifically denies the presence of Celts.

There were numerous conflicts between Massaliotes and the Ligurians and Celts, but eventually the superior military technology, wealth, political organisations and sea power of the Greek city brought her to a position in which she could dominate her environment. Livy (5.34) tells us that in the reign of the elder Tarquin, the Celtic king Ambigatus sent one of his nephews, Segovesus, with an army in the direction of the Danube, and the other, Bellovesus, was sent to the conquest of Italy, which he attempted to approach over the Alps with great difficulty. At some stage he decided to help the Greek settlers against a Ligurian tribe called the Salvii. However, there were two tribes with this name, one near Massalia, and the other dwellers in the Alps. This may be a source of confusion in Livy's account. The mission of Ambigatus' nephews was much later. He may be alluding to a conflict between the Northern Salvii and a different party of Celtic warriors. Trogus relates that the Celts aided the Phocaeans against their Ligurian neighbours (Justin 43.4.7). This may very well have been the case, but it is impossible to be precise about times and events.

In the years preceding the Celtic sack of Rome (390 BC), Massalia reached a level of power and wealth which provoked fear and jealousy in the other peoples of Southern Gaul. Trogus describes the situation as follows:

> After this there were great conflicts with the Ligurians and equally great wars with the Gauls, which increased the city's glory by the addition of victory to victory, and made her famous among the neighbouring peoples. Also she defeated the armies of Carthage when war broke out over the seizure of fishing vessels, and created security for those who had been oppressed. The city also formed alliances with the tribes of Spain, and almost from the beginnings of her history she remained scrupulously faithful to a treaty concluded with Rome, and energetically aided her ally in all her wars by means of auxiliary forces. Since therefore Massilia was flourishing in abundance of wealth, distinction of achievements and the increasing glory of her strength, the neighbouring peoples gathered for the purpose of eliminating her very name, as if they were to extinguish a fire. The tribal king Catumandus was elected leader by general agreement. When he was laying siege to the city with a great army of his choicest warriors, he was terrified in his sleep by the vision of a menacing woman who said she was a goddess, and he straight away made peace with the Massiliotes. He asked if she might be allowed to enter the city to pay his worship to the gods of the city. When he came to the temple of Minerva on the citadel, he saw in the portico a statue of the goddess he had seen in his dream. Immediately he exclaimed that this was the goddess who had terrified him in the night, the goddess who had ordered him

to relinquish the siege. He congratulated the Massiliotes for being under the protection of the immortal gods, and he presented the goddess with a golden torque and made a treaty of perpetual friendship with the Massiliotes.

Now that peace had been obtained and concluded, ambassadors of the Massiliotes on the way back from Delphi, where they had been sent to give gifts to Apollo, heard that Rome had been taken and burned by the Gauls [390 BC]. When this event was reported in the city, the citizens mourned it with a public funeral and collected public and private funds to make up a sum of money to pay the Gauls, from whom, as they learned, peace had been bought. For this service trade immunities were granted to them by the Romans, a senatorial seat was allocated to them in the auditorium for the games, and a treaty was concluded on terms of equality.

(Justin 43.5ff)

The author of this material quoted from Justin is Pompeius Trogus, a Celt of the tribe of the Vocontii. His grandfather had received Roman citizenship from Pompey the Great for his services in the war against Sertorius. His maternal uncle had led squadrons of cavalry under Pompey's command in the war against Mithridates. Trogus' father occupied an administrative post in the army of Julius Caesar: he was in charge of letters and negotiations with the Gauls, and was keeper of the seal. Both by his Celtic origin and by the accumulated experience of his family, Trogus was in a good position to understand the relationships between Celts and Romans. We have seen from the passage quoted above that his association with the ways of Rome had in no respect attenuated his understanding of Celtic ways of thought.

Catumandus was frightened, we learn, by the appearance of a goddess of menacing appearance (*torva* is the adjective used to describe her). Now it seems very likely that he took her to be one of the Celtic war-goddesses, who are named amongst the ancient Irish as Bodbh, Badbh, or Morrigu. His presentation of a torque to the goddess would seem to support this identification on his part — and no doubt an archaic Athene-statue could have a look which could be legitimately described as *torva*, which suggests a formidable, indeed a dangerous glance.

This passage also suggests that the Celts were present in strength in the vicinity of Massilia at the end of the fifth century

BC, but that they had not displaced the Ligurians. It is impossible to determine the date of the treaty which is mentioned. Whenever it was struck, it was probably the revision of various earlier agreements between the two cities (Toynbee 1965: I. 421) which from their earlier periods had much in common strategically and economically.

Trogus dated the earlier amity between the Massiliotes and Rome to the reign of the elder Tarquin (Justin 43.3.4). According to the tradition, the Phocaeans on their way to the West had put in for a time at Ostia. Whatever the truth of this story, it is certain that their continued friendship rested on a basis of mutual interest: a restraint was applied to their common enemies by the balance of power which the two cities in concert represented. That Massilia should remain a force to be reckoned with by the Celts of the Rhone valley was of considerable consequence to Rome, and would continue to be so; the check that Massilia maintained against the Etruscans and Carthaginians was of cardinal importance to Rome. Both cities were strong and realised that they lived in a world of danger from which neither could expect to be immune.

As their relative strengths altered, Massilia was ready to act in a more auxiliary role as the principal ally and support of Rome in the Gallic domain, and with a particular view to her own interests in the west, in Spain. From time to time she could be argued to have been an over-zealous watchdog. This may have been the case in the early stages of manoeuvre which led to the Second Punic War (218–201 BC), during which she remained firmly attached to the Roman cause (Str. 4.15).

Rome's intervention in Spain was at least partly in response to Massiliote fears for the security of Rhode and Emporion within the zone of operations that the Romans, hard pressed by the Gallic problem in the north of their own peninsula, had seen fit to delimit in Spain for the Carthaginians and themselves. The limit was Saguntum. It was in Rome's interest to keep Hasdrubal from extending Carthaginian power to the Pyrenees. If he were allowed to establish a base there, he would be in a position to raise Gaul in alliance with the Carthaginians. Massiliote influence weighed with the Romans in their decision to make the immunity of Saguntum the pivot of war with Carthage; but wider and deeper strategic interests were at issue (App. 2.7). Massilia lost no opportunity of stimulating Roman fears and keeping evergreen her memory of the earlier war with Carthage (Lazenby 1978: 28). At a later stage, in 125 BC, when Gaul seemed to be increasing in warlike strength and intent, Massilia faced a threat from a northern Celtic tribe called the Sallurii. The Massiliotes appealed to Rome in the terms of the ancient alliance, and received aid. This move on the part of the Sallurii may have indicated a renewed capacity and improved organization amongst the tribes of continental Gaul whereby they might once more be able to invade the Mediterranean world in numbers which recalled the irruptions of past centuries. There can be little doubt about the increase of their power. Like the Germani, they had considerable ability to replace even the most massive losses (Ebel 1976: 64–5). The fear of Gaul which remained lively in the Roman mind was realistic: indeed it was most terribly realised in an unexpected way when Julius Caesar crossed the Rubicon in 49 BC, bringing an army against the Republic, which, though it did not consist mainly of Gauls, was based on the wealth and resources of the personal empire which he had acquired in Gaul.

Caesar distrusted the persistence of vigorous political independence in Massilia. This was in a style which in many ways resembled that of the old cities of Classical Greece, and which had virtually disappeared elsewhere in the Greco-Roman world. He could not fail to be influenced by the continuing goodwill of the Massiliotes towards Pompey, dating from Pompey's successful campaign against Sertorius in Spain in the seventies of the first century BC. In the event, Massilia hesitated to take sides in the civil war. Ultimately the city was forced to surrender to Caesar's lieutenant, Domitius, who had placed it under siege (*BC* 4.2.32). Caesar established a colony at Arles (Suet. *Tib.*; Haarhoff 1920: 9) which took much of Massilia's trade, so the older city declined in prosperity during the Principate until in the reign of Marcus Aurelius (161–180 AD) the Massiliotes were forced to abandon their ancient constitution and alliance for the usual relationship between city-states and imperial Rome.

Massilia throughout her history continued to be a blend of Hellenic, Roman and Celtic cultural characteristics. As some of the references we have considered seem to suggest, the process of mutual borrowing may have begun early in the life of the city. An anonymous Periplus of the fourth century BC mentions, as does Ephorus (4th century BC), that the Celts were admirers of Greek civilisation and on friendly terms with the Greeks. This certainly seems to have been true of Massilia and the Celts of her environs and even beyond. There is evidence of trade in goods of high value and artistry between the Massiliotes and the Celts of Gaul from the sixth century BC. The author of the Periplus refers to the prominence of music at assemblies of the people in Massilia. Is it possible that we have here a shadow of bardic influence from the neighbouring Celtic tribes? At Celtic assemblies, genealogical poetry and song in praise of the chief men was a general custom. Influence also moved in the other direction in the sphere of artistic and intellectual custom. Celtic bards and 'philosophers' are said to have learned to sing in heroic verses: in particular, the 'philosophers', that is the druids, were occupied in the study of the natural universe (Amm. 15.9). Although we may not wish to accept these Hellenisations at full strength, it would be ridiculous to deny cultural interactions of the kind which they broadly reflect. We need not doubt the story that the Celts learned to draw up their legal contracts in Greek.

We may recall that a triple statue of Hecate (or what has been taken to be this goddess) has been found in Massilia (Clerc 1929: 452). Even if we make allowance for the triple character of Hecate in the Classicial tradition, this object nevertheless calls to mind the Celtic tricephals of insular Celtic provenance, and the triad of goddesses, the *tres matres*, or *matronae*, of widespread cult in the Celtic world. We have mentioned the possibility that one alarmed Celtic leader may have identified Athene with the war-goddesses of his own people.

It has been suggested that Massilia's restrictive laws on the behaviour of women may have had the intention of controlling the vivacity of Celtic wives married to earlier generations of citizens, or that they were passed to slow up the rate of intermarriage between Greeks and Celts (Ebel 1976: 30; Dunbabin 1948: 186). Strict propriety in the manners and customs of social and family life were characteristic of some of the cities of Cisalpine Gaul in Classical times. Later Burdigala (Bordeaux) enjoyed a similar reputation. An easy answer would be the narrowness of a self-conscious provincial ethos staking its claim for civilised status in a frontier zone; and this would explain the actual framing of laws intended to stem the progress of barbarisation. Another possible explanation, one which also takes account of mixed marriages, is the intense and passionate view of marital fidelity which is exemplified in several stories handed down about the loyalty of Celtic women: the story of Chiomara is one of these (see Chapter 13).

The allegations that the Massiliotes persisted in the sacrifice of human beings may relate to a Celtic element in the culture of the citizens. This is asserted by Lactantius Placidus (6th century AD) in his comment on Silius Italicus 15.178. The hint that the principal character in the surviving fragments of the *Satyricon* of Petronius Arbiter narrowly escaped being sacrificed (in the sense of being nominated as a *pharmakon* (scapegoat) in Massilia, may point to a comparable strand of ceremonial conservatism which has been reinforced, if not actually introduced, by Celtic influence (Rankin 1971: 57). Later, as a mere provincial city of the empire, bereft of its old independence, Massilia retained still a distinct identity which to some extent reflected its mixed background and composition.

3

Notices in Some
Fourth Century BC Authors

The capacity of the Celts to inspire terror, their quality of *to
kataplektikon*, was not a marked characteristic of their identity for
the Greeks until their invasion of Greece at the beginning of third
century BC (see Chapter 5). Relevant passages from the *Periplus*
attributed to Scylax, which may be as old as the mid-fourth
century BC, are free of this feeling, as are other fourth century BC
references to Celts. They were certainly regarded as usable
mercenaries and are mentioned in this capacity by Xenophon in
his *Hellenica* (7.120.31) in his discussion of the events of 367 BC,
when Athenians, Spartans, and others were opposing the rising
power of Thebes. They are mentioned in company with Iberians,
and it may be that they also are from the Iberian peninsula. They
are more likely to be splinters of the hordes who invaded Italy and
sacked Rome in 390 BC.

Dionysius I of Syracuse (430–367 BC) sent two thousand such
auxiliaries to help the Spartans and their allies against the
Thebans in the Peloponnese (Diod. 15.70). The Spartans seem to
have approved their fighting qualities.

In his *Laws* (637de) Plato makes a specifically anthropological
observation about the Celts: along with Scythians, Persians,
Iberians, Thracians, and Carthaginians, they are both hard-
drinking and warlike. This is what any fourth century BC Greek
would expect of distant, and by definition, less civilised tribes. We
may take it as barely possible, however, that the *Laws*, a work in
progress in the last years of Plato's life (d. 352 BC), may reflect
growth of rumour and information about Celtic national
character. The participants of the dialogue in the *Laws* have before
their attention the question of how they should moderate the use
of drink in their proposed new city-state. They agree that total

abstinence is not to be entertained as a practicable option but it is remarked that some peoples make more vigorous and unrestrained use of drink than others. Excess, such as that of the Celts and others, was not admitted. The kind of indulgence to be found at certain Greek festivals was cautiously accepted by these planners of a new society.

According to Plutarch (*Camillus* 22.4), Aristotle had heard of the Celts sacking Rome, but thought that it was Lucius Camillus who had come to the rescue of the city. If this allusion is correct, Aristotle had heard of the intrusion of the Gauls in 348 BC, when they withdrew from a Rome which was well prepared. His comments on the Celts sometimes appear to show the influence of early sources.

In a discussion of the Caucasus region in *Meteorologica* 350 ab, Aristotle states that the Istros (Danube) rises in Pyrene, a mountain which is near the western equinox and lies in Celtic territory. The Istros flows, he goes on to say, through all of Europe into the Euxeinos. Most of the other rivers flow northwards from the 'Arkynian' mountains. In this account, he seems to be following the general story of Herodotus and his sources. In his treatise on the *Generation of Animals* 748 a25, he refers to the coldness of the Celtic lands which are situated beyond Iberia. Information about the Celts was still hard to obtain in his time; they made no strong impact, as yet, upon his world.

Ephorus (*c.* 405–330 BC) was not an analytical historian, but a promulgator of interesting historical material. Yet his view about the extent of the territory occupied by the Celts is not excessively exaggerated by the standards of the fourth century BC. At this time they did indeed occupy an area roughly equal, as he says, to the size of India. We should not accept Strabo's criticism of him for extending *Celtike* too far into Iberia (4.4.6). He reminds us of the theme of Celtic hardihood mentioned by Aristotle (see Chapter 4), when he remarks that obesity is held to be a punishable offence amongst them.

Theopompus (4th century BC) speaks of the Celtic capture of Rome in 390 BC; he also records that the Celts offered alliance to the *tyrannos* Dionysius I. According to Theopompus' history of Philip II of Macedon, the Illyrians were greatly given to ceremonial feasting. Consequently, when the Celts were making their way into Illyria in the fourth century BC, they invited Illyrian men of power to a feast, and put drugs in the food with the result that the guests, helplessly afflicted with diarrhoea, were easily killed or captured (Ath. 443 bc). The Celts were as well acquainted with ceremonial feasting as the Illyrians. They thoroughly understood that a tradition of hospitality offered convenient opportunities for the elimination of enemies.

Pytheas of Massilia was a navigator and geographer who was at the peak of his career about 310–306 BC. There is every likelihood that he travelled round the British Isles, and possibly beyond. At least he says that Thyle is six days' sailing from Britain (Fr. 6a Mette). In his opinion, Britain's position lay parallel with Borysthenes on the Pontus. He seems to have had knowledge of the seasonal differences which were so marked in Celtic lands and other parts of Northern Europe. In saying that Britain lies to the north of the country of the Celts, he is probably using the designation 'Celt' particularly of those tribes which lived near his native city in Southern France and perhaps also the Celts of Northern Spain. He seems to have distinguished Germanoi from Keltoi (11a Mette).

Pytheas is frequently criticised by Polybius and Strabo, but he had in fact travelled and had seen for himself many places previously unvisited. He estimates the circumference of Britain at four thousand miles (Str. 2.4.1). Cantion, the ancient name of modern Kent, he says is a few days' sailing from Gaul: Britain itself is two thousand miles in length and is rich in cattle, millet, and vegetables, including roots; but the place is cold in winter, and is not very productive of fruit. Because of the unfavourable climate, the corn is threshed indoors, and then stored (Str. 4.5.5.). Pomponius Mela (1st century BC) quotes Pytheas on the subject of the Cassiterides, the 'Tin Islands', which may perhaps be Cornwall. The same author also says that Pytheas refers to an island opposite the Osismici in which priestesses called Senae performed mysterious rites to Bacchus, and were capable of changing their shape (*De Situ Orbis* 3.6).

According to the Periplus which is possibly by Scylax, the Celts are already in the north of Italy as residents: they live next to the Tyrrheni or Etruscans, who in turn are situated next to the Umbri. The fourth century BC flavour is perceptible enough; the author continues to inform us that beyond the Celts are the Veneti and, on the further borders of these, the Istri and the Danube basin. He thinks that the Celts came up the Adriatic by ship.

The genuine Scylax of Caryanda, a geographer in the employ of King Darius of the Medes and Persians, accompanied the king in his first expedition into Scythia in the late sixth century BC. He is not a very likely authority for the comments in the preceding paragraph, which seem to reflect Celtic incursions into Italy even later than the early fourth century BC. The genuine Scylax, who is mentioned by Avienus (370), is a link between the geographical writers of the late Archaic period and those of Classical and Hellenistic times. Our earliest record of the original Scylax is in Herodotus (4.42) where there is an account of the journey he made both to the east and the west. He is attributed with personal knowledge of the world that lives beyond the Pillars of Heracles (Gibraltar). He is also reputed to have made a 'periplus' of Libya. It would not be unreasonable to expect such a writer to have something to say about the Celts.

There is a certain archaic primitivism in the way in which the extant 'Periplus' describes the layout of the territories of exotic tribes: after the Keltoi, the Venetoi, the Istroi, with the river Istros flowing into the Pontus. The Istros is said to turn towards Egypt. However this apparent patina need not be taken to affirm the genuine antiquity either of the essay as a whole, or that this particular section stems from a lost work by Scylax.

With the end of the fourth century BC, the Celts moved from the background of Herodotean rumour and material for analogical anecdote into the midstage of Greek history, in which they proved to be more terrible than earlier primitivising romantic imagination had ever envisaged.

4

Anthropology and Heroics

Distant tribes were a perennial source of fascinating commonplace for Greek and Roman authors. We begin with the picture of the Cyclops' isolated pastoral incivility in the *Odyssey*. He is ignorant of the ways of the city-state. Homer considers him the worse for this. Herodotus (1.153) thinks that the absence of an *agora*, which is essentially the absence of the city-state, promotes honesty and innocence. Where there is no money, only goods, there is less temptation to evil (Schröder 1921: 31). This idea became a commonplace, or topos of literature and oratory. Its constituent themes were freely transferred from one natural folk to another by the sophisticated intelligentsia of the Mediterranean. Clitarchus' opinions about the Indi are applied by Julius Caesar to the Galli (*BG* 6.19.3) and are matched by Pliny's view (*NH* 6.89) about Taprobane, which is modern Sri Lanka (Schröder 1921: 30). Poseidonius (1st century BC) took Herodotus' account of the Scythians (*Skythikos Logos*) as his model for his description of the Celts of Gaul. Poseidonius' information is embedded in the texts of Strabo, Diodorus and Caesar. Tacitus in his *Germania* sees in the Germanic tribes a primal purity resembling that of the most ancient Roman tradition. Not specifically Roman, but none the less to be wondered at, are such customs as the sacrificial killing of a wife when her husband dies, if he happens to be a chief; eating the bodies of the dead, or slaughtering the aged for the same purpose.

The so-called 'Archaeologia' at the beginning of Thucydides' history describes the ethos of very early Greece as being like that of the barbarians of the author's own times (1.5). He stresses that a wandering life of rapine was preferred to the sedentary routine of agriculture, a preference which Herodotus had attributed to most barbarian peoples. Later, Poseidonius says it of the Iberes, and Ammianus attributes it to the Alani. Thucydides says also that the Greeks of very ancient times went about armed, and that most contemporary barbarians observe this custom. Ephorus and Poseidonius report that the Celts carry weapons, and the same is said by Tacitus of the Germans and by Ammianus of the Persians (Schröder 1921: 48).

Many savage peoples were thought to be notably just and decent in their way of living, like Homer's Aithiopes, 'the most just of mankind'. In the *Iliad* (13.3) the Abioi, a northern counterpart in decency of the former, are said to be favoured by Zeus. Our main source for the nobly savage character of remote tribes would seem to be Herodotus. Later authors add local detail to the core of this established topos. We need not suppose that Herodotus was the inventor of the idea in its explicit, non-Homeric form. Hecataeus made a notable contribution to the *Skythikos Logos* (Hdt. 4.49: Schröder 1921: 48). Also, the Scythians may have been mentioned by Hesiod in a work quoted by Strabo (7. 300-2) and in Aeschylus' lost *Prometheus Unbound* (Lovejoy and Boas 1935: 288).

Another topos noted that primitive peoples worshipped the moon, stars, and natural forces, as distinct from irrationally conceived anthropomorphs. This was an idea which understandably interested the sophists of the fifth century BC, such as Prodicus, who criticised the accepted attitudes of their contemporaries. Celtic belief in the power of destiny was likely to raise sympathetic echoes in the thought of Stoic writers such as Poseidonius. Natural tribes were held to practise a pure and natural worship uncontaminated by the artificialities of Mediterranean civilisation. Lucan (1st century AD) follows Poseidonius in saying that the Celts 'worship in the woods, without temples' (1.453), but he does not omit to mention their cruel religious practices. Tacitus also draws attention to the simplicity of German and Jewish religious beliefs and thus follows the line of the topos, which in itself, if excessively simple, was not entirely untrue.

From these commonplaces of ancient anthropology we may construct in outline a picture of the tribes of Northern Europe and Eurasia, wanderers who do not necessarily take up settled habits when they decide to make their home in a country, inveterate warriors, contemptuous of agriculture and given to feasting: Herodotus describes Persian *convivia* (1.133), and Poseidonius was influenced by his description when he came to discuss the feasting customs of the Celts (Schröder 1921: 50–4).

Some aspects of primitive culture were not so admirable as manifest simplicity of character and an imprecise and apparently philosophical notion of godhead. Herodotus relates that the Scythians habitually flayed the heads of enemies (4.64). Ammianus said that the Alani were head-hunters. The Celts were notorious practitioners of this custom (Str. 4.197). Poseidonius managed to accustom himself to the distasteful sight of heads nailed up at the doors of houses. It was a point of Celtic hospitality to draw the attention of visitors to the heads of particular foes (Str. 4.198). Livy describes how the Boii took the head of the Roman commander Postumius (23.24.11). The head of Ptolemy Keraunos eventually was fixed on the end of a Celtic spear. Not merely the Thracians, but the Celtic Scordisci, were capable of using the skulls of enemies as drinking-cups (Ammianus 17.4.4).

Greek intellectuals from the sixth century BC onwards criticised the polydaemonism and the anthropomorphic imagery of the religious tradition. Xenophanes of Colophon suggested that if cattle had gods these would, on the analogy of current human practice, look like cattle. He thought that God was a unity and in no way similar to man. Heraclitus and Empedocles also criticised elaborate temples and images. This kind of viewpoint seemed to find a natural reflection of itself in the elemental worship practised by primitive nations. The Roman polymath Varro says that the ancient Romans were without *simulacra* of the gods for a long time. This is said of the Alani by Ammianus (31.2.23). Herodotus had already pointed out that the Persians and the Libyans worshipped natural elements of the cosmos. According to the Epicurean writer Philodemus (1st century BC), the sophist Prodicus (5th century BC) held that early man honoured as gods the natural substances that support life (DK 77B5). Names of great inventors of benefits for our species were added in time to the roster of deification: the sun and moon and natural forces were given the status of gods (Sext. Emp. 9.18). Nature was the paradigm for the philosopher, and those who lived lives apparently closer to nature, such as Celts and Scythians, seemed likely to have a pure and uncorrupted form of belief. Even if some items of their ritual were unattractive, their simplicity of belief remained as a standing reminder of the decline of man into complexity of myth and ceremony.

Some early peoples were supposed to eat the bodies of their dead (Hdt. 1.216.2–3; 3.99). Some were believed to press involuntary euthanasia on their parents, when these reached the ages of sixty or seventy (Sext. Emp. 3.210). In the fourth century BC, Diogenes of Sinope, the Cynic philosopher, and an advocate of natural practices as far as he was advocate of anything, defended cannibalism on the anthropological ground that 'other races do it'.

Neither this custom nor that of leaving corpses out to be devoured by wild animals was imputed to the Celts, though in their great battles in Greece they seemed careless about recovering their dead for burial. The custom of leaders taking with them into the next world by means of funerary sacrifices the human beings and animals they loved or found useful in this world is imputed to the Scythians by Herodotus (4.7); Caesar did not find it observed by the Celts whom he encountered in Gaul, but it was remembered from an earlier time (*BG* 6.19).

Ideas of personal survival of death were thought to prevail amongst northern primitive tribes by the writers of Classical antiquity. It has been argued that Pythagoras, the alleged innovator of a theory of personal immortality amongst the Greeks, was influenced by northern, shamanistic notions of the soul's ability to maintain itself in separation from the body (Dodds 1951). An understandable corollary of this view about northern tribes was their reputation of holding death in contempt. The Getai were 'a most courageous and most just people' (Hdt. 4.93), who do not know fear in war (Str. 7.297). So also were the Trausi (Hdt. 4.43). According to Poseidonius, the Celts were similarly fearless as the result of the teachings of their druids (Str. 4.197) and on this point he is followed by Julius Caesar (*BG*.6.14.5). Lucan echoes this theme in his poem on the great Civil War: northern peoples are indomitable in war and in their love of death (*Phars.* 8.764). Pompeius Trogus regards the inhabitants of Spain as equally unintimidated by the prospect of death (Just. 44.21).

The ferocity of primitive peoples was a recurrent theme. All Greece used to walk abroad armed: Thucydides refers to this necessary custom of rough old times: *pasa hē Hellas esidērophorei* (1.6.7). Aristotle repeats the idea, and indeed, the verb, *sidērophorein* is in his *Politics* (1268 b39). Ephorus uses the same word of the Celts: *Keltoi sidērophorountes* (Fr.105 Nic. Damasc.). Most primitive people, it was agreed, even primitive Greeks, preferred war to agriculture, of which the tasks were best left to women (Silius Italicus *Pun.* 3.350). In this connection, we may recall Thucydides' perceptive comments about the frequency of migrations (*metanastaseis*:1.2) in earlier times which had the effect of displacing populations and were more in keeping with raiding and a pastoral economy than with agriculture. This style of life, consisting largely of war and robbery, was preferred by the Thracians, especially the Tauri (Hdt. 4.103). As a proof that brigandage was a widespread and acknowledged way of making a living in the early Greek world, Thucydides offers the customary question asked in the *epos* of strangers: 'are you pirates?' (1.51). Caesar says that the British and Germans followed this ancient tradition of theft as a way of life (*BG* 6.35; 5.12). Tacitus supports this (*Germ.* 35); and Ammianus finds brigandage rife amongst Achaians and Alani (31.2.21). The *TBC* has as its definitive plot the theme of cattle-rustling.

Of any tribe's customs, those most liable to misunderstanding by alien observers are those which concern sex. The Greeks, who were strictly protective of the nuclear *oikos* and its women and children, interpreted the apparently freer customs of foreign peoples as promiscuous, or representing the possession in common of women and children. The Greeks had in their midst a primitivistic, still alien, and widely misconstrued set of sexual mores in Sparta. Herodotus reports communism of women amongst the Massagetai (1.2.16), the Libyans (4.172), and the Indians (3.161). The Libyans are quoted as a similar example by Aristotle in his *Politics* (1262 a19). Plato may have used stories of the Sauromatides and other barbarians as sources of his argument in the *Republic* that women should have more freedom to participate in the running of the city-state and that to this end marriages should be temporary and women and children no longer be attached to the nuclear patriarchal family (Rankin 1964: 92). Coexistent with the idea of promiscuity amongst barbarian peoples was another facet of commonplace which claimed that there was a higher standard of sexual fidelity in these wilder societies than in Greece or Rome. We shall consider an example of remarkable constancy in Chapter 13, when we discuss the Galatian Chiomara and the revenge she took on her violator.

In the essay on 'Astonishing Narrations' (*peri thaumasion akousmaton* 837a ff), some adherent of the Peripatetic school shows himself aware of the well-used road from Italy up through Celtoligurian and Celtic territory, which is protected by a series of tribes who are hospitable to strangers and punish anybody who harms them. The writer has a notion of the largely homogeneous culture which stretches through the regions in question, but he may not have known in any detail of the customs and attitudes underlying the hospitality. His words convey the impression of a degree of organisation of traditional practices between tribes which goes beyond local individualism and rivalry. It may be that the source of the essay describes a state of affairs as early as the fourth century BC. The tumultuary hordes of Celts that attacked Italy from the beginning of fourth century BC may seem from the Mediterranean point of view to be devoid of order and organisation, but there must have been a developed network of bonds within the Celtic army to get it started and keep it on the road.

Aristotle and his school may have known more about the Celts than appears in the texts we possess. His constitution of Massalia no doubt contained information about them. In the *Magicus*, possibly a lost dialogue, Aristotle is said to have mentioned druids and holy men amongst the Celts and Galatai. We cannot regard this as hard evidence that Aristotle knew about the druids, for the inclusion of the word Galatai raises some questions, even if these are not taken to be the invaders of Greece and subsequently of Asia (see Chapter 14 below). If they are, then the *Magicus* cannot be a work of Aristotle (384–322 BC). However, we may reasonably take Galatai to be the name for the Celts who moved on Italy and the Balkans during the fourth century BC. If we could accept his reference in the *Magicus* (1497 a: D.L.1.1), it certainly would complete for us a set of remarks in Aristotle that sums up the main characteristics of the Celts as a culture or cultural aggregation: that they are hospitable and protective towards strangers; that they have a distinctive attitude towards nature, that they have a class of holy men or philosophers, and that they are warlike and ferocious.

On the subject of that almost definitive activity of the Greek city-state, warfare, Aristotle brings Scythians, Persians, Celts, Thracians and Macedonians into comparison for their warlike qualities with the Dorian warrior-states of Sparta and Crete (*Pol.* 1324 b). The list is almost identical with that of Plato in his *Laws* (637 de). We are, I am sure, looking at an established topos. In the fourth century BC the Celts were becoming increasingly well known to the Greek world. Their name was added to the register of barbarians whose unusual customs could usefully be cited in argument. Like the Scythai, Amazones, or Antiphon's entirely imaginary Skiapodes, or 'Shadow-feet' (5th century BC), the Celts could provide a premiss for the criticism and analysis of Greek assumptions about their own inherited customs. This was an amplification of the attitude to distant and strange tribes which we see in Hecataeus and Herodotus.

According to Aristotle, the Celts imposed a harsh regime on their children. They hardened them to cold by allowing them very little clothing in the face of a severe climate (*Eth. Nic.* 1336 a). This is a likely comment about any northern nation. He also says (*Pol.* 1269 b 26–7) that although it is to be noted that most belligerent nations are much influenced by their women, this is not true of the Celts, who openly prefer attachments between males. —

Athenaeus echoes this comment (603a) and so also does Ammianus (30.9). It seems to be the general opinion of antiquity. It may have its origin in the essentially warlike character of early contacts between the Celts and the Greeks in which the Celts, like other primitive warriors on campaign, would be governed by a ritual abstinence from women. This would be in no way discordant with the occurrence in insular Celtic tradition of powerful and warlike women, such as Scathach, one of several great female teachers of martial arts (Thurneysen 1921: 404), or the ruthless queen Medb. Nor can the historic Boudicca have lacked predecessors.

The Celts erupt into Aristotle's discussion of fear and courage as representatives of the extreme of rashness:

> Of those who run to extremes in this matter, the man extreme in his absence of fear has no specific name to describe his condition (I have already said that extreme conditions often have no precise name to describe them). Anybody would be mad or completely bereft of sensibility if he feared nothing; neither earthquake nor wave of the sea, as they say of the Celts. (*Eth. Nic.* iii 5 b28)

Aristotle thinks that courage should be purposive and for the sake of some good end: *kalou dē heneka*. The character he sees in the Celts is boldness for its own sake, and this is irrational. That in their temerity they do not even fear the waves of the sea is said of the Celts in the essay 'On Astonishing Narrations' (837a ff); but consider also the *Eudemian Ethics* 1229 b28, which comments that some people know the dangers of thunder and lightning but face them through boldness of spirit (*dia thymon*), just as the Celts take up arms and go against the sea.

All barbarian courage is based on this *thymos*, this 'daring spirit', and the word carries the implication of lost or absent self-control. Fighting the sea is attributed by Ephorus (*FHG* 44: Str. 4.4.6) and Aelian (*Ver. Hist.* 13.3) to the Cimbri. This tribe, in alliance principally with the Teutoni(es), inflicted severe defeats on Roman armies in the first century BC until they were eventually destroyed by Caius Marius. The Cimbri originally lived on the coast of the North Sea. So also did tribes more generally agreed to be Celtic. Poseidonius suggests that the story of the Cimbri fighting the sea is fictitious (*FGH* 31: Str. 7.2.1–2) and that the same applies to the rationalising interpretation that they moved from their home territories because they were frightened by tidal floods. The nature of the tides, he thinks, would be sufficiently well known to them and need not be a cause of panic. He argues that they put these stories about because they were looking for a pretext to go on a raiding expedition.

Were the Cimbri Celtic? According to Pliny (*NH* 4.95) and Solinus (19.2) the part of the northern sea that edges the land of the Cimbri was called 'Morimorusa' in Celtic, meaning the 'Dead Sea' (Goidel. *muir marbh,* Bryth. *môr marw*). Beyond this is the sea Cronium, meaning 'withered' (cf Ir. *cron*), or possibly 'frozen'. These placenames do not prove that the Cimbri spoke Celtic at the time referred to by the authors, or indeed, at any time of Classical reference. What they indicate is the presence of Celtic speakers in the area at some time, and that they were in residence long enough to give lasting names to places. The British placename 'Morecambe' means 'curved sea' (*mor com*) in Celtic, but it is a considerable number of centuries since speakers of Celtic lived on its shores.

On the flat lands of the northern European coast inundations of the sea frequently destroyed life and dwellings. In spite of Poseidonius, the plundering journeys of the Cimbri and their associates may have been caused by such flooding of their tribal lands and, as an alternative to migration, it is possible that some of the warriors may have put on their armour and fought with the sea. Ephorus said that more Cimbri died of drowning than were killed in battle. Taking arms against the sea was not necessarily a purely symbolic act: more plausibly it was a heroic embrace of honourable death which would ensure the immediate transportation of the soul to a good afterlife. The sea was a living entity, a god well worthy of combat, just as in the Homeric *epos*, river-gods can be attacked and put to flight by mortal heroes. This belligerent attitude to unfriendly natural forces is not confined to Celts or Germans, but the tradition about the Cimbri may form the basis for the remarks in Aristotle and Aristotelian writers on the extreme fearlessness of the Celts.

The same tradition may also be connected with the story of Caligula leading his army to the sea-shore opposite Britain and ordering his soldiers to gather up shells (Suet. *Gaius* 46; Xiphilinus 166.36: Dio 59.25.1–2). It is tempting to interpret the incident as a piece of late Julio-Claudian dementia; on the other hand it might have been a calculated assertion of power over the sea, and by inference, what lies beyond the sea. The lighthouse which the Emperor built on the Channel coast is accessible to a similar interpretation. This was sufficient to have him hailed as 'Britannicus' by his army (Dio 59.25). Both acts may have been in response to an appeal by Cunobelinus' son Amminus, who wanted the Romans to intervene in British affairs to his advantage. They may have been enough to satisfy Amminus' immediate requirements. The prestige of Rome's numinous presence as an ally may have been more useful to Amminus than the actuality, which could have had some inconvenient aspects. His British compatriots might see the Roman emperor by these acts making himself master of the protecting sea, and therefore of Britain herself. A diplomatic victory was obtained without putting ill-disciplined legions to the test of battle. The legionaries themselves would console bruises to their dignity at being told to gather shells by the reflection that at least they would not be called upon to cross a dangerous sea and fight. As P.J. Bicknell has pointed out in his ingenious article on this affair (1962: 74), the legion contained a proportion of Gallic soldiers who could understand and approve the manoeuvre, and Caligula himself had some knowledge of Celtic traditions and ways of thought.

Another, later descendant of the theme of fighting the sea may be identified in one of the several versions of the story of the Ulidian hero Cu Chulain's reaction to his discovery that the young stranger he has fought and killed is in fact his own son. In the version which was followed by W.B. Yeats in his verse-play *On Baile's Strand*, Cu Chulain is so enraged when he finds out the identity of his opponent, that he rushes into the sea and fights it until he dies. Versions of the story in the Irish literary tradition do not represent Cu Chulain as responding to the terrible event in this way, though he still dies in the sea. In the death-tale *Aided Enfiri Aifi* from the *Yellow Book of Lecan* Cu Chulain does not displace his anger against fate and himself towards the sea: instead, a cry of lament is raised and for three days no calf is allowed to be with a cow throughout Ulster (Meyer 1904). In the metrical *Dindshenchas* (Gwynn 1924: 134–6) we find another variant of this story of the death of the son Cu Chulain begot on the foreign warrior woman Aife; in this, the lament over the young man's grave has become a standard ritual amongst the Ulstermen. Other stories, long preserved in the oral tradition, have the hero fighting the sea and meeting his death in it. A version of Cu Chulain's killing of his son Caonlaoch which comes from oral sources in north-west Ireland says that, after the death, Cu Chulain is tied up on the shore to fight the sea and that he does this for seven days and nights until he dies. The other Ulster heroes have bound him, so that the anger he feels may not turn against them. A similar version is transmitted by Augusta Gregory in *Cu Chulain of Muirthemne* (1902): according to this story, the king Conchubar instructs Cathbad the druid to draw magic circles round Cu Chulain, so that for three days he fights the sea and expends his anger on it rather than on the Ulstermen. These versions come from oral tradition of the eighteenth and nineteenth centuries AD; Yeats' version would appear to be derived from them (Bjersby 1951: 27).

The theme of fighting the sea is clearly both ancient and potent in the Celtic cultural tradition. In its light we may observe a people driven by a heroic fury which is alien to Archaic and Classical Greece and to the whole Classical tradition, except perhaps for Achilles at his most daemonic. Greek sentiment attributed the failure of Xerxes' invasion of Greece in no trivial measure to his having had the impudence to chastise the Hellespont, a god, with lashes for its bad behaviour to his bridge of ships. He also treated it like a slave when he bound the pontoons across it with chains and ropes (Hdt. 7.33–7; Aesch. *Persae* 746ff). Nevertheless, Homeric heroes fight with gods and even wound them, as in the *Theomachia* (*Iliad* 16), the battle of the gods, without incurring punishment for *hybris*. Close to the Celtic fight with the sea is Achilles' combat with the river Scamander (*Iliad* 21) in which the hero is rescued from defeat only just in time.

We might also wonder whether collective attacks on the sea were not at the same time a useful method for cooling the courage of a tribe's warrior-group when no expedient object for their aggression presented itself. This could at certain times and places be related to frustration at not being able to fend off the sea's incursions on tribal land. We may call to mind the incident in *TBC* where Cu Chulain is thrust into a vat of water to cool his dangerous, manic rage, though we should not forget another possible explanation, namely that the story represents an unfocused reminiscence in a later, Christianised era, of the sacrifice by drowning, such as may be illustrated on the Gundestrupp cauldron. Another transmogrified version of the theme may be seen in Cnute's deliberate and ceremonial failure in commanding the sea to go back. This may be the vestige of an ancient custom appropriate to tribes who lived in places subject to inundation; and possibly Cnute was demonstrating that old ideas about fighting the sea and about the power of sacral kingship needed modification in the modern world of the eighth century AD. Notwithstanding these speculations, Aristotle and many who came after him were impressed by what seemed to be a trait peculiar to the ancient Celts, their capacity to launch into a condition of manic ferocity in which they knew no fear. This was one of the characteristics which made them extremely frightening to the Greeks when they invaded Greece in the third century BC. People who were daring enough to fight the sea were capable of anything. Whatever the explanation of their wars with the sea, it would be hard to find any action more alien to the Greek spirit of propriety in relation to the gods and humane good sense.

When Aristotle speaks of the Celtic lack of fear in the face of such phenomena as earthquakes and decides that they are rash rather than courageous, he uses words such as *mainomenos*, 'crazed', or *analgētos*, 'lacking in normal sensitivity' (*Eth. Nic.* 1115 b25). There is some evidence, however, of professed fear of natural forces on the part of ancient Celts. When Celtic ambassadors discussed a treaty with Alexander the Great, Aristotle's distinguished pupil, they admitted fear of nothing, except, perhaps that the sky should fall, and he thought them merely vainglorious (Str. 7.38; Arrian *Anab.* 1.4.6). He may have misunderstood the meaning and intention of their statement. True, they were declaring themselves free of fear of *him*; but they were probably also using a formula of emphasis in support of their desire for a treaty of equals with equal. Whether or not they felt completely secure in such an implication is another matter. Their form of words, which may have been close enough to an oath, actually referred to a substantial fear that the world might sometime end (Livy 40.58.4–6; Jullian 1906). In the Irish law tracts the oath which relates to the proper ordering of a contract (*aitire*) commits not only the individual party's corporeal integrity in keeping the bargain, but involves the natural elements also:

'oath of breast and cheek, heaven and earth, sun and water' (Thurneysen 1928: 22). The Celts certainly were frightened of such manifestations of natural power as thunderstorms, because they thought that they might presage the end of the universe. Their religion had an elemental bias. The weird weather at Delphi contributed to their panic and defeat (see Chapter 5 below) in psychological as well as physical terms.

Drink and feasting were an important component of the ethos of Celtic and other IE societies. One of their functions was the forging and maintenance of close bonds between the leaders and the main body of the warrior-group (Lévi-Strauss 1972: 339). Greek memories of earlier customs are stored up in the passages of the Homeric *epos* which describe such feastings, which as well as being effective bonding rites, could also be impediments to warlike efficiency in the time and substance that they consumed. The Classical Greek symposium was a descendant of the ancient feast, which itself may be descended from a much earlier custom of sharing out food amongst the members of the hunter-group.

Celtic ceremonial feasts involved honour contests⁻ for the 'champion's portion' (Ir. *curadmír*). Single combats were held between banqueters, and occasionally individuals entered into contracts whereby they would agree to be killed for the payment of a determined reward. Some of these features of the Celtic feast have left traces in the Irish sagas: *Fled Bricrend*, *'Bricriu's Feast'* (*FB*), *Tain Bó Cúalgne* (*TBC*), and *Scél Muice Meic Dathó*, 'The story of Mac Datho's Pig'. Poseidonius was aware of similar customs in the Celtic tribes of his own time (1st century BC):

> Belligerent in their customs, they often have single combat at dinner in which real injury is possible and even the death of the combatants. There is great rivalry for the champion's portion. They are also known to allow themselves to be killed for an agreed sum or properties.
>
> (Ath. 154c: *FGH* 16)

The violent activities of the *FB*, including the intrusion of monstrous characters making arrangements with Cu Chulain to cut off his head, are, no doubt a mythologised version of the tradition. Like *TBC*, the *FB* presents a condition of ancient Ireland, predominantly that of the first century AD, not much later than Poseidonius' own time. The *fled* (Bryth. *gweledd*) may be etymologically related to the Homeric *eilapine*. Keating (*FF* 1.13) describes a contest for the *curadmír* in Emain between Conal Cernach and Laoghaire. The former of these characters could be an avatar of the horned god Cernunnos, still known in Britain as Herne the Hunter. We may conjecture that Poseidonius heard of the custom of *curadmír* from some old story like *FB* or *Scél Muice Meic Dathó* (Dinan 1911: 314). Both *FB* and Poseidonius mention the champion's contract in which a man allows himself to be killed for a price (MacCana 1977: 89–90). Poseidonius had seen what he regarded as Celtic barbarities at first hand, and he had become hardened to some of them. We could suppose that he had heard of feasts of this ferocious sort carried on further off in the wilder parts of the Celtic domain which he had not visited. He seems to know of the rough custom of earlier times by which each hero at a Celtic feast would rush for the champion's portion so that challenges and fights arose from the scrimmage (Eustath. 1606.14; Dinan 1911: 332–3). We may observe that ancient Irish law laid down punishments for illicit seizure of the *curadmír* (Henderson, *FB* xiv). There is no indication that Poseidonius regarded these uncouth activities as mythical. He sees them as old customs (Ath. 4.40; Diod. 5.28.1–6).

The champion's portion occurs in *Iliad* 9.208. Here we find Agamemnon offering Aias the best piece of the animal's back, the hindquarter of pork which is supposed to be particularly choice. In the section of the *Odyssey* that is set in Phaeacia, the poet Demodocus is served with an especially fine piece of meat at the suggestion of Odysseus.

Poseidonius says that armed men were in attendance at the Celtic feast and that an order of precedence was observed amongst the guests. We learn from *Scél Muice Meic Dathó* (17) that the men-at-arms could influence the contest for the *curadmír* both by making an intimidating wall of shields and by using the ritual of bone-casting or bone-pointing. Meat was generally eaten, but fish was available in coastal areas; wine imported from Massilia or Italy was drunk by the upper classes; the poor people drank korma, a kind of mead. The cupbearers served drink from right to left, the direction which was observed in the worship of the gods. Poseidonius also testifies that the eating and drinking habits of the Celts were leonine, but clean; on this point he is clearly speaking from personal observation.

The feasts of Mycenaean heroes in the Homeric *epos* were frequent and lavish but they did not have any noticeable effect on the progress of the siege and warfare against Troy. Achilles' heroic temperament was a much greater impediment to the achievement of victory. The Phaeacians of the *Odyssey*, on the other hand, live on a peacetime footing, and enjoy a noticeably higher standard of comfort than the army before Troy: their feasting is regular, and obviously part of the bonding ritual we have mentioned. A variant of this may be seen in the perpetual feasting at the expense of an absent host on the part of Penelope's suitors. When the Olympian gods are in residence on Olympus, their feasting is understood to go on without cessation. However, we need be in no doubt that the feasting custom of the Celts significantly impaired their military efficiency, especially when they were at war with more tightly organised forces. Diodorus records that Celtic mercenaries employed by the Carthaginians brought about the defeat of their own side at the hands of Caecilius at Panormus in the First Punic War (3rd century BC) through their drunkeness (23.21).

In *TBC*, when Medb reviews her forces, she decides to exclude or kill a section of them called Gálioin because their military efficiency and briskness of organisation makes the rest of the army look foolish. These Gálioin probably were part of the pre-Goidelic population of Ireland who were taken into the service of the Goidels in the long struggle against the Ulaid (Ulstermen) with whom they probably share an ethnic origin. They did not indulge in protracted ceremonial feasting, and so made better headway against the Ulaid than did the Goidels. A Goidelic genealogy was later invented to assimilate them (*EIHM* 95). Medb did not implement her original decision; instead, the Galéoin were dispersed through the rest of the army, so that their effectiveness would be less noticeable.

In the aftermath of their invasion of Greece in 279–278 BC, the Celts were greatly injured by quarrels which broke out amongst themselves in their army. Polybius (2.19) explains this as the result of too much food and drink. He is right up to a point. The ceremonial feast provided the ideal scene for the outbreak of quarrels and recriminations after a defeat. The consumption of food and drink in great quantities was a consequence of the potlatch type of social obligation that pressed upon Celtic leaders and chiefs. Given the independent status of chiefs in a heroic or 'Iliadic' way of living, individual quarrels on points of honour could easily cause wider conflicts.

Wily and unscrupulous chiefs could manipulate the feasting custom with an eye to its potential for generating quarrels. The eponym of *FB*, Bricriu, held a feast from which he was himself by prior agreement absent, but which he watched from the comfort of his *grianan* ('sun-room'). He managed to bring the men and women guests into two sets at violent cross purposes by carefully devised challenges and innuendo. Like Thersites in the *Iliad* (*FB* xi), Bricriu was not completely accepted as a member of the heroic society of the Ulaid, and he skilfully makes use of its mores to throw it into confusion and dismay. In another example of such management, Mac Datho deploys the competitive element in the heroic feast to take the baleful pressure of powerful neighbours off his back. Mac Datho is king of the Lagin, who are of similar stock to the Gálioin. Both Medb of Connacht and Conchubar Mac Nessa, king of the Ulaid, wanted a wonderful dog that Mac Datho had, and each sent delegations to intimidate him into giving it up. Mac Datho manoeuvred the two groups into conflict over the honour-portion of an immense pig which was the centre-piece of the feast he held for them. His plan was to get two powerful parties at loggerheads in order to free himself from the pressure they were putting on him, for he had a much weaker kingdom than either Medb or Conchobar. The customs of the feast provided him with levers which he could operate in his own interest.

Hannibal's treatment of some Celtic prisoners he took while he was crossing the Alps also reveals a skilled exploitation of the Celtic honour-code for the purpose of entertaining his own men who were weary and worn out by their sufferings in the transit of the Alps. According to Polybius (3.62) he set up a competition amongst his young Celtic prisoners who had endured very harsh treatment, being lashed and loaded with chains on the march. He put them in a space in the middle of the army and set before them suits of arms of the kind used by Celtic chieftains in single combat. Horses and rich cloaks were also put up as prizes. Lots were drawn. The Celts prayed for good luck, and the fortunate winners were set to fight each other in pairs. The prisoners who were not fighting congratulated the dead as much as the victors who survived. The former were at least at an end of their hardship. Polybius comments that Hannibal's soldiers were at this stage very much of the same opinion.

Hannibal knew enough about Celtic customs to manipulate them for the sadistic enjoyment of his troops. He had good reason to be knowledgeable in this field, for he hoped to benefit from the enmity towards Rome of the Celts of northern Italy. In the Celtic community, the whole issue of victory or defeat could be decided by single combat between leaders, and the Celts accepted the application of this custom in wars against non-Celtic peoples. Manlius Torquatus got his cognomen from the torque he took from the Celtic prince whom he killed in an agreed duel. This custom of decision of a war by single combat takes the heroic ceremonial of Celtic warfare to the extreme bounds of its honour-centred motivation.

Ptolemy found, in the course of his war against Magas (see Chapter 5 below), that his Celtic mercenaries were planning to take over his kingdom of Egypt. In leading them to a desolate island in the Nile, he knew that he could rely on their individualist, heroic pride to make them turn on each other when it was exacerbated by starvation: it would not suggest to them that they should co-operate to escape. He was a shrewd enough anthropologist to realise that the trait which made them good mercenaries, eager for glory and reward rather than moved by loyalty to cause or race, also made them vulnerable to the kind of pressures he had devised for them.

Bricriu, Mac Datho, Hannibal, and Ptolemy had interests which lay outside the code of the honour-portion, feasting and heroic ceremony which was part of the Celtic ethos. They were free to deploy this ethos against those who were its firm adherents. Yet in general, hospitality was an obligation of the weightiest kind in all quarters of the Celtic world, and its rules were only seldom perverted in the interests of policy. Celtic chieftains were under a social compulsion to give hospitality and gifts to dependants, followers and kin. As in the potlatch custom, the act of giving conferred prestige on the giver. Desire for prestige entails the need for publicity: there were poets who spent their professional lives disseminating the glory of princely openhandedness. They came to be in a position in which they could demand their price, for they could also create the opposite of prestige by satirising a chief's meanness, like the unknown Irish poet who expressed his disappointment in the memorable epigram: 'I have heard he does not give horses for poems/he gives what suits his nature: a cow.' Poets were sometimes employed as malign diplomats. When a prince wanted to stir up trouble for a rival, he could send his poet into his enemy's country with the instruction to make judiciously provoking satire or create a *casus belli* by refusing as unworthy the gifts offered for his poems (Rhys 1898: 324–5).

The description by Poseidonius of an amazing example of potlatch is preserved in the text of Athenaeus' *Deipnosophistai*

(151e–152f). Louernius, the son of Bityes, a Galatian prince whom the Romans had conquered, wanted to bid for the leadership of his tribe. He used to drive over the plains in his chariot scattering gold and silver to the enormous crowd of people following. He fenced in a space twelve stadia square, set up wine presses in it and brought in vast quantities of food. Anybody who wished could be entertained most lavishly and politely. This went on for a number of days. A poet from some barbarian people arrived late and, when he met Louernius on the road, produced an ode to his generosity, sorrowing over his own unfortunate lateness. As the poet ran along beside his chariot, Louernius called for a purse of gold and threw it to him. The poet may not have been a Celt, but there is no doubt that he knew the appropriate idiom of adulatory verse. He continued his ode, singing that the very footprints of Louernius brought benefit to the human race. The imagery and the effusive gratitude could easily be paralleled in the Irish bardic tradition, even as late as the seventeenth century AD, when Eoghan O'Rahilly was praising the last Gaelic patrons.

Phylarchus of Naucratis (2nd century BC) tells another story of prodigious spending. His story of Ariamnes of Galatia is also preserved for us by Athenaeus (150b–f). Ariamnes announced that every year he would give a feast for all the Galatians. Throughout all Galatia he divided out the countryside by measuring the roads, and built, at determined intervals, banqueting halls, each of which was capable of holding four hundred guests. Each had had a large cauldron of stew which was kept boiling all the time. Not only his compatriots were eligible for hospitality, but passing strangers were pressed to come in and share in the feasting.

These two instances may remind us of the stories of the great hostels, the *bruidne*, of Irish mythology. These places of hospitality were patronised by kings and seemed to have a religious significance (*EIHM* 120f). They may be taken to occupy a location overlapping this world and the next. Louernius and Ariamnes marked out the areas for their hospitality in a way that could suggest the making of ritual precincts and not merely acts of capable administration. In Irish mythology, the Bruiden Da Derga, and the Bruiden Da Choca, are, as their names imply, under the patronage of deities. These establishments, of which there were six, according to the tradition, were places of considerable danger: some of them were destroyed by fire and heroes perished in them; which may be an additional indication of their sacral or sacrificial function (Ross, *PCB* 82–6).

The cauldron in the story of Ariamnes may be more than merely an instrument of generosity. In the archaic Greek world, cauldrons and tripods were prized possessions, carrying with them an aura of prestige from the time when the age of metal was young. By the same token, in the Celtic world they were not simply status symbols, but frequently had a cult significance (*PCB* 57). They were associated with gods, as was, for instance, the cauldron of Da Derga which provided unending sustenance for his tribes and at the same time had a regenerative function, bringing life back to the dead (*PCB* 233) on a larger scale than the cauldron of Medea.

Who paid for this prodigality? It was the redistributed product of the tribe's efforts in agriculture and war. The chief of a tribe was supplied plenteously by its lesser members and dependants. The difference in status between chief and ordinary tribesman was considerable (Caes. *BG* 6.13), but the relationship between them was not that of landlord and tenant until Roman times, for the Roman bureaucracy could not grasp that tribal territory could be a possession of the tribe as a whole rather than the assignment of a chief or prince.

The example of the Vaccaei may illustrate this question of land-ownership. Poseidonius (Diod. 5.43) records that it was the custom of this Spanish tribe to divide their lands up every year, to make the harvest common property and divide it amongst members of the tribe, with the provision of punishment for anybody who took more than his share. This account has some of the atmosphere of a topos about primitive communism, but it may also be a shadow of a distinct fact of Celtic social usage.

The custom of redistributive generosity had to have its limits. In the life of St Brigit we find that her family objected to her inveterate habit of giving all she could lay hands on of their property to the wretched, needy and poor. So far as we can regard her case as historical, we may see in it a radically pagan Celtic obligation at the point of metamorphosis into a Christian virtue (see Chapter 13 below). In any event, the burden of her charity was borne not only by her family but also by their clients. The biography of Brigit (*Bethu Brigte*) is quite clear that her tendency to give was regarded by her family as a serious menace to its economic survival. Of course, it was not her business to do the giving but that of her father, who was in a better position to judge what the family could sustain. In the two instances which we have discussed there is a definite bidding for power and prestige on the part of the conspicuously generous princes. Brigit is in some respects parallel, in that she is pursuing a spiritual state by comparably generous material acts.

An ancient Celtic warrior in a seizure of fighting fury was a fearful adversary to face; and Greek horror at the invasion by such in 279 BC was well founded and hardly exaggerated. Until his condition changes, he is as likely to be a danger to his own people as to the enemy. Consequently, a displacement trick is needed to turn his energy in some less deadly direction. When Athene in the first book of the *Iliad* prevents Achilles from killing Agamemnon, we have a relatively late and sophisticated version of such a trick. In *TBC* there is another means of defusing heroic wrath.

Cu Chulain is more ferocious and labile than is Achilles even at his most murderous. He is a raw original of the old IE version of Achilles which is concealed in the Greek *epos* under a layer of Aegean art and civilisation. When Cu Chulain achieves his first real distinction as a hero for the slaughter of the sons of Nechta, the king, Conchobar, views with apprehension his return to his own people:

> I know that chariot fighter [he says]; it is that young fellow, my sister's son. He went to the border [between Ulaid and Ireland] and his hands are very red. He has not had enough fighting, and if he is not met, all the young men of Emain [the capital of Ulster] will be killed by him.
>
> (*TBC* 1183–5)

The following device was used: one hundred and fifty naked women were sent out to meet him. He hid his face against the side of the chariot to avoid the sight of their shame and this enabled him to be lifted down safely to have his anger cooled in three successive baths of cold water, which vaporised with explosive rapidity, and he blushed from the top of his head to the ground. His good humour and his usual handsome appearance, which had been distorted by fighting mania, were restored (*TBC* 1186–99).

The Greeks and Romans saw in the Celt a survival of the heroic code of life. In the statues of the 'Dying Gaul' there was expressed the stern determination of an Aias choosing death by his own hand rather than enduring to live with dishonour (Tierney 1960: 198). There is also in this heroic picture more than a trace of the Stoic gentleman's philosophised version of the ancient rule of honour.

The physical character of the Celt is described as tall and blond (they even whiten their hair with lime). Their nobles grow moustaches and shave their cheeks (Pos: Diod. 5.27). The Greeks thought that moustaches were odd and probably unhygienic. One of the Archaic *rhētra* (ordinances) of Sparta commands the warrior-class of *homoioi* ('peers') to shave their moustaches and keep the laws. The general appearance of the Celts was 'terrifying' — the adjective *kataplēktikoi* is used to express this, and its meaning is emphatically precise in this regard. Their voices were deep and very guttural (*baryēcheis kai pantēlōs trachyphōnoi*). In conversation they were brief and allusive (*brachylogoi*): most of their meaning they leave to be inferred. Yet when they are praising themselves or abusing others — presumably in the preliminaries of a fight — they are full of eloquent exaggeration. Their manner is menacing, stressed and highly dramatic (Pos: Diod. 5.30).

This could easily be a word-portrait of the men of the Irish sagas. It might even contain a suggestion of tendencies to aspiration and hiatus which we find developed in later extant Celtic language. Their talk sounded harsh and throaty to the tonally attuned Greek ear.

Poseidonius says that the main fighter on a chariot is a noble. The driver of the chariot is from a humbler grade of society (like Cu Chulain's charioteer Loeg) though presumably he is of free status. We are told that the warrior challenges his enemy before fighting and recites as part of the challenge his distinguished genealogy, which both authenticates his right to challenge a noble adversary and in addition may constitute a ritual of intimidation. These genealogical declarations not only celebrated the challenger's own origins, they could also include ridicule of the opponent's character and family (Diod. 5.29, Dinan 1911: 317). Genealogy had an important function in Celtic warfare and knowledge of noble ancestries was kept alive by the poets.

The Roman historian Claudius Quadrigarius (Peter 1906–14: 1.207) is said to have described the encounter between Manlius Torquatus and a Celtic leader in the Gallic war of 361 BC. His account of the incident is preserved by Aulus Gellius (2nd century AD). It has also been used by Livy (7.9.6). The Celt fought naked but had a shield, two swords, his torque and armlets. He is said to have put his tongue out and laughed at Manlius.

Nakedness in combat was not invariable. According to Poseidonius, some Celts wore iron breastplates, and had helmets elaborated with frightening ornaments and excrescences (Diod.

5.29). He mentions that they had two-edged swords, which were, we may suppose, not unlike the Highland *claidheamh mòr*. The lack of manoeuvrability of these weapons at close quarters often was an important cause of Celtic defeat. The nakedness in the case we are considering may have had a ritual significance: single combat may have had some of the character of a divine trial involving the sacrificial death of the defeated. As Livy tells the story, the Celt went into the fight singing some kind of battlespell (*cantabundus*, 'singing', is the neutral word which Livy uses), and the historian contrasts this with the staid steadiness of his Roman opponent (7.9.6). Again we may have the aroma of ritual penetrating the fog of Roman prejudice. Livy praises Roman contempt for barbaric customs in war such as colourful clothes, gold ornament, singing, boasting and empty clashing of arms (ibid.; cf. 6.42.2). Of course, Manlius killed the Celtic chief, and took his torque as a trophy, earning the cognomen of 'Torquatus' for himself and his descendants.

In spite of their habit of collecting the heads of enemies and other rituals alien to Greco-Roman notions of decent military efficiency, the Celts were acknowledged to be a gifted people. They have acute intellects and are quick learners, Poseidonius admits. They have intellectual classes: these are bards who compose poems of praise and satire and accompany their recital on the harp; philosopher theologians called druids; and prophets. These latter observe the flight of birds and inspect the entrails of sacrificial victims as methods of divination. Human sacrifice provides predictive guidance by the way a victim falls when stricken, the convulsions of his dying limbs and the flow of blood from the wound (Diod. 5.31). No sacrifice was allowed to take place without a *philosophos*, a druid, being in attendance. It was this class who understood the supernatural world and was in contact with it. They were mediators between humanity and the gods. Not only this, the druids were people of great political influence both in peace and war. In the case of the bards, not only friends, but enemies pay attention to their songs, and their influence has been known to bring wars to an end.

With their mixture of cruelty and theory, intellect and superstition, the Celts were not seen as mere fighting maniacs but as a society with its own philosophy and accumulated learning. As Julius Caesar points out, this learning was orally transmitted and no serious use was made of writing in connection with it. We hear, however, of Celts writing letters to the dead and incinerating them so that they will reach their intended recipients in the next world: this custom may have developed after the Celts had come into contact with the Greeks of Massalia and the art of writing.

A poetic class in a society postulates a formal training in the art of poetry involving a system of oral composition and transmission. To sustain this, there is need of a body of information classified under headings which facilitate memorisation from which students and practitioners can draw material for their individual works. The same, we may note, can also be true of an educational system which makes use of writing, like that of the Greco-Roman world, if it also places importance on rhetoric and speechmaking, as that world did for many centuries. The triads of Ireland and Wales, three-fold proverbial utterances on a wide variety of subjects, may be descended from an oral repertory of themes. Also there may well have existed in the Celtic world of Classical times some genres of composition not unlike those which survive in the older Irish literature, whose *scéla* ('stories') fall readily into such categories as: battles, deaths (of heroes), courtships, elopements, massacres, plunderings, birth-tales, hostings, feasts, other-world adventures, migrations, eruptions of rivers, and visions (MacCana 1972: 75).

This list, it will be noted, contains most of the themes treated in the *Iliad* and the *Odyssey*. Descriptions of places, such as those preserved in the Irish *Dindshenchas*, draw in part on ancient thematic sources of this kind. These old vestiges of an oral tradition survive in several manuscript copies of which we may mention the *Book of Ballymote* and the *Yellow Book of Lecan*, both of the fifteenth century AD. The material in the collection belongs to different periods: one of the earliest verse articles is attributed to Mael Muru (Othna) who died in 887 AD (Gwynn 1935: 93). Nobody knows exactly when the topographical poems and articles were first collected and written down, but the idea of such a conglomeration of knowledge may go back to very early times, when it was part of the education of important members of a tribe to know in detail localities and their features and names. We might also suppose that these items had some relation to the geographical and historical course prescribed for the eighth year of the course of poetic training. Such knowledge would be of clear practical value to a warrior. We are told (*Lebor Uidre* 5102–7) that Cu Chulain had to learn all the places and their names that were visible from the boundaries of Ulster.

This information would be useful to a society which was engaged in tribal and border warfare and was moving slowly into the territory of its rivals. But spying out prospective possessions and learning the features of new land also could be a serviceable tactical technique for a horde that was moving more quickly. However, in less fluid conditions, this packaged topographical knowledge could be of the utmost utility to a poet: knowledge of places and their associated myths could assist his livelihood as a maker of honorific songs for patrons in these neighbourhoods (Gwynn 1924: 91).

Much of the information from Classical sources which we have been considering in this chapter will also underlie the one which follows. It comes mainly from the texts of authors such as Strabo (64 BC–21 AD) and Diodorus Siculus (1st century AD), and also Pausanias (2nd century AD). These writers are not so late as to be completely out of touch with a credible ancient tradition about the subjects they discuss. Strabo and Diodorus present us with much that comes from the Stoic writer Poseidonius. Pausanias' account of the Celtic invasion of Greece in the early third century BC (the subject of our next chapter) is based on the work of a number of writers who lived nearer to the time of the events and who are not to be neglected as evidence, whatever we may think of their bias or rhetorical habits. When Pausanias chooses to imitate Herodotus' account of the Persian Wars of the fifth century BC, we know where we are in terms of literary and historical intent: he is expressing an analogy between the struggle with Persia and the threat to Greek civilisation and freedom represented by the Celts. However, we cannot be so clear about the sources he used who belong to the third century BC.

Hieronymus of Cardia is a likely informant of Pausanias. He lived at the time of the Celtic invasion of Greece, and his work is quoted twice by Pausanias. Since Pausanias was far from being an obsessive researcher, we might easily overestimate the influence of Hieronymus in his account of the Celtic invasion (Hornblower 1981: 72). The fact that Diodorus also mentions Hieronymus, not as a writer, but as a historical figure, may indicate that he also used his writings (Hornblower 1981: 72). The web is tangled, especially when we try to trace the influence of Timaeus, who was in exile in Athens during the crisis. He also may have taken something from Hieronymus. Some have supposed that he was a source used by the Celtic author Pompeius Trogus, whose work survives in that of Justin. According to Polybius, Timaeus made a close study of Gauls, Iberians and Ligurians. Trogus, Diodorus, and Pausanias all may have used Menodotus of Perinthus and

Agatharchides of Cnidus. There may be an early origin for the tradition distinct from that followed by Hieronymus and Pausanias about the fate of Delphi in the invasion. Livy seems to have had access to a source which says that the Celts actually sacked Delphi (28.48.2).

Our present discussion is more concerned with the evidence of two historians, Polybius and Poseidonius, men of sophisticated insight and critical acuteness. The work of the former is extant in large portions; the latter is quoted and referred to by Strabo, Diodorus and Athenaeus (3rd century AD).

Polybius was a citizen of Megalopolis who was deported to Rome, with other Greeks, on the orders of Aemilius Paullus after the Battle of Pydna in 168 BC. He had been active in Greek politics from an early age. He was the son of the Achaean General Lycortas, and a friend of Philopoemen, the last statesman of an arguably free Greece with a claim to personal distinction. In Rome, Polybius became friendly with Aemilius' family. He learned to understand the captors of his country and himself and to appreciate their system of government.

In his general history, Polybius is interested in the Celts mostly as cultural contrasts and military threats to Rome. In his view the Romans had been induced by their long-standing dread of the Celts to engage in the continual reorganisation of old legions and the enrolment of new ones, and they had busied themselves with such tasks even in 226 BC, though they had defeated the Celts many times since those early encounters when they had been routed by the fury of the Celtic charge (2.23). By implication, the Celts, as perennially imminent invaders, had been an important formative influence on the development of Roman military power. For Polybius, the conflict between Romans and Celts was essentially the contest between reason and the irrational (2.35). The Celts were incapable of forward planning or consistent practice (3.14). In their temperament there was no reliability, but an instability (*athesia*). This unpredictable volatility made the Romans unwilling to use the Cenomani as allies against the Insubres in 223 BC. Polybius sees this *athesia* as a moral defect. He does not connect it with the heroic lability of temper which is to be seen in the main characters of the Greek *epos*.

He provides a description of their way of life which was later to be useful to Livy. They are, he says, a nomadic people, not unlike the Veneti (2.17), whose pressure upon Celtic territories led them to abandon their siege of the Roman Capitol in 390 BC

(2.18). The Veneti have a different language. The Celts live in open villages (2.17). They have no permanent buildings; their beds are on straw, and they mostly eat meat. War and agriculture (the latter in the case of Cisalpine Gaul) are their principal occupations, and they have no organised body of knowledge or any art. Their main notion of property is cattle and gold, which are portable. Their highest value is placed on friendship. Clienthood is part of their social organisation and a man is estimated by the number of his clients and friends.

We may connect this last proposition with the conspicuous efforts of Louernius to purchase obligation and popularity. Polybius shows little appreciation of the poetic and philosophical culture of the Celts: he is too keen to represent them as unintellectual children of nature to investigate their thinking. Not that we need suppose the highest level of Celtic culture to have been spread evenly amongst all Celtic people, any more than literary, scientific and philosophical interests evenly pervade our own world. Also, the tribes which impinge on his attention are on a war-footing, and consequently less preoccupied with the finer arts of living. The importance attributed to friendship brings to mind what may be a Celtic cultural trait in the Roman poet Catullus (1st century BC), who was of Cisalpine origins. He was most acutely conscious of his friends' good faith towards him, their constancy in attachment and the opposite of these characteristics. When he suspects, no doubt rightly, that he is betrayed, his pride and sensibility are agonisingly irritated in a way that recalls Achilles rather than a more Classical Greek or Roman temper of mind. In our own times, two distinguished men of a country which retains Celtic characteristics, namely James Joyce and Sean O'Casey, were notable not only for their poetic genius, but for the bitter resentments which they nursed throughout their lives at certain bad friends.

Polybius seems to have acquired a clear understanding of the gradual building up of the Celtic threat against Rome and its early allies, and of the original intrusion of Celtic tribes into the Po valley, in which they destroyed its Etruscan cities such as Melpu (in 395 BC), which was to become Mediolanum, one of several of that name in the Celtic domain, and is now Milan. Though he had a well-developed sympathy with the Roman view that the Celts were a menace to Roman security, he was able to isolate this view and observe it as a distortion of perspective on their part in that their preoccupation with the Celtic threat, which was by no means

an unreal danger, had obscured a greater peril in the growth of
Carthaginian power in Spain (2.22). His disregard of Celtic
culture is its higher forms does not necessarily mean that he was
completely unaware of it: he had visited Celtic countries in person
(3.59). He was interested in Celts as wagers of war and does not
interest himself in any aspect of their customs which has not some
relevance to their military capacities. As a historian, he has the
right to select in relation to his subject, and his summary of the
Celtic wars of Rome before the conflict with Carthage became the
predominant issue of her survival is extremely useful.

He is interested in the visual impression created by Celts on the
field of battle: the bright clothes of the Insubres, notably the
trousers (a sure mark of barbarism in the Greco-Roman world),
and the bravado of the Gaesati, who rush into battle naked. The
name of this Alpine tribe is probably connected with *gaisos*, which
means 'javelin' and is a word which has been given an Iberian
origin in Athenaeus 273f. It may also be related to OIr *gai* 'a
spear'. Polybius translates 'Gaesati' as 'mercenaries' (2.22),
which, if its original meaning is something like 'spearsmen' in
Celtic is by no means an unreasonable secondary meaning, when
we consider such words as Greek *doryphoroi*, the attendant
bodyguards of tyrants and dictators. He explains that the Gaesati
threw away their clothes for fear that brambles should impede
their fighting by entangling them (2.28): this is obviously the
viewpoint of a plain Roman legionary rationalising a ritual
nakedness that he could not understand; nor has Polybius an
interest in scrutinising the matter further. Also described is the
great noise of trumpets, horns and battle-cries that emanates from
a Celtic army. The gold ornaments worn by the fighters in the
front rank, the principal warriors, make a formidable appearance.
In another part of his account, Polybius mentions the wearing of
heavy leather trousers and breastplates, which contrasts with the
nakedness of front-line fighters who were defenceless against the
javelins of the Roman legionaries. He tells us that the Celtic shield
was of inadequate size and the sword unsuitable for battle against
legionary formations. The sword, in addition, was sometimes of
inferior quality (2.23). No aspersion is cast upon the ferocious
courage of the Celtic fighters. Polybius sums up the defeat
inflicted on the Celts by the Romans in 225 BC, shortly before the
outbreak of Rome's long conflict with Carthage in which the Celts
were destined to play an important part, by emphasising that the
Celts had no capacity for rational planning, but conducted their

whole campaign on impulse. Polybius' own career in the military and political life of Greece, his experience of Roman society and its discipline, his admiration for the latter and his intention as an historian, all help to explain his attitude to the Celts. To him they were wild fierce barbarians who had almost destroyed the civilisation of Greece and the growing power of early Rome, and who had continued to be too useful an ally to the Carthaginians. We have no grounds for thinking that he cared to know much more about them than that. He knew about Brennos, Bolgios and Achichorios, who were Celtic leaders against Greece in 279 BC (1.6.6), but he had known in person the great Philopoemen.

Poseidonius (b. *c*. 135 BC) continued Polybius' historical narrative from 145 BC to 82 BC. Of the historians of the ancient world who discuss the Celts, he is the one who not only saw for himself their way of life and customs, but who also was prepared to learn from what he saw. He had the analytical intellect of a philosopher and the intuitive insight of an anthropologist. He visited Spain, considerable portions of Gaul, and the land around the Alpine region. He may have visited Britain about 100 BC. His account of the Celts was used by Julius Caesar in his commentaries on his campaign in Gaul.

Celts had once again become prominent inhabitants of the Roman consciousness as a result of the war waged by the Romans against Transalpine Celts from 125 BC to 121 BC. This continuing prominence stimulated the historian to take an interest in them (Tierney 1960: 199). Although he had the sensibilities of an anthropologist, Poseidonius was no more free from prejudice than many other similarly gifted observers. His criticism of some features of Celtic ethos, such as boasting, drunkenness, human sacrifice, head-hunting and excessive faith in divination (Str. 4.4.25) reflects his Stoic distaste for irrationality and superstition. As Tierney points out (1960: 211), Poseidonius' comments on Moses are by no means fulsome. Yet it is much to the credit of his percipience that he draws a parallel between the champion's portion contest of the Celtic feast and the passage of the *Iliad* (7.21) in which Aias is honoured after his successful fight with Hector by being given the best portion of the animal. His handling of the story of Louernius is intended to demonstrate the importance of wealth in Celtic politics (Tierney 1960: 221). His attitude was scientific in its regard for the theory that the development of people and their societies is affected by the nature of their physical environment. This view is to be found in the Hippocratic treatise on *Airs, Waters and Places*: it eventually became embedded in the teaching of the Peripatetics and was long maintained there. There may be an early evidence of its influence in the argument in Plato's *Republic* which seeks to associate phases of the individual human mind with related sections of the social and political order (Tierney 1960: 190f, 220).

Poseidonius admits that at first he was disgusted by the Celtic custom of preserving and exhibiting the heads of enemies, but he says that he became inured to it after a time (Str. 4.5.4). This was one of the cherished customs of the Celtic world to which the Romans put an end in areas under their rule. His comments on these heads and his reaction to them show some of the pertinacity and breadth of mind that we should expect in a field anthropologist. Other items in his description suggest hearsay rather than personal testimony. His reference to solid ice in the sky is one of these: perhaps it is an excessively dramatic description of a hailstorm, but it is more likely to refer to harsh freezing, since he speaks of rivers turning into natural bridges (Diod. 5.25). There is also the story of winds strong enough to blow the clothes off people. This could be based on some unusual but actual happening (Diod. 5.22).

Poseidonius rejects fables: Strabo says that he acutely conjectured that the nomadic life of the Cimbri prevailed as far as the Sea of Asov. He thought that the Cimmerian Bosphorus derived its name from the Cimbri (Dinan 1911: 349f). He was influenced here not only by the type of etymology which many intellectuals of the ancient world, and especially the Stoics, believed in; but by the tendency of the old geographers to divide Northern Europe and Eurasia on the one hand between Celts in the West, and on the other, Cimmerians in the East. The Cimmerians were subsequently replaced by Scythians. He mentions the Boii as resident in the Hercynian Forest. They repelled the wandering Cimbri when their territory was invaded by them. The Cimbri gradually moved towards the Danube and the land of the Scordisci. From there they moved on in the direction of the Taurisci. When eventually they came in contact with the Helvetii, these formerly peaceful people decided to join them in a life of depredation.

Poseidonius also speaks of British tin-mining; of the thickly populated nature of Celtic countries (the fecundity of the tribes was no doubt a cause of their warlike migrations); but our credence is strained when he says that British kings live largely at peace with each other (Diod. 5.27). Even by the belligerent standards of Greek and Italic city-states, the Celtic cantons could hardly be described as largely pacific in their neighbourly relationships. Nevertheless, Julius Caesar (*BG* 5.12) reproduces Poseidonius' view on this as on many other matters of Celtic culture. Poseidonius sees the British use of chariots in war as an archaism reminiscent of the methods of fighting in the Trojan War.

His description of the use of chariots is also close to that attributed in the Ulster cycle to the principal heroes on both sides. The chariots are drawn by two horses. The warrior throws his javelins from the chariot, and then steps down to fight naked with his adversary. We are indebted to him for his account of the *trimarcisia* (three-horse) technique of chariot-fighting, which was an arrangement of replacements in a battle. The chariot at this time was particularly characteristic of British warfare, and seems almost to have become extinct in other Celtic countries.

He is impressed by the innocent archaic courage of the Celts in battle, and mentions their dependence on the impact of their first great charge at the enemy (Str. 4.43). Yet this simple nature and absence of cunning is accompanied by sharp intellect and a great capacity for learning. The Celts and Germans he regards as similar: the Rhine is the boundary between them (Str. 4.41.2f). Amongst the Celts, the form of government is generally aristocratic, and it is their custom to elect a new leader every year. Military leaders are elected by the whole population of free men (Str. 4.43). Kingship persisted amongst the Insular Celts in Classical and later times. Julius Caesar confirms that there was a ruling class of nobles in Gaul. Slavery may be inferred not only from the testimony of Irish texts but from the discovery of what appear to be slave chains in pre-Roman Iron Age sites (Salway 1981: 15).

Strict discipline was observed in tribal assemblies, which seemed to be more like those of Sparta than Athens. If a man spoke out of turn or caused annoyance, a piece of his clothing was cut off by an official appointed for that purpose (Str. 4.4.3). The fact that such an official was needed itself indicates that good order was more of an ideal than an actuality. The assembly of the Greek army before Troy in the second book of the *Iliad* shows us Thersites asserting himself above his station and being put down in a brawl by Odysseus.

Poseidonius does not neglect to mention Celtic hospitality, according to the rules of which strangers were not asked who they

were or where they came from until they had been fed and cared
for; a piece of archaic good manners which reminds us of the
Phaeacians in the *Odyssey* who were prepared to wait for information from Odysseus about his identity and adventures until they
had discharged their obligation as hosts. This is the politeness of
a frontier society where a bandit may appear off-duty in another
district as an entirely harmless traveller. Thucydides was well
aware of the circumstances and motives which formed the basis of
this old-fashioned politeness (1.5.2).

We may probably attribute to Poseidonius the following
comments, which are not without anthropological interest, but
which have the air of being compressed and derivative:

> The women [of the Celts] are as large as the men and as
> brave. They are mostly very fair-headed when they are
> born. The tribes of the north are extremely ferocious. The
> Irish and the British are cannibals. They used to be known
> as Cimmerioi; now they are called Cimbroi. They captured
> Rome and plundered Delphi and ended by dominating a
> great part of Europe and Asia. They mixed easily with the
> Greeks and this section of them became known as
> Gallograeci or Hellēnogalatai. (Diod. 5.32–3; Str. 4.43)

Poseidonius does not attempt to palliate the fact that the Celts
on a number of occasions defeated large and powerful Roman
armies; but he points out that consonant with their martial
ferocity they practise weird and unholy sacrificial customs.
Criminals are kept for five years and then are impaled and burned
on large wicker shields as sacrifices to the gods. They also sacrifice
prisoners of war and they torture and burn or otherwise destroy
the animals they capture in war (Diod. 5.32). Another method of
human sacrifice is described which seems to involve drowning
(Str. 7.2.3).

We learn from Poseidonius that the Celtic women are
beautiful, but that the men pay little attention to them. He
elaborates slightly the comment we have already noted in Aristotle's *Politics* about the prevalence of homosexuality amongst
Celtic men. The young men will offer themselves to strangers and
are insulted if the offer is refused. He mentions that the men all
lie down together on skins (Diod. 5.32). Possibly some kind of
bonding ritual within the warrior group is involved which requires
abstinence from women at certain times.

According to Poseidonius, the Celts not only believed in the immortality of the soul, but adhered to many of the tenets of Stoic physical theory (Tierney 1960: 223). The druids were the guardians of this philosophical tradition. At the same time the Celts were still using human sacrifice as a means of divination, and carefully preserved the skulls of their enemies. The inconsistency need not trouble us any more than the observance of Roman religious ceremonies by philosophically educated Romans of the late Republic and early Principate or the attendance of these same gentlemen at capably staged barbarities of the gladiatorial games (see Chapter 14 below). If indeed the Celts held the view that the cosmos was animate, animated and purposeful, and that the individual soul was immortal, they were not too far from the general Stoic position. There can hardly be any doubt that their religious thinking was interpreted in a more philosophical fashion by Poseidonius than was warranted by the reality. Caesar, on the other hand, may have exaggerated the social and political function of the druids in Celtic society. The more virulent he could make the druids appear as fanatical instigators of war, the stronger his case for the annexation of Gaul (Tierney 1960: 211).

Caesar's use of Poseidonius is an example of one eyewitness perverting the evidence of another to suit his own very different intentions. Caesar was not a historian: he was a political war-lord in need of good public relations material with which to confuse both friends and enemies in Rome about the true nature of his activities in Gaul. Caesar did not see so much of actual Celtic life as did Poseidonius. While it was necessary for him to have some understanding of the people against whom he was waging war, he did not need to know more than was necessary to accomplish their defeat. Unlike Poseidonius, he did not see the Celt as natural man, the noble savage uncorrupted by the complexities of urban civilisation. Poseidonius recognised their ancient heroic code for what it was and saw some analogy with the way of life described by the *epos* and he also observed that their way of life was moderate (*tas te diaitas euteleis*). When he adds that they have no contact with the luxury produced by wealth (Diod. 5.22), he is scarcely convincing, except in so far as a people can have a naïve greed for gold, either for its own beauty or for ceremonial purposes, without being corrupted by it.

It is hard to square any of this with the gold-hungry raiding Celtic armies which devastated large tracts of the civilised Mediterranean world. Poseidonius himself mentions the great quantities of gold which the Celts possessed, though he says that much of it was consecrated to the gods; much of it was nevertheless regarded as personal wealth. In this connection he refers to the wearing of gold torques (Diod. 5.27). In this whole question we should remember that very few social phenomena are narrowly univalent: the torque may have been a convenient instantiation of wealth and prestige, but it also had a ceremonial significance beyond the value or otherwise of its metal. We can neither confirm nor reject Poseidonius' opinion that the Celts remained in general innocent of the corruption carried by gold. He admits that they allowed themselves the luxury of imported wine, which replaced their native mead (*zythos*). The Celts seemed to like gold and they also admired, as their princely burials attest, beautiful works of art. Their liking for these may have been a trifle more innocent than that of such Romans as Caepio, who robbed a sacred Celtic pool of the rich offering that had been sunk in it (106 BC).

Certain common themes are evident in Poseidonius' anthropological comments on the Celts: primitivism; extreme ferocity; cruel sacrificial practices; the strength and courage of their women. Poseidonius is a reasonably detached observer. His account is a condensation of Greco-Roman tradition and experience of the Celts up to his time, together with some analysis and some eyewitness observation. He would like to see Celts as natural men with a leaning towards Stoicism; for a Stoic, there is nothing more natural than to find Stoicism in a natural state in the wild. His Hellenic prejudices against barbarism and the irrational are fairly well under control.

Polybius is willing to emphasise the bad faith of Celtic mercenaries (2.7) rather than their heroic characteristics. He does not ask himself why Celts should feel themselves bound to richer and more powerful aliens whom they would in other circumstances regard as legitimate prey and plunder. Their role as mercenaries was, after all, only another phase of their vocation as invaders who extorted money from cities by threat. Poseidonius' knowledge of them is deeper and is irrigated by the universalist sympathies of the Stoic. Yet he is affected to a degree by old Golden Age topoi about the uncorrupted innocence of savage foreign races. When we consider the traumatic and at the same time stimulating effects of the Celtic invasion of Greece in the third century BC upon the Greek ethnic consciousness, and the terror inspired in the Roman soul for centuries by the Gallic *tumultus*, we can only feel respect for the reasonableness of our historians. They represent the distinctive enquiring aspect of the Greek mind. Another approach to the problem posed by the Celts was the attempt to assimilate them into the body of Classical myth.

The answer was not hard to find: Hellenic Galatia was said to have been named after Galatos, the son of Cyclops and Galatea (*Et. Mag.*; Dinan 1911: 145). According to Caesar (*BG* 6.18) the Gauls looked on themselves as autochthonous, and the children of Dis pater. Timaeus said that they were descended from Polyphemus and Galatea or from a giant called Keltos (*FHG* 1.200). The Cyclops, we recall, is the type of natural uncivilised man in the *Odyssey*: he would seem to be an appropriate ancestor for these wild large-limbed fighters. Another account makes Heracles their ancestor, who, in the course of his wanderings in the West begot Galatos or Keltos (Diod. 10.24; Amm. 15.9.36; Parthenius 30). Athenaeus (284c) informs us that Callimachus wrote a poem called *Galatea*. It presumably argued that the Galatai are descended from Galatos, the son of the Nereid Galatea. Callimachus mentions the Celts in his *Hymn to Delos* (171ff):

when Brennos from the Western Sea
led hosts for the overthrow of the Greeks.

It is a pity that we do not have more on the subject from this most distinguished of Hellenistic poets. Another significant Hellenistic writer has left us his neat summary of the myth. In one of his *Erotica*, or love-stories compiled for poets to adapt, Parthenius of Apamea (1st century BC), a teacher of Virgil and friend of the poet Cornelius Gallus (d. 26 BC), tells how Heracles wandered through Celtic countries when he was bringing the cattle of Geryon from Erytheia. He came to (the king) Bretannos, who had a daughter called Keltine. She fell in love with Heracles and hid his cattle, refusing to give them back to him before he had made love to her. Now because Heracles was in a hurry to recover his cattle, and even more because he was struck by the beauty of the girl, he had sexual intercourse with her. A son was born to them in due time. He was called Keltos, and from him the Celts got their name (Parthenius 30).

This is a typical Hellenistic *aition* or explanatory mythical story. Its origin can hardly be earlier than the Celtic invasion of Greece in 279 BC. Heracles, the friend of man and civilised ways and, incidentally, a canonical hero of the Stoics, is used to assimilate the wild invaders into the Greek tradition, just as hundreds of years earlier (11th century BC) another set of invaders, the Dorians, claimed descent from Heracles and were called Heracleidai: the story was that they were not alien, but the descendants of Heracles come home at last from their northern exile. The story of the barbarian princess who compels the wandering hero to sleep with her is a familiar topos. Calypso in the *Odyssey* is an obvious example. Parthenius is supposed to have used the story of Keltine in his poem *Heracles*. It is not extant.

Timaeus tells the story that the Argonauts found the Black Sea blockaded by the forces of Aeëtes, King of Colchis, and so were unable to return home by the way they had come. They dragged the *Argo* overland, and according to Timaeus, they dragged it to the head of a river, the Tanais, which discharges into the Northern Sea, and in this way they were able to return to Greece. A proof of this was the fact that the Celts, an indubitable northern people, worshipped two prominent Argonauts, Castor and Pollux (Diod. 4.56). Perhaps Cernunnos and Smertullus were the Celtic gods who seemed to correspond with the Dioscuri.

The Celts themselves were not slow to respond to the blandishments of mythopoeia. The Galatians of Asia Minor would not eat the flesh of the pig, because the divinity Gallus, whom they had adopted as an eponymous hero, had been killed by a wild boar (Paus. 7.17). In view of Celtic fondness for pork, this was a serious matter: Celts lived mostly on milk and meat (Pos: Str. 4.4.3; Polyb. 2.15). The Aedui thought that they, like the Romans, were descended from Trojans, and this sense of kinship underwrote their long alliance with Rome (Amm. 15.95; Lucan 1.428).

The next two chapters will consider the varied contacts between Celtic peoples whose values were those of the age of the epic, and the two most highly organised contemporary societies, those of Greece and Rome, who had not forgotten the ideal of heroic achievement, but had so adapted it to the city-state community that they had difficulty in understanding the raw original when it confronted them.

5

The Second Finest Hour of Hellas

When Celtic warriors in a furious horde invaded Greece in 278
BC, her inhabitants saw in their eventual victory over this
northern terror a glorious renewal of the triumphs against the
Persians in 490 BC, and 480–479 BC. Some stimulant for their
national pride was needed. Since the victory of Philip II at
Chaeronaea (338 BC), Greece had been substantially under the
power of Macedon. There were restless movements amongst the
cities from time to time: attempts to regain the old freedom for
destructive rivalry. One such attempt after the death of Alexander
was crushed after a deceptive initial success. Yet Athens and the
others still retained enough illusory independence to become
resentful at each setback to old pretensions and irritably willing to
risk another futile throw in a game which they could no longer
afford to play. The city-states were haunted over generations by
the ghost of their defunct importance and were unwilling to
discard their claims to individuality and liberty of action whether
the imminent suzerain was Macedonian or Roman.

A fragment of poetry on a papyrus of the third century BC has
a reference to Celts, possibly in connection with some Hellenistic
king, and compares the 'wild Celtic warrior' (*thouros anēr Galatēs*)
with the Mede (J.U. Powell 1925: 131). The Celtic attack became
embedded in the great drama of Greek mythopoeic history. The
invasions were indeed savage and severe in their effects and the
fear which they inspired can hardly be exaggerated. The Greek
cities rose to the occasion, but in fact the peril was less than in the
Persian Wars. They did not face an enormous and well-organised
empire led by rulers of the calibre of Darius or Xerxes, who were
intelligent and determined leaders whose considerable strategic
and political gifts enabled them to sustain their policies and plans

over a longer period in command of vast and disparate hosts. The Celts were a partly concerted horde of heroic individuals not unlike in temperament those much admired figures of Greek epic, Diomede and Achilles, in their least co-operative moods.

At the same time, the Celts in action were of an unrestrained savagery that had not previously been encountered in enemies of this strength and number. Further, they did not seem to care what became of the territory they entered so long as it provided booty. Pausanias deliberately sustained the parallel between the Celtic incursions and the wars against the Persians. In this he was following his own sentiment and taste, especially in the favour he shows to Athens in his account. His emphasis, however, was broadly in tune with Greek tradition in the matter. The defeat of the Celts was a mighty salvation. A national festival in its memory, the *Soteria* or 'Salvation', was instituted soon afterwards.

From the north had come the earliest layers of IE speakers into the Greek peninsula, bringing, perhaps, a language not unlike Luwian, and thereafter dialects which became Mycenaean and probable related varieties of speech. In mythology this pressure from the north, as well as from the Aegean, is a recurring motive. Achilles is a northern hero, sometimes as much a menace as an ally to the lords of Mycenaean Greece. The exiled Heracleidai came home from Epirus in the guise of Dorian invading tribes, descendants of primeval banished ones. The Persians invaded from the north, both by land and sea. The security of lines of communication in the Thraceward region was a preoccupation of the Athenians throughout the Peloponnesian War: hence their dismay at the loss of the important base of Amphipolis, which they tried to recover not only in the course of this war, but for many decades, even in the time of another northern threat in the shape of Philip II of Macedon. This area was in Classical times essential to the security of Athenian food-supply from the fertile shores of the Pontus. It held back the barbarian aggressor from the jugular of civilisation. From the lands north of the Vale of Tempe, even those north of Thermopylae, little but trouble could be expected with certainty, and no alliance was dependable.

There was no single inheritor of the vast empire which Alexander had acquired and which stretched from the Aegean to the Punjab. Greek city-states of the old dispensation had participated in this great work of conquest as satellites, not principals. After Alexander's death, the city-states revolted, and were firmly put down by Antipater in what has become known as the Lamian

War. The successor generals of the dead conqueror became fiercely competitive warlords, who struggled to divide the conquered territories between them. They were in effect satraps, ruling over wide tracts of Asia. In Egypt, Ptolemy wisely staked his claim, but our interest in this chapter is directed more in the direction of Macedon and Thrace as well as Greece itself. It could be said that Antipater, the veteran general of Philip's time who succeeded Alexander in Macedon and Greece, had been able to hold the empire together after a fashion, in that while he lived his influence helped to prevent it from falling into chaos and conflict; but when he died (319 BC) rivalries turned into wars.

Wars promised well for the profit of northern tribes who were watching the situation. Fragments of history probably ascribable to Alexander's general Ptolemy, son of Lagus, describe the Celts of the Adriatic discussing a treaty of friendship with Alexander in 335 BC. As we have seen, they maintained that they feared nothing except that the sky might fall (Str. 7.3.8; Arrian *Anab.* I.4.6). They were safe enough in their assertion, for they knew very well that Alexander had no intention of invading their territory but had his gaze turned towards Asia. Still, if the sky were not about to fall, they could value the goodwill of such as Alexander, who gave them their treaty, hoping that they would be the less troublesome while he was occupied in other directions. Arrian also tells us (perhaps on the authority of Ptolemy) that in 323 BC a delegation of Celts came to Babylon along with representatives of other nations to pay their respects to the conqueror. This was the first time that the Macedonians had seen Celtic war-equipment and armour. If this is consistent with the story of the embassy that sought a treaty in 335 BC, then at that time we may suppose that Celtic warriors were not a familiar sight in the region — indeed they may not yet have been sighted at all. We should suppose that the ambassadors of 335 BC would not have come to negotiate peace fully arrayed in arms. Primitive warriors would not usually hesitate to do so. Indeed they would be ill-advised to go to negotiations unarmed in many circumstances. These Celts, in spite of their heroic formulae about the sky falling and the like, had perhaps become shrewd in the diplomatic ways of the southern world even at this relatively early stage of contact.

They were no doubt speculators, like most migrating tribesmen, whatever their tongue or race. The later embassy to Babylon would no doubt include a survey of the prospects for predatory raids. They knew that a time would come when Alexander would be no more, and that this might be an opportunity for their people. In accordance with the style of their own wandering expeditions over Europe, they attached great importance to individual leaders chosen for the purpose of some great enterprise, and such leaders were in the nature of things vulnerable to misfortune. Alexander's role would lend itself readily to interpretation in Celtic terms.

Although we do not intend to study the destructive square dance of Alexander's successors, we need to be aware of the effects of their activities, which can have done no other than raise Celtic hopes for a prosperous future. Cassander in Macedon and Lysimachus in Thrace were in alliance with Ptolemy against Antigonus, whose ruthless military energy had made his the stronger power in Asia. Seleucus, whom he had driven from his base in Babylon to seek refuge with Ptolemy, was restored. Demetrius, the son of Antigonus, managed to engage the help of the Greek cities by declaring them free from Macedon and Cassander. The cities had another intermission of their slavery which, though merely apparent and temporary, was nevertheless welcome. In the drama of succession, there were parts even for minor actors.

Demetrius succeeded in repelling Cassander in his attempt to retake Greece (304 BC). Cassander had been encouraged to make this effort by Demetrius' preoccupation with a lengthy siege of Rhodes. In 303 BC, Demetrius recreated the league of Greek states centred on Corinth, a body originally instituted by Alexander. At Ipsus in Asia Minor, a battle was fought in 301 BC in which the forces of Lysimachus and Seleucus defeated the armies of Demetrius and Antigonus. Antigonus was killed, but Demetrius escaped. As a result of this Lysimachus came to possess a substantial portion of northern Asia Minor. In Mesopotamia Seleucus was supreme, and also in Syria, although Ptolemy occupied northern Syria as the price of his support for Seleucus. Cassander ruled in Macedonia. Demetrius retained power by sea and in some of the cities of Greece and Asia Minor. The Athenians' renewed taste of liberty remained unchallenged in this chaos of conflicting aspirations until Demetrius occupied the city in 295 BC. In 297 BC Cassander had died, and his sons quarrelled among themselves about the inheritance: they fell prey to Demetrius' ambitions, and Macedon was seized from them. Pyrrhus, king of Epirus and later the invader of Italy, was also defeated by him. He began to entertain wider ambitions towards Asia Minor.

In 288 BC Lysimachus and Pyrrhus seized Macedon, and Athens rebelled against Demetrius' rule with the aid of Ptolemy I. Demetrius' campaign ended in a disastrous defeat at the hands of Seleucus in Asia Minor in 285 BC. He was taken prisoner and in a year or two had succeeded in drinking himself to death.

Lysimachus increased his power as a result of the eclipse of Demetrius. His domination embraced Macedon, Thessaly, Thrace and parts of Asia Minor. The other strong man who emerged from the conflict was Seleucus. A struggle for power between the two was inevitable. Seleucus came to an agreement in 283 BC with Demetrius' son Antigonus Gonatas, whose mother had been a daughter of Antipater. Ptolemy's exiled son Ptolemy 'Keraunos', who had been dispossessed in favour of his half-brother, Ptolemy II, became involved on Lysimachus' side. Lysimachus was married to Arsinoë, who was the half-sister of Ptolemy 'Keraunos', who owed his nickname 'Keraunos' ('thunderbolt') to his impetuosity. These offshoots of the founding Ptolemy conspired to bring about the murder, at the instigation of Lysimachus, of Lysimachus' son Agathocles. Disaffection and discredit followed this act. Seleucus crossed to Europe and defeated and killed Lysimachus. Ptolemy Keraunos assassinated Seleucus, whose period of glory as the sole ruler of Alexander's empire was dramatically brief (281–280 BC). Ptolemy claimed that by this action he had avenged the killing of Lysimachus.

In his lifetime, the power of Lysimachus had kept back wandering groups of Celts and other aggressive peoples. Although Ptolemy Keraunos was able for a time to keep control of Macedon, his rule, like his personality, was unstable, as his transactions with the Celts will illustrate.

The Celtic migrations which had harassed Italy since the beginning of the fourth century BC had been give a temporary but effective check by the defeat the Celts suffered from the Romans at Sentinum in 295 BC. In the next decade, however, large groups began to build up in the Danube valley and Illyria. About 279 BC the dam burst: one Celtic army moved north-east against the Triballi and the Thracian tribes. This was led by Cerethreus; Brennus and Achichorius led their force east against the Paionians; and Bolgius moved south-east into Macedon.

There had been an attempted invasion of Macedon and Thrace under the leadership of Cimbaules, but it had no effect because local resistance was too strong (Paus. 10.19). The first serious incursion was led by Bolgius (the name is probably a ceremonial leadership name) in 281 BC. Ptolemy Keraunos emerged from his welter of murderous intrigue to become in 281 BC the first arguably Greek leader to die at the hands of the Celts. The country had been weakened by its recent troubles, but it could have been effectively defended against the invaders, had it been competently led. Ptolemy misread the situation. He had already rejected both warnings about his peril and offers of help from the Dardani, a Thracian tribe, who found that they had no option but to join forces with the Celts. Ptolemy misunderstood when the Celts, in a characteristic *démarche*, offered to refrain from attacking if he gave them a sufficient sum of money: he thought that they were suing for peace rather than blackmailing him. So he told them that he would accept the idea of peace with them, if they handed over their leaders to him as hostages. This proposal amused them (Justin 24.4). Ptolemy joined battle and was defeated. The Celts took his head and placed it on the point of a spear.

By a minor irony of history, the leader of the Celts who defeated Ptolemy had a name or ceremonial title which matched that of Keraunos. He was called Bolgius, which also has the notion of a flash of light in its meaning. The Fir Bolg were an early layer of the successive invaders of Ireland, and the name is embedded in many placenames throughout the island in this context. 'Bolg' is the genitive from a nominative plural 'Builg'. It has been suggested that the Builg took their name from a deity called Bolg (nominative singular) (*EIHM* 42). The name may be connected with /bheleg/, 'shine' or 'flash', and the god in question, who no doubt gave the Belgae their name, was a thunder-god like Zeus or Juppiter (*EIHM* 51ff). A Latin inscription from Gaul, near Lyons, *Iovi Fulguri Fulmini*, suggests this function of deity. The coincidence is less surprising, if we remember that we are discussing peoples who were all of the IE family and worshipped sky-gods.

The next Celtic onslaught was in 279 BC, and was under the leadership of Brennus and Achichorius. 'Brennus' also seems to be a titular name, possibly having a kingly meaning (Bryth. 'brennin', 'king'), and it has been suggested that it was the title borne by Achichorius. Macedon would have been swamped by the vast Celtic army had it not been for Sosthenes, a man of modest origins, who gathered an army together and defeated the Celts (Justin 24.5). His initial successes were not decisive. The Celts were not only numerous, but vigorously led, and soon there was nothing to prevent them from moving south into peninsular Greece.

When Antigonus had made peace with Antiochus, he returned to Macedon and found himself confronted by the Celts whom Brennus had left behind in setting out to invade Greece itself. These had already demolished the armies of the Triballi and the Getae (Justin 25.1) and now they threatened to take over Macedon. They sent ambassadors to Antigonus to see whether he would buy peace from them and also to combine some judicious spying with the negotiations. They came back with enthusiastic accounts of his wealth and simplicity of character, and it was decided that they had to do with another Keraunos. They came by night to make a secret attack, but they found Antigonus' camp deserted. Overcoming their suspicions, they occupied the empty camp and in due course they went off towards the coast with all the valuables they could find. Here they were suddenly attacked by the sailors and part of Antigonus' army which had withdrawn on his orders (Justin 25.2).

Pausanias' account of the Celtic invasion of Greece seems to have been strongly influenced by the lost history of Hieronymus of Cardia. According to this source, the Celts (referred to in Greek fashion as 'Galatai') originally were inhabitants of northern regions on the shores of the Great Sea (Paus. I.3.5). Hence they had been making their way gradually towards the Ionian Sea. The Greeks, we are told, were not enthusiastic in defence of their country because Greece had been so seriously debilitated by Alexander, Philip, Antipater and Cassander (1.4).

The narrative in Pausanias' work tends to favour the Athenians, who, it says, though they were profoundly weary because of the protracted wars they had endured, went to block the pass at Thermopylae against the invaders. This was a volunteer force which included soldiers from a number of cities, and it was commanded by Callippus. Although Athens was strongly eclipsed by Macedonian strength at this time, she was still the most potent city-state in the Greek world, with the possible exception of Syracuse.

The Celts by-passed Thermopylae by means of the same path across the mountains which the Persians had used in 480 BC when Ephialtes of Trachis had guided them in order that they might be able to attack Leonidas and the Spartan force from the south. The Athenians were now themselves to face the uncomfortable, though distinguished prospect of being surrounded in defence of their country by overwhelming odds at the pass of Thermopylae. The Celts, once past the obstacle of the mountain, defeated the Phocians and in spite of residual opposition they moved quickly towards Delphi and its treasures. Their primary aim was that of the Celts who had attacked Rome in 390 BC: they were interested in treasure rather than settlement, though as we see in Italy and elsewhere, settlement could follow depredation.

The Athenians and the others were with great difficulty evacuated from Thermopylae by the Athenian fleet. This is how the narrative goes; but doubt has been expressed whether the Athenians did in fact send ships to Pylae. The doubt rests on the absence of inscriptional evidence for so dramatic a move. If such evidence were available, it seems likely that Pausanias' pro-Athenian leanings would have prompted him to mention it (Nachtergael, *Sot.* 144). He makes a particular point of the Athenian leadership of the army: he says this was on account of their ancient repute as defender of Greece (*kat' axiōma to arkheion*: 10.20.5). However, the doubt is based on silence, after all; and unless the whole scene at Pylae has been grossly exaggerated, the Athenians would have suffered as famous a massacre at the hands of the Celts as the Spartans did in 480 BC, if ships had not come to take them off.

Pausanias' account tells how the Celts failed of their objective. When the Phocians and the Aetolians, once a byword for backwardness, but at this stage reaching the full development of their power, came to do battle with the Celts near Delphi, thunderbolts and rocks fell from Parnassus, and phantoms of warrior heroes appeared for the encouragement of the Greeks. Two of these apparitions were from the far north, the Hyperboreans Hyperochus and Amedochus. There was also a more local hero, Pyrrhus, son of Achilles. He was formerly regarded by the people of Delphi as an enemy.

This phase of Pausanias' narrative describes how the Celts went to Asia Minor and tells of their adventures there. Another account which he gives goes into greater detail about the campaign in Greece (1.4). Pausanias' first account of the Celtic invasion is linked to his description of the memorials to past Athenian military glory which were hanging in the *bouleutērion* at Athens. His more detailed narrative, which we shall follow in due course, is attached to Delphi (10.19–23). One of the most alarming aspects of the Celtic war was the threat which it offered to that extremely holy place.

We have seen that the Celtic horde split into three streams: Cerethreus against the Thracians and Triballi; Brennus and Achichorius moved towards Paeonia; and Bolgius to the Macedonians and Illyrians. After the death of Keraunos, Brennus advocated an attack on Greece, which was both weak and wealthy. Achichorius was to combine with him. Pausanias reports greatly inflated figures for the Celtic armies: one hundred and fifty-two thousand infantry and twenty thousand cavalry — indeed sixty thousand cavalry in total, if account is taken of the Celtic custom of providing two reserve attendants for each cavalryman to take his place if he is put out of action. This was the famous 'trimarcisia': the 'three-horse' system (Ir. *marc* Bryth. *march*, 'horse'). Clearly Pausanias is following the Herodotean tradition which seeks to magnify the scale of the conflict. He wants to make the war against the Celts comparable in importance with the great double conflict against the Persians, even to the extent of having two waves of invasion.

In one important respect the Celtic war was more frightening in prospect than the wars with the Persians had been. In spite of the sackings of cities, massacres and other atrocities committed by the Persians, the ultimate object of Persian policy would appear to have been that the cities of Greece should become dependencies of the Persian Empire. The Celtic invasion, by contrast, seemed to have as its end merely pillage and destruction, and the fighting style of the Celts seemed murderous and full of an entirely alien viciousness. It looked as if the Greeks' very survival were in the balance.

In spite of being weary of war and deficient in energy and morale for effective self-defence, the Greeks were forced to the task by desperation. They could only remember the atrocious treatment suffered by the populations of Macedon, Paeonia and Thrace, or what was currently happening to the Thessalians. Pausanias is at pains to compare the various components of the Greek forces in the Persian Wars with those in the army assembled to fight the Celts. Callippus, the son of Moerocles, was the commander of the joint Greek army in 278 BC. To the Athenians was allocated the supreme command because of that *axiōma* of which we have spoken. Antiochus sent a force from Asia to participate in the campaign, and Antigonus managed to send help from Macedon.

Following Pausanias' more detailed reprise in Book 10 of his earlier narrative of the war, we find that the first Greek move was to break the bridges across the Spercheius, above Thermopylae, and to place a holding force on the river bank. The Celts ordered the local people to repair the bridges, and they could do nothing else but obey. More important, Brennus, whom Pausanias describes as being a very able general (for a barbarian), sent some of his warriors to a part of the river where their tall stature enabled them to ford it, thus bypassing the Greek move. As a consequence, the Greeks had to fall back to Thermopylae. Brennus decided to take the road across Mount Oeta which Hydarnes the Persian had used to bypass the Spartans at Thermopylae in 480 BC. Though he did not succeed in taking Heraclea, which guards the entrance to the paths across the mountain, he intimidated the population into helping him, which they did through hope as well as fear; for they saw some chance of having him out of their district.

Brennus made his attack on the Greek position without prior consultation either of omen or seer. At this point, Pausanias, or his source, wonders whether the Celts have the custom of divination. With no defensive arms but their shields, the Celts rushed into battle in a wild charge. The Athenian ships came in close to the land and fired missiles at the enemy, who went into a disordered withdrawal in which many of them were trampled into the mud of the marshes. In this battle at Thermopylae, the Athenians were accounted to have been the most courageous of all the Greek contingents. The bravest among the Athenians was Cydias, whose first experience of battle was his last. His shield was dedicated in the temple of Zeus Eleutherios. Centuries later, Cornelius Sulla, who respected neither god nor man nor the memory of honour, saw fit to steal it.

Of the two concealed paths which lead over Mount Oeta, one goes into Aetolia; the other is more suitable for a larger force to pass. This is the path used by Hydarnes in 480 BC, and it leads to the sources of the Cephissus (Cary 1949: 67) Heraclea had been constructed by the Spartans during the Peloponnesian War in 426 BC, to guard the northern entrance to these paths. We may suppose that the Greeks' initial intention to hold the Celts at the Spercheius took into account a possible use of the path against them. Not only had the path been an important part of the Spartan system of communications during the Peloponnesian War, it also was used by Philip II of Macedon. The path was not a secret, except by tradition.

From their defensive line at Thermopylae, the Greeks were

compelled to hope that the Celts would not make use of the path, and the failure of the Celts actually to take Heraclea would have given this hope some nourishment. As the Celtic foray into Mount Oeta against the temple of Athena shows, they were investigating the region and no doubt soon became acquainted with the path and its earlier use. The temple had a garrison under the command of Telesarchus, who won lasting glory for his conduct of its defence. It was not taken. The fact that it had been given a garrison shows that the Greeks envisaged the possibility of a Celtic move in this direction. The Celtic force which invaded Aetolia took one branch of the path. They went on to destroy the town of Callium with the infliction of every kind of cruelty. The other path took the Celtic warriors towards Phocis and Delphi.

The Celts were helped in their negotiation of the pathways through Oeta by a strange daytime mist. In fact the Phocians were in a position where they could have blocked the Celts' exit from the path, had they not been deluded by the mist. This felicitous concealment must have seemed to the Celts, as it certainly would to their descendants, to be of supernatural origin. We hear of a magic mist (*ceo druidechta*) in the saga *Fled Bricrend* (Windisch 1880: 39), and much later in the song 'Maidin Luain Chíngcíse' (Whit Monday Morn), about an episode in the abortive Irish war of independence in 1798 AD.

The Phocians were driven off the pass, and retreated towards the main body of the Greek army. The fleet at this stage began the evacuation of Greek forces hemmed in at Thermopylae, and contingents from the various cities departed for their respective homes. Brennus did not wait for the other Celtic army under Achichorius to join him but pressed on towards Delphi on his own initiative.

Although the Celts had suffered heavy losses at Thermopylae, the edge of their aggressive impetus was in no way blunted. They astonished the Greeks by not pausing to bury their dead. Brennus is described as the only Celtic leader who was not depressed by setbacks, and on this occasion he was determined to seize an important tactical advantage without delay. The force which he had sent into Aetolia was large enough to draw off the Aetolians, one of the most vigorous components of the allied army, to defend their own homes. The vicious destruction of Callium may have been a piece of calculated terrorism to break the cohesion of the Greek defence by distracting the Aetolians. It may also have been an effusion of exasperated mania. Pausanias' account compares the behaviour of the Celts to that of the Laestrygonians and the Cyclops in the *Odyssey*. Possibly, Greek propaganda added to the story of Callium the item that the warriors ate the flesh of infants and drank their blood. Those women who could summon up enough courage killed themselves or ran on to the swords of the Celts: those who did not were raped so repeatedly that they died from the injuries they sustained, or else were left to starve to death. The Celts are said not to have abstained from intercourse with the dying or the dead. History is so rich in authenticated horrors that we should be careful of falling into facile incredulity about such stories as this. Nevertheless, we may recall a similar story in Herodotus (8.33) of women killed by multiple rape in the Persian invasion of Phocis.

Accordingly the Aetolians made for their home country as quickly as they could. An army from Patra, an Achaean city, met the enemy head-on with a hoplite force and was severely mauled. The Aetolians, however, augmented by many volunteers not only of fighting men but women and the aged, made a continuous ambush along the road taken by the enemy, and harassed them as they passed very effectively by means of missiles. This did the Celts great damage, because they had no armour but their shields to defend them. The size of the Celtic army which went into Aetolia is given as forty thousand men, of which only twenty thousand, it is said, managed to reach Thermopylae.

In the face of the imminent peril, the god of Delphi reassured the frightened citizens through the agency of his oracle: 'I will defend my own,' he said. That Pausanias' narrative was influenced by Herodotus' account of the Persian invasion of Greece is nowhere more obvious than in his description of the Celtic attack on Delphi. Herodotus tells how the god of Delphi tells the people not to remove the treasure from the temple, because he himself is capable of protecting it from the Persians (8.36). This was a recurrent theme of Delphic reassurance: in 371 BC, much the same message was given out in face of a threat from Jason of Pherae: 'It will be my concern.' (*Sot.* 149).

Nevertheless, forces from the Greek cities came to defend the god in his shrine. Other events of a fortuitous and favourable character also made their contribution. Achichorius had left a large part of his army at Heraclea to guard the accumulated booty. As he came south with the rest, Aetolians and Phocians captured his baggage and supplies.

Then came the remarkable events of earthquake, thunder and

lightning at the time when the Greeks were organising their allied army to meet the Celtic attack. Again in Pausanias' account there is mention of the manifestation of ancient heroes to aid the Greek cause. In this second account of the affair, in Pausanias' tenth book, the heroes named are: Hyperochus, Laodoces, Pyrrhus, and Phylacus.

Frost and snow caused rock falls which greatly injured the Celts. The Phocians, who knew the terrain, persistently harassed the rear of the Celtic army. The Celts fought hard but were forced to retreat. They killed their own wounded. Brennus himself was wounded and carried off the battlefield. In the night the Celtic army was seized by a sudden collective dread. In their panic they could not recognise each other, or even understand their own language; and they feared that Greeks had got into the camp and were in their midst. This could suggest that there were different Celtic dialects in the army that gave rise to misunderstanding in a moment of stress, or that there were non-Celtic allied contingents amongst them. In any event, the Celtic warriors began to fight promiscuously among themselves and many were killed. Their attempts to retreat the next day were hampered by the Phocians whose attentions would not allow them time to forage for food.

At this time the Athenians and Boeotians rejoined the Greek force and played their part in the campaign of attrition. The two branches of the Celtic army were now reunited, though Achichorius' force was still being hounded by the Aetolians. Brennus is said to have killed himself by drinking neat wine: his wound would certainly not be helped by such a beverage. Another version of the story says that he drank the wine and then committed suicide (Diod. 22.92). As the Celts struggled back to the Spercheius, the Thessalians and Malians were waiting for them, eager for revenge and, according to Pausanias, hardly one of the Celts got away safely from the expedition into peninsular Greece.

Another version of the reassurances issued by the god of Delphi makes him say that 'the white maidens' would effectively protect the gods (Diod. 22.95). The white maidens have been interpreted as snowflakes, part of the wild conditions that depressed Celtic morale and led to disasters. We might ask how much effect snow would be likely to have on the morale of a northern people (*Sot.* 157). Snow was not the only trial in terms of natural phenomena with which they had to cope. Also, they would tend to regard such events as of supernatural causation. Their susceptibilities would be sharpened by the sacred reputation of the place they intended to attack. Further, we may assume that a considerable number of them were not of northern European birth or experience, though we should also bear in mind that the Alpine and Balkan regions can provide plenty of snow and ice. I think we must imagine the combined effects of bad weather, unexpected natural disturbances and superstition, upon an army ill-disciplined by southern standards, badly provisioned and driven much too hard. Such an assembly of factors could easily lead to an outbreak of mass hysteria of the kind which has been described.

But, at last, who can be certain in this matter? Napoleon's army in Russia was not greatly appreciative of snow, nor was Hitler's. No attacking or invading army is likely to find it helpful. Another suggestion makes the white maidens *Moirai Kēres*, goddesses of fated death, or *daimones*, 'saviour spirits'. They were indeed saviours as far as the Greek cause was concerned, and goddesses of darkness and death in the nocturnal panic of the Celts. Again we may be seeing shadowy reflexes of the Celtic war-goddesses — though the whiteness is hard to explain in such a context, except in terms of snow.

There may have been a sacral element in Brennus' suicide. By sacrificing his own life he would die a death analogous to that of the warrior in battle. Again, no explanation is simple or certain. For the ancient Celts, in spite of their marked energy and resilience of mind and body, the prospects of life for the defeated, especially the defeated leader, whose honour and credit with his followers would be entirely dissolved by defeat, were dismal: consider Boudicca's suicide, and that of the famous 'Dying Gaul' and his wife in the Hellenistic sculpture. Many examples of suicide are recorded amongst Celts and Celtiberians (Dottin 1915: 148). Assuming that Brennus did not actually commit suicide in the sense of stabbing himself but simply decided to neglect his wound or exacerbate its effects by drinking wine, we should have an example of the heroic custom by which Celtic warriors enlarged their wounds in order to make them honourably conspicuous (Livy 38.21). Such actions, and the attitude which prompted them, could conceivably lead to death.

Brennus may be classed as a very able and courageous general, who, if he had been leader of a more disciplined and better supplied army, could have crushed Macedonian power and established Celtic rule over Greece. Greek tradition does not underestimate his quality. The fact that the Celts were still able to expand towards Asia and the establishment of a Celtic kingdom at Tylis in Thrace provide clear indication that the force of the Celtic migrations was not spent and that the defeat in Greece, serious though it was, did not decisively reduce Celtic power.

After the repulse of the Celtic invasion of 278 BC, a festival of commemoration called the *Soteria*, the 'Salvation Festival', was instituted in Greece by the Amphictiones, that highly respectable and ancient religious assembly of the Greek states. The ceremony was reorganised by the Aetolians, who regarded themselves as the main architects of victory, and, as might be expected, the *Soteria* provided the cities with material for controversy over the years (Diod. 22.3–5, 9; Justin 24.4.8; Paus. 1.4, 10; 5–13). In regard to Delphi, we might reasonably ask: what precisely was being celebrated, the salvation of the shrine from rapine, or the clearing of the god's precinct of its sacrilegious pillagers?

An inscription from the island of Cos, which was published in 1904 AD, says that the Galatai did not pillage the Delphic sanctuary. Yet some historians maintain that the sanctuary was in fact wrecked. It is possible that it was partially occupied for a while (Parke and Wormell 1956: 256–7), but if this were so, the absence of traces of that occupation remains to be explained. Parke and Wormell suggest that the story of its complete immunity from violation may have been part of a subsequent Delphic propaganda effort. If the Celts never entered the sacred place how can we explain, except in terms of rhetorical commonplace, Brennus' alleged mockery of the Greeks' anthropomorphic idols (Diod. 22.97)? Unless the Celts' stay in the sanctuary was very brief, they can hardly have failed to pillage it. The Cos inscription refers to the temple as still in being and presumably intact. There is no talk of repairs:

> Diocles Philinou proposer: Whereas the barbarians having made an expedition against the Greeks and the temple of Delphi it has been reported that some of them that attacked the temple have been given their just deserts both by the gods and at the hands of men who came to the aid of the temples in the barbarian onset and that the temple has been preserved and adorned with the captured arms of its attackers and the rest of these have been destroyed in engagements between themselves and the Greeks: in order that the people [of Cos] should be manifest in their joy at the victory that has been gained and in the making of offerings

to the god for his epiphany in the crucial engagement in the environs of the temple and for the safety of Greece: it has been resolved invoking good fortune by the people that the *architheōros* and the *theōroi* [chief sacral ambassador and ambassadors] who have been elected when they may come to Delphi shall sacrifice to Pythian Apollo and Zeus Saviour and Victory and let them also sacrifice to each of the other gods a fully grown animal.

The law goes on to ordain the day as a day of celebration and thanksgiving for all citizens and residents, and it votes sums of money for the various purposes of the resolution (*Sot.* 402).

Another authority, the poet Callimachus, lived at the time of the Celtic attack. In his *Hymn to Delos* (4.181–5) he has the god speaking of the Celts as 'already beside my tripods'. This might be poetic exaggeration, were the event itself not so momentous. The passage which mentions the Celts (71–185) is part of a prophecy made by Apollo from his mother's womb. Naturally, Callimachus takes the opportunity to incorporate in his poem a sufficient praise of the Ptolemies:

'I say that there will come to us in the future a struggle we all wage together, when, raising barbaric sword and Celtic war, latter-day Titans will rush upon us like snow from the very far West; or as numerous as the stars when at their thickest they pasture the sky. And forts and [villages of Locris and the Delphic high places], the Crisean plain and the narrow [valleys] of the mainland will be crowded all around and we shall see smoke from a neighbour house burning, not simply hear of it; soon beside the temple they will see the armies of hostile men, and next to my tripods swords and vicious sword-belts. And their hated spears which will lead their owners, the mindless tribe of Celts, on a journey which comes to no good. Some of their shields will be my trophy; others the prize of an energetic king [Ptolemy] when they have seen those that wear them perish in the flames.'

The last few lines refer to Ptolemy Philadelphus who hemmed up his Celtic mercenaries on an island in the Nile after they had seemed to have become dangerous to him. There they died of starvation and the desperate quarrels that arose amongst themselves.

As we have mentioned, Ptolemy had hired them as mercenaries in his war against Magas, close to the time when their fellow Celts were invading Greece.

Another element in the discussion about the Celtic attack on the shrine is the story of the gold that the Celts are supposed to have sent home to their tribal lands in the West. In 106 BC, the Romans dispatched Caepio with an army into Narbonese Gaul to put down turbulence amongst the Volcae and Tectosages. He took Tolosa, sacked the town, and seized its votive treasures which were sunk in its sacred lakes. He was defeated by the Cimbri in 105 BC. Later he was sent into exile on the grounds that he had hired a group of gangsters to steal the gold on his behalf on its way from Tolosa to Rome.

This was not in itself an improbable arrangement, as the career of Verres in Sicily amply demonstrates. Timagenes' opinion (*FGH* A88.F.11) preserved by Strabo (4.1.13) and by Justin (3.3.36), is that Caepio was afflicted with bad luck because he was plotting to steal sacred objects belonging to the god of Delphi which the Tectosages and others had brought back from Greece to their kindred in Gallia Narbonensis. Apparently Poseidonius took a different view. He said that the Phocians had already used up the Delphic treasures for their own purposes during the so-called Third Sacred War (356–354 BC). Nor are the artistic representations of Celts fighting with divinities over sacred objects to be regarded as firm proof that the temple was actually sacked (*Sot.* 102ff). The material from Tolosa is more likely than not an accumulation of motives representing the worship of generations of Celts, who frequently dedicated precious objects in wells, lakes and rivers.

It is difficult to conclude that really serious damage was done to the Delphic precinct in the course of the Celtic war. This is not to diminish the magnitude of the threat posed by the Celts or the sufferings they inflicted on Greece. The Greek world was deeply stirred by the war and its outcome: epic poems called *Galatika* were composed by several poets, but only pieces of these works remain embedded like fossils in the texts of later authors. Their story must remain unclear.

The Aetolians never managed to impress on the rest of the Greek world the magnitude of their merits in the defence of Delphi. Their sufferings had been the severest in the war and their general contribution to the defence of Greece must be regarded as decisive, even though the Phocians were the nominal victors of the battle near Delphi itself. Aetolian resentment never died out and it manifested itself later when, in 243 BC, they took over the *Soteria* festival from Delphi. This did not enhance their popularity. Under their charge the festival declined, despite considerable injection of funds.

After the war, the Celts continued to find employment as mercenary soldiers, as they had, to some extent, before the invasion of Greece. From their point of view mercenary service was a contractual extension of their way of life as raiders who extorted money from cities as the price of leaving them in peace. In 274 BC, we find them in the army of Antigonus. They tended to find employment in the armies of rulers of Macedonian origin, who early perceived the potential usefulness of a people not too different in culture and incivility from many of their Macedonian compatriots. Antigonus' army was routed by Pyrrhus after his return from Italy. He dedicated spoils from this battle in the temple of Athena Itomia, which lies between Pherai and Larissa (Paus. 1.13). His dedication was celebrated by an epigram:

Pyrrhus hung up these shields in honour of Athena.
    They are spoil from the bold Celtic warriors.
He destroyed the whole army of Antigonus: no wonder:
    Both then and now, the sons of Aiacus could fight.

Pyrrhus' allusion to his glorious ancestry would have been understood by his Celtic enemies; so also would his tribute to their courage.

We have mentioned that Ptolemy Philadelphus hired Celtic mercenaries in his war against Magas of Cyrene (Paus. 1.7). We have referred to this event and its dire consequences as having taken place near to the time of the main Celtic invasion of Greece. In fact, there is considerable uncertainty about the date. It may have been as early as the invasion of Bolgius, or as late as the mid-fifties of the third century BC. The earlier date may be likely, or perhaps the mid-seventies. Ptolemy's acquaintance with the Celtic ethos is already sufficient to enable him to manipulate the Celts to their own destruction by exploiting their Homeric individualism and high temper. These Celts were still so uninitiated in the way of the Mediterranean world to suppose that they could plot without being spied upon, and may have trusted to the language barrier and main force for success in bringing their plan to fruition. A relatively early stage in the relationship of Celt and

Greek is suggested, though perhaps not before 279 BC.

Antiochus I, the son of Seleucus, succeeded his father shortly before the Celtic invasion of Greece and became embroiled in a war with Zipoites and Nicomedes, kings of Bithynia. Not even Lysimachus had been able to subdue Zipoites. Nicomedes brought in Celtic mercenaries to help him against Antiochus, as they had previously done in his quarrel with his brother Zipoites. These Celts soon acquired the Greek language and became known as 'Gallograeci' (Justin 26.2). Antiochus was driven out of the northern part of Phrygia, which became part of Galatia, and he was also deprived of the north-western portion of Lydia, which became Pergamos. Antiochus' one success against the Celts in 275 BC earned him the name *'Soter'*, 'Saviour', but he was killed in battle against them near Ephesus in 261 BC.

A more extended account of the Celts in Asia Minor belongs to Chapter 9 where we shall discuss them under the name which is familiarly used of Celts in this zone: 'Galatians'. At this point we shall follow Polybius' compressed history of them (4.46) from 279 BC to 220 BC. According to his summary, the Celts who left their original home with Brennus and survived the defeat at Delphi, came to the Hellespont where they settled around Byzantium, conquered Thrace and made Tyle (Tylis) their capital. The Byzantines used to buy them off in the time of their early invasions under their king Comontorius. This gradually turned into a species of tribute. In the time of their king Cavarus, the Celts were attacked by the Thracians, and completely crushed (200 BC).

Livy (38.18) describes how the Celts ranged through Asia Minor, a recurrent menace to its constituent powers, and were capable at the peak of their strength of exacting tribute from the rulers of Syria. Eventually they were defeated in 189 BC by Attalus of Pergamos.

Although Brennus' army, to its own eventual despite, retained many of the characteristics of an inflated raiding party rather than an organised host (Walbank 1957–79: 1.195.7), there is no doubt that it was a genuine menace to the survival of Greek civilisation in the peninsula of Greece. Thus there was some justification for the Greek view that their struggle against this invader was comparable with the Persian Wars. They were ready to celebrate their victory as a resurgence of national power, a regeneration of their ancient glory which was especially exhilarating in view of the defeat received by the Macedonians, their conquerers and oppressors, at the hand of Celts whom they themselves had now contrived to defeat. Indeed Macedonian power had been relatively weakened by the wars of succession which followed the death of Alexander; but unfortunately for Greek hopes of liberty for the cities after the Celtic defeat at Delphi, the Macedonians were soon to dominate them once again. The Greek states, as so often at crucial times in their collective history, debilitated themselves by mutual strife.

Yet there were gleams of hope still for the old Greece. That Macedon had been weakened by wars of succession was beyond doubt, and it was this weakness which gave the Celts their opportunity to invade. The impact of their invasion did further damage to Macedon. This is evidenced by the fact which we have been considering, namely that the successor Macedonian powers employed Celts as mercenaries after their elimination from Greece in order to recover the old dominance.

Even as early as 280 BC, the cities of the Achaean League, which had been forcibly dismantled in 300 BC, were beginning to negotiate with each other again. As this federal group grew in power and confidence, it came to represent as close a realisation as possible of Classical Greek independence, until Roman power overshadowed it, along with its rival Aetolia, and also the Macedonians, whose king, by his understanding with Hannibal in 216 BC, provoked Roman intervention. Yet this Achaean phantom of earlier glory and its contemporary, the late blossoming Aetolia, owed much of their rise and influence to the effect of the Celts upon Macedon and the recreation of Greek confidence which was the outcome of the Celtic attempt upon Greece.

6

Tumult, Prejudice and Assimilation: Rome and the Gauls

An abiding preoccupation of the Roman mind remained vivid throughout the history of the city: this was the vulnerability of this Italic peninsula to invasion, especially from the north. The impact of frequent Celtic invasions was a powerful factor in the formation of the attitude with which the Romans apprehended real or imagined menace from foreign peoples. Acts of bad faith which Roman commanders in Gaul and Spain sometimes committed against Celtic adversaries may be seen not entirely as instances of heartless finesse applied against innocently heroic tribesmen: they were at least partly the results of desperate fear arising from a history of suffering at the hands of invading hordes. The *tumultus*, that declaration of a state of defensive anxiety and preparation against a barbarian invasion, is a characteristically Roman formalisation of a terror that was never completely laid to rest. That fear, even at the time of Rome's abundant power in the period of the early Principate, prompted efforts to stabilise barbarian frontiers with Rome thousands of miles away from Italy and to base these limits on natural features which would obstruct intending invaders. In the case of the invading Celts, the Alps had proved to be ineffective barriers in themselves. We have noted the tradition that Ambigatus sent out his nephews with armies of conquest towards Italy and towards the Hercynian forest.

Livy's chronology (5.34–5) wrongly places this movement of Celtic warriors in the time of the elder Tarquin's kingship in Rome: more probably it relates to much later events in the fifth and fourth centuries BC (*Sot. 5*). Archaeological evidence suggests the presence of wandering groups of Celts in the Po valley in the fifth century BC (*Sot. 6*). These were the corm of the army that was to ransack Rome in 390 BC, not only inflicting terrible physical damage on the growing city-state, but injecting an uneasy and lasting prejudice into the tissue of the city's life.

Livy implies that the expeditions inspired by Ambigatus involved the removal of a surplus population of the tribes (5.34). In his narrative he describes how the various Celtic tribes dispossessed the Etruscans from northern Italy, made their way into Etruria itself and from there into Latium. The men of Clusium first felt the threat of Celtic invasion in 391 BC. They appealed to the Roman senate for assistance. No help was given; but three ambassadors, members of the family of the Fabii, were sent to negotiate with the Celts and persuade them to leave the harmless people of Clusium in peace. Otherwise Rome would make war, though the senate preferred to have a friendly relationship with this nation which they had never met before (Livy 5.35).

The Gauls said that there would be no war, if the people of Clusium gave them land to settle in: the Romans then asked what right they had to make such a condition to the inhabitants of any country, and what were they doing in Etruria anyway? The Celts replied that their right was in their swords. Livy stresses desire for land as an important motivation of the Celtic invasion, as it was in Greek colonisation of various parts of the Mediterranean world. The Celts, however, were not exclusively interested in land: they would take either booty or land, and were not averse to having both. As a result of these discussions fighting broke out immediately and the Roman ambassadors infringed international custom by taking part in the battle themselves (Livy 5.35).

Quintus Fabius is said to have killed one of the Celtic leaders in the battle. This is the first scene of personal combat between a Roman and a Celtic grandee, in which the Celt is killed. We should be cautious about accepting this achievement as historical. It may be Roman propaganda concocted after the battle to cover the disgrace of Roman infringement of the honourable customs regulating the behaviour of ambassadors; more likely it is part of the wider campaign of self-persuasion by which the Romans for some considerable time attempted to conceal the ugly fact that the Celts often defeated them in battle.

When the Celts observed that the ambassadors were taking part in the fight, they decided to leave the Clusini in peace and concentrate their aggression on Rome. The older counsellors of the Celts had some difficulty in restraining the younger element from marching on Rome straight away. At last they decided to send envoys to demand redress. Livy says that the Fabii behaved more like Celts than Romans in the affair at Clusium: a sufficiently prejudiced comment, but Livy was never troubled by doubts on the subject of Roman national superiority. He concedes that the outcome of the subsequent battle between the Romans and the Celts would have been different, if the Fabii had been possessed of more sense. When the Celts came to complain about the diplomatic indiscretion committed by Rome's representatives, the Senate admitted that the Fabii were at fault but was reluctant to prosecute them. In fact they were elected consular tribunes for the following year — the year of the disastrous defeat of the Romans at the Allia. We may doubt whether punishment of the Fabii would ultimately have provided Rome with immunity from Celtic attack. It might however have provided her with more able generals for the coming year.

The Fabii proved to be arrogant and careless tacticians. It was substantially their fault that the Celtic victory was so overwhelming. Livy sees an element of tragic inevitability in the unfolding of the events of 390 BC. He concedes that the Celts had right on their side and that their leader was a better general. This man's name was Brennus, as was the name of the Celtic leader of the attack on Greece in 278 BC. It may have been a ceremonial title rather than a purely personal name (see Chapter 5 above).

In spite of his recognition that the Celts were behaving in this matter in a perfectly understandable way, Livy nevertheless describes them as a race naturally prone to tumult, who indulged in wild war-cries and battle-songs that filled the air with a horrendous noise (5.37). This is one brief distillation of inherited Roman prejudices about the Celts.

The battle of the Allia was a shattering blow to the prestige of Roman arms and it left the way to Rome open to the Celts. The capacity of the Roman army to defend the city was broken and only the Capitol held out. The Celts destroyed the rest of the city with a thoroughness which suggested a desire for revenge as much as rapine. Plutarch tells us (Numa 1) that Rome's ancient records perished in this destruction of the city and that afterwards they were reconstituted by forgers in the interests of distinguished houses and aristocratic families and were inflated with irrelevancies in order to give these as glorious a history as possible. There can be little doubt that the Romans had a distinct creative talent in the fabrication of early history. Stories reflecting credit on various heroes of the Celtic sack proliferated.

Appian quotes Cassius Hemina and other authors for the story that when the Celts were trying to storm the Capitol and not succeeding, a young man called Caius Fabius Dorsuo, a priest of Vesta, made his way through the besieging lines with the utmost coolness in order to carry out the yearly ceremony in honour of the goddess whose cult was the particular charge of his family. Even though the temple was burned, he made sacrifice on the ritually required spot and returned uninjured (Fr. 19 P). He was protected by the power of the divinity, and as Livy sees it (5.46), by the superstition of the enemy. It is perhaps no accident that Fabius Pictor also tells this story of Fabian distinction.

According to another early historian, Quintus Claudius Quadrigarius (Aul. Gel. *NA* 17.2.24), a certain Quintus Comminius is said to have made his way through enemy positions to communicate with the Senate on the besieged Capitol, and to have departed by the same way carrying their mandate for the return of Camillus from exile (Livy 5.46.8; D.H. 13.9). Camillus was the heroic general of Rome's wars with Veii and other neighbours of his city, but he was exiled for alleged maladministration of the booty won in the war. After his restoration, he is said to have gathered the fragments of the defeated Roman army which was sheltering in informally fortified positions near Veii, and with this force he is supposed to have inflicted two defeats on the Celts on their way home to the north.

If Dorsuo and Comminius did what the historians say they did, then they deserve at least as much credit as those less conscious, but no less effective, patriots: the geese whose honking warned the garrison of the Capitol that the Celts were mounting a night-attack. The Celts knew little about investing cities, and their siege-lines could easily have been penetrated by anybody of moderate courage who knew the terrain. More important, the Celts were thinking of departing in any case. Their siege, which was as much as anything an act of blackmail, was proving unproductive. They were encamped in places where there was a maximum risk of fever, and disease was diminishing their numbers and their morale. We may doubt whether Brennus could have held his army in place for a protracted siege. It was in his interest and that of the Romans that they should arrive at an accommodation. The price of Celtic withdrawal was one thousand pounds of gold.

Pressure from the Veneti in the northern lands from which they had come was another incentive which brought the Celts back from the wreckage of Rome. The Veneti exerted this pressure largely because other tribes beyond their territories were pressing upon them (Polyb. 2.17). This domino model of tribal unsettlement, consequent wandering and tumultuary attack on more settled zones may be taken as having some validity. As they made their more dispersed and less enthusiastic way north, the Celts who had attacked Rome were more vulnerable to harassment from the partially revived Roman forces. We should remember that the Celts were not yet securely fixed in the areas of northern Italy in which they had come to predominate. War was in progress everywhere. It was only in 396 BC, on the day on which Camillus took Veii, that the Insubres, Boii and Senones (Brennus' tribe) got possession of Melpum, the Etruscan city which they called Mediolanum. It was, according to Cornelius Nepos (Pl. *NH* 3.125), a very rich prize. We need not suppose that all the Celts left the southern part of Italy as a result of Brennus' arrangement with the Romans. The north was not yet definitely their home.

There is an element in the Celtic conflict with Rome at this time which lies outside the conceptual framework of naïve raiding in search of plunder. The incursion of 390 BC was the first of a series of attacks which drove towards Rome in the fourth century BC. Some of these were encouraged, if not actually promoted, by Dionysius I and Dionysius II of Syracuse. Syracusan interests would not be served by the growth of Rome's power over her neighbours (Toynbee 1965: 1.25ff). Livy says that the base of the raids in the mid-fourth century BC was Apulia. Syracuse was an employer of Celtic mercenaries.

Possibly Rome's unwalled condition and the difficulties she had in keeping her recently acquired domination over the Latin cities made her seem an attractive target. Certainly the Celtic invasion gave Rome's Latin allies the opportunity they needed to defect. After the disaster of 390 BC, it took the Romans thirty years to regain their authority over the Latin communities (Polyb. 2.18). Roman accounts of the catastrophe, especially as represented in Livy's narrative, do not suggest such a resultant weakening. The slowness of Roman recovery is not surprising, particularly if the Celtic invasions of 367 BC and 365–363 BC were financed by the rich state of Syracuse. Perhaps Camillus' victories over the departing Celts belong to the realm of historical myth. There is no mention of his success before the second century BC. The story could be a reflex of the victory gained by the people of Caere over the Celts as they withdrew from Rome (Toynbee 1965: 1.373). Yet it seems reasonable to suppose that the Celts in retreat, with their heroic fury at a low ebb, would be susceptible to real damage from a regrouped Roman army, feeble though it might be. Also, the Roman Senate would have every reason to show its allies and not merely the Celts that their city was still a force to be considered. In short we may have here a performative as well as a literary act of face-saving.

There can be no doubt, however, that Rome was actually weakened by the Celtic attack. The fact that M. Manlius Capitolinus, the defender of the Capitol in the Celtic siege, attempted to seize supreme power in 385–384 BC may indicate that the domination of the patrician families was temporarily enfeebled by the magnitude of the disaster that had fallen on the city. This may mark the beginning of the process by which the plebeians, exacerbated by debt and shortage of land, eventually in 367 BC extracted from the patricians the arrangement that in future one of the consuls should be a plebeian.

The *Annales* of Q. Claudius Quadrigarius take account of events from 390 BC. They are said to have mentioned (Aul. Gel. *NA* 9.13.7–19) another Manlius who in a Celtic invasion of 367 BC fought and killed a Celtic chief, and took his torque, winning for himself an eternal glory, and for his family, as well as himself, the cognomen of 'Torquatus'. Livy describes this event, which is supposed to have taken place in a battle in which the Celts were defeated at the river Anio (6.42). Livy is inclined to place the duel several years later. His description of the event refers to 361 BC. In his carefully staged account, the self-assertive war-dance and battle-chant of the Celt, his size, arrogance and colourful armour are placed in contrast with the businesslike character of the small Roman, who has taken the precaution of arming himself with a short Spanish sword suitable for infighting. The blade of the great Celtic sword whistles idly past the Roman champion who, by the benefit of his relatively short stature, stabs the Celtic leader upwards through the loins and belly.

There is another example of single combat attributed to 348 BC: in this also the Roman succeeds in killing his Celtic opponent; and again the Roman victor gains a surname to commemorate his distinguished act. We could suspect that this heroic deed of Valerius 'Corvinus' was merely a doublet of the fight between Torquatus and the Celtic chieftain, but we should also remember that the settlement of wars by single combat was a known custom of heroic Celtic society. A Roman, whose technical skill, equipment and manoeuvrability was superior in such a situation, might readily offer to fight an adversary whom he had sized up as being less formidable than he looked.

According to Quadrigarius and Livy (7.25) there was a great incursion of Celts into the Pomptine area in the consulships of L. Furius and Claudius Appius (348 BC). When the Celtic and Roman armies were ranged against each other, a gigantic Celtic chief came forward and arrogantly made his challenge. The tribune Valerius obtained permission from the consuls to answer his challenge. He went forward with a modest but courageous step, in contrast to the Celt's contemptuous attitude. Suddenly a crow came to perch on Valerius' helmet, and it proceeded to attack his opponent's face and eyes, after which it flew back to sit on the Roman's helmet. Livy explains the occurrence of the crow as a sign of divine intervention: this may echo the tradition of how both Celts and Romans understood the happening. Celtic goddesses of war appeared in corvine form. The Celt would probably have found such a manifestation especially intimidating, if he were affected by this belief, and would immediately fear that the patrons of battle had rejected him. In the Irish tradition, these sinister birds perched on the shoulders of the dying Cu Chulain. Nor did the Romans regard crows and ravens as particularly favourable omens.

In 334 BC the Romans concluded a treaty with the Celts. The increase of Rome's power and influence made this seem to be a useful move from the Celtic point of view. The Romans, on their part, were freed for a time of the Celtic menace and were enabled to proceed with the subjugation of Italic peoples such as the Samnites. A balance of power was created which also removed the likelihood of Etruscan interference with Roman expansion in the peninsula.

The Celtic parties to the treaty seem by this time to have become settled in their homes in the good lands of northern Italy, but they found themselves under threat of invasion in 299 BC from other Celtic tribes who lived in mountain areas which were less favourable and fertile. By a mixture of bribery and appeals to common ethnic origin, they persuaded these highland tribes to turn their hostility against Rome and, as a pledge of the sincerity of their arguments, they decided to join the move against Rome themselves. They made their way through Etruria where they were joined by a number of the inhabitants who were anxious to do the Romans some harm. Although these expeditionaries obtained considerable plunder which they managed to take home, they were weakened by internecine quarrels of the kind, Polybius says (2.19), which arise from excessive eating and drinking.

In 297 BC the Celts and Samnites joined together against Rome and defeated a Roman army at Camertium. But the Celts were chased out of the territory of Sentinum by Roman consular armies. Samnites and Celts suffered substantial losses. Another Celtic invasion in 284 BC brought the Romans a defeat under the walls of Arretium. They had come to relieve the town. The Roman praetor was killed, and the ambassadors whom his successor sent to negotiate the release of prisoners were murdered by the Celts. The Romans sent a punitive expedition which utterly routed these Senones. A Roman colony called Sena was established in tribal territory near the mouth of the river Po.

The power of the Senones to give trouble was neutralised. The Boii, that formidable and widespread family of tribes, continued to be a potential danger. Experience of the Celts as allies indicated to the Etruscans that enemies could be preferable and the Roman alliance was increased by the adherence of a number of Etrurian cities.

These events took place three years before Pyrrhus invaded Italy at the request of Italiote-Greek cities who were becoming increasingly alarmed at the growth of Roman power in the peninsula. Five years had still to pass before the Celts who invaded Greece were defeated at Delphi. Throughout this period, Polybius comments, war raged like a plague amongst the Celtic peoples (2.20). Polybius also makes the point that as a result of the experience of war that they gained in fighting the Celts, the Romans were the better able to face the challenge of the war with Pyrrhus (280 BC), and also to make war successfully against the Carthaginians.

These years saw a turning point in the military relationship between Romans and Celts. The Romans were weary of living in fear, not merely of intrusive raids but of the risk of being overwhelmed and destroyed by the numbers, vigour and ferocity of tribes who now occupied the valley territory of northern Italy. By their debilitation of Etruscan power, the Celts had contributed to the growth of that of Rome, but at the same time they had themselves become a resident menace on northern boundaries of Rome's sphere of influence. Rome could now call on vast reserves of manpower, but her difficulty was that many of these forces came from allied states who might defect if an advantageous prospect were set before them.

Polybius' theory of successive waves of tribes pressing on each other was substantially correct. Celtic intrusions which seemed to have wealth and adventure as their principal objectives were more remotely set in action by pressure from tribes who coveted the lands of more settled and prosperous tribes. And we must remember that the Celts who tried to intimidate Clusium had alleged that they wanted land. By dispossessing the Senones and planting a colony at Sena, the Romans taught the tribes a lesson; but they taught them not only to be frightened but to regard revenge as the last resource of survival, so that they seized every opportunity to ally with Rome's enemies, as the Hannibalic war was amply to prove.

Polybius (2.20) describes how the Boii reacted to this move against the Senones. In 283 BC, this powerful tribe gathered an enormous army, and with the help of some of the Etruscans, moved against Rome. At Lake Vadimonis, they were routed by the Romans, and half of the Etruscan force was annihilated. Few of the warriors of the Boii survived the battle. The next year they tried once more, and shortage of manpower compelled them to arm young adolescents. (This may be a Greek rationalisation: traditionally, the warriors of the Celts were often remarkably young.) Complete defeat of this army persuaded the Celts to attempt negotiation again.

There was then a period of peace between the Celts of north Italy and the Romans which lasted for nearly forty-five years. A new Celtic generation grew up, however, which had no immediate acquaintance with the terrors and hardships of war and thought of nothing but revenge upon the Romans. Every small incident inflamed the ruling Celts against their ancient enemy. It was mainly the dominant classes of Celtic society, whose strong feelings of heroic honour were still uncleansed of the effects of their former defeat, who were most enthusiastic for the renewal of war. Only certain chiefs were involved in negotiation with fierce mountain tribes, and it was a most unpleasant shock for the Boii when a large army of strangers from across the Alps arrived at Ariminum.

In the foothills of the Alps and in the Rhone valley lived Celtic tribes who scrupulously followed the old ways of a warrior tradition and were available for contracts to undertake expeditions. These Celts passed almost imperceptibly in the third century BC from the character of freebooting cattle-receivers and raiders to the profession of mercenary soldiers. Perhaps we see an intermediate stage when they entertain the suggestions of some leaders of the Insubres and Boii. These outlanders were described as 'Gaesati', which Polybius (2.22) thinks has the meaning 'mercenary'. The word is more likely to be connected with Greek *gaison,* meaning 'spear' (cf. the *gai bolga* of Cu Chulain; Gk *chaios*: Skt *hésas*: Stokes 1894: 109). The leaders of these Gaesati were duly bribed, and it was pointed out to them that there was an immense amount of wealth for the taking in Rome. Historical arguments also, we are told, were deployed to persuade them. They were reminded that their own tribes had in times past taken Rome without much resistance, held it for seven months and left it only when they felt like doing so. No doubt the Gaesati were impressed by this version of history. We are not told that they asked their suborners and employers why, if the matter was so easy, they did not undertake the expedition themselves.

Roman intelligence sources were equal to the crisis. An army was levied and supplies were collected. An advance was made to the frontiers of Celtic territory as if the Celtic attack were already in progress. Polybius makes the important point that the Celts, by threatening Rome, diverted Roman attention from the consolidation of Carthaginian power in Spain. The Romans were not unaware of this proceeding: they were obliged to overlook it, for they had made the settlement of the Celtic question their priority. It seemed to be a reasonable enough holding-operation to make a treaty with Hasdrubal, who was active in Spain. The Celtic threat was nearer home than Spain (2.22).

Some of the Boii made plans to thwart the warlike intentions of their leaders. They killed their own two kings, Atis and Galatus. Then the strangers and the Boii liquidated their mutual suspicions by a pitched battle in which both sides suffered severely. The Roman pre-emptive force was able to return home without fighting.

In 232 BC a Roman move had agitated the fears and suspicions of the Boii and must be accounted as at least a partial cause of the troubles that led to the introduction of the Gaesati. Gaius Flamininus procured legislation which divided the territory of the Senones amongst the landless citizens of Rome. Polybius disapproved of the measure, not only because of its democratic character, which as a friend and dependent admirer of Roman *nobiles* he was bound to find subversive, but also because it was bound to generate occasions of conflict between the Celts and the Romans. The Boii in particular were suspicious of Rome's intentions with regard to their own territory (2.21). It has been suggested that there were remnants of the displaced Senones still residing in the territory of Picenum which Flamininus was proposing to subdivide, and that the prospect of these being dispersed amongst the free tribes of the Po valley was an immediate cause of Boian exasperation (Toynbee 1965: 1.167). Certainly the forceful injection of refugees into their lands would convey the impression that the Romans had scant regard for the territorial integrity of a supposedly allied people and would add to their fears that they might be the next to be expropriated. That there were residual Senones in the territory from which the tribe had been officially expelled need not be doubted. Before the evolution of modern technology, a clean sweep of population was not a practicable proposition.

When the Gaesati entered the Po valley in 225 BC, the Insubres and the Boii remained faithful to their agreement with them. The Cenomani and the Veneti took the Roman side. By a series of drafts the numbers of the newly formed Roman legions were quickly filled. Now that enemy forces were marching through Etruria, the allied cities supported Rome, not merely out of loyalty, but for sheer survival. Deeply implanted in their minds was the ancient dread of Celtic attack. The great size of the force which Rome was able to deploy at this time, including one hundred and fifty thousand frontline troops, illustrates the extravagant boldness of Hannibal's subsequent invasion of Italy (Polyb. 2.23).

The First Punic War had prevented the Romans from dealing finally with the Celtic menace. It was after this war that the Celts made their concerted attack of 225 BC: it may have been intended as a pre-emptive attack by the Celts (Toynbee 1965: 1.88) but it was much too late for this purpose. Then came Hannibal's invasion of Italy, which prevented the Romans from bringing the Celtic question to a conclusion for a number of years. Just before the Celtic invasion of 225 BC, the Romans granted full citizenship to the Roman settlements of northern Italy, which had previously had only limited franchise. This was a prudent move intended to neutralise any tendency the municipal settlers might have had to ally themselves with the Celts against the metropolitan power. In this war the fighting was savage and, from the Roman point of view, the outcome cannot have seemed certain. The Celtic army penetrated far into Etruria, but their great force of seventy thousand men (exclusive of families and dependants) was pinched between two Roman armies at Telamon (225 BC) — one of the

Roman armies had just landed fresh from Sardinia. The Celts were completely routed after a furious resistance. A Roman consul was killed and his head was taken on a spear to the Celtic king. One of the Celtic kings, Cocolitanus, was captured; the other, Aneroestes, escaped but committed suicide afterwards. The surviving consul, L. Aemilius, took a vast amount of booty including torques, which he dedicated on the Capitol. Of the ten thousand prisoners, he took a large number as slaves. Forty thousand Celts were killed in the battle (2.31).

The Celtic threat was in effect demolished, but the Romans decided to remove the possibility of its recrudescence by subduing completely the land of Cisalpine Gaul. They were unable to complete the task in the next three years; Hannibal's invasion intervened. After Telamon, there were several significant military actions. One of these, at Clastidium in 223 BC, was notable for another example of single combat. The consul M. Claudius Marcellus killed the Insubrian leader, Virduromarus.

The war of 225 BC was the last great venture of the Cisalpine Celts against the Romans though other uprisings were to follow. The Romans were to spend the years 203–191 BC in retaking Cisalpine Gaul after the Second Punic War and the Boii were not broken until 190 BC. In these campaigns, the Romans had to face Celts who were hardened by the Punic War and encouraged by their experience of Roman reverses at the hands of Hannibal. They also had the benefit of being led by officers left behind by Hannibal. We may note that on the eve of Hannibal's invasion, the Roman commissioners were busy with the task of dividing up the lands of the Boii.

Polybius gives a vivid account of the noise generated by a Celtic army going into battle in his description of the battle of Telamon. We might ask whether his rehearsal of the terrifying aspect of the Celtic host at this stage (225 BC) is not somewhat coloured by commonplace. Yet there can be little doubt that the Gaesati must have provided a daunting sight and sound. He says that the Celts made use of trumpets and horns and the human voice to such effect that the whole landscape seemed to be alive with noise. The gold ornaments of Celtic notables were also intimidating, though they encouraged the Roman soldiery with the compensating promise of spoils (2.30). The long sword of the Celts could cut, but not thrust. We have reason to believe that Celtiberian swords were different. At the battle of Telamon, the discharge of Roman *pila* ('javelins') against the Celts caused terrible loss, because Celtic shields were not big enough to give adequate protection.

There can be little doubt that the military technology of the Celts was inferior to that of the Romans. It was still moulded and guided by the cultural assumptions of the Bronze Age. Their tactics were also too much affected by heroic and traditional ideas to give them good chance of success against the Romans. Polybius is right in his assessment (3.14) that they failed to work out their tactics rationally, by means of *logismos*, rather than by heroic battle-fury, *thymos* — he uses the word that occurs so often in the Homeric poems to designate the proud aggressive spirit of heroic warriors. This spirit was certainly shown by the Gaesati who rushed into battle naked except for weapons of offence (2.28). They were locked into a ritual concept of war which taught that a fighting death transported the liberated soul immediately to the immortal sphere.

When Hannibal entered Italy in 218 BC, he had no shortage of Celtic recruits. Yet overall the response was disappointing. Celtic fighting power had been debilitated in the years following Clastidium. If the Carthaginian invasion had been somewhat earlier, he might have had more substantial help and the outcome of the war might have been different. He was all the more angry because he represented himself as the liberator of Italic Celts from the oppression of Roman rule (Livy 21.52). The role of liberator is seldom completely rewarding.

The Boii and the Insubres had revolted, with good reason, before Hannibal arrived. The Boii were still a force to be reckoned with, but Hannibal and Hasdrubal looked on the Celts as useful and expendable battle-fodder rather than first-rate soldiers. Aided by their environment of woods and swamps, the Boii stopped the advance of a Roman army in 218 BC, and destroyed another in 216 BC. In 201 BC, they defeated a less organised Roman force which was destroying their crops (Livy 31.2). The Celts had the idea that they should be ravaging other people's land and not suffering the devastation of their own. In their disappointment, they began to transfer their hatred of the Romans towards Hannibal (Livy 22.1). Livy dwells on the poor performance of the Celts in Hannibal's army on the march through Etruria (22.2). The Celtic race, he says, does not easily endure hardships of the kind faced by the mixed force on its way through marshy and difficult terrain. Some lay down and did not get up but were sucked into the mud. Men and animals suffered alike and only those who buoyed up their mind with hope could sustain their bodies by the efforts of their minds. The Cenomani, who were unenthusiastic in their enmity towards Rome, made peace in 197 BC.

In 218 BC some of the Cisalpines appealed for Roman aid against Hannibal. Others preferred to wait for some sign of which side would prevail before committing themselves. Hannibal's initial depredations in Celtic territory were in part a means of obtaining supplies to recruit the energies of his soldiers, who were in bad condition after crossing the Alps. They were none the less ill taken by the Celtic inhabitants, who did not find robbery more palatable because it was committed by a professed ally in the cause of their own liberty.

The end of Hannibal's campaign did not bring the end of Roman fears of Celtic intrusions from the north. When there was a revolt in Liguria in 193 BC, and Ligurian tribesmen entered Etruria, the threat was serious enough, but it would be hard to see how it posed an immediate danger to Rome. Yet it was sufficient cause for the Romans to raise a special levy of soldiers, as they had after such major disasters at the hands of Hannibal as Cannae and Trasimene (Livy 34.56). A similarly sensitive reaction is to be noted in 181 BC, when a proconsular army encountered more trouble than it expected in dealing with a remote tribe of Cisalpine Gaul.

The Romans were mindful of their own inherited fear and also, to some degree, of the sense of independence still entertained by the Celts of the Cisalpine zone. Even after many decades of war and suffering and great losses of manpower, the region was not without strength, and no 'province' of Cisalpine Gaul was instituted by Rome until 81 BC (Toynbee 1965: 2.266). But there was no question after the Punic War as to where the real power and authority lay and, as often in their history, the Romans too readily made cruel and unconstructive use of their advantage.

The potential for repression and sadism in Roman rule seldom remained hidden for long, and it is not surprising that the Celts of northern Italy grasped what opportunity for revolt they could over the course of the years. Though many Boii of high standing had made their peace with the Romans in 192 BC, we find that in the same year T. Quinctius Flamininus murdered a Boian chief. The man and his family had arrived to capitulate, and the proconsul apparently killed him to entertain a sulky boyfriend (Livy 39.42; Plut. *Cat. Min.* 17). Flamininus was taken off the senate roll in 182 BC by Cato the Censor for this and other acts, but from the Celtic point of view, justice must have seemed to be tardy and attenuated.

After years of exemplary loyalty, the Cenomani defected from their alliance with Rome and took the Carthaginian side in 200 BC. We have noted that they made their peace with Rome in 197 BC. In 225 BC, they had taken no part in the Celtic attack on Italy, nor did they join Hannibal in 218 BC. The Roman general in command of the Cisalpine region decided to disarm them in 187 BC. They complained to the Senate: the consul M. Aemilius Lepidus, who was empowered to look into the question, reversed the decision to disarm them. Disarmament was a very likely prelude to dispossession and dismemberment of the tribe. Not all appeals to the government at Rome were so successful.

At the same time a Roman might reasonably suppose that the flow of dangerous Celtic population from across the Alps which started centuries before was still in progress. A body of Celts which included twelve thousand fighting men came over the Carnic Alps in 186 BC. A praetor with a Roman army went against them in 183 BC and forced their capitulation. Eventually they were sent back whence they came. They seem to have had peaceful occupation in mind after some plundering, for they had begun to build a city.

The Roman authorities had marked out for settlement by their own citizens the district of Aquileia. Squatters from the tribe of the Statielli attempted to found a city there and M. Claudius destroyed it.

When the Statielli surrendered in 173 BC, M. Popilius Laenas razed what remained and sold the people into slavery. He auctioned their property. Protests to the Senate brought no redress. The consul was determined that the land should be subdivided for inhabitants of Rome. Consequently he obtained sufficient political backing to avoid having to undo his atrocity. Some of the Statielli were released from bondage but there was no restitution of their property or land.

Displacement of population in northern Italy to make room for settlers from Rome or for the ex-soldiers of Roman war-lords became an established pattern in Roman dealing with the region. It was still suffering in this way in 41 BC, when land was being taken over for the veterans of Octavian's and Antony's army. Restitutions were exceptional. Virgil's Ninth Eclogue may have been a plea for the restoration of his family farm near Mantua. The Romans would have found it convenient to remove the

Celts from the whole north Italian area. Such a wish would not be hard to understand, after centuries of turbulent history between the two nations. They had neither the resources not the ultimate will to effect such an act of genocide, brutal though some of their actions against the Celts undoubtedly were. The Celts refused to become extinct, even in heavily Romanised districts. Their culture was not savage, though it was inferior in technology — especially that of war — to that of the Romans. They had learned much from the Etruscans whom they encountered and displaced in the Po valley and, in many respects, they had refined their skills and style of life since their first invasion of the region in the fourth century BC. It was in the Roman character to be patronising about other peoples: Livy (36.40) describes silver vessels captured from the Celts as 'not badly made for this kind of work'. Toynbee (1965: 2.256) is sure that this means that they were fine works of art.

In the Celts, Rome had a formidable enemy with resources of population that must have seemed interminable. Even though Roman knowledge of European geography was far from accurate at this time, they had some awareness that the Celtic world stretched far into the wilderness of northern Europe and even Britain, and eastwards through the Balkans as far as the middle of Asia Minor. They probably felt as if they were confronting a superpower with an inexhaustible supply of fighting men. The Alps were not a reliable barrier, much less the river Po. When the Massilians, as automatic as watch-dogs in their reactions, sought Roman aid against the Ligurians in 154 BC, it took them nearly thirty years before they could lead their old ally into Transalpine responsibilities which brought about the foundation of the Roman province of Narbonese Gaul and made the rapid growth of Julius Caesar's power a practical possibility in later years. Roman campaigns against the Ligurians brought them into conflict with the Allobroges, who refused to give up a refugee Ligurian chief. Before long they were involved with the Aedui and the Arverni, over whom Q. Fabius Maximus won a crushing victory in 125 BC. This, with the establishment of Narbonese Gaul, had the advantageous result for the Romans that they were now provided with clear communications as far as the Pyrenees. The way was secured by a colony of veterans at Narbo. Though Roman influence stretched far up the Rhone valley, the Roman government at this stage had little ambition to become embroiled in the problems of wild Gallia Comata — 'long-haired

Gaul'. It was becoming more difficult for the enemies of Rome to use the Celts against her, as they had repeatedly managed to do, beginning with the Latins in 361 BC until the second Punic war. A Roman of Romans, C. Julius Caesar, was to deploy the resources of Gaul as a lever to overturn the Roman Republic, and by his success to provide an example for future generations of ambitious generals in provincial zones throughout the course of imperial history. Inhabitants of Roman settlements in Cisalpine Gaul were given Roman citizenship in 90–89 BC. Citizenship was extended to all dwellers beyond the river Po in 49 BC, but the region could not be regarded as completely pacified until the tribes who lived in the foothills of the Alps were conquered early in the Principate. In 42 BC, Cisalpine Gaul became officially part of Italy.

We need not regard Roman fears of the north as ill founded or paranoid even in their continuance beyond the point where the dangers seemed effectively to have been liquidated. The Romans cloaked their fear under prejudice and contempt. The large numbers of slaves, able-bodied and untamed, which the wars had provided for the rich men of Rome created the fear of locally generated *tumultus*. The real vulnerability of Rome in the face of such a menace is well illustrated by the slave-revolt led by the gladiator Spartacus in 73 BC.

A large part of the army of this enslaved Thracian prince was Celtic; many were Thracian. The Celtic custom of single combat rendered captive tribesmen all too likely recruits for the murderous sacrifice of the Roman games. The Celts who joined Spartacus seemed to see the whole undertaking as a replay of the earlier Celtic raids into Italy. This is not to attribute to them a consciousness of history, though they must have had some folk-memory of earlier glories. It is more a question of their culturally conditioned assumptions and their current situation which would tend to lead them to such a view. The horror of their lives as gladiators and rural slaves would be likely to make them as indifferent to death as the Celts who invaded Greece two centuries before. They could hardly be expected to act in any other way than as a primeval warrior horde. Return to the supposed freedom of their ancestral lands would not necessarily be their most favoured option. Thus they preferred, after the heroic fashion, to hazard all on each successive throw, rather than make their escape while the going was good. The revolt racked Italy from end to end in the years 73 to 71 BC.

Spartacus' strategic ability and capacity for organisation enabled him to threaten the fabric of Roman Italy more seriously than any enemy since Hannibal. In spite of the degradations of a gladiatorial life, he preserved a sense of honour and liberty worthy of the line of Thracian princes from which he came. He was in many respects the moral superior of his Roman adversaries. The various ethnic groups in his army had different interests, and divisions amongst them debilitated the enterprise as a whole. In particular there was tension between Celts and Thracians. Spartacus depended on the support of two able and courageous associates, the Celtic gladiators Crixus and Oenomaus. Both fell in battle before the final defeat of the revolt. Crixus had already separated himself from Spartacus, but friendship evidently was maintained: when Crixus was killed in 72 BC, Spartacus sacrificed three hundred Roman captives. This was one of his few cruel acts, and it may be seen, not merely as a gladiator's fitting revenge on a society which had done all it could to defile him, but also as an archaism from the same world as Achilles' sacrifice of Trojan captives on the pyre of Patroclus.

We shall not recount the successive and well-merited humiliations suffered by Roman commanders at his hands, before M. Crassus and Pompey eventually brought the situation under control in 71 BC. If Spartacus had been able to enforce cohesion on his enormous host of slave volunteers, he would have succeeded in tearing the Roman state apart. The success he achieved in the almost impossible task of imposing discipline could only be partial, but was impressive. Too many of his soldiers thought in terms of plunder and revenge rather than the strategic victory which would have brought reward beyond anything they might imagine. They forced his hand, and he engaged them, against his wish and judgement, in the battle that went decisively against him at the river Silarus.

In this episode, which brought such danger to the doorsteps of the Roman people, Roman custom must be held responsible for the barbarism, unamended after centuries, of putting gladiators in the position where, being doomed to die in the games, they had nothing to lose from rebellion. The same holds in the case of the slaves kept in such harsh conditions in the countryside that their expectations of life must have been similarly shortened. One of the most cruel results of economic changes since the Hannibalic war was that which had made Italy into a country of *latifundia* worked by these human beasts of burden.

It was necessary even for the most intelligent and self-conscious Romans to express contempt for what was so generally feared. Marcus Porcius Cato (243–149 BC) speaks in his *Origines* (Fr. 39 P) of the Celts as brave, quarrelsome, superstitious and with a capacity for apt speech — the last he did not intend as a compliment. Later, Silius Italicus (25–101 AD) says much the same in his *Punica* (4.190), when he refers to Celtic *furor*, and mentions the alleged Celtic tendency to run away when their leader in battle is killed (4.300): they are, he says, a loquacious race and volatile in mind (8.17).

Marcus Tullius Cicero, who must be considered one of the most humane as well as one of the most gifted of all the citizens of the Roman Republic, makes use of this ingrained prejudice against the Celts, with all the skill we might expect, when it suits his case. In his speech defending Fonteius, Cicero makes use of every item in the Roman repertory of ideas hostile to the Celts.

Fonteius had been *praetor* in Narbonese Gaul in 75–73 BC and it was not until 69 BC that the case of the inhabitants against him was brought before the commission *de rebus repetundis* (extortion). This was a busy court with a backlog of work. The complainants were Narbonese Gauls with a history of friendly association with Rome, but the population of their province and its sentiments about Rome were mixed. The chief city, Massilia, was, as Cicero admits, a respectable ally of Rome, but he goes on to speak of the accusers as if they were the same wild men who had so often invaded Italy and were by their very nature and tradition settled in their hatred of Roman civilisation. Only the colony of veterans at Narbo Martius, he makes out, stands between Rome and people like these accusers.

'How could Gauls be believed in money matters?' he asks. Everybody knows that Roman traders keep accounts. No Celt ever does business without a Roman being involved. Cicero defies anybody to produce accounts that would incriminate this respectable public servant, Fonteius. His argument along these lines is devised to appeal to the *equites* and *tribuni aerarii*, middle classes largely engaged in business, who since the *Lex Aurelia* of 70 BC were allowed to sit on juries. The *equites* in particular were susceptible to arguments supporting their economic interest in the provinces. Cicero tells the jury that Fonteius is one of themselves. In all his arguments prejudice is the dominant theme: not even the most respectable Celt is to be placed on the same level of credibility as the basest Roman, let alone a distinguished citizen like Fonteius (27). This gem is linked to many others. Cicero sees fit to remind the jury that the Celts attacked Delphi in 278 BC, and that they had a century earlier (390–388 BC) attempted the Capitol at Rome.

Cicero does not fail to mention the matter which Romans seem to find especially offensive: the alien dress of the Celts, in particular their trousers (33); there is arrogance also, he says, in the uncouth fashion in which they walk through the forum at Rome, mouthing menaces in their harsh tongue. We need say no more. The continuing strength of Roman xenophobic feeling is evident. When Cicero accuses Piso, he makes it a point of his denigration that Piso had an Insubrian grandfather (Fr. 9). Views not substantially dissimilar were held about the Greeks, and this abuse also remained fresh and lively over the centuries. Cicero, the most Hellenised Roman of his time, does not hesitate to conciliate the ignorant prejudices of his fellow citizens in his fourth speech against Verres, where he makes appealingly philistine remarks about Greek ineffectiveness and love of the arts (*Verr.* 4.134). Yet he mentions the druid Divitiacus, the friend of Julius Caesar, with considerable respect as a gentlemanly student of the physical universe (*De Div.* I. 90). It is not a question of what Cicero thinks about the Celts — no doubt he entertained some unfavourable opinions of them — but rather what, as an advocate, he felt bound to say about them to a set of average Romans. He had no qualms about attempting to rehabilitate the thoroughly rascally Galatian, Deiotarus, in the eyes of Caesar.

It is no doubt an oblique, but none the less distinct example of ethnic prejudice that the fellow conspirators of Catiline against the Roman state should have tried to enlist the help of Allobroges who were in Rome on a mission on behalf of their tribe. In brief, the conspirators intended to slaughter the leading men of Rome and the Senate and set fire to the city. No doubt they thought that such a project would appeal to both the Celtic imagination and sense of tradition.

In his account of the conspiracy, the historian Sallust (86–85 BC), presents the Allobroges in a way that reflects both Roman prejudice and the actual mannerism of Celtic culture which the Romans found so annoying. His Allobroges behave with the assertiveness of archaic heroes and are given to exaggerated speech, but they have a distinct capacity to calculate their advantage. They do not appear as an inferior people, except in so far as they have some consciousness as members of a subject nation that they are facing a manoeuvre in power politics which is likely to take them well out of their depth and could easily end in disaster for their tribe and themselves. Their swift changes of intention and aptitude for intrigue are reminiscent of Julius Caesar's description of chiefs with whom he had to deal in Gaul.

The Allobroges, according to Plutarch, were in Rome to complain about the maladministration of their territory by Roman officials. In his Life of Cicero, Plutarch tells us that there were two commissioners from the Allobroges. Lentulus, one of the conspirators, approached them to see whether they would be prepared to join with his friends and himself in a revolution which would free them and their people from the debt in which they were entangled. Their communities were heavily in debt and so were the commissioners themselves, Sallust tells us (*Cat.* 40). So also, we note, was Catiline, and he saw revolution as a possible solution of this and other personal problems. We recall that a provincial community like the Allobroges was not likely to have swift or sure redress (if indeed they got any at all) from the legal organs of Rome. The commissioners and their tribe were victims, no doubt, of the Roman habit of forcing loans which were not needed and could not be repaid on provincial communities and their chief men. The indebtedness became a form of slavery to Roman financiers and officials and was a long-standing source of trouble between Rome and the provinces. Their indebtedness would therefore recommend these Gauls to the conspirators as material for the revolutionary plot. Also, says Sallust, Gauls were known to be fierce and warlike.

Sallust also reports that a man called Umbrenus, who had experience in Gaul as a merchant, was delegated to make contact with the Allobrogan commissioners. In conversation, they gave him to understand that they were hostile to the Senate for giving them no relief, and as far as they could see, only death would bring an end to their sufferings. Apparently Umbrenus, in spite of his experience amongst Celtic people, put too literal and Roman a value on these expressions of heroic pessimism, for he decided that they were precisely the men that the conspiracy needed and arranged with great secrecy that they should be informed of all the details of the project.

The conspirators' intention in attempting to recruit the Allobroges was not ill founded. At this time there was considerable unrest in Celtic regions (Sall. *Cat.* 42) as well as in southern Italy. Muraena had arrested a number of potential leaders of revolt in

Cisalpine Gaul (Cic. *Mur.* 41). From the point of view of Catiline and his associates, it made sense to exploit Celtic discontent.

Nothing was gained from these two delegates. They may indeed have felt that there was much in the conspiracy that merited their sympathy, but they were also constrained by fear. They may have felt themselves compelled to agree that they become party to the conspiracy; they may have felt that in immediate terms this was the price of their release from a strange house in a strange city (Sempronia had arranged the meeting in the home of her absent friend, Decimus Brutus). When they were alone, they were afflicted by doubt. When they weighed the gain that might come from the revolution with the sure reward offered by the Senate (*certa praemia*), that Celtic quality of acute realism, which cohabits with heroic assertion, revived in them and they informed the authorities in the shape of their tribe's patron, Q. Fabius Sanga, who in turn told the consul, Marcus Tullius Cicero. The consul's shrewd advice was that they should pretend to embrace the cause of the conspirators and ask to meet other members of the movement; also that they should promise their support. Further, they should get assurances in writing from the conspirators; these, they should say, would be needed in order to convince their compatriots at home. They obtained copious documentary evidence in letters from Lentulus, Cethegus, Statilius, and Cassius. Volturcius was to accompany them from the city on behalf of the conspirators. By previous arrangement with Cicero, they had agreed to allow themselves to be arrested at the Milvian Bridge. Consequently, they, Volturcius and the written evidence fell into the hands of the consul. Volturcius reneged on the conspiracy and offered his testimony to the state. The conspiracy was broken and Cicero enjoyed his hour of greatest political glory. The Allobroges and Volturcius received rewards from the Senate (Sall. *Cat.* 50).

The first Roman thoroughly to exploit *Gallia Comata* as a source of power and wealth was Julius Caesar (100–44 BC). One of the most remarkable pieces of empire-building in history began when Caesar had *Gallia Comata* added to Cisalpine Gaul, Narbonese Gaul and Illyricum as his proconsular province in 58 BC. He had estimated the potential of Gaul when he was using the southern part of it as a base for communications during his campaigns in Spain. The possession of Gaul, in the first instance for a term of office of five years, would enable him to lay the foundations of a personal power so great that it became impracticable for the

Senate to remove him from office. He was ultimately to have strength enough at his disposal to wreak his own Roman *tumultus* upon his own city. By this means he would sweep aside the old machinery of the senatorial Republic. Its frame would remain for centuries to mock memories of the liberty he had destroyed.

Gaul was at that delicate stage of social development when kings have been replaced by aristocratic oligarchies which have not yet settled down into an establishment of peers. There were many rivalries within and between tribes which a foreigner could exploit. Caesar saw his opportunity and used it ruthlessly to organise the as yet inarticulate power of a formidable nation. If he could subdue the ferocity of a people who traditionally were the terror of the Roman world, what could he not subdue? He was also a brilliant author and publicist, and what he has to say of the Gauls and Britons in his *Bellum Gallicum* is the more effective for its avoidance of cruder forms of prejudice.

Also available to his enterprise was the Danube area to which his governorship of Illyricum gave him access. If Gaul could be said almost to have invited him to intervene in his affairs, his judgements about the strategic importance of Transalpine Gaul correctly led him to accept the invitation. This was demonstrated in the war between his nominated heir and successor Octavian and the remaining triumvir, Marcus Antonius. Octavian was being hard pressed after the indecisive issue of the Perusine war. In Spain and in the south he was threatened by the forces of Sextus Pompeius, and from the east by Ahenobarbus at Brundisium. He tried unsuccessfully to negotiate with Pompeius, but the key to his survival proved to be the good fortune which placed Gaul in his hands. The younger Calenus handed Gaul and its army over to Octavian when the elder Calenus, who had held it for Antonius, suddenly died.

Julius Caesar's operations in Gaul really begin with the Aedui. This tribe, which had a long record of friendship with Rome, was being pressed by the Sequani in the east and the Arverni in the west. The Sequani called in Ariovistus, a German and prince of the Suebi, to help them. This move from across the Rhine can be seen not merely as the response to an appeal, but as part of a wider movement of tribes in the east and north which had been in progress for some time. As early as 120 BC, the Roman general Papirius Carbo led a campaign against the Cimbri who were attacking the kingdom of Noricum, an ally of Rome. Strabo describes the defeat that the Romans suffered. He calls the tribe the Teutones. The battle took place near the city of Noreia, which may be the modern Magdalenenburg (Alföldi 1974: 35-7). The Cimbri and Teutones were to be a major threat to Roman security at the end of the second century BC. These convulsions in the eastern Alpine zone, where the Boii had been powerful since the fourth century BC, continued in the time of Caesar's governorship, and add point to his authority over Illyricum as well as the three Gauls.

This was not a good period for Celtic independence. The Boii, who had been displaced from Dacia by Bourebista, invaded Noricum and, according to Caesar's account, besieged Noreia and entered the territory of the Helvetii in 60 BC. They probably joined the Helvetii in their movement outwards into Gaul. Stiff resistance on the part of the people of Noricum had prevented them from settling in that country. Voccio, the king of Noricum, had a sister who married Ariovistus. This marriage is significant of a need to counterbalance, by means of a new alliance, the combined power of Helvetii and Boii. It seemed to be a felicitous manoeuvre, for the Romans at this point designated Ariovistus as 'king and friend' (*rex atque amicus*) (Alföldi 1974: 40).

At the end of his friendly duties towards the Sequani, Ariovistus refused to leave and compelled them to allow him and his followers to settle in the country which is now called Alsace. The Aedui had already complained to Rome in 61 BC about the situation, which they saw as dangerous, but they had received no effective response from the Senate. Indeed it was Caesar who arranged in 59 BC for Ariovistus to be nominated to the honour which we have mentioned. By this act Caesar was perhaps playing for time until he should be able to arrive in Gaul with enough strength to suppress Rome's new friend.

In 59 BC, the Helvetii, who came from what is now Switzerland, made an attempt to settle in rich lowland Gaul. They asked permission from Caesar to cross the territory of the Allobroges in the southern province of Gaul. He did not simply refuse: he appeared with an army, defeated them and turned them back in the direction whence they had come. Including their families, they numbered nearly half a million souls. They chose another route which took them through the Sequani, who gave them passage, and proceeded to the lands of the Aedui, which they thoroughly ravaged. Caesar defeated them at Bibracte and sent the survivors back to their original home. This rapid campaign involved him in the politics of 'Gallia Comata'.

He had now to meet the challenge of Ariovistus' ambition. Ariovistus and his warriors were thrust back over the Rhine. From our point of view, his portrait of Ariovistus in his Commentaries holds particular interest. Caesar delineates him as a monster of fierce, arbitrary cruelty, boastful arrogance and formidable cunning. This picture of the Germanic chief is made all the more repellent to the Roman mind by the attribution to him of political insight as well as military craft. In generalship he was certainly more than a match for the Sequani and the Aedui. Caesar also makes Ariovistus clearly aware of the opposition that Caesar himself may have to face in Rome if things go badly for him in his administration of Gaul. In conversation, Ariovistus is made to say much about his own virtues and little about the matter in hand. This Caesar stigmatised as mere barbarism (*BG* 1.44.1), but he knew very well that it was a negotiating ploy on the part of the German which was within the ancient tradition of warrior peoples, and from a Germanic or Celtic point of view, a legitimate diplomatic diversion. It is interpretable as a version of the ritual challenge, insult and recital of glories that precedes a Homeric or Celtic contest between heroes. At the end of the colloquy, Ariovistus proposes further talks, since he obviously intended the present ones to have no concrete result.

Caesar comments that Ariovistus is not entirely savage or inexpert in politics (*BG* 1.44.9). This may be a mischievous admission that he has been deliberately depicting Ariovistus in a way that would titillate Roman prejudices and fears (Sherwin White 1967: 18). His account of the German leader makes him appear to be some kind of primal brute, like the Cyclops in the *Odyssey*, who in some respects is an exaggerated and primitivist caricature of the heroic type more respectfully portrayed in Achilles. Caesar even uses 'key' words repeatedly (like epic epithets) to describe the barbarian as 'fierce' or 'ignorant'. Caesar needed to blacken the character of Ariovistus, whose defeat in real and public-relations terms gave an initial imprint of respectability to his own acquisition of an empire in Gaul. His description of the Celts of Gaul need not be regarded as so sharply angled towards prejudice (Sherwin White ibid.).

Ariovistus was set up as a paradigm of barbarity against which the Celts of Gaul could be measured. In his account of his campaign against the Nervii (*BG* 2.15.5) he uses the same adjectives denoting ferocity and belligerence as he uses of Ariovistus and his war-horde, but he also attributes to these barbarous

Belgae the Aristotelian quality of greatness of spirit which enabled them to fight an effective and aggressive war (*BG* 2.27.5; Sherwin White 1967: 18).

In 57 BC, these Belgae of northern Gaul had begun to seem menacing: Caesar's pretext for attacking them was his obligation to the Remi, who chose Roman friendship rather than being crushed by the Belgae. Caesar had the assistance of contingents from the Aedui and other friendly tribes. Jealousy among the Belgic septs enabled them to be defeated singly. The situation was not essentially different from that which favoured the Anglo-Normans in their earliest interventions in Ireland. There was no national organisation capable of offering a unified defence, whereas there were many actively divisive forces operating in the country at large. It could not be said that Gaul was even culturally uniform. It is significant that Caesar begins his book by stating the three main differing ethnic groups: Arverni, Celtae and Belgae. These all may have had a common interest in being left to pursue their several ways of life undisturbed, but they had no mechanism for realising this purpose.

After their defeat, the Belgae, a group of mixed Celtic and German origins, were treated with comparative moderation. This was the Roman policy in the case of the Nervii, who proved to be an extremely resistent and warlike group. The Aduatuci claimed descent from the Teutones, who had caused great terror to the Roman world together with the Cimbri, when they had cut a swathe through Gaul and Spain, defeated Roman armies and shaken Roman confidence. These were attacked by Caesar on the pretext that they had broken their truce, and were sold into slavery as a whole population. We cannot help suspecting that their ancestry stood against them, whatever their actual misdemeanour. Their fate, as well as providing an example of Roman severity which would encourage loyalty in others, enabled Caesar to be seen as the conqueror of a tribe whose ancestors had shaken the world.

The Veneti, a people who lived on Gaul's northern coast, were made anxious by what they saw as the inevitable supplanting of their trade with the Britons, when, as seemed inevitable, Roman merchants would manage eventually to persuade the governor to invade Britain. They attempted to divert this anticipated competition by preventing the invasion from ever taking place. They and other tribes of the region began a revolt which Caesar successfully put down. The Germanic Usipates and Tencteri were also defeated when Caesar took the opportunity of attacking them while they were under truce.

Caesar made his landings in Britain in 55 and 54 BC. Dumnorix, whom Caesar intended to take with him to Britain in 54 BC, escaped, was caught and executed. This Aeduan chief had been brought as an unwilling travelling companion along with others as guarantees of their compatriots' passivity during Caesar's absence in Britain. The greater part of Roman power in Gaul had been directed towards the expedition across the Channel. The usually pro-Roman Aedui were deeply angered by the death of Dumnorix.

Many of the Celtic leaders argued that Caesar's power was now as extended as his resources would permit. His decision to do little more in Britain than conclude a few formal alliances encouraged such a view. Increasing acquaintance with the economic apparatus of Roman rule also sharpened discontent. In 53 BC, the Romans quickly suppressed revolts which broke out but the spirit of discontent still remained alive. Acts of rebellion were met by measures of extreme severity: land, crops and people were impartially destroyed. The Roman position was perilous, but at the end of 53, Caesar felt secure enough to cross the Alps into Cisalpine Gaul in order to transact the business of his other gubernatorial responsibilities.

But the people of the province had found a leader for their attempt at a more concerted resistance to the increasingly burdensome yoke of Roman rule. This was Vercingetorix, a prince of the Arverni. In Caesar's absence across the Alps, Vercingetorix gathered his forces. These forces inflicted horrifying damage on the Romans and their dependants in Gaul, and in reprisal atrocities were inflicted on the population of Gaul. The Romans experienced a serious setback at the beginning of the war in their failure to take Gergovia. After the battle at Avaricium, the Romans were savagely unsparing of their defeated enemies. The impetus of the revolt eventually was broken at Alesia, and Vercingetorix surrendered. In 51 BC, the last strongpoint, Uexellodunum, was taken. Vercingetorix was kept a prisoner for six years and eventually was ritually slaughtered as part of the celebration of Caesar's triumph.

Caesar took many serious risks in the urgency of his efforts to gather together a personal empire in Gaul. The revolt of Vercingetorix was strong enough to have overturned all his achievements, had it only been better co-ordinated. Celtic social patterns did not admit of tight enough organisation of military resources to inhibit Caesar's movement in the province. Celtic military science was learning rapidly from contact with that of Rome, but it could not advance quickly enough to meet the challenge posed by a general of Caesar's genius. There was no shortage of talent or courage among the Celts of Gaul, but the social and political organisation of the country was too loosely articulated to produce a result commensurate with their energy and hatred. In Gaul there was none of the concentration of patriotic stubbornness that often characterised the Mediterranean city-state.

At the time when Julius Caesar took over the governorship of the Celtic provinces, those of Narbo and Cisalpine Gaul were appreciably advanced in Romanisation. Yet little is known about the details of their social organisation at this time and much less about the substantially untamed world of 'Gallia Comata'. It seems that a warrior aristocracy predominated. Caesar reports that the majority of people were in the position of servitors and slaves to a ruling class composed not only of warriors but also of druids. The generosity attributed to Celtic chiefs in antiquity suggests that they may have had as one of their kingly functions the redistribution of goods produced by their communities, a primal duty which still remains in modern vestiges of royal prerogative and patronage. Caesar does not specify who owns the land on which the tribe lives. Later the Roman authorities would register the land as being in the possession of the tribal chiefs, but there is no evidence that this was a system native to the country. The Vaccaei of Spain seem to have regarded the land as the property of the tribe. Caesar attributes this latter tenure to Germans, whom he, like other ancient authors, seems to think of as a more primitive and ferocious species of Celt. The introduction of Anglo-Norman notions of law into Ireland and Scotland enrolled native chieftains and princes as the owners of the land. The tribesman's status changed as a result and he became a mere tenant instead of an integral member of a society in which his status was assured by ancestry and mutual duty in relation to his chief. This is to be seen in the changes which took place in Scottish Highland society as a result of the defeat of the Stuart cause in the war of 1745 AD. Chieftains, who formerly would have regarded their clansmen as bound with them in a community of kinship and obligation, were able to send them off the land and replace them with sheep, later to be replaced by grouse.

Whatever the situation was with regard to the ownership of

land in first century BC Gaul, there is no doubt that Celtic society there and elsewhere was very far from being a primitive democracy. The fact that Celtic chiefs were expected to indulge in lavish displays of expenditure and could afford to do so is sufficient indication of the immense difference in wealth that subsisted between them and ordinary members of the tribe, who were the providers of the substance for conspicuous largess. Orgetorix, the leader of the Helvetii, is said by Caesar to have had a *familia*, which here means something like 'personal establishment', of ten thousand people, and in addition to these many clients and dependants. Their obedience and loyalty was the basis of his power and, influence amongst the Helvetii and enabled him to exercise an almost unlimited authority (*BG* 1.21). Clientship was an important bonding mechanism in Celtic society (*BG* 13.1.1–2; 15.1–2). We are not informed in detail by Caesar, or indeed anybody, about the social structure of Celtic life in the Gaul of this time. This does not mean that there were no interesting complexities to record, if it had been in an author's interest to report them. Caesar only tells us what he thinks will support his own cluster of theses about his activities in Gaul. There was no expressed social structure like the constitution of a city state or an obvious complex of institutions like that of Rome which Polybius was stimulated to describe. All that Caesar tells us about the warrior-nobles' function in society is that they are occupied in war, and that they have retainers and dependants in proportion to their wealth (*BG* 6.15). The bond between client and chief was capable of being maintained by force: Vercingetorix, according to Caesar (ibid.) raised his army from the tribesmen by threats of death, torture or mutilation. This was worth Caesar's while to report, since it illustrated the barbarism of his enemy.

Some of the customs attributed to the Gauls of Caesar resemble those of the earlier Romans. Others have a barbarous peculiarity. Some of the material came to Caesar from observation; much from reading books such as that of Poseidonius. A Roman-like custom which he mentions is that whereby the father of a family had power of life and death over his children (*BG* 6.19).

When a man of some distinction dies and there seem to be grounds for suspicion, his widow can be examined under torture, as a slave might according to the Roman custom. In marriage, a man has to put up as much property as the woman. The surviving partner of the marriage inherits the property, together with such increments as it has acquired over the years. Celtic funerary customs are described by Caesar as sumptuous by the standards of a relatively poor culture (*BG* 6.19). Animals and other valuable property are burned on the pyre with the dead. Not long before Caesar's time in Gaul, it was the custom also to immolate a chief's clients and slaves at his funeral. It is not impossible that Caesar owes this piece of antiquarian lore to the druid Divitiacus.

Caesar also reports a custom which forbade children to be seen publicly in their father's presence until they were grown up. This would seem to a Roman to be a barbarous oddity. We can scarcely guess its purpose. Psychoanalytical explanations present themselves, but any ostensible advantage to society from the prohibition remains a puzzle. Nor do we know whether it was confined to some regions. Since it seems to refer to children who were below the age of military effectiveness, it clearly means boys only: sons are specifically mentioned (*BG* 6.18.3). The custom seems to have a certain analogy with Gaelic fosterage, which had the effect of binding families of the tribe in closer relationship, or the boys' regiment of Emain Macha, in which Cu Chulain was trained. Caesar's note on the practice does not suggest that the children could not see their fathers in private, but we might suspect that the element of taboo that is implied might make this unlikely.

The finding of what are obviously slave chains in Llyn Cerrig in Anglesey and elsewhere indicates that the institution of slavery was maintained by the Celts of Britain. There was probably a slave trade between Britain and Gaul. Caesar attests the nearly servile status of the lower social classes who have no say in government and are not allowed any initiatve (*BG* 6.13.1–2). These can fall into actual slavery, in which their position is in all respects analogous to that of the slaves in Rome. Debt can bring about this misfortune (*BG* 6.13).

In general the Gauls were not ill prepared by the nature of their own way of life to adopt many of the ways of Roman civilisation (Salway 1981: 15). Their much publicised political volatility and their tendency to individual assertion when the opportunity presented itself are not much different from the independent attitude adopted by Rome's unwilling Italic allies from time to time in the history of the Republic. The pride of Gaulish grandees in revolt, whatever the differences in the cultural flavour of their motives, was not categorically different from the arrogant ambition of some of the Roman warlords and intending warlords in the last decades of the Republic.

Caesar depends on Poseidonius for some of his comments on

the nature of Gaulish society. In spite of his intention to mould his account of the country to his own propagandist purpose, he exhibits a surprising breadth of appreciation in commenting on matters that he decides to include. Strabo is substantially not entirely dependent on Poseidonius in his account of the Romanisation of the tribes of Gaul and Spain. What he says of the advance of Roman mores and customs amongst the Volcae and Turditani, for instance, must have been based on his own information, since it was only during Caesar's dictatorship that these changes took place (Sherwin White 1967: 2). Also, his knowledge of the Germanic tribes may be related to an increase of knowledge about them during the wars of Augustus' Principate (ibid.). Strabo and Caesar on the whole agree that civilisation is a qualitative and material condition of living which can be measured by its similarity to Greco-Roman ways of life. Caesar, however, is more liberal in his estimation of Gaul than is Strabo or his source (Sherwin White 1967: 33). Caesar admits that the customs followed by the inhabitants of Gaul are not notably distinct from those of most other peoples: Celtic gods are very like those worshipped by the Romans. The Germans, apart from having no druids, and different gods, are wilder and more warlike than the Celts (*BG* 6.21). They worship the sun and the moon and a god who seems to be Vulcanus. They have no knowledge of other gods, have no developed agriculture and do not consider robbery to be an offence. They do not have personal ownership of land but divide it up each year, a system reminiscent of that of the Vaccaei of Spain, except that brute force rules among the Germans to such an extent that the stronger can oust the weaker from his allocation of land. In Caesar's opinion, this way of managing land meets the requirements of a warlike society. Ownership of land would induce softness and would be a cause of contention within the tribe. It is almost as if Caesar perceived the Germans as a warrior-caste like the Spartans who were compelled to keep their distance from the working of the land which was alloted to them, or the class of 'guardians' in Plato's *Republic* who have nothing to do with primary production so that they will not be corrupted by greed or other economic vices. Whatever the system of land tenure in Gaul might have been at this time, it is clear that Celtic chiefs in that country were well provided with power, wealth and obedient servitors. Although we are aware of the difficulties of coming to any formulated view of the system that was followed in Gaul, it is reasonable to suppose that its society was more complex than that of the Volcae Tectosages who lived in a condition close to that of the Germani (*BG* 6.24.5–6). In a corresponding fashion, the German Suebi were more Gallicised, through contact with the more advanced consuming and trading society of Gaul (*BG* 4.3).

The large physical size of the Celts of Gaul is explained by Caesar as the result of their being allowed to live as they wish when they are young, freely and without the rigours of *disciplina* (*BG* 4.5). Their bulk also is caused by the kind of food they eat. Caesar differs from the view expressed in Strabo (and possibly Poseidonius) in placing less emphasis on the absence of city-state organisation as a distinctive feature of Celtic culture (Sherwin White 1967: 21). But when he speaks of the Celts' amazement at the siege machinery and other mechanical technology of the Romans (*BG* 2.12; 4.25) which they appeared to suspect was operated by divine influences rather than human agency (*BG* 2.30, 31), he makes them out to be mere children of nature, unaccustomed to the ways of an advanced society. Caesar used their wonder to his own advantage by constructing elaborate works of engineering as often as he could. It was an effective psychological tactic. But even the cataplectic effects of Roman engines of war were only temporary (*BG* 7.22.1). The Celts were too quick-witted to remain long in a state of bafflement before these military refinements. They soon showed themselves capable of taking up Roman inventions and using them for their own purposes. They became adept at countermining, building towers quickly out of scaffolding, and other methods of opposing siege techniques.

Caesar's description of the druids makes them a much more formidable group than a collection of witch-doctors: he presents them as students of natural science, but understands that their influence has a religious basis. They are essential participants in all services to the gods, including the sacrifice of human beings (*BG* 6.15). The philosophical emphasis in his explanation of their teaching may have been influenced by Divitiacus, the druid of the Aedui and brother of Dumnorix. More probably he is continuing the Greek interpretation of the druids as a species of Pythagorean philosopher. In this, he once more represents himself as the conqueror of no weak, primitive or disorganised people, just as his praise of the fighting qualities of the Belgae in effect praises himself as their vanquisher.

His most dangerous enemy, Vercingetorix, he speaks of with due tribute to his courage in his struggle for national liberty (*BG*

7.89. 1–2). This feeling of respect did not prevent him from having Vercingetorix executed after six years of what must surely have been agonising imprisonment, but he did this as a matter of political necessity and presumably there was no acrimony in it. He saw that it was only natural that the Celts, like any other race, should want to be free (*BG* 3.8.4, 10.3). Their levity (*levitas*) and unpredicability (*mobilitas*) he does not hold against them, for he takes it into account that they are among the most warlike of the world's inhabitants, and it is to be expected that they will resist conquest (*BG* 5.54.4–5). These qualities led the Celts to make military decisions on the basis of vague rumours: they had no rational means of gathering intelligence (*BG* 3.18.6).

Caesar puts a speech into the mouth of the Celtic prince called Critognatus which makes an unfavourable comparison between the methodical and unrelentless oppression inflicted by Roman tax-gatherers and other exploiters in league with them, and the terrible but passing terror of the Cimbric and Teutonic raids (*BG* 7.77ff). The barbarians, when they have gone, at least leave the inhabitants their native laws and way of life intact. These words may be taken to be Caesar's and not those of the Celtic prince. This was in keeping with the manner of ancient historiography. Even though comparison between one form of rule and another was part of the curriculum of exercises in the schools of Rhetoric, this speech is not a mere formality, but a telling comment. Caesar was aware of the rapacity, bullying, and bureaucratic overload implicit in the Roman process of pacification and he knew that nothing was done in a Roman province that was not to the advantage of Romans.

For the majority of those who lived in the provinces, the Roman Republican administration of their lands was, at best, an authoritarian domination and, at worst, a cruel and selfish tyranny which spared neither lives nor property and was made all the more distasteful by a promise of judicial redress which was seldom redeemed. This regime was riddled with national prejudice, allowed limited social mobility and was incapable of providing an administration of the law immune from the inter-ference of influential members of the Roman ruling class. Caesar's destruction of this appearance of *libertas* in the Civil Wars brought some hope of relief to subjects both provincial and domestic. Under the Principates, especially those of the Julio-Claudians, the poison of Roman rule conglobulated at its centre, in Rome. In many cases the government of the provinces was better regulated, though they would always, from time to time, become fields of contest between rival generals who desired to become emperor. In frontier areas, such as Britain, abuse of authority by comparatively minor officials could still create major wars, as in the case of Boudicca's revolt in 61 AD.

Critognatus' purported speech looks forward to the speech which Tacitus attributes to the Caledonian leader Calgacus in the *Agricola*. This contains the memorable sentiment that when the Romans take over a country, they create a desolation and call it peace. Caesar also seems to anticipate the dreadful fact that in the fifth century AD, many Roman citizens in the provinces would find the rule of Germanic barbarians easier to bear than that of the Roman bureaucracy. Critognatus' point remained valid: nothing remained free from the grasp of Roman rapacity. There is no question about Caesar's authority to speak on such a subject: he despoiled Spain of twenty-five million sesterces, and from Gaul he took so much plunder in captives and gold that when all was put up on the open market, the current price of gold fell by a sixth.

Caesar balances these implicitly anti-Roman comments by professing horror at the savagery of one of Critognatus' proposals, which we might conjecture was actually part of what the man himself may have said. The speech is supposed to have been made in besieged Alesia. Critognatus proposes that the defenders sustain themselves by cannibalism, and that the old and feeble should be put down for this purpose, as had been done in the wars against the Cimbri. This idea runs counter to a profound taboo in the Greco-Roman world. The man-eating Cyclops of the *Odyssey* is depicted as utterly repellent (*Od.* 9.215) and as knowing neither law nor morality. The Thyestian feast of a ragout of infant limbs generated a curse on the house of Atreus which could only be worked out in the grief of disastrous generations. Herodotus' story of the Indian Calliatai (3.38) who ritually devour dead parents and are scandalised by the Ionic custom of cremating them shows that in the fifth century BC a wedge of critical relativism had been inserted into the traditional prohibition. The pool of enlightenment on this subject was narrow and evanescent. Caesar may have known about the Calliatai, and he may also have been acquainted with the advocacy of cannibalism in the teachings of some Cynic philosophers. Even if he did not know of these opinions he would probably have heard of the anthropophagy that occurred in the city of Saguntum when it was besieged by Hannibal and of the pathetic evidences of similar acts of desperation found in

Numantia when Scipio reduced it. Both these instances are from Spain, and happened in Celtic or part-Celtic environments. It may be that like their fellow Indo-Europeans, the Indian Calliatai, the Celts did not find the prospect of eating human flesh under such circumstances so horrifying as a Greek or Roman might. It would be possible to flesh out the contents of a rhetorical topos on this subject; perhaps there was one in the repertory of the schools (Rankin 1971: 100–5). At the same time, Critognatus may have made some such proposal. We need not believe that Caesar was genuinely shocked.

In the course of this chapter, we have seen that Livy (59–17 AD) did not hold the Celts in high regard. He is not concerned with their history as such. His sincerely tendentious programme is to celebrate Roman national character and achievement. For this to be done effectively, he cannot allow Rome's enemies to appear as too soft or easy opponents, though their inferiority of culture and morale must be made clear. He is not so generous in his estimate of the Celts as Caesar is in the *Bellum Gallicum*. He harps on their instability of temper in war. Typical of his judgement is his statement in 10.28 that the Celts have no lasting stamina: they fight at the beginning of a battle with more than human fury, but when they become tired, as they soon will, they are weaker than women.

This same theme of Celtic instability is taken up strongly in 38.17, in his account of Manlius' operations at the river Halys in Galatia (189 BC). A speech which might well be called racist is attributed to the consul in which he accuses the Celts of combining softness and ferocity, of wearing long ruddled hair, of having excessively long swords and big shields (which they beat), of indulging in war-dances, battle-songs and wild shrieks to intimidate their enemies. His soldiers should bear in mind that for the last two hundred years, Romans had been able to defeat Celts. If only they could hold that first ferocious charge, which Celts make in such an access of fervid temper and blind wrath, the giant limbs of the enemy would soon slacken with sweat and weariness. Dust, heat and thirst would do for them without the Romans lifting a sword. Anyway, these were the degenerate descendants of the men who had conquered so much of Europe and Asia. The way of life in Asia had softened them. Not only are they Celts; they add to this the decadent character of Asiatics.

Allowance has to be made for the fact that the speech is represented as a general's encouraging words to his army before a battle. He was not in the business of doing the Celts scrupulous justice in such a situation. Yet the speech sums up Roman ethnic prejudices against the Celts. Apart from courage — and that of a disorderly kind, in Livy's view — Celtic virtues were different in kind from those of Rome, and inferior.

Narbonese Gaul with its ancient Greek layer, its southern climate and its old alliance with Rome was in many ways part of the Greco-Roman Mediterranean. The elder Pliny says that it is 'Italy, rather than a province' (*NH* 3.31). Its Hellenised civility was somewhat diluted by the foundation in it of colonies of Roman veterans. From its Romanised upper classes came educated officials and military commanders of merit. An equestrian genera-tion was succeeded by a senatorial one (Tac. *Agr.* 4.1). The first Narbonese consul came from Gallic Vienna: he was Valerius Asiaticus, consul in 35 AD. His city was the former tribal centre of the Allobroges (Syme 1958: 456). Next to be elevated to this rank was Domitius Afer of Nemausus in 39 AD. There was at this time a gradual increase of Senators whose names commemorate early grants of citizenship: Domitii, Valerii, Pompeii. This influx was not confined to families from Celtic regions. Spanish, Illyrian and Oscan names are recorded (Syme 1958: 590). Earlier, the poet, soldier and administrator Cornelius Gallus (69–26 BC) was from Forum Iulii. It has been suggested that his father may have been given citizenship through the influence of Pompey's lieuten-ant, Cn. Cornelius Lentulus, for services during the war against Sertorius (Syme 1939: 75).

Another notable son of Narbonese Gaul was Pompeius Trogus, who lived in the time of Octavian. His historical writings are epitomised by Justin (3rd century AD), though some fragments are preserved in other sources. Trogus' *Historiae Philippicae*, which occupied forty-four books, were modelled on the Histories of Theopompus (4th century BC). As a world history, this work of Trogus inevitably reduced in perspective the importance of Rome, which it treated as one of a number of great civilisations. Apparently it included interesting material on Massilia and Spain.

Justin records that Trogus mentioned his Celtic ancestry and said that he was of the tribe of the Vocontii. His grandfather had obtained citizenship from Pompey the Great during the Sertorian war and his uncle had been a cavalry commander in Pompey's campaign against Mithridates. His father, however, served in the army of Julius Caesar.

We shall speak of the poet, soldier and administrator from

Forum Julii, the versatile Cornelius Gallus, in the context of other poets in Chapter 7. We shall now consider the problem raised by a friend and correspondent of the younger Pliny, the famous historian Cornelius Tacitus. No hard facts are available about his origins. Attempts neither implausible nor conclusive have been made to place him in the Celtic country of northern Italy. In a letter which the younger Pliny writes to him, he asks Tacitus about a point concerning the appointment of a schoolmaster in Comum. He seems to expect that Tacitus will know something about such a subject. This is suggestive, especially when it is considered in company with the fact that in Tacitus' early work, a dialogue on rhetoric and style (*Dialogus de Oratoribus*), several of the participants in the conversations are from Gaul, though they are not from the Cisalpine region (Syme 1958: 614).

More suggestive is the story related in a letter written by Tacitus to Pliny (9.23.2): Tacitus is in conversation with an *eques* at the games; they talk about literature and life, and the *eques* asks Tacitus whether he is Italian or from the provinces. Tacitus says: 'Your knowledge of Roman oratory should tell you who I am. Then the man asks: 'Are you Tacitus or Pliny?'

Did Tacitus (asks Syme 1958: 619) have an accent not unlike that of Pliny? The answer would appear to be affirmative. It would be a Romanised Celtic accent, probably attenuated by metropolitan life.

Tacitus had plenty of information about Gaul and knew people who could keep him in touch with events there. His time in Gaul in charge of the financial administration of Gallia Belgica and the two Germaniae was well spent from the point of view of his future writing of history (Pl. *NH* 7.76). He would know the people of Colonia Agrippinensium in the lands of the German Ubii; also he would be in contact with the important members of the influential Treveri — one of these had been procurator of Britain in the principate of Nero (Syme 1958: 452).

Tacitus' evident distaste for the immorality and corruption of the imperial family and court in the Julio-Claudian principates could suggest that he was a provincial. He was, in fact, conscious of the distance in customs between the capital and the towns of the provinces, and he knew that provincials could be shocked when they came in contact with Roman practices (*Ann.* 16.5.1).

Brixia (Pl. *Ep.* 1.14.4) and Patavium had the repute of old-fashioned severity (Martial 10.16.8). We have no reason to place Tacitus in either. Old values were not a monopoly of Cisalpine communities. In his *Agricola*, he introduces a digression about the British and their ethos, and he is able to make comparison unfavourable to the Romans. Cn. Julius Agricola was the father-in-law of Tacitus. He was from Narbonese Gaul. In the office of military governor of Britain, he gave distinguished service. He fought and won several important battles with the tribes of Britain. Tacitus' discussion of the Britons can hardly be seen as propaganda for a barbarian nation. It has more of the quality of a rhetorical topos in which the natural virtues of a wild and barbarous people are idealised in order to point up the decadence of a more mature and civilised Mediterranean community. The fact that the British are supposed to possess interesting virtues is merely contingent. They happened to be the people against whom Agricola's victories were won. Their virtue adds to the glory of his achievements.

Nor can we make much of the compressed epigrammatic style of Tacitus. It might remind us of the terse, riddling proverbialism attributed to Celtic conversation (Diod. 5.31.1). This could hardly be isolated as a distinctive proof of nationality. The style of the *Annales* suits the subject matter. The *Dialogus* is different in texture. The *Historiae*, which are later than the *Annales*, are not so intense or epic (Syme 1958: 616–7). We are left with the hanging opinion that Tacitus may have been some kind of Celt. If so, he was more probably Narbonese than Cisalpine.

From the Narbonese town of Forum Julii came the father of Agricola, L. Julius Graecinus, to enjoy both distinction and a tragic end. He entered the senate under Tiberius, and became praetor. He became a well-known writer on botany and agriculture. He was of such integrity that he would not accept from aristocrats of known bad character their contributions towards the games which it was his official duty to present to the inhabitants of Rome. Caligula had this valuable citizen killed when he refused to prosecute on the basis of the Emperor's whimsicality.

His son Cn. Julius Agricola (b. 40 AD) was educated at Massilia and, as he seems to have admitted, studied philosophy with an un-Roman enthusiasm. He served with the military governor Suetonius Paulinus in Britain. Although anxious for distinction, he bore in mind that he lived in times when it could be dangerous to draw attention to oneself; 'a good repute', said his son-in-law, 'was more perilous than vicious notoriety' (*Agr.* 5.4). Agricola's wife came from a notable family of Narbonese

Gaul. The marriage improved his prospects of a career and he became quaestor, an office whose term he served out tactfully in the province of Asia where temptations were so plentiful and where the prospects of many a promising man had been ruined. In Rome, he lived quietly and his inconspicuous style of living enabled him to survive the dangers of 66 AD and the Neronian terror which cut away talent by swathes, often for no better reason than that it was talent. He even survived his praetorship in the last year of Nero's Principate. Such a survivor was marked out for future advancement. He commanded a legion in Britain, was governor of Aquitania, became consul and member of the patrician order in 77 AD. Vespasian made him governor of Britain, where among other military achievements, he defeated the Caledones and their allies at the battle of the Mons Graupius. His career ended quietly and in an atmosphere of official neglect.

Others whose roots were in Narbonese Gaul reached imperial level. It has been suggested that Ceionius Commodus, who was nominated heir of Hadrian (*Imp.* 117–138 AD), but who died, could have been from Bononia (Syme 1958: 601). Another conjecture makes him Hadrian's illegitimate son. Pompeia Plotina, the wife of Trajan (*Imp.* 98–117 AD) may have been from Nemausus. The Emperor Antoninus Pius was of Narbonese origin (*imp.* 136–161 AD).

It was the Emperor Claudius who formed the policy of trying to canalise the flow of talent from Gaul into channels useful to the empire. The prominence of some of the individuals we have mentioned must owe something to his policy, but his efforts were only partially successful. He did not cure a powerful country of its desire for independence and revolts would still break out; but he tried to move in a constructive direction. In 48 AD, he made a speech in the Senate recommending that important men of the Aedui be appointed to the rank of Senator. The text of the speech has been preserved in an inscription found at Lugdunum (Lyons), his place of birth. Tacitus also provides us with an edited version of his recommendations.

A national spirit had survived Caesar's conquest of his powerful and dangerous group of peoples. Roman rule had been seen as at least providing a protection for Gaul from the intrusions of Germanic raiders. Men of the Celtic tribes had been willing to join in Roman expeditions into Germany. The defeat of the Roman legions by Arminius in 9 AD discredited this aspect of Roman suzerainty. Under Quinctilius Varus, three legions had been completely destroyed in the so-called *'Clades Variana'* ('the Varus disaster') of the Teutoberger Mountains. This was not only a sharp blow to Celtic confidence in Rome but a defeat for Roman confidence in the superiority of Roman arms. There was no further plan for the subjugation of Germany. Not surprisingly, the Celts of Gaul wondered — and the Romans suspected them of wondering — whether they might also hope to accomplish as much against the armies of Rome (Syme 1958: 454). It may hardly be doubted that the legions which in the Principate of Tiberius were stationed along the Rhine, ostensibly to keep the Germans out, were not just as well placed to cope with internal disruptions in Gaul. This seemed to be particularly likely in the case of the legions at Argenorate (Strasbourg) and Vindonessa, which confronted regions with hardly any German population (Syme ibid.).

Some aspects of life in Gaul mirrored that of Italy. There were large tracts of land owned by a few people and worked by those who, if they were not in fact slaves, must at least have been held in a condition near serfdom. The difference peculiar to Gaul was that the Celtic tribesman was bound to the land he worked by tribal bonds and loyalties to chiefs, who corresponded to the Roman grandees who owned the *latifundia* of Italy that actually were worked by slaves. Under Roman laws, the Celtic aristocrats were regarded as having the title of personal ownership of the lands. This state of affairs persisted well into late Antiquity and provided a model for the society which was to evolve in later centuries (Syme ibid.). The cities of the Celtic regions often bore the name of their local tribe for which they provided a centre, for the tribe remained important.

Of the northern troubles which occurred between the *Clades Variana* and the accession of Claudius, the most serious was in 20 AD, when major portions of the Treveri and the Aedui came out in rebellion. Tacitus is our main informant about the revolt.

Rome's willingness to allow its richer citizens to enmesh provincials, individuals and whole tribes in debt by forcing loans on them was bound to produce trouble. It was an important cause of the rising of 20 AD. Two individuals distinguished in their respective tribes, Julius Florus of the Treveri, and Sacrovir, a prince of the Aedui, organised a rebellion which promised serious dislocation of Roman rule. The story is told in characteristically dramatic terms by Tacitus in his *Annales* 3.40–46. The disaffection was widespread and the revolt gained sympathy in many cities and settlements. It was nationalistic in character: its ostensible inspiration was the recovery of former liberty and the reassertion of the military glories of the Celtic past. Some sentences of rousing oratory are put in the mouths of its leaders by Tacitus. A main motive, however, was this indebtedness and disgust at the arrogant behaviour of Roman officials. The project was not likely to succeed unless the soldiers of the legionary garrison, who also were sufferers from the abuse of authority, could be persuaded to join the rebels. Their resentment at the alleged murder of Germanicus was used as propaganda to win them over, but with limited success. Widespread and dangerous though the revolt was, it was soon brought under control. The forces of the Treveri and the Aedui were insufficiently trained and equipped to face regular Roman units with any hope of success. Florus was defeated in the midst of a collection of tribesmen and bankrupts as he made his way to the relative safety of the Ardennes. He escaped, but was eventually hemmed in by the enemy and committed suicide.

The Aedui came out more strongly in revolt, but they too were overcome. They managed to seize Augustodunum and for a while they held it. It is interesting that Sacrovir was able to recruit there many students from distinguished Celtic families. In enlisting these idealistic Classical scholars, he at the same time obtained the support of their families. We cannot help being reminded of the Roman students at Athens, who, like Horace, were almost automatic volunteers for the cause of the Republic at Philippi. These young Celts no doubt hoped to become the rulers of an emergent new nation that could rival Rome. The army of the Aedui had many soldiers as well equipped as the legionaries of Rome: some former gladiatorial slaves were so heavily armoured that the Roman soldiery could only kill them with hatchets and pickaxes. The defeat of Sacrovir's forces was crushing. He and his followers killed themselves in Augustodunum. They had set the town on fire, and Romanised though many of them undoubtedly were, their death has about it an element of primitive ritual. We may recall the stories of ancient Irish heroes perishing in the conflagration of their *bruidne*.

By a touch of irony, both the leaders of revolt bore the name 'Julius'. Both were of the Romanised ruling class of Celtic nobles. They were well acquainted with the problems faced by the Roman government in Gaul and planned to exploit these. Both seemed shrewd enough to know that without the help of defecting Roman soldiers from the legions they had no hope of victory. In a species of double bluff, Sacrovir at one point urged Celts to fight on the Roman side. According to Tacitus, morale on the Celtic side was low. In following the ancient Celtic custom of the defeated leader's ritual suicide, the two Romanised revolutionaries not only made a last assertion of national honour, but avoided the shameful fate of being executed by the Romans. Gaul was far indeed from being effectively Romanised.

Claudius was born at Lugdunum in 10 BC, and he retained a sentimental regard for the region. Though Tacitus altered some of the text of Claudius' famous speech at Lugdunum, he conveys most of its ideas, improving, at places, the logic. One geat fallacy of the speech is the citation of the precedent of Narbonese being made Roman Senators in support of the proposal that important men from the rest of Gaul should be brought into the Senate. The categorical error lies in the fact that the inhabitants of Narbonese Gaul were much more Roman in their assumptions about life than people from the rest of the country. The proposed Senators were still the chiefs of their tribes, no matter how Romanised in language and manner they might appear to be. In contrast to Narbonese Gaul, the rest of this vast country had not yet begun to provide Rome with senior soldiers and officials.

Conciliation of Gaul and the avoidance of revolt no doubt formed the basis of Claudius' proposal, but it would be unfair to derogate from the constructiveness of his intention. He argued that the grandees of Gaul would be less willing to revolt when they had become more integrated with the Roman establishment. Tacitus adds to Claudius' case the wealth and civilised attainments of the Celtic ruling class at this time (Syme 1958: 461). The fact was that they were potentially dangerous warlords, no matter how smooth their manners.

In spite of Claudius' liberal expression of intent, and its acceptance, there seems to have followed no impressive flood of new names from northern Gaul into the list of known officials of state. We can suggest that this indicates a strong persistence of cultural identity, a certain unwillingness to co-operate with the Roman official system. The princes of the region remained too Celtic to feel happy as Roman Senators (Sherwin White 1967: 56–7).

These differences could not be removed by declaration. That there was good reason for any *princeps* to feel concerned about the loyalty of Gaul's great landowners is well indicated by the rebellions of Vindex and Civilis. The revolt of the latter in particular aspired to a unified empire of Gaul, which would have been fraught with dire menace for the security of Italy.

Claudius' efforts to bring the great men of Gaul into the senatorial establishment could be said to have produced a not entirely unpredictable result in the case of Julius Vindex. The father of Vindex was a Senator, presumably of Claudian creation. Vindex himself was *legatus* in charge of Gallia Lugdunensis. The temptation to make use of his opportunities was too great: for, according to Dio (63.22.1) Vindex was not only a Roman Senator, but a descendant of the princes of Aquitania, who could call on the sentiments of many tribesmen. He was supported by many chieftains and their thousands of clients.

He came out in revolt in 68 AD. In spite of the strength of the support he received, he was defeated by the Roman general Verginius Rufus at the battle of Vesontio (Besançon). It appears that Verginius had entered into conference with Vindex at this place. Either by a contrived accident or in a moment of genuine suspicion, Verginius' soldiers attacked Vindex as he was entering the city, and he killed himself in the conviction that he had been betrayed and trapped.

We may doubt whether Vindex wished to replace the emperor at Rome. He may have been disgusted by what he had heard of Nero's reign, and certainly Roman procurators were a persisting plague that spoiled Gaul of much of its wealth in the interests of an increasingly parasitic Italy; but we have no clue as to any extensive ambition he may have entertained. When Nero died, he offered his support to Galba. Verginius Rufus was the only governor of a Roman province who did not elect to support Galba: his own soldiers encouraged his ambition to become *princeps* himself. On the whole, the motivation of Vindex and his supporters seems to have been nationalistic, but their ultimate object remains ill defined.

In the revolt of the Batavian chieftain Civilis in 69–70 AD, Treveri and Lingones swore allegiance to an *imperium Gallicum*, an empire of Gaul and the Gauls. Their enthusiasm for this new state was repressed by their defeat at the hands of Petilius Cerialis at Trier. Again we may note that a vigorous sense of ethnic independence must have promoted the concept of an *imperium Gallicum*, which itself strangely prefigures the power and influence that Gaul later was to possess in the history of the Roman Empire, when factors such as declining economic potency and decrease of population were making themselves more apparent in the life of Italy.

Julius Classicus, a prince of the Treveri, joined the movement which originated with Civilis; but not at the outset. Classicus had been the commander of an *ala* of Celtic cavalry in the army of Vitellius in 69 AD. He seems to have had sympathy with the idea of Gaul as an independent nation. This idea may presume to have been atmospherically present among the ruling class of Celtic society for a considerable number of years. But at the beginning of Civilis' rebellion, Classicus and his associates held to the Roman side.

Civilis was animated by a patriotism which had been sharpened by a sense of personal resentment against Rome. His brother had been executed on a false charge of treason and he himself had suffered the humiliation of arrest and transportation to Rome. His anger was not mitigated by his acquittal by Galba. Classicus' view of the rebellion's chances of success was changed by the death of Vitellius and even more by the death of the enfeebled *legatus* of Upper Germany, Hordeonius Flaccus. Consequently he entered into negotiations with Civilis. Hordeonius had pusillanimously requested Civilis to pretend revolt in order that his own Roman soldiers should be kept loyal through fear. In all fairness, we should remember that the man was old and sick and in other respects unfit for his command. When he had left the scene, Gaul hatched flocks of rumours about secret oaths taken by chieftains that they should finally get rid of the Romans. The first step would be to block all the passes from Gaul into Italy.

Civilis was a brilliant and unscrupulous diplomatist. He had, as Tacitus says in a patronising phrase that echoes Julius Caesar's estimate of Ariovistus, 'a more than barbarian cunning'. This led him to avoid complete committal to the empire of Gaul, and to attempt to show himself still loyal to the Emperor Vespasian (*Imp.* 69–79 AD).

Messages were sent to the tribes of Gaul recommending the seizure of the present opportunity together with the Alpine passes and listing the names of Roman general officers whom it would be useful to kill. The legions could be brought round to the revolutionaries' way of thinking once their *legati* had been removed. The position of the Roman commander Vocula was so weak that he had to allow himself to become involved in a spurious expedition together with Classicus and purportedly against Civilis. Classicus made an arrangement with the forces of Civilis and withdrew his own forces from the line, leaving Vocula no option but retreat. Classicus then instigated a mutiny amongst Vocula's troops and procured his murder by means of a plot. At this point Classicus felt that the time was ripe for him to assume the insignia of the emperor of the empire of Gaul. But Petilius Cerialis disappointed his ambition by his defeat of the Treveri at Trier, and Classicus was obliged to join Civilis across the Rhine. He was involved with Civilis and the Batavians in a last stand in one of their islands. Civilis capitulated. We do not know what became of him, nor do we know how Classicus ended.

After the revolts of Vindex and Civilis, fewer Senators are noted as originating in any of the three Gauls. Spain and Narbonensis remain as suppliers of the establishment. Galatians of princely family and Celtic origin also begin to enter the Senate (Syme 1958: 462).

The *Histories* of Tacitus are a main source for the account of Civilis and Classicus. We have seen how important his *Annales* are for our understanding of various events in the history of Gaul under the Empire. It must be said, however, that nothing he says ever suggests he had any interest in non-Roman peoples in their own right. In the time in which he lived, there was no Romantic idea that there was something stimulating or intrinsically attractive about barbarian nations. Also the Romans had lived with barbarians and had to cope with their peculiarities for a long time (Sherwin White 1967: 49). His occasional ridicule of barbarian customs and temperament does not prove in him a deeply implanted hatred of Gauls, Britons and Germans. He had the civilised Roman's automatic contempt for those who were not Roman. Whether he had this attitude from the tradition of his family or had carefully acquired it as an instrument to advance his career — a protective colouration in a Roman environment — it is impossible to say. It proves nothing about his own origins. The Irish Classical scholar J.P. Mahaffy (19th–20th centuries AD), himself possessed of a Gaelic name, had nothing but vociferous contempt for Gaelic language and culture.

What Tacitus says about Celts and Germans is saturated with rhetorical topoi, and is unrelated to any scientific intention to inform us about alien cultures. The Celts and Germans are clothes-horses for the draperies of commonplace. Though he cannot help conveying some useful and important information about them, they become in his texts the spokesmen of liberty against oppression and of ancient discipline and morality against modern decadence, as if they were fully subscribed members of a group of Stoical oppositionists at Rome. There is in this a historical unrealism, but there is also a sincere political philosophy, inspired by a genuine love of decency and an affection for *libertas*, which we would probably conceive to be a restricted form of human liberty. There is no question of his approving democracy, any more than it would be approved by people like Vindex or Classicus. Tacitus' republican, aristocratic predilections lead him to represent the initiators of rebellion against Rome as advocates of a *libertas* which barbarians and Romans alike have lost to a power-hungry Principate and its vulgar satellites. This theme of freedom is strongly imprinted in his *Agricola*: both in his description of Boudicca's motives and in the speech of Calgacus to the Caledones. He does not stress barbarian cruelty either in the case of Boudicca's destruction of Verulamium (*Ann*. 14.33.6), or in the sacrifice by the Germans of their Roman captives after the defeat of Varus (*Ann*. 1.61).

He describes the Germans (*Germ*. 15.1) as inert in times of peace, given to drunkenness, and inveterate in their love of gambling. In contrast to the disgraceful practices of contemporary Rome, they respect marital fidelity, are ascetic in lifestyle and their custom of keeping freedmen in their place wins his approval. They are in many ways unspoiled primitives, not unlike the legendary Romans of the early days of the city's history. He makes the German leader, Arminius, deliver a speech to his compatriots urging them to defend an untrammelled freedom as yet untainted by the dishonour of Roman rule and the oppression of Roman taxation. It is already an unexpiated disgrace for the Germans to have seen the despised *fasces* and *toga* between the Elbe and the Rhine. He is ferociously critical of his father-in-law, Segestes, who is prepared to acquiesce in Roman domination of his country. The deification of Augustus (valid in the provinces) and priesthoods dedicated to the worship of mere human beings are matters of derision for him. The capture of his young pregnant wife infuriates him and he is eager for revenge (*Ann*. 1.59ff).

The speech of the British rebel Caractacus (*Ann*. 12.35) is shorter and more concerned with ethnic freedom than that of the individual, nor is it especially directed towards moral questions, such as the status of conquest or conquerors. His phrase about the recovery of liberty is intended to be read in a Roman context by Roman readers who do not much love the Principate but who, at the same time, have little regard for foreigners.

When he is at last brought before the Emperor, Caractacus requests rather than begs for clemency (*Ann*. 12.38). According to

Tacitus' account, he argues that it was only natural that he should have defended his property and land against the Romans' desire to possess them. There is no natural law which maintains that people should take on the yoke of Roman rule without resistance. Clemency to him would be a glory to Rome. His execution would be a trivial event soon forgotten.

Claudius pardoned him, his wife and family. This is a matter of history. Yet it is difficult to accept that his speech was exactly as Tacitus describes it. The manner and basic argument were no doubt impressive, and Claudius was capable at times of listening to reason. But Caractacus spoke as if he had just stepped out of a school of rhetoric.

Another striking speech is that of Calgacus to his army before their terrible defeat by Agricola at the Mons Graupius. His speech is paired, as is often done, with that of the enemy commander to his soldiers. Calgacus argues vigorously for a free people's right to remain free. He utters a crushing condemnation of Roman provincial rule which spares neither the property, chastity nor liberty of the person. What he says has little to do with Celts or their way of life. It could as easily be the speech of any citizen of Rome whose rights are being annihilated by the emperor or his servants. His speech is memorable for the equation of Roman peace with desolation. He speaks like a Cato or a Thrasea rather than a Celtic chief, whose ideas of abstract liberty need not be assumed to be so liberal as those which occur in this speech.

Agricola's speech (33–4) encourages his weary men. He reminds them of their Roman virtues and of the unstable, fugacious character of the enemy that confronts them. These, he says, are the survivors of other, braver British armies: they are only alive today, because they fled from other battles. In any case, the barbarian soldier is capable of being thrown into panic by the mere noise of battle.

Tacitus does not suppress the Roman case. He allows the benefits of Roman rule to be expounded eloquently by Petilius Cerialis, the opponent of Classicus and Tutor in the revolt of Civilis. Cerialis is soon to go to Britain as its governor (*Hist.* 4.73).

He argues that since Gaul is the scene of inevitable warfare between petty kingdoms, the only defence against chaos is the Roman presence and this has to be paid for by means of taxes. This purports to be a speech addressed to the Treveri and Lingones at Colonia Claudia. The settlement was in a frontier zone and accessible to approaches like that of the Tencteri, a

German tribe from across the Rhine. These had suggested to the inhabitants on grounds of their common racial origins (the townspeople were of mixed German and Celtic stock), that they should dismantle the walls and kill all the Romans in their territory. The townspeople admit that they, as Celts, have the same origins as the Germans, but they claim that they have no foreigners amongst them. They are a people with their own identity (*Hist.* 64ff).

Part of the argument of Cerialis is that no distinction is made under Roman government between Roman and native; that Celts and Romans alike are eligible to command legions and hold high office — no small exaggeration. The inhabitants of Colonia Claudia must have perceived the disingenuousness of both approaches. By this time they would have been hardened by experience to the ambivalences generated by their frontier location and racial mixture. In this episode, we can almost observe the conception of a new national identity.

From this period Gaul remained relatively free from major upheaval until the great imperial crises of the third century AD. In many parts it became prosperous: its rich and fertile land responded generously to an increasingly organised agriculture. But Gaul was in no respects immune from the operation of deleterious economic forces which began to make themselves felt at the end of the second century AD and in the third century AD all over the empire. The causes of a gradual but universal decline in prosperity in the empire are uncertain: all we can say with certainty is that they were plural, not singular. The winding down of Roman military effort when the frontiers of empire ceased to expand induced contraction in other areas of Roman life. The Roman economy had been more dependent than was realised upon accessions of foreign wealth and slaves from conquered territories. The growing energy of barbarian tribes on the frontiers was an effect of this cessation of growth and a cause of further social and economic disruption. Excessive taxation to meet the needs of the army and an ever-increasing and centralised bureaucracy, the rigidity of the class structure, the system of land tenure and a neglect of such technology as was available, all these can be and are cited as causes of a decline which became increasingly obvious to Rome's enemies and made her rule more burdensome to her friends.

Gaul was not unaffected by these seismic forces. Towns once more had to be fortified. Local consciousness revived and became aggressive, as trade and communications declined (Drinkwater 1983: 216–7). The towns tended to atrophy; tribal groups became uneasy. The tribes were still aware of their identity.

Only after 250 AD were the most severe effects of the general instability felt in Gaul (Drinkwater 1983: 225). The Alamanni, a formidable congeries of tribes (the name itself means 'all-men'), came over the German frontier. Gallienus restored this situation but soon removed his Roman army away from the Rhine. The capture of the Emperor Valerian by the Persians in 259 AD threw the whole empire into crisis, and encouraged the return of the Germanic tribes in the west. Postumus, the rival of Gallienus, decided not to race for Rome and supreme power. A kind of order was restored in Gaul which resulted in the creation of what was virtually an independent Gallic empire. Successive invasions continued to injure the economic base of the country. Small farmers and traders were eliminated. The growth of *latifundia* was facilitated by the harsh economic climate, just as the Hannibalic invasion of Italy had led to the concentration of land holdings in the hand of relatively few people. Soon landowners such as Victoria, a Celtic aristocrat and the mother of the Emperor Victorinus, had the resources and influence to set up in power her kinsman Tetricus as one of a succession of pretenders to the emperorship.

Vicious contention between rivals for supreme power did half the work of the barbarian invaders. Postumus had been able to hold off the Germanic threat, but subversive elements among his soldiers compelled him to accept Victorinus, a member of his staff and a Celt, as his colleague. There was a rival claimant, Laelianus, who was defeated at Moguntiacum (Mainz). Postumus infuriated his victorious army by refusing to allow it to plunder the city, and he was murdered by his soldiers (270 AD). Victorinus succeeded and soon also was murdered. It was then that Victoria put forward P. Esuvius Tetricus, who ruled in Gaul until his defeat by Aurelian in 274 AD. Gaul and Britain were reabsorbed into the empire, but the punishment sustained by Gallic society as a whole in consequence of its period of stormy quasi-independence removed any further hope of creating an *imperium Gallicum* and weakened the country's capacity to resist invading tribes.

The fourth century AD was another period of relative stability in Gaul, except for the frontier zones which were under constant pressure from the Germanic tribes. Areas remote from the troubles, like Burdigala, were flourishing centres of education.

Here the tradition of humane studies and rhetoric, which had implanted themselves firmly in Gaul, was maintained by such men as Ausonius, whom we shall consider in a later chapter (Chapter 12).

Peace did not last. Alaric's attack on Rome in 410 AD was followed by others. It was deplored by the poet Rutilius, who in his mistaken bardic confidence was sure that it would not happen again. In 415 AD, Wallia succeeded in establishing his Visigothic kingdom in southern Gaul and Spain. Genseric founded the Vandal kingdom of North Africa in 429 AD. Italy was rent by the Hunnic invasion of 452 AD. Rome escaped destruction then, but was sacked in 455 AD by Genseric. In 486 AD Odoacer finally unhinged the old decaying structure of empire. In the general collapse Gaul became Frankish. Its late Classical revival was over. The poet Sidonius Apollinaris represents the last stand of preciosity against brutality.

7

Cisalpine Literary Talent

In spite of Polybius' assertion (2.35.4) that by his time the Celts had been driven out of the Po valley, the incidence of Celtic inscriptions and Celtic names in these inscriptions tells a different story (Chilver 1941: 71ff). Even in imperial times a name as Celtic as Boduac Tritiac occurs. But already in the second century BC the process of Romanisation had begun, as is suggested by bilingual inscriptions such as that of Todi (Polomé 1983: 519). People had begun to change their names from Celtic to Roman forms: Briona becomes Quintus (Chevallier 1962: 367). Celtic cults persisted: Belenus was worshipped; also the Matronae, who are no doubt the triple goddesses known elsewhere in the Celtic world. We hear of the Fatae Dervones (*dervos*, 'oak') who possibly were connected with woodland precincts.

In a sequence of generations of Romanising families, names change from Celtic to fully flowering Roman triplexes with wonderful suddenness. In addition, we must not forget the influence of Italian settling families, such as the Caecilii and the Valerii (Chilver 1941: 75), whose gentile names were taken over by friends and clients. Celts mixed readily with Ligurians and Veneti as well as Italic and Greek people. Assimilation also took place on the level of material culture, but this did not mean that local culture disappeared. There appears to be evidence that in the second century AD the Celtic language still survived (Aul. Gel. *NA* 2.7.35) — unless the abverb *Gallice* simply means 'speaking with a Celtic accent'. Romans, like Anglo-Saxons, found the speech of other nations diverting, from the mere fact of its difference. Some Cisalpines liked to have their children educated at Rome, but there were those who preferred the excellent local schools. Virgil, whose family was probably not of Celtic descent (Gordon 1934), was educated in Cremona and Mediolanum (Holland 1979: 11). Celtic Italy was early prepared to contribute to metropolitan civilisation. Schools were established soon after Rome began to be dominant in the region in the third century BC.

Northern Senators were appointed by Julius Caesar to enliven a house that had become effete. This provoked an outbreak of comic verse about Gauls taking off their native trews and putting on the purple-striped toga of their new rank. Mock resolutions of Senate were circulated providing that no citizen shall show any strange Senator where the Senate House is (Suet. *Div. Jul.* 80). Caesar knew that the new men were his men and that they were not bound by traditions of loyalty to the optimate ascendancy. His experience of the sluggish degeneracy of the senatorial class of his time was deeper than that of most contemporaries except, perhaps, Cicero. Other men had come to Rome from the northern country before these, but they had come to make their way in literature and drama, since politics was not yet accessible to them as a career. Catullus was to attempt a public career, but for various reasons he had no success, though it seems that he may have had some patronage from the Metelli.

Of all Cisalpines, Gaius Valerius Catullus is the one whom we can claim to know as a person, because his small body of poetry, much of which is poignantly related to himself and his feelings about his life, has substantially survived. But before we discuss him and his contemporaries, and those later distinguished men of the Cisalpine region, such as Pliny and Tacitus (who perhaps was one of its sons), we shall consider some earlier representatives of Celtic intellect and the attitudes which they encountered in Rome.

Caecilius Statius (or Statius Caecilius) of Mediolanum was Celtic. He had his origins in the tribe of the Insubres. He is said to have combined lyical quality in his comedies with a broad Aristophanic humour. He was also strongly attracted by poets of the Athenian New Comedy, such as Menander, and he tended to make these his models. His native vitality could not always be kept within the confines of this more manicured species of comedy. Yet he was praised by Horace for his *gravitas*, that most Roman quality, which, if it can be translated at all, contained some of the meaning of 'moral and intellectual seriousness of purpose'. Caecilius 'flourished' about 179 BC. A man of great comic invention was Lucius Pomponius of Bononia who was active around 90–89 BC. Amongst scores of titles of Atellan farces which are attributed to him, is one called *Galli Transalpini*. No doubt it was devoted to the mockery of wild tribesmen of the hills. It is a pity that we do not possess the text. We cannot tell whether he was the first Celt to satirise his own compatriots in order to amuse the lowest level of the oppressing nation. Perhaps, as an urbanised inhabitant of the region, he had the same feelings about the Transalpines as a citizen of medieval Galway would have about the O'Flaherties and was anxious to strike a blow, even verbal, against them. Nor do we know that he did not regard himself as entirely Italic in race! However, he also wrote a farce called the *Campani*. We may suppose that local characteristics were thoroughly satirised in it.

The Cisalpine voice and style made an individual impression in Rome. Not only in the time of Catullus was this individuality criticised. Later commentators, such as Quintilian (*c.* 40–96 AD) had little good to say of it. One of the few northern characteristics of speech and composition that can be clearly isolated in ancient literature that mentions them, is that combined eccentricity of hiatus and elision which involves vowel clashes between juxtaposed words. Cicero's criticism and Horace's implied disapproval (by avoidance) of this feature of poetic expression give backing to the view that it is of the north (Holland 1979: 11). We learn from Greek sources that the voices of Celts were deep, rough and guttural. We have noted already the capacity of surviving Celtic languages to cope with hiatus and frequent aspiration between and within words. It is possible that this process, of which extant languages may show the evolved result in some of their morphological and syntactic arrangements, may have been already in an early stage noticeable to the trained Greek ear in the Classical period. Even if they had ceased to be commonly used, the Celtic dialects could still have continued to influence Latin speech in the districts where they had once predominated. Recent study has shown the extent to which Hiberno-English is influenced by the sounds and syntax of Gaelic (Sullivan 1976).

　Though Celtic influence remained strong throughout the province in Catullus' time (*c.* 85–54), Romans in general fought against its influence and were prepared to borrow only equestrian terms from Celts. Strabo (5.1.6.) speaks of Mediolanum as the chief town of the Insubres (Holland 11ff). Cicero disliked the Celtic accent and thought of it as the opposite to the urbane (*Brut.* 171). We have seen (Chapter 6 above) how he makes it a matter of denigration that Piso has an Insubrian grandfather. He mentions another Insubrian, T. Catius, who was a writer on

Epicurean philosophy (*Fam.* 15.16.1): neither attribute claimed Cicero's approval. Catius was a fellow-townsman of Cornelius Nepos. Quintilian admits a qualified admiration for Catius' style (*Inst.* 10.124).

In *De Oratore* 3.171 and *Orator* 150–2, Cicero criticises the hiatus and elision between open vowels in Celtic speech — he is referring to Celtic speakers of Latin. The powerful conjunction of consonantal sounds struck heavily on his sensitive ear. With regard to his estimate of poets, it must be said that Cicero, to judge from the fragments of his own verse, had not the most developed appreciation of verse rhythm. He is said to have remarked that if he had his life over again, he would not waste time with the lyric poets (Sen. *Ep.* 49.5; Holland 1979: 15). The 'new poets' of Rome, of whom Catullus and other Cisalpines were the most striking representatives, were unattractive to him. Horace also ridiculed the Cisalpine accent (*Ep.* 1.70; *Sat.* 1.10, 36 *et al.*). He regarded it as absurd. In his composition he avoided hiatus and elision wherever he could. As he developed in his art, Horace moved further away from the individualism and, as he saw it, the irresponsible self-consciousness of the preceding literary generation of Cisalpine Hellenistic poets.

Another characteristic of the northern poets was their fascination with onomatopoeia and word-play, which need not be attributed to outright bilingualism, but could easily be stimulated by the linguistic and cultural influence of a Celtic substrate. Quintilian did not like such effects, and possibly his attitude to them contributes to his relatively low estimate of Catullus (10.1.87). Lucretius' genius does not seem to have been appreciated by him, any more than it was by Cicero in 54 BC (*QF* 2.9[11]3). Titus Lucretius Carus (*c.* 98–55/54 BC) is not known to have been from the north, but his style has arguably northern characteristics (Holland 1979: 48ff). He is the author of a monumental and passionate epic poem on 'The nature of the universe' (*De Rerum Natura*). His style resembles that of Catullus in his apparently deliberate use of elision either strongly marked or artistically suppressed for a designed effect. Consonants are used in his poetry in a way which sometimes seems to be purposefully evocative of mood: sometimes they are downright imitative in their effects, as when he uses *m*'s violently to describe an animal eating its prey (3.888). The same consonant appears in concentrated repetition in Catullus' thirteenth poem to indicate greedy eating at a dinner-party. Lucretius makes *m* exude tragic sadness in his famous and highly critical description of the sacrifice of Iphigeneia at Aulis to produce favourable winds for the Greek fleet which is about to set sail for Troy.

We can have no certainty about Lucretius' origins. I incline to the view that he was from Celtic territory, but this cannot be demonstrated beyond doubt. His cognomen 'Carus', which occurs in the *subscriptio* of one of the important manuscripts of his poem and some of the lesser, has suggested to Friedrich Marx (1895) that he was from a Celtic or Celtiberian land: a name like this, which suggests endearment, might be an indicator of Celtic or Roman/Celtic clienthood, or even ex-slave status. Marx quotes such names as Boduacus Karus from Cisalpine inscriptions. Also to be taken into account is the humility with which the poet addresses his undoubtedly unsatisfactory patron, that quintessential man of his time, Memmius, a third-rate political gangster — who might have had Cisalpine connections, for he appointed Catullus to his staff for his term as governor of Bithynia. The fact that 'Carus' occurs as the cognomen of respectable persons of some public standing in the early Empire may be set against Marx's view, but it does not dissolve its plausibility.

We might suppose that these clashes of vowels and other peculiarities which have been linked to Celtic influences (Holland 1979: 16ff) simply indicate the development of Latin verse in itself: in the late decades of the Republic techniques were gradually growing towards the kind of virtuosity we see in Virgil and Ovid, but verse still retained some of the native rugged character of the Latin language, which was not well suited to the adoption of quantitative metres involving many short syllables such as the Greek hexameter. Lucretius speaks feelingly of his struggles in attempting to write on Greek philosophy in a Greek metre in the Latin language. But even if these characteristics designated as northern were merely marks of the primitivism of Latin literary techniques, they could at the same time be just as eligible to be identified as northern when it is recalled that Catullus and several other important poets of the time (including, perhaps, Lucretius) were of Cisalpine origin. We remember also that Cicero was producing verses with very few of these objectionable exhalations, and if the fragments are any indication, he was doing so with considerable dullness.

Catullus is the most important of the poets from Celtic territory of northern Italy and he deserves to be taken as our main representative of the school of 'new poets' in the second half of the first century BC who took the poetry of Hellenistic Alexandria as their literary model. There are difficulties involved in comparing the work of poets who are known to us only from fragments with the largely extant poetry of a poet like Catullus, but there is no indication that any of them, Cisalpine or Roman, was his equal, let alone his superior. We might cautiously insinuate that the survival into Renaissance times of a single manuscript of his work in his home town of Verona was not entirely an accident of history. This manuscript was soon lost, but not before copies had been taken.

Other poets of this school were Valerius Cato, Helvius Cinna and Furius Bibaculus, who, like Catullus, satirised Julius Caesar. Caecilius, whom Catullus mentions in his Poem 35 as living at Novum Comum, was another member of this vivid group. Caecilius is said to be working on a learned poem about the 'Magna Mater', the great goddess of Dindymus in the East, who may have been of special interest to a Cisalpine of Celtic associations because of local cults of the 'Matronae' (Holland 1979: 80). Catullus also devotes a poem (63) to her fearful cult and its dire effect on the life of her worshipper Attis. There was also Terentius Varro of Atax, a Transalpine Celt (b. 82 BC) who was associated with this literary movement. He wrote satires, an *Ephemeris* (or *Epimenides*), love elegies, as did all the others, and a war epic after the manner of Ennius called the *Bellum Sequanicum*, which may have touched upon Caesar's activities in Gaul. A line or two of this remains, inconclusive as to subject. Of his *Argonautica*, more considerable fragments remain.

Perhaps at this point we might mention Cornelius Gallus, a Narbonese from across the Alps who was younger than these 'new poets' or 'neoterics' but who carried on their Hellenistic interests. He came from Forum Julii in Narbonese Gaul where his family had been settled in 69 BC. His birth year may have been 62 BC. Octavian rewarded his efficiency and allegiance by making him governor of Egypt; but he fell from favour, probably because of his wayward individuality. He may have been trying, or gave the appearance of trying, to carve out a personal kingdom for himself in Egypt. The *Princeps* renounced his friendship with Gallus. He had then no option but to kill himself; which he did, in 26 BC. One verse of his poetry survives from literary quotation: a few more verses recently recovered from an Egyptian papyrus may be his (Anderson, Parsons and Nesbit 1979). He was an accomplished poet in elegaics, and his book of *Amores* celebrated

a lady whom he chose to call 'Lycoris', as Catullus called his love
'Lesbia'. Gallus' love affair and his jealousy in it are mentioned
in Virgil's tenth *Eclogue*.

Volusius, whose *Annales* Catullus ridicules as being no better
than lavatory paper (36) was his fellow Celt from the north of
Italy. In another poem (95), Catullus says that his compatriot's
great work will die at Padua, where he may be presumed to reside.
In this poem, the *Annales* have as their suggested use wrappings for
marinaded mackerel. Perhaps this Volusius is really a certain
Tanusius Geminus whom Suetonius used (*Div. Jul.* 22) as a source
for his life of Julius Caesar. If Tanusius was, as we might
conjecture, not unfavourably disposed towards Caesar, this could
be as good a reason as any other for Catullus to attack him. But
the motive is more likely to have been personal and literary than
political.

Furius Bibaculus (or Vivaculus) of Cremona was older than
Catullus. His lifespan seems to have been from *c.* 103 to *c.* 25 BC.
He wrote personal epigrams about Valerius Cato which may have
anticipated the conversational and not unfriendly satire that
Catullus sometimes addresses to his friends. He seems at first to
have favoured Caesar's cause and then to have turned against
him. His line in which Juppiter is described as spitting snow over
the Alps is criticised by Quintilian as being too artificial in its
metaphor (8.6.17). That his satire could also be biting seems to
be indicated by the fact that Tacitus speaks of him together with
Catullus as satirists against Julius Caesar (*Ann.* 4.34). Catullus'
remarks about Caesar and his adherents were severe and
scurrilous. A few surviving lines of abuse directed against Caesar
by Licinius Calvus, who was not from Cisalpine Gaul, but who
was an enthusiastic 'new poet' and a friend of Catullus, give us
some idea of the standard of outrageousness required in treating
this subject. No doubt Furius could match both Catullus and
Calvus in imaginative obscenity, if his excessively vigorous
metaphor is any indication. We may note that, with admirable
impartiality, Calvus heaped abuse on Pompey also: these individualist poets did not care for the coming men of power in the
Republic.

Brixia, the town of the Cenomani, was the home of Helvius
Cinna. Some Celtic words occur in the fragments of his poetry,
but they are mostly of equestrian interest. He seems to have had
no objection to conflict of vowels between words. He is described
by Catullus as writing a long and complex poem called *Zmyrna* full

of elegant and convoluted exposition of myth in the Alexandrian manner.

Cornelius Nepos (*c.* 94–24 BC) was some years older than Catullus. He also was from Cisalpine Gaul, but his place of birth is not known. Besides his famous annalistic history, the *Chronica*, and his extant biographies of prominent men, he also composed erotic poetry. He was a respected senior Celtic intellectual of his time and perhaps, to some degree, the patron of Catullus and others from his native country. Catullus dedicated his collected poems, his *Libellus*, to him (1). Cicero and Atticus seem to have been amongst his friends.

The Alfenus who appears in Catullus' thirtieth poem and the Varus who attended lectures on philosophy with Virgil could be the same man. Our information on this point comes from commentators on Virgil in antiquity. He may also be identical with the Alfenus whom Horace mentions with little respect (*Sat.* 1.3.130). Of humble birth in Cremona, he came to Rome and studied the law with Publius Sulpicius Rufus. He reach high public office: in 39 BC, he was consul and he may have been able to help Virgil in his efforts to regain some of his family's land from confiscation at the end of the Civil War. He was the first man of his region to attain the rank of consul. Philosophy was his main intellectual interest and he is said to have written ably on it. This was the kind of career that the father of Catullus may have wished for his son. Alfenus rose above the disadvantages of his poor material background. Horace, who surely had no right to do so, mocked him for the family trade of barber which he had to practise in his early years.

Catullus may have had some of his education in Rome. We might surmise that he did not have all of it there, for in many ways he was imperfectly Romanised. He tells us that his family had a house near Rome in a marginally fashionable district and that this house became heavily mortgaged (44). We do not know whether this came from a decline in the family's prosperity or was the outcome of Catullus' prodigality. Catullus' father was a friend of Julius Caesar and had given him hospitality (Suet. *Div. Jul.* 73). The family was probably typical of the ruling class of Cisalpine towns, many of whose members were in receipt of Caesar's patronage in return for their support. The region's former allegiance to Pompey was mostly transferred to Caesar. Yet some Cisalpines were to be found in Pompey's army occupying responsible positions. The services of Pompey's father in obtaining Latin rights for the region were never entirely forgotten. Ronald Syme (1939: 74) thinks that Catullus may possibly have been under the patronage of the Metelli: Metellus Celer, husband of Catullus' 'Lesbia', was governor of Cisalpine Gaul in 62 BC.

To be opposed to Caesar was more than an intellectual fad for Catullus and his associates. Although they were most of them outside politics either from choice or lack of patronage, they seem to have had some kind of intuition of the coming tyrants. From what Catullus tells us, he was unwilling to compromise with the inevitable dishonesties of the trade — witness his disastrous tour of duty with Memmius in Bithynia. Also, Catullus may have been in reaction to his family's adherence to Caesar in deciding that he wanted nothing to do with that potential dictator: 'I'm not much interested in being in your good books, Caesar, and I don't care whether you're dark or fair' (93). Caesar, himself an intellectual, would seem all the more sinister to a fellow intellectual like Catullus: he would think that he could understand his dread intents more precisely than he could read personalities like Pompey or Crassus. The poetic movement which Catullus and his friends took as model for their own consisted of Greek poets of the conscious and sophisticated community of Alexandria who had applied fearless and detached psychological scrutiny to myths which dealt with such difficult themes as incest. This was the subject of Helvius' *Zmyrna*, which was to take him nine years to complete.

The artistic effort of delving into the recesses of the human soul and the transformation of primal sin and furious passion into polished literary artefacts required no small ability in self-analysis. In his less formal poems about his own sexual adventures, both homosexual and with female whores, Catullus shows a boldness in exposure of his behaviour which amounts almost to an arrogant rejection of shame. These vignettes were placed by him in relation to his poetry of passion for 'Lesbia' in the organisation of his book deliberately to give an ironic view of life as he experienced it. If such a man devotes even a portion of his attention to summing up political figures of his time, he is not likely to have come to favourable conclusions. He attacks Caesar's friends with the scrupulous obscenity that he does not hesitate to apply to his own acts.

Catullus may have characteristics which are capable of being argued as distinctively Celtic within the confines of the cultural tradition in which he lived and worked, which was that of the dominant Roman society. His work could also be considered to have elements in common with poetry of a much later date in Celtic. Catullus' name may be of Celtic derivation (Dottin 1920: 112). If it is connected with /catus/ 'battle', this might indicate warrior origins in a Celtic context; or it may be from /catos/ 'clever'. Doubtful also is the name of 'Cathbad', the druid and teacher in the Ulster saga. Catullus' home town, Verona, was not a Roman colony: it was a place of different tribes and languages.

Clearly any suggestion that particular elements in his poetry or that of his Cisalpine associates are distinctively coloured by the traditions of a Celtic region or familiar ways of thought which show characteristics shaped by Celtic origins can only be speculative. Yet there is an undeniably non-Roman flavour in much of his poetry and this may at least in part come from regional and background influences, as well as being the expression of a unique individuality.

There is an acrid strain in surviving Celtic poetry from insular sources which may come from druidic and post-druidic customs of composing curses and spells. It is tempting to see some element of this in the attacks that Catullus makes on his enemies. Within the Greek and Latin poetic tradition, we have to go back to Archilochus of Paros in the seventh century BC to find comparably scalding abuse levelled at individuals. The suggestion of an ethnic tincture in the poems of attack which Catullus directed at certain individuals does not necessarily carry with it the implication that he was conscious of the ancient association of poem, curse and spell (Elliott 1960). 'Flyting' in Scots poetry had its origins in Gaelic custom and could be recognised as a disreputable archaism by poets such as William Dunbar (15th century AD) even as he was practising it against an enemy (Scott 1966: 171ff). We cannot tell whether Catullus was aware of any ancestral satiric tradition in his country, but his temper was attuned to satire as a weapon of offence and revenge. The kind of society which sets a high value on individual sense of honour, the 'shame society', readily finds a use for satire as an integrated counterbalance to the overweening claims of heroes in its warrior class. In ancient Ireland, satirists were feared by the ruling class and achieved a species of backhanded domination which itself was oppressive. Catullus' intense ferocity of attack can be seen as his means of defending his own integrity and honour which ultimately derived from the blending of these and other and unknown cultural traits. He was determined not to serve in a society of rigid castes and prejudices like that of Republican Rome. His failure in making a career, even of a moderate kind, may have come from a regional stubbornness which had in it some of the last vestiges of heroic pride.

Other men from Cisalpine Gaul played the Roman game with success. We have already mentioned Alfenus, who would seem to Catullus to be on the way to success even at the time when they were acquainted. Later there would be others. There is another factor, however, which comes into an assessment of Cisalpine attitudes to Rome, and it is not Celtic. It is the old-fashioned character of provincial society. Standards of personal, familial and public morality in provincial towns were more reminiscent of the strictness attributed to the Rome of centuries earlier than the sophisticated capital which Catullus knew in the latter years of the Republic. Cisalpine Gaul had a reputation for strictness of ethos. Brixia, for instance, was said to be very strait-laced. In Gaul in the fourth century AD, Burdigala would enjoy the same repute of severe respectability. Italians from non-Celtic parts of Italy could find themselves surprised and disillusioned by the laxity and corruption of the city they had been brought up to admire. Cicero of Arpinum never ceased to persuade himself that he was living in a city which, if it had ever existed, was the Republican Rome of centuries earlier. He kept fuelling his patriotism with his own rhetoric in his speeches and letters, but sometimes he shows us that he recognises the raffish reality. His career, even more than anything he recorded in literature, indicates how successful he was in persuading himself of the actuality of his ideal. Catullus saw clearly what the life of the capital really was and he lashed himself and others in his anger at ever having thought well of people and affairs.

Of those Cisalpines who made a distinguished contribution to literature, Publius Vergilius Maro, whether his name be interpretable as Celtic or Etruscan, can hardly be denied the savour of his native region. In one of his early poems about a muleteer (*Appendix* 10) he parodies Catullus' fourth poem closely. In other parts of his work, especially the *Eclogues*, he shows an intense local loyalty and affection for place of the kind that we see in Catullus' poems about Sirmio and even 'Colonia'. The poem about the muleteer contains clear Cisalpine references. Memory of Catullus remained strong in the Cisalpine country. In one of his letters, the younger Pliny speaks of a friend of the poet Vestricius Spurinna who could write poems in a Catullan style, but not so well as the original (*Ep.* 4.27.4).

We need not deny Celtic influences in the background of Virgil's life. Etruscan and Ligurian elements can be suggested with no greater assurance than Celtic can be excluded. The region of Mantua was mixed in population. There is no reason to deny that there was a Celtic component in the local culture. Even if only some of the poems included in the *Appendix* genuinely represent his early work, Virgil still qualifies as having some of the mark of a 'new poet' in the salad days of his poetic career. The *Eclogues* deal with some identifiably local problems of land expropriation (a curse which has pursued the Celts through the ages). And we recall that the tenth *Eclogue* provides a connection with Gallus and his love affairs. Virgil's great epic poem, the *Aeneid*, has much of the impersonality of its genre. A Celtic flavour has been perceived in it, but with little plausibility.

No one could say that the historian Livy (Titus Livius, 57 BC–17 AD) is an outspoken admirer of the Celtic peoples. His literary object is the justification of the progress of Rome from hill-settlement to world empire in terms of an ancient discipline whose constituent virtues of courage, good faith and endurance, he sees conspicuously deficient in the Rome of his own time (*Pref.* 5). He was from Patavium, and while he may show in his writings some of the eloquent vitality of the Celtic spirit as the Romans observed it, he has little good to say of Celts. He describes them as being of highly emotional temper (*fervidum ingenium*: 2.8.17). This makes them prone to engaging in tumultuary raids: they are bold at first in battle and almost inhumanly ferocious, but they soon fall off into a weakness that he describes as being more than feminine. They cannot endure hardship and are essentially unpredictable. He brings them out as a foil to Roman fortitude and virtue. He speaks of them either as one who is proud not to be a Celt or as a Celt who is ashamed of being one and is at pains to conceal the fact — an all too familiar figure in the history of the Celtic peoples.

The origins of his family are unknown. The region where he was born was mostly Venetic. Whatever early environmental influences bore upon him, his style has richness and sinuosity which distinguish it from that of any other prose author in Latin. Livy's imagination is that of an epic poet rather than a scientific historian. His critical faculty is by no means underdeveloped, but he makes it serve the interests of the great flow of Rome's history, regulated by destiny and the virtues of the Roman people. His immense narrative filled one hundred and forty-two book-rolls, of which the contents of thirty-five are extant. All his life he was a supporter of the Republic. So great was his admiration of Pompey, that Octavian used jokingly to call him the 'Pompeian' and chose to respect his genuinely held but harmless sentiments (Tac. *Ann.* 4.34). He received generous patronage from the *Princeps* which his republicanism gave him no reason to refuse. In addition to his history, he wrote philosophical works which have not survived. Asinius Pollio said that Livy had a quality which he called 'Patavinitas' — 'Paduanism' (Quint. *Inst.* 1.5.56). This may not so much refer to an alien element in his mode of expression, as an archaic puritanism of values in his approach to historical interpretation (Syme 1939: 485; 1958: 202).

The author of *Historia Naturalis*, Plinius Caecilius Secundus (23–79 AD), was another distinguished native of Cisalpine Gaul. His nephew, scarcely as distinguished, but just as well known, Gaius Plinius Caecilius Secundus (61–113 AD) was born in the town of Comum (Como). This younger Pliny was the author of a copious correspondence (much of it with northern compatriots) and a *Panegyric* on the Emperor Trajan, under whom he was consul in 100 AD. The Caecilii, Pliny's family, had lived for a considerable time in Comum: we recall that Catullus invited a friend called Caecilius to come from Novum Comum to see him (35). The attachment of people from Cisalpine Gaul for their native region and compatriots even after years of absence was strongly maintained (*Ep.* 1.14.1).

Beyond doubt, the region was fertile in literary talent. This distinguished crop of poets and literary men in many instances have arguably Celtic origins and backgrounds. There is no doubt also that there was a sense of community amongst the writers who came from this region to succeed or otherwise in Rome. We have tried to identify traits which might conceivably be Celtic in the case of one or two of those of whom something more than the merely fragmentary is known. We remain aware that in this essentially multiracial area little is known of traits which we could confidently fasten to Etruscan, Ligurian, Venetic or even Italic origins.

8

Celts and Iberians

In a legend preserved by the Romantic mythologist Parthenius, Iberos is mentioned together with Keltos as offspring of Heracles by the nymph Asterope (Parthenius 30). Asterope is the daughter of Atlas. It may not be coincidence that Eber is one of the mythological ancestors of the Irish. Eratosthenes distinguished between the Spain of 500 BC, in which Celts were not so prominent a portion of the population, and that of his own time, in which they were. He was writing in the third century BC. He was criticised by Polybius and Strabo, who misunderstood the distinction which he was making. The myth is not inappropriate, for the cultural stratification of the Iberian peninsula in antiquity is complex, and it is not easy to identify traits which belong to the various components of the population. Yet the Celtiberes or Celtiberi seem to have been a blend of Celts with a previous population of Iberians. The Celtiberians were the most belligerent of the Iberian peninsula's inhabitants and they inflicted terrible losses on the Romans in the course of their long struggle against Rome.

After the second Punic War during which Rome had perforce become a major power in Spain, the confederations of the Lusitani and Celtiberians were a constant source of trouble and expenditure to the Republic. The persistence in hostility to Rome of these groups in the period after the Hannibalic war can be considered as the military factor which more than any other brought about the transformation of the Roman army from citizen levies into a professional fighting force (Toynbee 1965: 2.61).

The Celtiberians had a distinct ethnic character in the ancient world. There was a strong Celtic element in them. Other tribes, such as the Lusitani and Vaccaei, seem to have been of Celtic or part-Celtic culture and speech. Some of the Lusitani appear to

166

have spoken, or understood, or at least used for inscriptional purposes, an IE language which had some features in common with Celtic and which was of a very archaic and conservative linguistic type (Tovar 1973: 195ff). There were also the Celtici, a southern Spanish tribe of Celtic character and connection. The Celtici lived near Gades and Tartessus. Archaeological evidence seems to suggest that Celts (or people who lived like them) were in the lower parts of the Guadalquivir valley as early as the sixth century BC (Arribas 1981: 46). Avienus' account of the region may reflect this. Tumuli in Andalusia could be interpreted as the burial place of Celtic leaders: if so, these graves represent a culture influenced by Mediterranean ideas and themes.

The tribal name of the Celtiberi (we shall usually speak of 'Celtiberians') suggests a definite, indeed a possibly deliberate, mixing of tribes. Celtiberia as such was a relatively narrow area in the north-west of Spain (Pl. *NH* 3.20). 'Celtiberian' is sometimes used in a more extended meaning which covers the whole Celtic phase of the Iberian and Celtic cultural mixture in western and central western areas of the Iberian peninsula.

Poseidonius is no doubt responsible for the following remarks about the Celtiberians in the text of Diodorus 5.33:

Celtiberes are a fusion of two peoples and the combination of Celts and Iberes only took place after long and bloody wars. Both were very warlike and this, with the fertility of the country that they occupy, has made them well known. Their armament differs from that of the Celts. They are noted for their hospitality and they regard strangers as being under the protection of the gods.

Celtiberes wear black clothes, hairy like a goatskin: some have shields of the lightly-constructed Celtic type; others a round shield of the kind more familiar in the Greek world. The iron of their two-edged swords, shorter than the Celtic great sword, is capable of cutting anything. The process of manufacture involves burying the iron from which they are to be made so that the softer layers of metal are peeled away by corrosion and only the harder part remains to be forged into a sword.

The Iberians, as distinguished from Celtic and Celtiberian tribes, predominated in the eastern parts of the peninsula in its coastal regions and also in the south, though there were many areas of symbiosis with the Celts and Celtiberians. Saguntum, the town which was to be the fuse of the Second Punic War, was the boundary between Iberians and Celtiberians. The Iberian language seems not to have been IE, and there is disagreement about its affiliations. The candidature of Basque is not certain and the connection of Iberian within the language presumed to have been spoken by the inhabitants of Tartessus is merely speculative. One of the earlier examples of the Iberian language is written on a lead tablet in Ionic Greek letters: it dates from the sixth century BC. There are several scripts which are thought to have a much earlier origin.

Writing of earlier origin survives in alphabetic and syllabic forms and in a mixture of the two. Much of it may be of Phoenician origin, but some similarity to elements of the Mycenaean Linear B script and the Cypriot syllabary has been discerned (Tovar 1961: 15). Not only the Iberians, but the Celtiberian people of the peninsula kept old syllabic signs in their writing well into the Roman period because these seemed to be more suited to expressing some of the sounds of Celtic (Arribas 1981: 87).

Celtic language seems to have persisted in Spain until at least the second century AD. Most of the Celtic seems to have been an archaic form of q-Celtic, which may have been superimposed on a previous non-Celtic, but IE-speaking layer of population. There was also evidently an infusion of later p-Celtic speakers whose language was of the Brythonic or Continental Gaulish species (Tovar 1961: 98–9). Lucan (4.10), followed by Appian (*Hisp.* 2), reports that the Celtiberes were from Gaul and had come into Spain to escape famine. The story may be based on Poseidonius. The word 'Gallus' is seldom used of the Celts of Spain. Pliny (*NH* 3.3.11) provides one of the few examples. This could be mere chance, but it could also indicate that the Celtiberes had a strongly differentiated national identity for which the name 'Gallus' seemed inappropriate except to an antiquarian. Evidences of p-Celtic in some of the placenames, especially those of the *-dunum* type, do not necessarily suggest a major influx of Celts from Gaul. That such an immigration did take place is widely accepted, but it cannot be precisely connected with the linguistic remains. With some caution Tovar suggests (1961: 98) that the relatively small number of *-dunum* names in comparison with those which end in *-briga* may indicate that the p-Celtic speakers were a more recent and smaller group of arrivals in the peninsula. He notes that the *-dunum* names are found mostly in Catalonia and not far from the passes of the Pyrenees (ibid. 105–6). Though the *-briga* type predominates in Spain, it also occurs in Gaul (Dottin 1915: 440ff). Nor are names in *-dunum* necessarily associated with the speaking of p-Celtic in a given district: 'Sen-dunon' in County Cork is certainly in a zone associated with q-Celtic speech: Ptolemy mentions an Irish city called 'Dounon' (2.2.9; Dottin 1915: 429ff). But whether or not we agree with the theory that p-Celtic preceded q-Celtic in Ireland, it seems clear that some p-Celtic was spoken there at some time. The evidence from these placenames has to remain tentative, though its suggestions are helpful. The evidences of Hallstatt and La Tène cultural traits in Spain do not lead to any firm attribution to the former of q-Celtic speakers, or to the latter of those who spoke p-Celtic. The Hallstatt phase may even antedate the arrival of any speakers of Celtic in the peninsula. A certain amount of La Tène material is found, but most artistic and craft material represents an extension of Hallstatt ideas in a local idiom. In general it is difficult not to match at some level the evident predominance of Hallstatt themes with the prevalence of q-Celtic and forms of speech related to it.

A number of ancient authors agree (obviously in accord with some old source of information) on certain main points about the Celtiberian character. Like other Celtic populations, the Celtiberians are celebrated for ferocity and dedication to the practices of war, and are hospitable. Strabo (4.18), Valerius Maximus (2.1), Silius Italicus (1.22 etc.) and Justin (44.2), not forgetting Livy (22.21), present the portrait of a people fearless in the face of death and gifted with a vital curiosity in anything new or unusual. They take readily to gladiatorial combat (Livy 28.21) and are given to duelling (Silius 16.537; Florus 1.33). When Scipio Africanus held games in Nova Carthago in 206 BC to honour his father and uncle who had died in the Spanish campaigns, he had no lack of applicants for gladiatorial duels from Celts who wished to settle some point of honour outstanding between them. The Celtiberians, like other Celts, thought it a criminal act to abandon their chief when his life was in danger, or to survive him in battle (Str. 3.4.18; Plut. *Sert.* 14.4; *et al.*). They considered it a glory to die in battle, but had a taboo against being cremated. They believed that the souls of those killed in battle go straight to heaven if vultures eat their bodies (Silius 3.340). If they have devoted their lives to the success of a battle, they regard it as dishonourable to survive in defeat (Val. Max. 2.6.11): this may provide a commentary note on the famous statue of the wounded Gaul, who has killed his wife and is killing himself: he is avoiding for both of them the disgrace of capture and slavery, but more than this, he is avoiding the dishonour of even surviving the defeat of his tribe. The prejudice against cremation and the wish that the body of the fallen dead should be devoured by birds may to some extent explain the indifference of the Celts who invaded Greece to the burial of the bodies of their dead — the reverse of Greek feelings on this subject. Most of the warriors may be supposed to be free men of client status to their chiefs, like the *ambacti* of Gaul or the *soer-chéli* of the ancient Irish. The warrior ethos is aptly summed up by Cicero: the Cimbri and Celtiberi exult in battles and lament in sickness (*Tusc.* 2.65).

They were not too distant from the Greeks in their beliefs that the gods looked kindly on those who were friendly towards strangers (Diod. 5.34). A minor, but peculiar, anthropological fact about them, which is very alien to Greek and Roman practice, was probably recorded by Poseidonius, though the poet Catullus seems to have known of it: the Celtiberians used stale urine to clean their teeth. Catullus mentions this as one of the unsavoury attributes of that perpetual and unseasonable smiler, Egnatius the Celtiberian (37.20; 29.17ff). Strabo (3.4.16) and Diodorus (5.33), who also mentions the custom, probably got the information from Poseidonius. It was a fact likely to stick in the memory of any (non-Celtiberian) historian. A more acceptable habit was drinking wine mixed with honey (Diod. 5.34). So also the Irish of the sagas drink 'mid' as well as 'curm', or beer (Gk *korma*). At least some of the Celtiberians — the Vaccaei are specifically mentioned — appear to have had the custom of dividing their land amongst the tribesmen each year, and sharing the harvest communally. This is reported by Diodorus (5.34), who may be informed by Poseidonius. The view that the tribal land was the property of the tribe, rather than the king, or chief, was a widespread Celtic view.

We are not informed in any detail about the religion of the Celtic peoples of Spain. Strabo (3.4.16), again, we may suppose, following Poseidonius, says that they were *atheoi*, meaning that they worshipped gods who by his standards were vaguely conceived and lacked anthropomorphic definition. There is no direct evidence of druids in the life of Celtic Spain, but the occurrence of placenames of the 'Nemet'-type in Spain (Ir. 'nemed': *Actas* 138) may well indicate the ceremonial groves associated with druidic religion.

The picture which emerges from writers of Greco-Roman

antiquity who mention the Celtic and other inhabitants of Spain is that of a rugged collection of tribes, hardened by a severe terrain and a traditional warrior ethos based upon a concept of heroic honour.

No more than other Celts were those of Spain to remain untouched by the conflicts and interests of advanced contemporary states of the Mediterranean world. Carthage and Rome intruded on their remote, traditional ways of life. They themselves had not been responsible for any large-scale intrusions on the territory of the great powers of the Mediterranean basin. They had not, like their kinsmen, invaded Greece or ravaged Italy or settled in large tracts of south-east Europe and Asia Minor. They had the misfortune to be placed between the sphere of influence of Carthage and that of Rome. Their story is that of a painful, slow, but never entire integration into the world-empire of Rome, to the life of which they made energetic and original contributions.

In the latter part of the sixth century BC, Carthage absorbed the old kingdom of Tartessus, but she began to encroach more purposefully upon Spanish territory after her defeat at the hands of Rome in the First Punic War (264–241 BC). By the terms of the peace, other spheres of action were forbidden to her; and even in Spain, treaties delimited her potential growth. In the war, she had lost control of Sardinia and Corsica; her power was broken in Sicily and she was virtually expelled from the island. The mercenary army of Carthage revolted against their employers and almost overwhelmed the state. A substantial proportion of these soldiers were of Spanish origins. When the revolt was settled, with some help from Rome, the Carthaginians attempted to recover Sardinia. They failed, but they succeeded in alienating Rome. The best potential sphere of expansion that remained for them was Spain, and here they made a rich and powerful empire for themselves with remarkable speed. The colonising movement was initiated by Hamilcar Barca in 237 BC; he was succeeded by his son-in-law Hasdrubal, who founded Nova Carthago in 228 BC. This man's son, Hannibal, expanded Carthaginian domination up the peninsula as far as the river Ebro.

The effects of the Carthaginian presence on the Iberians no doubt in relative terms accelerated their development as a society. They had been affected by commercial contacts with Greeks and Carthaginians for some time, but now foreign influence was more direct and political. The Celtiberians had a long tradition of mercenary service in the armies of Carthage (Polyb. 14.7–14). A composite army of Iberians, Celtiberians and Africans provided Carthage with an excellent fighting machine. Inevitably it would sometime be put into action. The Romans were not reassured by what they learned of these developments. For a long time, however, they remained inert and were awakened to the growing danger of the situation only by the appeal of Massilia, that ancient ally of Rome. The Massiliotes feared that eventually the Carthaginians would strip them of their trading connections on the Spanish coast.

For the immediate and ostensible purpose of repelling Iberians who were harassing Carthaginian settlements in Spain, Hamilcar Barca, from his base in Libya, had built up a powerful army in Spain and attached its loyalty firmly to himself and his family (237 BC). He managed to allay Rome's anxiety about his proceedings for a time by expressions full of diplomatic vagueness. Hamilcar died in accidental circumstances in 229 BC. It was the policy of his successor Hasdrubal that alarmed the Massiliotes.

Hasdrubal tried to meet this problem by assuring a Roman delegation that he would not go across the Ebro. The Romans were fully occupied with wars against the Cisalpine Celts and the Illyrians, and they took no notice of the Carthaginian advance until they received an appeal from Saguntum, a town lying just south of the Ebro, whose citizens feared that the Carthaginians were about to seize it. Saguntum and Rome had concluded an alliance in 223 BC, but Hannibal took advantage of quarrels between a tribe allied to Carthage and Saguntum and took the city in spite of Roman warning. This was the efficient cause of the second major war between Rome and Carthage (218 BC), which involved, amongst other horrors, Hannibal's lightning dash into Italy and the infliction of a devastation from which southern Italy has probably not yet fully recovered to this day. Hannibal added to his army Celtic warriors of Cisalpine Gaul for his protracted laceration of Italy.

In this war, the Romans were not content with a policy that confined their armies to the task of defeating Hannibal within Italy. It was typical of the confidence which they felt in spite of the crushing defeats they had sustained in set battles against Hannibal, that they should decide to move forces to Spain, in order to attack the main source and core of Carthaginian power. If they could possess Spain, Hannibal's army in Italy would be a severed head, frightful, but in effect harmless.

The Roman army was sent to Spain early in the war, in 218

BC. The disaster of Cannae in 216 BC, together with the revolt of Capua from the Roman alliance, did not divert Roman policy from the master strategy of detaching Spain from the Carthaginian war-effort. Publius and Gnaeus Scipio were appointed to command in this theatre of war, and their expedition initially made good progress. The task of the generals was not made harder by the fact that Hasdrubal was at the beginning of the campaign absent in Africa. By means of a series of actions successfully mounted against Carthaginian forces both on sea and land, the Romans had by 211 BC taken control of a considerable portion of Spain and recovered Saguntum. The Roman army contained many Celtiberians, who showed a tendency to desert at crucial times. Success was not to be continuous. In 210 BC, the Romans were divided in two for the purpose of separate campaigns and both sections were defeated with the death of both generals. The Romans had to evacuate Spain as far as the Ebro. By this time Hannibal's army was beginning to weaken in Italy, and the Carthaginians did not find themselves in a position to exploit their advantage in Spain, which, if it could have been done in co-ordination with Hannibal's continued presence in Italy might have brought some significant victory. The younger Publius Cornelius Scipio, son of the general Publius who had been killed in 210 BC, was appointed to command in Spain. His strategic talent, which was perhaps superior to that of Hannibal, inspired him to make moves of such boldness and speed that in 209 BC he seized Nova Carthago by a surprise amphibious attack and with this stroke deprived Carthage of her main base of supplies in Spain. In 208 BC, he defeated Hannibal's brother, Hasdrubal, at Baecula, and soon felt sufficiently secure in his victory to transport his forces to Africa.

In spite of his defeat, Hasdrubal managed to evade the occupying Roman forces and reached Cisalpine Gaul with the intention of bringing badly needed reinforcements to Hannibal. His army was defeated at Metaurus and he was killed, with the consequence that his severed head was thrown into Hannibal's camp in order to disedify an already disappointed army.

When Scipio left for Africa, the inhabitants of Spain had time to reflect. Their enthusiasm for Rome cooled as some of the implications of Roman dominance in their country began to be apparent. They had little to gain by being ruled either by Rome or Carthage, and their tendency to change sides in the war reflected this indecision at an early stage of its development, though it was characterised by the Romans as a natural Celtic unreliability.

One important result of the war in Spain was that Rome found herself in control of the silver mines near Nova Carthago and in the Sierra Morena, where gold also was mined. Copper was mined at Luxia, now Rio Tinto. Many thousands of pounds of precious metal were transported to Rome in the six years following Scipio's departure for Africa.

Money began to be minted soon after the Roman occupation of the country, and Roman taxes were to be paid in coin and ingots. There were also the less formal, but less endurable exactions of Roman governors, who came into office soon after 205 BC. The activities of these men, who from 197 BC were of the rank of propraetor, eventually brought about the remedial establishment in Rome of the standing commission on extortion (*quaestio perpetua de rebus repetundis*), which gave little relief in fact to the victims of gubernatorial greed.

In 197 BC two provinces, Hither and Further Spain, were created by the Romans, but no immediate pacification of the country was achieved. The initiative to revolt came in 197 BC from the otherwise quiet Turdetani. In 196 BC, they were defeated at Turta by the Romans, but not before disturbance had flowed into the Hither province. This area remained uneasy. In 195 BC, M. Cato was sent with an army and landed at Emporiae. His campaign was innocent of decisive success; he did, however, contrive to alienate the Celtiberians during the course of an otherwise unspectacular attempt to take Siguenza and Numantia. Yet Cato managed to seize silver mines in the upland districts of Catalonia. In 195 BC, the Lusitani, a Celtic people, revolted, causing Roman forces to be moved against them from as far south as Toledo. Aemilius Paullus lost a battle against the Lusitani in 190 BC. He was victorious in another, and for a time there was an unstable equilibrium, with no major event on either side. In 181 BC, further Roman permeation of the Ebro valley began to have irritating effects, at a time when Rome was occupied with the affairs of Greece and Asia Minor. The process of pacification was continued by T. Sempronius Gracchus in the years 179–178 BC. According to Polybius, T. Gracchus destroyed three hundred cities of the Celtiberians. Poseidonius maintains, rightly, that they were not cities but forts (Str. 3.16.2). We may suppose that they were typical Celtic hill-forts, like Irish *dúnta*. Gracchus, father of the popular reformers Tiberius and Gaius, offered the Celtiberians reasonable terms of peace. Soon conditions were settled enough for the foundation of colonies. In 171 BC, Corteia was established to be settled by the illegitimate children of Roman soldiers and native women.

The tightening noose of Roman taxation and other troubles imposed on a proud people by arbitrary rule were inevitably destined to stimulate further revolts. In 154 BC, the Celtiberians of Hither Spain and the Lusitani of the Further province rebelled against the Romans. Roman manpower was strained to its limits. In Rome, the tribunes, on behalf of an increasing number of people who were becoming subject to recruitment, vigorously opposed the draft for the Spanish war. The war was protracted. Two powerful tribal complexes were involved, both mutually heartened by the others' successes. The situation was so serious that Spain became the province of consulars, instead of pro-praetors. Fulvius Nobilior was defeated in the course of his march on Numantia, a prime centre of resistance, and he had no success in taking the place. In 151 BC, the Roman commander M. Atilius offered conditions of peace to the Lusitani which were nearly accepted. His successor, Servius Sulpicius Galba, opposed the treaty. His army suffered a serious reverse in battle. In the course of further negotiations, Galba practised an act of deceit against the Lusitani of the kind that has been practised against Celtic peoples at other times and places, and sometimes indeed by their fellow Celts: he took advantage of their traditional sense of honour and the sacred nature of hospitality. Representatives who came from the Lusitani to apologise for the infringement of Atilius' peace were slaughtered. It was an act of brutal bad faith comparable to the murder of the Galatian tetrarchs by Mithridates in 86 BC. Cato afterwards charged Galba in court with the crime of this incident, but the jurors would not convict him. Galba's campaign against the Lusitani was marked by bloodiness and treachery, and it was the cause of intense hatred of Rome on the part of the Lusitani and Celtiberians, which would cost Rome dear in the years between 149 and 133 BC.

While Rome was extending her influence in the East, the inhabitants of Spain took advantage of her situation. Rome had never in any sense subdued the strength of the tribes of northern and western Spain. From Lusitania, substantially modern Portugal, a leader called Viriathus emerged who was to succeed in prosecuting a most effective guerrilla war against the Romans until they procured his assassination in 140 BC. Their moves against him from 149 BC only increased his hold over his tribe and between 147 and 140 BC, he caused continual and serious damage to the Roman presence in Spain. A more open form of war broke out in 143 BC. A couple of years after this in 141 BC Viriathus managed to surround a consular army and force it to surrender. Being made hesitant by domestic factions and rivalries among his own followers, he released the Romans under treaty, only to be attacked by them almost immediately afterwards. Servilius Caepio, in command of the Roman army, made little headway, but he contrived through Viriathus' friends that he should be murdered. When he was killed, the Lusitanians gave up the war. Two hundred pairs of warriors are said to have fought in single combat in the celebration of his funeral ceremonies.

Between 143 and 133 BC, the war against the Celtiberians was carried on separately from that which was directed against the Lusitani. In 143 BC, Metellus cleared the valley of the Ebro of enemy forces: Pompeius, who followed him in his command in the region, was unable to reduce the town of Numantia in spite of having a strong force at his disposal. His peace with the defenders of Numantia was not validated by the Roman Senate. The fine that the defending forces paid as part of the terms of the treaty was not returned. Mancinus achieved a low point in Roman prestige in 137 BC, when twenty thousand of his soldiers surrendered. Again, negotiations in bad faith enabled the Romans to escape. Otherwise, Rome would have suffered a disaster comparable in magnitude to that of the Caudine Forks.

Scipio Aemilianus, the destroyer of Carthage in 146 BC, was appointed to the task of taking Numantia in 134 BC. Judiciously timing his encirclement of the town to prevent its people from collecting supplies, he starved it out, but not before the Numantines were reduced to cannibalism, an incident which was to provide material for the moralising rhetorical exercises of budding Roman orators for generations to come. Scipio razed Numantia completely, and its fall effectively reduced the Celtiberians' chances of gaining their freedom from the yoke of Rome.

In 105 BC, the Celtiberians still retained enough of their native vigour and ferocity to drive the Cimbri and Teutones from Spain, though these had crushed Roman arms in Narbonese Gaul, inflicting eighty thousand casualties on the Roman army which opposed them. The name of the Teutones must have sounded familiar to the inhabitants of Celtic Spain in the west and central zone, where 'teuta' ('people') occurs frequently as a component of placenames (*Actas* 85). An element of Celtic connection or borrowing is understandable enough in a largely Germanic tribe (Tac. *Ann.* 1.60.5).

Success against the Cimbri and Teutones and their satellites, together with the example of the success these raiders had enjoyed in their defeat of large Roman armies, inspired revolt once more in Spain, though it is not unlikely that the Lusitani had been preparing for action already for some time. No doubt the Celtiberians had some satisfaction from the thought that the consul who had been awarded a triumph for his victory over themselves in 107 BC, had been killed in battle by the invading northern tribes. There was no continuous integument of peace covering all of Spain in the following decades. Military governors fell too readily into the pattern of provoking the Celtiberians in order to earn triumphs in Rome for their achievements of unnecessary victories. T. Didius razed Temontia in 93 BC: this was a large town which had so far remained untaken, and he would not allow the site to be inhabited again. He also was guilty of a massacre of Celtiberi by means of treachery.

The process of absorption, however, was beginning. When, as a result of the so-called 'Social War', the allied cities of Italy south of the river Po obtained full Roman citizenship, the colonies of Ilalia and Corduba in Spain were also granted this status. In addition there were occasional grants of citizenship to individuals, procured usually through the patronage of important Roman personages who had some connection with the governing or economic exploitation of Spain. In the Social War, a whole troop of Spanish cavalry were admitted to citizenship as a reward for their services.

There was a certain Quintus Sertorius who served with distinction in the war against the Cimbri and Teutones. This man of great military and political talent was an associate of Marius and Cinna, and an adherent of their populist movement. His abilities incurred the jealousy and dislike of Cornelius Sulla. This hostile influence kept him from political office in 88 BC; but during the period when Marius was dominating Roman political life, the climate was more favourable to his ambitions, and he was elected praetor. In 83 BC, the year in which Sulla returned victorious over Mithridates and became dictator in Rome, Sertorius went as propraetor to govern Hither Spain. His aim was to establish a base for Marius' populist party in Spain, from which it might be possible to launch an attack on the dictator in Rome. Sulla understandably wanted to replace Sertorius with an appointee of his own. Sertorius was forced out of Spain and sought refuge in Africa.

After a period devoted to wandering and to mystical contemplation, Sertorius returned to Spain in 80 BC and took the lead in a revolt of the Lusitani. With these formidable warriors, Sertorius and his lieutenants inflicted bloody defeats on the Roman forces. The senior Roman commander, Metellus, was incapable of eradicating an enemy who used guerilla tactics so skilfully in a terrain that suited them so well. Sertorius wore down Roman power sufficiently to enforce its withdrawal to the South, and gradually he increased his authority until it covered the greater part of Spain. He established his own government and among other constructive measures, set up a school for the sons of Celtic chieftains. He also developed a naval base at Denia to accommodate his other allies, the Mediterranean pirates. After the abortive attempt at revolution by the radical leader and consul of 78 BC, M. Aemilius Lepidus, the remnants of his forces which had been defeated by those of the other consul, Catulus, were taken to Spain. M. Perpenna, who was in command of them, added them to the forces of Sertorius, and himself became a lieutenant of Sertorius.

Gnaeus Pompeius, who was to become 'the Great', and C. Memmius were appointed in 76 BC by the Senate to the task of removing what was growing to the proportions of an international menace; for Sertorius had established friendly relations with Mithridates through the agency of the pirates, who themselves constituted a major problem which it was to be one of Pompey's most notable achievements ultimately to solve. Pompey and his colleagues were not able to destroy Sertorius' forces in a set battle. When this was attempted in 75 BC, in the Sucro valley, Pompey would have been completely defeated if Metellus had not arrived with timely reinforcements.

In time, and with the aid of repeated additions of new troops, Pompey and Metellus were able to put increasingly severe pressure on the Sertorian forces. Many of the Lusitanian soldiers deserted and Sertorius felt obliged to inflict harsh punishments to discourage this. This policy further alienated the Lusitani, who already were sensitive to the tyrannical treatment they had received from some of the Romans on Sertorius' staff, who themselves were involved in internecine squabbling. In this atmosphere it was not too difficult for the Roman high command to inspire Perpenna with the suggestion that he should murder Sertorius. He did so in 73 BC, but his army was defeated by the Romans under Pompey, and he was taken prisoner and executed. When Pompey returned to Rome in the following year, he seemed to have solved the Spanish problem.

Sertorius is said to have kept a white doe which enabled him to communicate with the divine world. We might surmise that the Lusitani and his other Celtic adherents respected this pet as the impersonation of the horned god whom we know elsewhere as Cernunnos. According to Plutarch (*Sert.* 11) the doe was supposed to be his medium of communication with the goddess Diana. This may have been a propaganda trick to bemuse simple natives, but I can see no reason why we should think so, or why we should not do him the honour of accepting that he believed what he said about the creature. He regarded it as a mascot of his success and he was greatly disturbed when it was lost for a time at the battle of the Sucro.

Sertorius had the combination of intuitive understanding of people and creative imagination which is often found in great commanders and major poets. He was a brilliant master of guerilla tactics: his devices for winning the loyalty of tribesmen were no less inventive. He recognised the necessity of holding a visible balance of justice between the native population and the Roman settlers. He also understood the need to give the Lusitanian warriors plenty of gold to adorn their armour. Plutarch's life contains many other examples of his insight and leadership.

If Sertorius had enjoyed the good fortune to exploit the military possibilities of a country as rich in men and resources as 'Gallia Comata', he might have achieved success of comparable magnitude to that of Caesar. But he had no official standing in Spain and he had to rely upon Celtic soldiers who did not see themselves as soldiers, but as warriors who could go and come as they pleased. He had not enough Romans or Romans of good enough quality on his staff, and his cause was bedevilled by the presence of Roman settlers in the country who had already founded deep roots of resentment amongst the population. He was, however, an inspiration to Julius Caesar, and was himself an early example of the Roman man of power who in later times would intimidate Rome from a base in the provinces, when the 'secret of power', in Tacitus' words, 'got out that emperors could be made elsewhere than in Rome'.

When Julius Caesar came to Further Spain in 61 BC as

governor after his praetorship, it was with the intention of making, however belatedly, his military reputation. His visit in 68 BC to the shrine of Hercules on the island of Sanctipetri and his vigil there seem to have been a point of personal conversion for him. He may have been consciously following the mystical example of the charismatic Sertorius. As propraetor of Hither Spain, Caesar deliberately started a campaign in which, with suitable Herculean hardships, he won a victory over the tough Lusitani. Then he tackled the far north of the peninsula in an amphibious operation which gained him Brigantium, the modern Corunna, and completed Roman subjugation of the west coast of Spain. His wars with the Celtic and part-Celtic tribes of Spain were in a sense a preliminary trial for his later actions in a wider Celtic environment which would provide him with the greatest challenge of his career and also with a superlative military reputation and resources.

After his consulship in 55 BC, Pompey was appointed proconsular governor of Spain. His governorship was for an extended period which sought to balance Caesar's protracted proconsulship in Gaul. Crassus, the third member of the so-called First Triumvirate, was appointed to Syria, which proved his destruction. Pompey never exploited the possibilities of his appointment, nor did he construct a personal empire from his province, though that was at some level for him the purpose of his appointment: the Optimates needed some reliable warlord to counterbalance the frightening growth of Caesar's power. Pompey's reputation was high in Spain as a result of his campaigns there in the Sertorian wars. Hopeless and inevitably rejected courtship of the visibly degenerating senatorial Optimates kept him lingering in Rome to the distress of his more perceptive supporters. He was held back also by some vain unwillingness to compete which may have come from a suspicion that he was not fit to challenge Caesar and win.

When the long-foreseen conflict between Caesar and Pompey at last erupted in 49 BC with Caesar's crossing of the Rubicon (the boundary of his province and lawful military authority), Pompey was in no position to join his legions in Spain, but was forced to evacuate Italy. He and his supporters made their way to Greece. Caesar found it necessary to remove the threat posed by the Pompeian forces in Spain, which amounted to seven legions. He could not go against the forces of the Republic in Greece while Spain remained unsubdued at his back. On his way to Spain he blockaded Massilia (which had remained loyal to the Republic) and after an early setback, he managed to bring about the surrender of the army in Spain. As he returned, he received the surrender of the Massiliotes whom he fined heavily. He deprived the city of its territories and, for a while, of its ancient civic independence.

Caesar's defeat of the Pompeian forces in Spain was accomplished with some speed. Haste was particularly needful, not only for his wider strategy, but because the Pompeians had planned to play the Celtiberian game of attrition and guerrilla warfare. He was greatly helped by his cavalry from Gaul, whose activities enabled him to cut off enemy supplies while maintaining his own. When a pontoon bridge was torn away by a flood and an essential line of supply was broken, he made use of coracles, which he had seen in Britain, to rig an emergency crossing.

With surprising ineptitude, he appointed Quintus Cassius Longinus to be governor of Further Spain on his behalf. This man's reputation was far from savoury in the province from his time there in 54 BC as a member of Pompey's representative staff. He was an old-style Roman provincial governor of the kind whose simple, dedicated robbery of the provincials was already going out of fashion in 70 BC when Verres was prosecuted by Cicero on behalf of the despoiled Sicilians. An attempt was made on his life. His army threatened wholesale desertion. He was besieged in Ulia, a fortified town, and he was rescued from this predicament by Lepidus, Caesar's agent in Hither Spain, who later was to become a member of the Second Triumvirate with Octavius and Marcus Antonius.

Cassius had upset the equilibrium of his province sufficiently to encourage those adherents of the Republican and Pompeian cause who were not completely shattered by their defeat at Pharsalus to take advantage of the situation he had created. Pompey himself was dead, but his two sons Gnaeus and Sextus were able to come to Spain. After his victory at Thapsus in 46 BC, Caesar was able to turn his attention to Spain, now that Africa was pacified. At this time Pompeian forces in Spain amounted to thirteen legions, not all of which were of adequate, let alone first-rate, quality. Caesar brought about their defeat at Munda, by making use of their dual command, which placed them at an initial disadvantage. His own infantry was at a high pitch of training, and again he had the invaluable support of Gaulish cavalry in the rough Spanish terrain. Gnaeus Pompeius was captured and executed. Sextus escaped and survived to cause trouble in later years to Caesar's heir and successor.

After Caesar was murdered Sextus came out of hiding and gathered together enough forces to take the town of Nova Carthago. He was formidable to the extent that Lepidus, the Caesarean agent, felt it reasonable to come to terms with him. At this stage it was not certain whether the supporters of the Caesarean cause would prevail, and an arrangement with Sextus could be a prudent investment for the future. Accordingly, Sextus was allowed to expand into Sicily. Disaffection remained alive in Spain. Cassius was not forgotten. We find that in the battle of Philippi, which decided the issue against the old Republic and the supporters of the Pompeian cause, a large contingent of Iberians and Celtiberians took the Republican side. The Second Triumvirate allocated Spain to the governorship of Lucius Antonius, brother of the triumvir Marcus Antonius.

Sextus Pompeius was powerful enough to be taken seriously. Octavian and Marcus Antonius concluded a treaty with him at Misenum in 39 BC. He had under his authority Spain, and Sicily and Sardinia. Spain was the main basis of his power. The treaty agreed that he was to be consul and that he should have as provinces Sardinia, Sicily and Achaea for a term of five years; he was also to receive compensation for his father's proscribed property. Within a year the treaty was voided. Octavian took Sardinia, but failed in his attempt to recover Sicily. Spain was again the power base of a claimant warlord; but the end was to be defeat. Octavian and Antonius combined in an alliance of mutual need in a treaty they made at Tarentum in 37 BC. This released forces which could be used against Pompeius. In 36 BC he was defeated by Marcus Agrippa at Naulochus in Sicily. He escaped to Asia, but was captured and killed by Antonius' agents in 34 BC.

The battle of Actium in 31 BC eliminated Antonius as a candidate for ultimate power. A new regime could now be envisaged by Octavian and his colleagues. Spain remained restless. In 26 BC, Asturii, Cantabri and the tribes of Galicia tried to assert themselves against Octavian's rule and he was compelled to take action against them. Like his adoptive father Julius before him, he used Gaul as his base for operations in Spain. He became ill, however, and gave up his command in 25 BC. It was not until 19 BC that the Spanish war was concluded in Rome's favour under the heavy hand of Agrippa.

The Celtic peoples of Spain provided a major part of the manpower requirements of the Roman armies that held Spain during the imperial period. Under the Empire, and unlike previous times in her history, Spain's westernmost position brought her increasingly a life of peace, to which her inhabitants soon became accustomed. Most of the troubles of the Empire, until the northern barbarians began to exert their pressure, were in the turbulent east. In fact, Hadrian (*imp.* 117–137 AD), who himself was of Spanish origin, deplored the lack of military energy amongst his compatriots. The national temper had mellowed from long security. Celtic traits survived: in Tiberius' principate, Celtiberians were still using their own language, and they continued to do so for a considerable time after (Tac. *Ann.* 4.45). Pliny says that the Lusitanians spoke Celtic, and Silius Italicus tells us that the Gallaeci still used their native warsongs (3.345). Greco-Roman education was taking its toll of the inherited way of life. Little inscriptional evidence of native speech is available after the time of the first Principate.

Yet the imperial period before the times of the Germanic menace was not entirely free of alarums. In 170 AD, pirates from Africa invaded Spain and inflicted much destruction on Baetica. In 187 AD, Maternus disturbed Spain as well as Gaul with his army of irregulars. Spain took the side of Clodius Albinus in his violent candidature for emperorship in 192 AD, but its commitment to his cause was not deep. During the third century AD Spain was controlled for a number of years by Postumus, who ruled it, together with Gaul and Britain, as a Gallic empire.

The Germanic Vandals occupied Spain and became *foederati* of the Roman empire in 411 AD. They could defeat Roman armies, but not shortage of supplies. The Romans turned the Visigoths on the Vandals, as if it were possible to drive out one set of enemies by means of another. Making robbers into honorary allies was a measure of desperation which sometimes gave the appearance of success. The Silingian Vandals and the Alani who accompanied them were broken. The Alani and the Silingian Vandals coalesced, and asserted themselves with some vigour in southern Spain. Vandals were succeeded by Goths who eventually predominated in a country which was, nevertheless, destined to retain many vestiges of native and Roman culture in its language and ways of life.

We might say that the attitude of the Romans to the inhabitants of the Iberian peninsula was on the whole exploitative and suspicious. The country had been the source of the most serious attempt on the part of Carthage to destroy Rome. In it Carthage had an excellent recruiting ground and a supplier of food and precious metals. The Carthaginians could have made the more accessible regions of Spain into a powerful empire, which Rome at the time could scarcely have defeated. The Romans made no systematic attempt to possess the whole peninsula, once they had eliminated the Carthaginian threat from its territory. Exhaustion from protracted war and the calls of more urgent spheres of action kept them to their characteristic policy of taxation and extortion by governors, who by the very definition of their duty as commanding a *provincia* or 'military area of conquest' had an aggressive and greedy approach, unless they were being cowed by fierce tribes.

A principal source of conflict between Romans of the Republic and Celts of Spain was that, in their several ways, both sides were devoted to rapine. The former practised plundering under the cover of legal authority and the governmental practices of Rome; the latter were practitioners of the archaic variety of the game. It is hard to see how the Spanish peoples could ever have come to terms with the Roman presence while Spain was a strategic pivot of the western Mediterranean. The country was borne off in the whirlwind of war between Carthage and Rome, and then between Roman warlord and Roman warlord. The Celtiberi and the Iberes were acted upon cruelly by the politics of great powers, but their mountain stamina and heroic warrior-code (often betrayed by Roman deceit) enabled them to react formidably on a number of occasions and they kept their identity even when they were tinged to some depth by Classical culture. The elder Pliny reminds us that the country of the upper Anas was Celtic in culture, and that its inhabitants, of Lusitanian stock, still maintained their own religion, in which the goddess Turobriga was prominent, and still spoke Celtic.

Yet it must be admitted that many local artistic and cultural forms did not survive the long struggle against Rome from 200 BC to 50 BC. We have mentioned the foundation by Sertorius of schools for the sons of Celtic leaders. Pompey's arrival in Spain brought in its train grammarians and teachers of rhetoric. We hear of one of these, Asclepiades, who arrived at the same time as Pompey and taught in Baetica. He collected material for a history of the Spanish peoples and some of this survives in the work of Strabo. Inscriptions tell of the careers of teachers of Greek language and literature in various parts of the peninsula.

It soon became possible for talented Celtiberians to make their way to Rome in search of a career. An early contributor to the literature of Rome from this part of the world may be Egnatius the Celtiberian whom Catullus ridicules in his poems. Syme suggests (1958: 587) that he may be the Egnatius who, according to Macrobius (6.5.22), wrote *De Rerum Natura* ('On the nature of the universe').

It was not until the so-called Silver Age of Latin literature that writers of Hispanic origin became prominent. We cannot attribute Celtic origins to all the distinguished writers in Latin who were Spanish or of Spanish family. If we accept that environment is significant in the formation of a writer, we may entertain the possibility that the Celtic component in Roman Hispanic society had some influence on the formation of their minds.

The Annaei, the family of the Senecas (1st century AD), were of old Roman colonist stock, which does not exclude the likelihood of a native strain in their background. If so, it is not likely to have been Celtic. Corduba, their home, was a town in the territory of the Turduli, an Iberian tribe, possibly of Tartessian descent. M. Claudius Marcellus established the place in 152 BC. It may have been made into a *colonia* in Pompey's time. M. Porcius Latro, from Corduba, was one of Ovid's teachers. The town was a centre of rhetorical studies. Junius Gallo is remembered; also Sertilius Hena whose eloquence, according to the elder Seneca, was flavoured with a peculiar pronunciation (*Suas.* 6.27). Quintilian and Martial were from Celtiberia. Syme points out (1958: 618) that nobody has ever discerned a 'Celtic note' in their works. The great rhetorician and literary critic, Quintilian, was born in 30 AD at Calagurris in a Celtic zone: he hardly mentions Spain, except (1.5.7) to express his puzzlement at a Spanish word (Syme, ibid.). He may, of course, be trying to hide his origins from himself and others, having determinedly left behind him his country of origin. We can hardly follow this conjecture further.

The poet Lucan was the nephew of the elder Seneca. We might be tempted to see in the fervid republican eloquence of his poem on the Roman Civil War some of the passionate dedication to liberty that is evident also in some of Catullus' poems against Caesar and his satellites. But perhaps these upholders of old-fashioned *libertas* have nothing in common but their provincialism.

The geographer Pomponius Mela was born in Spain, in Tingentera, or Cingentera, on the bay of Algeciras. His lifetime in part coincided with the Principate of Claudius. There is a suggestion that the Roman *gentilicium* 'Pomponius' was taken by him through adoption, and that his real name was L. Annaeus Mela, brother of Seneca the philosopher, and father of the poet Lucan. His geographical writing seem to be based on very early sources.

The three generations of Annaei represent the most distinguished period of Spanish Latin literature in antiquity. Other authors of this time and a little earlier and later, Columella, the writer on agriculture, Pomponius Mela, whom we have mentioned, and Quintilian, fill in the background of a vigorous and creative period in the history of the Hispano-Roman population.

Martial is exceptional in that we have in his writings some frank assertions of Celticity. He was born in 40 AD in the Celtiberian town of Bilbilis: 'We are descended from Celts and Iberians', he says in epigram 4.55.8. He makes the same ethnic claim in 7.52, 10.65 and 10.68. He is perhaps the only extant classical author — certainly he is the only important one — to speak so clearly of his Celtic identity. Even Ausonius is not so vociferous on this point.

The barbarous placenames of Spain are humorously celebrated in 4.55:

We who are descended from Celts and Iberians
are not embarrassed at the mention of the
somewhat harsh placenames of our land.

Then he mentions Bilbilis and its fame in the making of ironwork. The same theme in almost the same words is taken up again in 12.18.10ff, where he talks about the crass names of places in the Celtiberian lands. He is clearly aware of the Celtic cultural theme and consciously identifies himself with it.

His poetic circle included Canius Rufus of Gades, Decianus of Emerita, Maternus of Bilbilis and Valerius Licinianus, all of them in their time notable for poetry, rhetoric or law. He was also strongly attracted to the circle of the Annaei until they were disgraced for their alleged complicity in the conspiracy of Piso in 65 AD. In 98 AD, Martial returned to Spain from Rome and settled in a comfortable small estate which had been given to him by a patroness.

Spain produced emperors, directly or indirectly: we may mention Trajan (b. 52 AD in Italica). The family of Hadrian was from Spain. Other men, famous in very different fields of endeavour, followed in the centuries that were to come. Priscillian, the bishop of Avila (4th century AD) is an outstanding representative of these. We cannot strike a distinctive Celtic note from any of them, not even the great Christian Classicist Prudentius, who was born in Celtiberian Calagurris (4th century AD). He wrote Pindaric poetry on the subject of the Christian martyrs in metre which was still strictly and Classically quantitative.

9

The Galatians

Saint Jerome, who had spent time both in Trèves and Ancyra, says that the Treveri and the Galatians have the same language. He says this in his commentary on St Paul's *Letter to the Galatians* (Migne xxvii 382). The history of these Celts who came into Asia Minor to plunder and to settle is turbulent. They seem to have been acted upon by others rather than to have been initiators in the drama of their history. Their effects, however, on the lives of their neighbours were sometimes drastic. They deserve to be considered separately from their kinsmen who invaded Greece. They made a nation. The invaders of Greece made nothing so lasting.

In 278 BC, large numbers of Celts crossed into Asia Minor at the invitation of Nicomedes of Bithynia (278–250 BC). Three tribes were involved: the Tolistobogii, the Tectosages and the Trocmi. They were more than a mercenary horde. They brought their wives and children with them. They were a people in movement. Only half their number were fighting men, and they were led by Leonorius and Lutarius. In the long term, they would tend to settle rather than raid. Their immediate employment was as mercenaries. Eventually they would pursue the old Celtic practice of mutual raiding and warfare between their tribal and cantonal districts. They had separated from Brennus' forces before the invasion of Greece. Of the survivors of Brennus' expedition, the Scordisci founded Singidunum in Yugoslavia; others made their way to Thrace and founded Tylis. In this region they came into contact with the culture of the Scythians. It was said of this part of the Scordisci that they did not mine gold, but preferred to steal it (Pos. Fr. 48 Jac.; Ath. 233d–234c) and for many years they extracted tributes from Byzantium.

Nicomedes used the three tribes we have mentioned in his war against Zapoites, and in his conflict with Antiochus I, who defeated them severely in the so-called 'Elephant Battle' *c.* 275 BC. Their robust capacity to cause trouble in Asia was not crippled by this. They seemed determined to remain and make a life for themselves after their own fashion. The kingdom of Tylis, on the other hand, tended to retain more of the character of a powerful establishment of bandits. Its history of extortion came to an end in 212 BC, when the Thracians revolted from its domination and destroyed it. According to Polybius, the last of the kings of Tylis, Cavarus, was a man of magnanimity and regal character (8.24). His name might be a ceremonial title with the same root as Irish 'caur', meaning 'giant' (Stokes 1894: 74). Cavarus, had, in fact, been of assistance to Byzantium, which was pinched in conflict with the Thracians on one side, and the Bithynians under Prusias on the other. However, his kingly abilities were not improved by the influence of a sycophant called Sostratus. Celts had spread from this region into the surrounding lands, even to north-west Bulgaria, where they were still recognisable in the Christian period (Hoddinott 1981: 127).

The Celts who moved into Asia Minor and were to become known as Galatians made a much greater impression on history and historians. Demetrius of Byzantium is said to have written thirteen books on their incursion into Asia (D.L.5.83), and he may be the source used by Polybius and hence by Livy for their respective accounts of the Galatians (Stähelin 1907: 7). Myths about the terror they caused grew up in the various cities. The story of the women of Miletus who were captured by the Celts while they were celebrating the Thesmophoriai became part of the romantic tradition of Greece in the strange and unpleasing tale of Erippe and Zanthus (Parthenius 8). In this the Celt who became the owner of Erippe turned out to be a man of some integrity, and Erippe the betrayer of her former husband and of her captor. The Celts in Asia Minor, however, had so bad a reputation for atrocities against prisoners that people would kill themselves rather than fall into their hands. Their reputation for monstrous behaviour towards prisoners had the effect of dampening Greek will to resist. We hear of taxes being voted, *ta Galatika*, which were for the ransom of prisoners taken by the Celts (*OGIS* 223).

As in peninsular Greece, myths became current about aid given to imperilled Greeks against the invaders by local divinities. Marsyas is supposed to have been helpful in Asia Minor (Stähelin

1907: 9). On the mortal plane, there is the more reliable story of the courageous services of a certain Sotas in defence of his native city of Priene.

The Celts were eventually contained in a broad strength of territory in the middle of Asia Minor which became known as Galatia. Here they settled, but they continued to emerge in a frightening fashion for their own purposes of raiding and large-scale extortion, and also in the pursuit of their concomitant profession as mercenary armies. Galatia is a stretch of territory in the northern zone of the central plateau of Asia Minor. It is generally from about two to four thousand feet above sea level, a monotonous country of bare hills with small plains between them. There are few trees. The land is fertile when there is enough rain, but it is frequently affected by drought and consequent famine. In antiquity, its main products were wool and slaves. Northern Galatia lay along the principal line of East-West communication, and from the time of the Hittites the region had been of some importance.

By 232 BC the Celts had been constrained to settle in this country in the midst of an already resident population. They did not take over their new home by conquest, but as the result of an agreement between the Hellenistic kings of the area who were anxious to solve the Celtic problem. For in coming to Asia Minor, the three tribes had intruded into an arena in which the successor kings of the empire of Alexander fought out their long and complex rivalries. The kingdoms involved were those of Syria, Pergamos, Macedon, Asia and Egypt.

From the outset Galatia was a mixed nation. Many of its people mentioned in inscriptions of Delphi as being, for example, freed slaves, are not Celts, who formed a ruling class, but came from the original population of Phrygians, who were only partly assimilated to Celtic culture. The Celtic Galatians and their descendants preserved the style and culture of warrior pastoralists, similar in some ways to the Dorians who invaded Greece at the end of the twelfth century BC, and whose descendants maintained the old ways of the original founders. Northern Galatia, the area of heaviest Celtic settlement was, like many other areas of this part of Asia Minor, inhabited by Phrygians, an IE-speaking people of similar stock to those who lived in the Troad. In the *Iliad*, Phrygians are represented as being a heroic warrior-race of horsemen. Their warlike capacities seem to have been blunted by the Cimmerian invasions. Between the tenth and seventh centuries

BC, Phrygia had been an independent state. In the third quarter of the seventh century BC the country was debilitated by the Cimmerians, whose last destructive writhings inspired Callinus of Ephesus to his famous elegiac exhortations to the youth of his city to resist. From this time until the middle of the sixth century BC, when it was absorbed in the Persian empire, the state of Phrygia was under the suzerainty of the kings of Lydia.

An ancient Phrygian thalassocracy had lasted for about a quarter of a century after 905 BC. The original Phryges had been a wandering people from Macedonia. Traditionally, it seems, they arrived before other tribes such as the Thynoi, Mysoi and Bithynoi who came into Asia Minor from the other side of the Bosphorus. The early Phrygian domain was split, apparently by the Mysoi, so that their land of settlement was divided into Hellespontine Phrygia and Great Phrygia (Ramsay 1900: 21). In their heroic phase they may reasonably be supposed to have been not unlike the Celts in their way of life. They had so declined from their old repute in war that they were capable of being dominated by a Celtic influx which can hardly have included as many as twenty thousand effective fighting men. In the southern areas of Galatia, the Phrygians had to some extent become Hellenised. From the third century BC, there is evidence that Galatia had become a centre of the slave trade. A possible cause of this commerce could be the displacement of Phrygian inhabitants from their lands: this, it has been suggested, could create a surplus population for disposal in the slave trade (Ramsay op. cit.). The trade persisted long after this problem had been solved: Ammianus reports that Gothic slaves were also on sale in Galatia (22.7.8).

Strabo assures us that the three Celtic tribes of Galatia spoke the same language (12.56). His term *'homoglottoi'* may be taken to indicate that there was no significant difference of dialect between them. They maintained their own customs, though these were modified in the course of time. We hear of a great sacred place of assembly called 'Drunemeton', a characteristically Celtic name. It may indicate the presence of the druid cult, though we have no other indication of druids in Galatia. The reference in Diogenes Laertius (I.I) to the Galatians having druids, in analogy to the *gymnosophistai* of India and other learned orders of other races, may not specifically refer to the Celts of Asia Minor, but to those of northern Europe. But the balance of likelihood is that the druid cult did exist in Galatia. The location of Drunemeton is not known. The only other evidence of Celtic religious practice is the report that they sacrificed their prisoners. Celtic peoples of whom we have more information had many goddesses in their pantheon. The Celts of Galatia seem readily to have taken to the worship of the Asiatic Mother Goddess.

Strabo also tells us that each of the tribes was divided into four sections, and that each of these was led by a chief (he does not say 'king'). Each of these sections was called a *tetrarcheia* or 'tetrarchy' and each had a general, two deputy generals and a judge. Could we suspect the judge of being a druid? The twelve tetrarchies sent a total of three hundred senators to the assembly at Drunemeton. Representatives of the tribes of Gaul used to meet in a similar assembly at Lugdunum, and the custom was Romanised in 12 BC. It took place in August, which is the month of the Irish Féil Lughnasa, the festival dedicated to Lugos or Lugh.

In common with other Celtic peoples, the Galatians did not establish city-states. This form of social organisation was alien to their tradition. They had hill-forts (cf. Ir. *dúnta*) which gave them protection for themselves and their cattle in times of trouble (Livy 38.18: 19). Many of the existing cities of Galatia were destroyed by the Celts in the progress of their colonisation of the country. Chiefs built themselves castles and strong points for defence. In the first century BC, Deiotarus ruled from such a 'dun', and not from Pessinus. Strabo refers to Ancyra, not as a city, but as a *'phrourion'* or strong point. Pessinus, the main religious centre of Phrygia, was not taken by the Celts. Gradually they came to live in it, and to achieve influence in the ceremonial life of its cult of the Mother Goddess.

Though the Celts and the earlier population blended to some extent, social distinctions remained which were based on original ethnic differences. We find that a man with a Celtic name like Gaesatodiastes can give his son a Greek name such as Amyntas. Similar phenomena can be reported of Gaul (Anderson 1938: 315). Yet the Celtic language seems to have survived at least to the time of St Jerome. This could scarcely have happened, had there not been a certain sense of exclusiveness at least in some parts of the Galatian Celtic community. This is distinct from the pretensions of some latter-day Galatians that they were the descendants of tetrarchs. The woman called Kamma, who is celebrated as the heroine of an actual tragedy by Plutarch (*De Virt. Mul.* 22) is said to have been kindly disposed to the subject race. This would indicate that in the second century BC (we cannot be certain of the date) there was still a marked distinction between the

Celtic ruling class and the rest of the population.

Livy (38.16.12) says that the three tribal divisions of the Galatians each had respective provinces for depredation in Asia Minor. His statement may be based on Polybius. Aeolis was the sphere of robbery for the Tolistobogii; the Tectosages moved inland into continental Asia Minor; and the Trocmi devastated the region round the Hellespont. The historian Apollonius is reported to have said that the Celts entered into alliance with Mithridates I of Pontus (302–266 BC) and it was he who settled them in the region of Ancyra. This act would not mean that these lands were in his possession at the time, but rather that the power of Antiochus was insufficient to hold north-east Phrygia (Ramsay 1900: 47). Mithridates was getting the problem of these turbulent allies out of his territory and into that of his neighbour. Antiochus I was on terms of hostility both with Mithridates and the Celts. His victory over the Celts was probably not decisive. His capacity to deal with them once and for all was reduced by the threat posed against him by Ptolemy. He was himself killed by a Celt in 261 BC. This could have been in a battle against Ariobarzarnes of Pontus (266–241 BC) or Philetaerus of Pergamum who was successfully founding his own independent kingdom.

Antiochus II was unable to impose his jurisdiction over the region around Ancyra which was occupied by the Tectosages. Seleucus II, his son and successor, in concluding a marriage settlement with Mithridates II (246–190 BC), gave with his sister as dowry the lands of Greater Phrygia. He was most anxious to be rid of Celt-infested dangerous territory, though he was also keen to be on peaceful terms with Mithridates. During this period Celtic raids were frequent and destructive in western Asia Minor. The Tolistobogii reached as far south as Apameia and Themisonium. Eumenes I of Pergamum (263–41 BC) had paid them ransom to leave him and his territories in peace. Attalus I of Pergamum (241–197 BC) refused to pay, and when the Celts came to collect the money in person, he defeated them in a battle at the sources of the Caicus, probably in 240 BC. In the war between Seleucus and Antiochus Hierax for the Seleucid possessions of Asia Minor, Antiochus employed a large force of Celts. Mithridates also adhered to Antiochus rather than his father-in-law Seleucus. Antiochus quarrelled with the Celts and barely escaped with his life. Celtic influence had increased in the alliance so that they were his substantive equals. Antiochus succeeded in gaining power over the Seleucid lands of Asia Minor. War broke out between him and

Attalus I of Pergamum. One of the four victories which Attalus won over an enemy army which included a force of Tolistobogii was in a battle near the shrine of Aphrodite near Pergamum itself. This suggests a bold quick raid by the Celts into enemy territory. In the other three battles there is no report of Celtic participation. Possibly they had sustained heavy losses in the battle at the Aphrodisium. It was not until 232 BC that they were at last confined in the territory which they had settled and made their own. A peace was made with them by agreement. Their role in the conflict between the Hellenistic nations was over. The end of this war saw Attalus supreme in Asia Minor, his power stretching as far as the Taurus in the south. From this time there is a recognisable 'Galatia'. The agreement seems to have accepted that the Celts were no longer interloping raiders in Asia Minor but an accredited nation. On the other hand, if their boundaries were to be respected, they would have to respect the integrity of the lands ruled by Attalus and restrain themselves from raiding them.

It may have been at this time, however, that a tribe called the Trocnades took over a portion of the Pergamene kingdom. They are usually supposed to have been a Celtic people, but there is doubt whether their name is really a Celtic ethnicon. The Celts were incapable of remaining still and quiet within the bounds of their new lands. Their old wandering habits impelled them westwards and, perhaps as Trocnades or perhaps not, they certainly infiltrated the districts surrounding the old sacral centre of Pessinus. It is not known whether the Celts took possession of the city itself at this stage or whether they simply occupied the lands round about it. Hemmed in as they were in the south by treaty and force, they are not likely to have been in a position to make so overt a move as the outright seizure of so important a sacred place: their opportunities for expansion lay more favourably towards the east. Apparently they had some sort of alliance with the city of Pessinus for about half a century, and its independence remained intact during that time.

The Celts, now 'Galatians' in our historial nomenclature, gradually blended with the older layers of population very much as the Phrygians and other incoming IE warrior-peoples had done in the past. In the later Empire, all the inhabitants of Galatia were homogenised, though there were some old families who still traced their descent from the Celtic tetrarchs of earlier times (Ramsay 1895–7: 249: *CIG* 4030). In course of time, the potent Hellenistic influence emanating from Pergamum came to be dominant in

Galatia, and would have prevailed completely, had not the residual cultural isolationist tendencies of the Celtic ruling class found some support from Roman interference in the region. Already there was a renewal, from the point of view of Galatia's Hellenistic neighbours, of Galatian potential for trouble-making and aggression. Within Galatia, the forces of Hellenistic influence in the country's way of life were in conflict with a traditional Celticism. The latter profited from Roman support, and the older Celtic mores became fashionable. Indeed, in the years following 189 BC, the Celtic warrior-idea presided over a more fused and united community of Celt and Hellenised Phrygian. A new and more cohesive national identity was forged, and Galatia began to be a genuine menace to her neighbours on account of her need to expand. From the contest with her Hellenistic neighbours, Galatia, with Roman support, was to emerge intact and vigorous. In the first century BC, the area ruled by people of Celtic descent in Asia Minor was greater than it had ever been. The Galatians had under their authority Lycaoni, Paphlagonia, Pontus and Armenia, as well as their own territories.

Let us return for a little to the later third century BC. We have seen that the Celts were not involved in the later wars of Attalus. His rule over the Cis-Tauric regions was not long. Seleucus III Soter (*reg.* 226–223 BC) intended to move into Asia Minor, but was poisoned by a Celt called Apatourus, who no doubt was the leader of mercenaries. We have the testimony of Polybius (8.53, 79) and Livy (37.8, 38) that Seleucid armies used Celtic mercenaries. They found employment also in Egypt. They were frequently agents of disruption in the armies in which they served and were open to enticement by enemy commanders. Celts were imported from Europe for mercenary purposes. Molon, the general who led a dangerously efficient revolt against Antiochus, also had Celts in his army (220 BC). Ptolemy Philopator had a force of Celts in his service, but they became demoralised at an eclipse of the moon. They fell into an undisciplined condition, and would, he saw, be useless because they believed that the eclipse portended defeat. There was nothing for him to do but take them back to the Hellespont, together with their wives and children who had accompanied them. He contemplated killing all of them, for they could easily in their state of mind have changed sides to Achaeus, the general and cousin of Antiochus. He was eventually restrained by his sense of decency from such a move.

Seleucus III was succeeded by Antiochus III, the 'Great', who brought back under his control former Seleucid dominions in Lydia and Phrygia. Achaeus was the general in command of the operation, and when he revolted, all these gains were imperilled once more (Ramsay 1900: 54).

Attalus now attempted to regain the lands he had lost. He brought in a Celtic tribe from Europe to help him (218 BC): these were the Aigosages. He made a foray with their assistance into Aeolis and across Lydia into northern Phrygia. After the campaign, he settled his Celtic mercenaries in Hellespontine Phrygia. Before long they began to make trouble in the Hellespontine area. They besieged Ilium, and devastated the surrounding country. The siege was lifted by forces from Alexandria Troas under Themistes. They were forced to leave the vicinity, but took possession of Arisba and continued with their vexations from this base. Attalus retained his influence in the territories he had repossessed with the aid of the Aigosages, but it is only reasonable to infer that he did so with the agreement of Antiochus, and that the two had arrived at an accommodation that included this question. Prusias I of Bithynia got rid of the nuisance of the Aigosages in 217 BC, by massacring them all, including their women and children (Polyb. 5.111).

Attalus and Antiochus allied against Achaeus, who was besieged in Sardis. The city was taken in 214 BC. In the following years, Attalus acquired Phrygia Epictetus, the north-eastern zone which bordered Celtic territory, and had been under the rule of Bithynia. Attalus had been at war with Prusias in 207–206 BC, and he may have obtained this piece of territory as a result (Ramsay 1900: 55). The influence of Attalus' power seems to have stretched as far as Pessinus, because he was able to take the Roman emissaries there in their quest for the great Idaean Mother Goddess.

The Celts of Galatia seem to have observed their original agreement with Attalus. They did not intervene in the west until he died in 197 BC. They tried to extend their power to the north and they may have made an attempt to take Heraclea on the Pontus at this time. After the death of Attalus, they moved against Lampsacus. The government of Lampsacus got from Massilia a letter in support of their case addressed to the Tolistobogii. This would appear to suggest that there was a continued sense of kinship and contact between the Celts of Galatia and southern France, who were of the same tribe. It would seem that the leaders of Galatia had abrogated their friendship with Pergamos before 189 BC.

This seems to show that their national temper had accommodated itself somewhat to the customs of Hellenistic diplomacy, rather than the simple practices of raiding.

In 205 BC the Romans were informed by the Sibylline Books that if they brought the Magna Mater, the 'Great Mother Goddess', from Pessinus, they would be enabled to get rid of Hannibal. Assuming the role of patron and guide, Attalus led the Romans up to Pessinus without consulting the Celts. They probably had little control over the city in any case. It was only later that they managed to infiltrate its holy institutions.

Romans came into conflict with the Galatians because they had been allies of Antiochus at the Battle of Magnesia in 190 BC in which the Roman victory had been savagely complete. Antiochus had provoked the Romans by his annexation of the Greek cities of the Asia Minor coast and by his intervention in mainland Greece which resulted in his defeat at Thermopylae in 191 BC. After their defeat of Philip V of Macedon, the Romans had declared Greece to be free, and Antiochus had deliberately ignored their settlement of Greek affairs. There was also the fact that Hannibal had been given refuge at the court of Antiochus and was inflaming his ambition with anti-Roman sentiments.

The Roman commander in the punitive expedition against the Celts was Cn. Manlius Vulso. He defeated the Tolistobogii and Trocmi with great slaughter at the battle of Olympus, near to Pessinus. According to Livy 38.18, following Quadrigarius, almost forty thousand prisoners from this battle, including women and children, were sold into slavery. Manlius occupied Ancyra, and defeated the Tectosages in a battle at a hill called Magaba. These successful acts of intimidation satisifed Manlius' policy for the region, and he made peace with the Galatians: one of the conditions was that they should not raid the western parts of Asia Minor. Manlius' severity was not only a sharp response to the threat that the Celts posed to the peace of the kingdoms of Asia Minor. It was also redolent of the inherited fear that haunted Romans when Celtic armies were on the loose (Livy 38.37).

Roman opinion was more reassured by the defeat of the Celts than by the crushing of the pretensions of Antiochus. The Romans had cleared the Eastern world for a time of the fears of a Celtic terror. They were not disposed to allow any local nation to achieve a position of predominance. In spite of Manlius' stipulation that they should not attack Eumenes (Livy 38.40), the Galatians were soon involved in a war with him. In this Pharnaces of Pontus and

Prusias of Bithynia were their allies (Trogus 32, Prologue). Even after the serious defeats they had suffered in 189 BC, the Galatians were still a formidable nation.

A chief of the Tolistobogii called Ortagion was ambitious for the unification of the Galatians under himself as ruler (Polyb. 22.21). His attempts at unification met with little success. In 181 BC, we find that a considerable number of Celtic cantons are mentioned together with their chiefs. This would seem to show that the tetrarchal system remained unshaken in spite of his efforts. Ortagion was evidently thinking in terms of the typical Hellenistic kingdom. Other chiefs who were in alliance with Pharnaces were more devoted to the traditional tribal system of the Celtic world. Polybius tells us (24.14) that he actually had a conversation with the wife of Ortagion in Sardis. It may be supposed that her presence in a Pergamene city meant that Ortagion's party had been defeated and that he had found it convenient to leave his own country.

Pharnaces had no difficulty in establishing his ascendancy over a loose alliance of Celtic chieftains and the situation of these tribal leaders began to be uncomfortable. The most enthusiastic supporters of the Pontic connection, Corsignatus and Gaizatorix (Polyb. 25.2) characteristically found the emerging tyranny hardest to bear and transferred their friendship to Eumenes II of Pergamum in 181 BC. A Roman interdict prevented the Galatians and their new ally from turning on Pharnaces.

The fact that Galatians are recorded as serving in Pergamene armies after 179 BC (Livy 42.55; 44.13) may indicate that the pro-Pergamene party ultimately prevailed in Galatia. But there was no more talk of unifying the country. Eumenes may have expressed objections to such a policy. Ortagion's policy was dropped in favour of a more gradual Hellenisation that was less likely to offend Celtic preferences for the old ways. It was also important not to irritate Roman susceptibilities by creating an obvious new concentration of power in the region. Eumenes' careful policy with regard to the Galatians and Rome perished on the rocks of Roman suspicion that he had been giving aid to Macedon. When in 167 BC the Galatians, encouraged by Prusias, invaded Pergamene territory under the leadership of Advertas and almost overthrew his government (Livy 45.19), the Romans would not allow him to retaliate. At the same time they were prepared to listen to complaints against him from the Galatians and the representatives of the Bithynian king. Eumenes' diplomatic talents won him suspicion rather than friendship from the Romans, who were also interested in maintaining a balance of power betwen the competing kingdoms of a still unsettled continent. Eumenes, however, managed to clear his country of Galatians and had some Roman support in making an agreement with them which provided that they should engage in no more raids (165 BC).

Rome's manoeuvres in this episode are not untypical of an intrusive imperial power anxious to secure its own interests by manipulating local sources of instability. For these purposes, the Galatians were ideal material and convenient instruments. Their fluid, loosely organised groups of tribes, following a way of life which was distinctive of Celtic and Celtic-descended peoples even down to eighteenth-century AD Scotland, made them the tools of aggressive, centralised governments whose policies they were ill equipped to fathom or circumvent. Their traditional political and social structures made them the victims of their own love of local independence and neighbourly rivalries. The nature of the land inhabited by the Galatians, particularly the wild stretches of north Galatia, enabled their archaic culture to survive longer than might have been expected. Their old traditions were consolidated by the treaty of 165 BC, which for a time diminished Pergamene influence in Galatia. In one example, tradition reasserted itself in a cruelly fundamentalist way after the treaty of 165 BC: they felt free to sacrifice to the gods the finest of the prisoners they had taken in the war. The remainder were simply executed, even though they were in some cases former friends and hosts who had given hospitality to Galatian leaders (Ramsay 1900: 61).

The habit of raiding was made almost necessary by the character of the Galatian social order. Between 164 and 160 BC there was a border dispute between the Galatians and Cappadocia. The Trocmi unsuccessfully tried to take possession of a strip of Cappadocian land. The Romans tended to take the side of the Galatians in this dispute. Ariathes, the King of Cappadocia, had to lay out a large amount of money in bribery to Roman ambassadors and senators in order to secure himself in what had been his own (Polyb. 31.13).

The Galatians gradually penetrated the most respectable and ancient local cults. Pieces of a correspondence have survived, in inscription, between Eumenes or Attalus II (King: 158–138 BC) and a high priest of the Mother Goddess at Pessinus. The name of this man was Attis, which may have been a ceremonial title, because we know that he was a Celt: the name of his brother was Aiorix (Ramsay 1900: 62). His political interventions in favour of the party of his people who were in favour of the Pergamene connection may remind us of the part played by druids in the political life of Gaul. But if, as is not unlikely, there was a druidic order in Galatia, its members can hardly have been entirely in sympathy with Attis' policy. It is not unlikely that the priesthoods of the goddess came to be allocated half to Galatians and half to local families of the older race, as the Celts became more settled and assimilated to the region.

The woman called Kamma, whom we have mentioned earlier in this chapter, was said to have been a priestess of Artemis. This Artemis is another phase of the Great Goddess of Asia Minor: she is most likely not an assimilated or Hellenised Celtic goddess. Kamma's story is told by Plutarch (*De Mul. Virt.* 20; *Amat.* 22). She was the wife of a tetrarch called Sinatus, who was killed by a man called Sinorix. Sinorix prevailed on Kamma to agree to marry him. The marriage ceremony involved the bride and groom drinking from a common cup. Kamma poisoned the drink and partook of it after Sinorix. She preferred to be dead rather than married to her husband's killer. The form of marriage seems not to have been Celtic. It may have been of an ancient Anatolian provenance (Ramsay 1900: 88).

Nevertheless, Celtic culture seems to have retained its strength and identity and to have been in no significant way weakened by such syncretisms. At times, the Pergamene influence seems to have prevailed, bringing an increased degree of Hellenisation into Galatian life; at other times, the connection with Pontus predominated, and this intensified the inherited Celtic patterns of custom. The latter tendency was generally favoured by the Romans. It provided a counterbalance against Pergamene power in the whole region.

We have seen that in the middle of the second century BC, the south was the only available path for Galatian expansion. The fact that the Galatians needed more room for living as well as plunder testifies to the continuing energy of what was now by no means a homogeneously Celtic warrior-nation. Between 189 BC and 133 BC, Lycaonia was not under the protection of Pergamum, and consequently, parts of it were added to the Galatian sphere of influence. By 160 BC the Galatians possessed added territories of considerable extent which were eventually regarded as part of Galatia.

Roman cultural forms were more readily adopted by the Galatians than were Greek. The Romans found the alien character of the Galatians in relation to the rest of Asia Minor potentially advantageous to themselves. A thoroughly Hellenised Galatia might become a mere appendage to Pergamum, and with it might possibly generate a major Hellenistic power which could embarrass Roman influence. Even Galatia itself, if it was sufficiently Hellenised, might become strong enough to challenge Roman authority.

The fluctuation between Pergamene and Pontic influences over the years in a sense insured the relative independence of Galatia from being absorbed by either power. Galatia, however, seems to have adhered to friendship with Pontus in the period when, after 130 BC, Great Phrygia was under the rule of Mithridates III of Pontus. Mithridates had been granted this addition to his kingdom by the Roman consul Manius Aquillius. He could never have held this gift in check without the acquiescence of the Galatians. Excessive growth of Pontus was not any more to the Romans' conception of their interests than the expansion of Pergamene dominion. Aquillius' move was not accepted: in 126 BC the Senate overthrew his allocation of Phrygia to Mithridates, but in fact it remained in the possession of subsequent Pontic kings, and the Senate behaved as if the original act of allocating it to Mithridates had been valid.

After 121 BC there seems to have been a reaction in Galatia against Pontus. Mithridates' successor, another Mithridates, was a minor under the regentship of his mother Laodice, and the Romans seized this opportunity of adjusting the balance of power by encouraging the party in Galatia which opposed the influence of Pontus.

The Roman dictator Cornelius Sulla in 85 BC made use of the Senate's repudiation of Aquillius' concession of Phrygia to Pontus, even though that repudiation had never been made effective. He declared Phrygia free, but in fact continued to treat the country as if it were a Roman dependency. The trouble started in 88 BC when Mithridates IV brought his army into Phrygia (Ramsay 1900: 67). This king of Pontus took possession of large tracts of Asia. His only serious opponents were the Galatians, and these he tried to neutralise by a vicious act of treachery. He had set up his court in Pergamum and he invited sixty Galatian chiefs to meet him there. He had them all killed, with the exception of one who managed to escape. The tetrarchs who had not been at

Pergamum he had killed by secret means. Only three of the tetrarchs of Galatia survived. Here again we have an example of the use against Celts of the Celtic attitude to the customs of hospitality. It appears that the families of the tetrarchs who accepted his hospitality were also killed (Ramsay 1900: 69).

The system of government by tetrarchies in Galatia was permanently crippled by this disaster. We can see that this must have been the intention of Mithridates: his killing of the families of the chiefs was probably politic as well as a reflection of his natural cruelty, for the succession would by this means be cut off. This severe blow to the Galatians pointed out the benefits that might come from a more cohesively organised state in which the constituent tribes worked more closely with each other and perhaps developed a more modern form of government. Mithridates' atrocity had the effect of persuading the pro-Pontic and pro-Pergamene factions in Galatia to join in hostility against him. He had not omitted in the general massacre to kill his own friends and supporters among the Galatians, as well as his opponents. One of the surviving tetrarchs, Deiotarus, drove out Eumachus, a satrap sent in by Mithridates to rule Galatia. This was in 74 BC. Lucullus' invasion of Pontus in 73 BC had the effect of clearing Galatia of hostile forces from Pontus.

From the time of Mithridates' attempt to extinguish Galatian national leadership at one blow until his final defeat in 66 BC, the Galatians were firmly in alliance with the Romans in their war against him. During this period of alliance, they took all the more readily to Roman ways of living and customs. It might be said with Mommsen (Ramsay 1900: 70), that the Galatians were at heart people of the West who had never completely accepted Asiatic culture. Vestiges of the old Galatian form of government seem to have remained until 64 BC, when Pompey, in the course of his great settlement of Eastern problems, instituted a system of three leaders amongst them instead of their numerous tetrarchs (Strabo 5.67). Pompey did not restore Lycaonia to his Galatian allies: they were granted some concessions in Pontus and Armenia Minor. The recipients of these lands were in effect the new rulers of Galatia, Deiotarus, the leader of the Tolistobogii, Brogitarius of the Trocmi, and another chief whose name is unknown to us. Each of these three new leaders was still called a tetrarch: the paradox of such a title for a member of a group of three is relieved somewhat by the fact that each was the leader of one of the three tribes which had been historically known as tetrarchies. In addition to his grant in Armenia Minor, Deiotarus, in recognition of his special services, was given Gazelonitis. The relationship between the three rulers was inevitably one of rivalry, and Deiotarus was best placed in respect of his possessions to prosecute a contest with his colleagues. He strengthened his already favourable position by concluding a dynastic marriage between Brogitarius of the Trocmi and one of his daughters; another daughter he married to Kastor, the son of the leader of the Tectosages.

We have seen that this remarkable man was a survivor of the massacre of the tetrarchs. He succeeded his father, who was, it is supposed, called Dumnorix. He had the capacity to make himself acceptable to Romans, and co-operated successfully with a succession of powerful men of widely differing temperaments, such as Sulla, Murena, Servilius Isauricus, Lucullus, Pompey, Bibulus and Cicero. He was well thought of by all of them (Ramsay 1900: 97). He introduced Roman methods of military training, organisation and tactics. The Roman art of estate management also attracted his interest in spite of its being alien to the aristocratic and pastoralist preferences of Celts. Cicero (*De Div.* 1.15.2ff *et alibi*) says that Deiotarus never embarked on any undertaking without taking the appropriate auspices. His procedure in this involved all species of birds, not merely a prescribed few, as in the Roman custom. We have no reason to believe that his auspicy was Celtic in type. We know that the Celts attached importance to auspices (Diod. 5.31.3), in spite of the statement in Pausanias that they did not (10.21). The worshippers of the Great Mother certainly did take auspices: the goddess guided birds to fly in significant directions, and her priests interpreted their movements (Ramsay 1900: 92). We can be sure that when Galatians prayed for the locust birds to come and counteract a plague of insects, they were not following a Celtic rite (Ramsay 1900: 93). Here, as in other customs, there may be a coming together once more of old strands of custom observed in their different ways by the various constituent peoples of Asia Minor from times of high antiquity.

Deiotarus received marks of the Senate's approval, and it was almost inevitable that he made the strategic error of backing the Senate and the old Republicans in the Civil War. He added his force to that of Pompey, who, from the point of view of the East, must have seemed a much better prospect that Caesar. Since we can reasonably infer communication between the Celts of Gaul and those of Galatia, we can hardly suppose that Deiotarus was ignorant of Caesar's brilliant achievements in Gaul or of the power that he had assembled. The messages, however, would have needed to be forceful indeed, if they were to occlude Pompey's repute in the East. Also, it would be thought that, no matter how formidable Caesar might seem to be in the West, he might very well find his resources stretched beyond their capacities if he were to attempt the subjection of what was, properly speaking, another continent. We need not impute to Deiotarus any feeling of loyalty to the Republic. He showed himself equally ready, in the aftermath, to negotiate with Caesar's representatives. The Civil War, after all, was a Roman quarrel; and it was for Deiotarus to make use of it in the interests of survival and, if possible, gain. At the beginning of the war he was already too feeble to get on his horse without assistance.

His family proved to be a more formidable menace to this tough, ruthless old operator than the warring Romans. Deiotarus' grandson (or son-in-law), Kastor, accused him of having conspired against Caesar during the latter's visit to Galatia. Cicero defended Deiotarus before Caesar as judge. Cicero had been on friendly terms with him since his tour of duty as governor of Cilicia in 51 BC. Now in 45 BC, he successfully presented his friend's case. Deiotarus went home and, it is said, put to death Kastor and his wife. It may, however, have been the elder Kastor who was executed as the instigator of the younger man's action.

Cicero reports (*Ad. Fam.* 12.2) that Deiotarus was in no respect generous in the reward he gave Cicero for speaking on his behalf. There was no question of princely Celtic potlatch here; Deiotarus was giving payment (or rather an honorarium) to a prominent Roman who, being a Roman, was in a position of advantage in relation to the Roman law, without occupying a position in the current Roman political structure that could in the least be considered intimidating. He would not gain any advantage amongst his own followers in Galatia by generosity to a foreigner, whose declining influence he was well placed to perceive. All had been won and there was no need for extremes of expenditure. Deiotarus died peacefully at an advanced age and was succeeded by his surviving son Deiotarus II.

We may mention at this point another ruthless, but less significant figure. Amyntas, a prince of Lycaonia, was the type of the fierce shepherd-king (Str. 12.569). In these troubled times, he made his way to prominence by calculated murder and intrigue, relentlessly swallowing more and more territory, without realising that for him and his like, time had already run out. He definitely entered the scene of international politics when he became, together with Deiotarus II, a supporter of Antony against Octavian. He subsequently had the wit to desert to the side of Octavian (Plut. *Ant.* 944c). When Deiotarus died, Amyntas made himself king of Galatia, and remained confined in this position. In a period of disturbance he had opportunistically filled a power vacuum in the middle of Asia Minor, but the configuration of much greater powers than he could command determined his limits. From now on, Galatia would be a province of the Roman Empire, and in the future, even more than in its turbulent past, it would respond to events rather than initiate them.

The Apostle Paul's message to the Galatians (*c.* 51 AD) can scarcely be supposed to have been addressed to the more Celtic lands of north Galatia. In his strictures on the Galatian Church, Paul does not seem to be referring to specifically Celtic traits. He attacks general human failings rather than the faults of character frequently attributed to Celts by Greeks and Romans. His direct address, 'O foolish Galatians' (*Galatians* 3.1), has no overtone of racial prejudice. Nor was he himself likely to have been so foolish as to speak to the Celtic element in the province, an aristocracy of warlike antecedents, in these terms. He is speaking paternally to members of a church, not paternalistically to wild tribesmen.

He urges the churches to support their teachers: converts to Christianity were not conspicuously willing to pay for this sort of thing, since they felt themselves at last relieved of the burdensome payments required by the pagan cults (Tertullian *Apol.* 13). There is nothing identifiably Celtic in this reluctance. In St Paul's time, Galatia was the name of a province, not an ethnic group. He might have been less likely to use Greek cultural assumptions to underpin his arguments, if he had been speaking in particular to Celts who were resistant to Greek culture (Ramsay 1900: 373). The Celtic people of North Galatia tended towards Roman ways rather than the customs of the despised Greeks. Yet the men of the north were not completely ignorant of the Greek language, which the Roman administration was trying to promote in their area. At this stage the religion of the Celts was more assimilated to that of Phrygia and much of its Celtic flavour may be supposed to have been dissipated by time.

Some families of later Galatia regarded themselves as descendants of kings and tetrarchs. Inscriptions which inform us of these claims no doubt reflect the same sort of romantic pride that modern Scots or Irish may feel in their descent from a notable Gaelic prince or chieftain. These inscriptions may presuppose a literary or poetic tradition by which the tradition of ancestral glory was communicated from one generation to the next. Nothing of the kind can be extracted from the scatter of inscriptions which has survived. We may safely accept that the Celts of Galatia did not use their own language as a medium for written literary composition.

In the fourth century AD, Themistius compares the Greeks unfavourably with the acutely intelligent and curious Galatians (*Or.* 23; *Soph.* 299). He seems to be speaking of a people stimulated by a relatively fresh acquaintance with Greek culture. In the same period, Libanius takes a similar view of the Galatians, though he may not have Celts exclusively in mind (*Ep.* 1333). The inhabitants are enthusiastic to study Classical Greek authors. He is referring to all the people of Ancyra. He also mentions the city of Tabia (Tavium) and recommends the appointment of a teacher for the citizens. The town may be on the point of setting up its first school of rhetoric. Ramsay (1900: 177) compares this with Tacitus' recommendation of a teacher for the new school at Comum (Pliny *Ep.* 4.13). We can accept that some of the Galatians mentioned by these authors were of Celtic or part-Celtic families.

In 74 AD, Galatia had been joined to Cappadocia as a single province by the Emperor Vespasian. At this time Cappadocia was beginning to be of greater strategic significance to the Romans because of its eastern position. The empire's eastern frontier was and would remain a point of weakness in the world dominion of Rome. Trajan separated the provinces in 106 AD: Galatia became somewhat isolated and the process of Romanisation slackened pace. Hadrian paid it more attention, but from this time there was an increasing tendency to separate pieces of its territory from it, and its diversity of character is recognised by the use of the plural *provinciae* in references to it. It is not part of our discussion to describe the various additions and subtractions to which it was subjected in the later centuries of Empire or the variations of its importance in the scheme of imperial strategy. It did not decline in significance in the centuries of the Eastern Empire. There was still a province of Galatia in the eighth century AD.

The historical experience of the region in which the Celts who became Galatians settled, together with the physical character of the country itself, entailed the continuation for centuries of the kind of frontier conditions and heroic mores which marked the period of earlier Celtic wanderings. The prolongation of this phase of national adolescence was conducive to the preservation of Celtic ways of thought and customs even in a potently influential Hellenistic environment. The most marked conservative trait was not the failure of the Galatians to make themselves into an organised state which could adequately defend and assert itself. This has been and remains a universal affliction of the Celtic and Celtic-descended countries and it evidently represents something deep in the tissue of Celtic culture. More significant was the failure of the Galatians to make a significant adaptation of the Classical civilisation or to make their own additions to it. The remarks of Themistius and Libanius might lead us to conjecture that the Galatians came to grips with the culture of the Greco-Roman world too late. For too long they had been swinging between the pendulum of Celticism and the influence of the Hellenistic world. In this respect Galatia differed from Gaul, which increasingly, as the central power of the empire waned, became the heir of Roman civilisation and its most effective executrix.

10

The Celts in Greco-Roman Art

The present chapter is an annex to its predecessors which have discussed the interaction of Celts with the city-states of Greece, the Hellenistic monarchies and Rome. Artistic representations of the Celts in the Classical world involved a degree of excited primitivism bordering on the baroque. The vigorous northerners were seen as living specimens of natural man whose archaic ferocity was balanced by innate courage and a certain heroic decency guided by an unpredictable sense of personal honour.

Greek art of the early Hellenistic period already shows this blend of romance and realism well developed in its depictions of these dangerous aliens. The heroic strength and violent posture of statues of the Celts remind us of the Lapiths and other Titanic figures of an earlier mythology. In the case of the Celts, however, the Hellenistic artist makes an attempt to represent a distinguishable ethnic countenance and expression.

Attalus I of Pergamum (*reg.* 241–197 BC) commemorated the victories won by Eumenes II and himself over the Celts by commissioning two (at least) sets of statues from sculptors of high repute. Epigonus, the son of Charius, was probably the Pergamene master-artist in charge of the construction of the sets. Pliny (*NH* 34.84) mentions other notable artists who collaborated in the grand project: there were Isogonus, Pyromachus, Stratonicus and Antigonus; a cross-section of the best talent of the Greek world at that time. Pliny actually says that their works commemorated the victories of Eumenes and Attalus. Pyromachus may be identical with Phyromachus of Athens (Pollitt 1986: 84; and, in general, Robertson 1975: 527ff).

One set of statues seem to have been set up on the Acropolis of Athens. This group, whose constituent figures were half-life-size, illustrated primeval wars between the Athenians and the Amazons in the time of Theseus; the Athenians fighting the Persians in 490 BC; and the victory of the army of Attalus over the Celts in Mysia. The originals were no doubt in bronze. Surviving copies are in marble. Pausanias saw a group of Attalid sculptures in Athens (1.25.2) which were about two cubits in height. Various museums of Europe hold specimens of about this size which are certainly Roman copies of the original groups. Marble examples of more than life-size statues also survive. These too are Roman copies of bronze originals. They are of Celts who are getting the worst of a battle. A well-known example is that of a Celt who with one hand holds up the body of his wife whom he has just slain and with the other pierces his own breast with his sword. This is in the Terme museum of Rome. Another famous piece, from the Capitoline museum, shows us a mortally wounded warrior slumped on the ground awaiting death. He wears a torque and beside him lies a curiously curved trumpet. This figure is heroically naked; the Terme male wears only a short cloak, though the female is draped. They die noble and savage deaths, as Greek and Roman opinion held was proper to their national character. The connection between Roman copies and Pergamene originals was first proposed by H. Brunn in 1853 (Pollitt 1986: 85).

The larger statues may represent a set which was put up in Pergamum itself; the vigorously posed smaller figures might seem to have been designed to allude to the battles of Lapiths and Centaurs on the Parthenon. Placing a set of important and expensive statues on the Acropolis of Athens was a tribute to a city which was the hereditary guardian of Hellenic freedom and the repressor of barbarian pretensions. There may also be the implication that this traditional role had now passed over to the kings of Pergamum.

Inscriptions from the precinct of Athena Polias Nikephoros in Pergamum provide more particular evidence for Attalus' monumental advertisement of his military achievements. In the precinct, a round base of about three metres in diameter was found which originated in the reign of Attalus I. The Romans remade it at some point in order to place the statue of an emperor on it. In doing so, they removed same capping blocks, which, when they were discovered, were found to have an Attalid inscription on them. It says that Attalus dedicates this thanks-offering to Athena, having conquered the Tolistoagii (Tolistobogii). The battle may have been that of 233 BC (Pollitt ibid.). Another inscription, recovered from stones which had been used in a Turkish wall, refers to Attalus and his general Epigenes fighting against the Celts and Antiochus. This could be a battle fought in 228 BC (Pollitt ibid.).

Another base from the precinct, a rectilinear one about nineteen metres long, has an inscription dedicating thank-offerings for success in a war. Again the dedication is, as might be expected, to Athena. The base is divided into eight sections, each one of which seems to have had a statue group upon it. Each section had its own inscription, describing the statuary above. Two of these inscriptions are sufficiently intact to make sense: they mention the Celtic tribe and where the victory over it was won. Over-life-size statues of Celts seem to have been dedicated on the island of Delos, as inscriptions show. Some of these large statues seem to have been made of Pergamene marble, which might suggest that they were contemporary copies of Pergamene bronze originals made to be set up in foreign temples as part of a propaganda effort in favour of Attalus.

We have seen that statues of Celts were given ethnic attributes by which they could be recognised. The males, who predominate in number in subjects that concern warfare, are given thick, wild hair, moustaches and bodies which, though classically muscular, yet hint at the length and sinewy texture of a Nordic people. Often the cultural identifier of the torque is shown. According to Diodorus (5.28.1–7), Celtic nobles shave their beards: the Capitoline and the Terme warriors are both beardless. Specimens of bearded Celtic men of the people are extant.

The faces of the Celts are emotional and expressive, showing wild anger mixed with despair, or harshly set in the anguish of death. Their concave profiles, high cheek-bones and narrow orbits contrast with the Mediterranean countenance. We may observe that the ethnic characteristics have been carefully noted. The Capitoline Gaul would, if suitably dressed, pass unnoticed in a Scottish regiment.

From the fourth century BC the art of Greece increasingly became interested in the individual person and the racial type, rather than the idealised and abstracted human specimen of the Classical period. This development accompanied increasing contact between Greeks and various foreign peoples. A comparable interest in individual personality and national character emerged in literature. The fury and the fear engendered in the Hellenistic mind by the advent of destructive and relentless invaders manifested itself in an excessively dramatic, almost expressionist style, which at times suggests a baroque giantism. Yet in a sense this style immunises the viewer from its subject's terrifying aspects even by its exaggerations. Lapiths and Centaurs were in the unplotted past: Celts were horribly immediate. To conquer such monsters in battle, as the commissioners of this art had done, was not just a military achievement of note, but also a triumph of the human spirit. It was a glory certainly not to be underplayed.

For an Italic interpretation of the Celtic threat in artistic terms, we may look to the Cales seals and the frieze from Civitas Alba (Civit' Alba). These exhibit the Celts as plunderers being extruded from temples by the intervention of the gods, a story which accords with one version of the Celtic attempt on Delphi (Bienkowski 1908: 100). We have seen that there is another version in which they never manage to enter the precinct. There are also many examples of this kind of event in the sculptural repertory of alabaster sarcophagi, grave monuments and urns from Etruscan regions. The inhabitants of these places had good reason to have strong feelings about the Celts and the menace that they represented. The predominant artistic theme is strife. The Celt is usually the stricken party. There is no doubt an element of apotropaic wish in this thematic choice, for there was no guarantee that the Celts would not return to plague the population.

Civitas Alba is in former Senonian territory. The terracotta frieze of great merit which was found there shows the Celts immersed in battle and plunder. The female figure who is resisting their theft is probably a goddess protecting her temple rather than a private individual opposing the pillage of her house. There is also a war-chariot represented on the frieze, which need not be seen as a proof that the Celts made use of such vehicles at the time commemorated. On pottery seals from Cales in Campania, which date from the late fourth to the late third century BC, Celts are depicted in their characteristic activity of plunder (Bienkowski 1908: 86ff). It may be that these scenes are imitated from sculptural models. In a third-century BC grave near Volaterra, a bell-crater was found which had painted on it the image of a warrior wearing a helmet of Greek-derived form, but conical and fitted with a finial. The warrior carries a large oval shield and is armed with a large sword (Bienkowski 1908: 30). The shield covers most of his body, but the portion which is left unconcealed suggests that the man may be naked apart from his weapons. This red-figure pot may well depict a Celtic warrior. The drawing is not of the highest quality. There is a slight absurdity in the figure, which is shown standing between large pieces of formalised vegetation. The picture may contain an element of apotropaic caricature. The impression is reminiscent of pottery drawings depicting rough, wild satyrs and Sileni. The artistic mode is quite distinct from the romanticism of the Pergamene sculptures, which show Celts as figures of tragedy, agonised but not debased.

Etruscan terracotta urns which depict battles seem to imitate Pergamene sculpture, rather than local experience of actual fights. A few, perhaps, may be said to reflect local spirit and events. Alabaster sculptures with inscriptions in the Etruscan language from Città della Pieve show fully armed warriors in what looks like hoplite armour who are identifiable as Celts only by the torques that they wear. One of these warriors is on his knees; his sword points to the ground and he is obviously stricken. A bird is shown tearing out his eyes. Bienkowski adduces Livy's story (7.76) of the raven attacking the Celtic chief who fought in single combat with M. Valerius Corvinus (1908: 81). Once more we may be reminded of the bird-goddesses of war in the insular Celtic tradition. The goddesses perch in bird form on the body of Cu Chulain in his death struggles. While it may be suggested that the Etruscan example does not involve a raven but a dove, which elsewhere is shown as sitting on the heads of warriors as a sign of their imminent death, we have to say that the bird under present consideration is behaving in a thoroughly undovelike fashion. It is pecking out the eyes of the dying man. In this it differs from other examples of birds who simply presage the death of a hero (Bienkowski ibid.). We do not need to connect the scene with any particular event in Roman mythological history, but the story told by Livy clearly belongs to the same general tradition. The companion warrior, who also wears a torque, is killing himself with his sword in the despair of defeat. The other part of the sculpture shows a gentleman, reclining at his ease and garlanded; the inscription is: Larth Purni Curce.

The representations of Celts do not tell us what the Greeks and Romans actually saw when they encountered the Celts, but rather what they thought they should be seeing. They wanted them to be defeated, distant and far removed from the sphere of actuality in which they wrought such palpable harm. Nevertheless the heroic style of the Celts and their wild courage struck chords of admiration in the hearts of Greeks and Romans brought up to revere the fighter for his people as admirable above all men.

11

Britain, a Source of Disquiet

Catullus used the Britanni as examples of remote, hairy barbarians (Poem II). In the late fourth century AD, Ausonius
published amongst his epigrams the anti-British sentiment: 'How
can a Briton be called "Bonus" ("Good")? "Matus" ("Drunk")
would be a more suitable name'. Even later, in 417 AD, Rutilius
Namatianus thought it suitable to use stock epithets of wildness in
referring to the Britons, who live at the edge of the known world.
Britain was no longer part of the Roman Empire, and Rutilius
was perhaps as entitled to keep alive the ancient commonplace of
British wildness, as Catullus had been nearly five hundred years
earlier. Britain's fierce northern tribes and its historic propensity
to generate untimely local emperors (Constantine III would be a
recent example), did not convey a convincing impression of
civility. In spite of centuries of Roman influence and in spite of
the blending of Italic and other foreign military elements into the
population, Britain was reverting to native Celtic type. Nor was
it any more free than other parts of the European empire from the
attacks of uncivilised Germanic tribes which even the firmly
grafted Mediterranean component of Britain's population was
hardly able to withstand. The Saxons and their associates made
a harsh condition of life no more amenable. Their attacks
promoted a recrudescence of Celtic tribalism, with its chiefs and
warlords who seemed to be needed to resist them effectively. From
this time on, Germanic names would appear in company with
Celtic personal names in the dramatis personae of British history.
The Romanised element would fade into the past.

Much of the history of pre-Roman Britain is based on the
evidence of local coinage, imitating models from the Classical
oikoumenē and given a stamp of native style. This was a prime

element of self-assertion on the part of Celtic rulers in Britain and elsewhere. It also indicated an increasing interest in trade with the Greco-Roman world. The presence of Belgic elements in the population of Britain is indicated by their distinctive pottery and their custom of cremating the dead. The Belgae seem to have arrived in Britain in the decades preceding Caesar's landings. The evidence of placenames would suggest that at the time of Caesar's invasion (55–54 BC) most of Britain was inhabited by speakers of Celtic (Salway 1981: 17). Coinage would seem to suggest that by this time Belgae had been immigrating into south-east Britain for about sixty years (Cunliffe 1973: 11). This movement may have originally been stimulated by the Cimbric and Teutonic disturbances of the first century BC and later continued because of Caesar's extensive military operations in Gaul, some of which were directed against the Belgae. By 55 BC Belgic chiefs and warrior-groups were gradually extending their hold over considerable areas of Britain, imposing their military aristocracy upon settlements of Iron Age farmers. Over this was to be laid the framework of Roman provincial military rule and financial administration. The burials of Belgic chiefs were ostentatious. Tumuli were reserved for a very select few. The large Belgic tumulus of Fitzwalter Road, Colchester, is of a burial at the end of the first century BC. Although it was robbed at some point in its history, it was found, when it was opened in 1924 AD, to contain a rich variety of imported artefacts as well as locally produced items of considerable elegance (Dunnett 1975: 17).

Julius Caesar's invasions had perhaps little value outside the sphere of public relations in the political contests of metropolitan Rome. Yet there was in the background the solid hope of profit and wealth for Roman merchants from this military venture, as well as the timely admonition of potentially troublesome tribes. Roman influence spread more rapidly because of Caesar's contacts with the British, but in the period between his landings and Claudius' invasion of 43 BC, the Celtic core of British social organisation remained unimpaired, as in an important sense it was destined to remain throughout the centuries of Roman presence in the island (E. Evans 1983: 955).

The Britons, according to Strabo, were taller and darker than the Gauls and their way of life was more primitive. Britain seemed to the Romans at first to be a somewhat lesser Gaul. It was probably best known in the Roman mind for troubles, exaggerated in the rhetoric of historians, than for anything else. The custom, long to be observed, of presenting Britain as a source of rebellion and a nest of barbarity not unlike Germany, was begun by Julius Caesar. The old Celtic custom of rivalries and wars between tribes and cantons was conscientiously observed in Britain before the Romans ever reached her shores and was assiduously maintained in the time of increasing contact with Rome between 54 BC and 43 AD. Pre-Claudian Britain is a landscape of dynastic strife and constant warfare in which a military aristocracy was staking its claims on the territory of an older but far from passive way of life. This involved the kind of chronic riot well described in the *Taín Bó Cúalgne*, which may reflect a long struggle in which Ulster was taken over by warrior groups from the south of Ireland.

We may begin with the Catuvellaunian king, Tasciovanus, driving Addedomarus out of his kingdom in Essex. This probably happened in 17 BC. Tasciovanus had begun to issue coins with his name and that of his capital city Verulamium. As a confirmation of his conquest, he also minted coinage with his name and that of the captured capital Camulodunum. This was not allowed to go on for long: Addedomarus seems to have returned; Dubnovellaunus followed him and supplanted him by force. He himself was replaced by Cunobelinus ('Cymbeline'), the son of Tasciovanus (Dunnett 1975: 12–13). The *Res Gestae* of Augustus record that Dubnovellaunus sought refuge in Rome.

Cunobelinus encroached upon the lands of the southern tribe of the Atrebates. After his death, his sons Caractacus and Togodumnus overwhelmed them. Their refugee prince Verica asked the Romans for help. His request provided a pretext for the Roman invasion. The main motives of this move had been suppurating in the minds of the rulers of Rome for many years and were: security of an awkward frontier, plunder, trade, patriotic diversion and the acquisition of military prestige necessary to the *princeps'* view of his own effectiveness in relation to his predecessors, impressing contemporary rivals and posterity. We have already discussed Caligula's apparently farcical gesture towards the conquest of Britain in 40 AD. This was ostensibly in favour of Animinus, a son of Cunobelinus who had quarrelled with his father. The policy of Caractacus and Togodumnus towards Rome was less friendly than that of their father. It was to the advantage of Rome that the south of Britain should not become solidified into a hostile unit. The achievements of Cunobelinus had already caused them some unease.

The Romans were ready to invade in 43 AD. Claudius did not

lead the expedition in person. In command was Aulus Plautius, an able officer. Cn. Hosidius Geta, later to be *consul suffectus*, was on his staff and his courage in a battle at the Medway is recorded. I shall not retail the events of the campaign which followed the three Roman landings. The Celtic army fought with characteristic bravery in the first onset, and its leaders tried to make intelligent use of their knowledge of the terrain. They did not take sufficient account of Roman engineering skill or its capacity to overcome natural impediments, nor did they envisage the special usefulness to the invaders of the Celtic auxiliaries who were part of the Roman force. The dread fact was that Celtic methods of warfare were based on different assumptions from those which underpinned the Roman military machine. In spite of the speed and brilliance with which some aspects of Mediterranean military science had been assimilated by the Celts, the armies of Britain were no match for those that confronted them. Updated Homeric heroism could not compete with a discipline which was both firm and flexible in its tactical movements. When Cassivelaunus confronted Julius Caesar, the core of the Celtic army had been four thousand chariots, a phenomenon more reminiscent of the *Iliad* than Hellenistic or Roman warfare. Chariots were still at large in Britain in 43 AD, and were to be used by Boudicca and her followers in 60 AD. They had fallen into obsolescence in Gaul before Julius Caesar began his campaigns there. Britain remained somewhat archaic. Plautius' victory was inevitable. Togodumnus and Caractacus and their respective armies were defeated. Togodumnus was killed at the battle of the Medway. Before long most of the lowland parts of Britain were under Roman control. Caractacus survived to trouble the Romans for a number of years, until Cartimandua, the queen of a powerful concentration of northern tribes called the Brigantes, betrayed him to the Romans.

After their success at the Medway, nothing stood between the Romans and Camulodunum, which they ravaged. This city had been named after Camulos, a god of war: it was of a size unprecedented in the Celtic world, with an area of thirty-two-and-a-half square kilometres (Dunnett 1975: 16). This was a suitably impressive captive capital for Claudius to enter triumphally during his brief visit to Britain. Some of the tribes became *socii* or allies of Rome and were allowed to continue to conduct their own affairs under Roman guidance. Others, who had an unfavourable record of resistance, were *dedicitii*, unconditionally surrendered people, who were under the arbitrary authority of the Romans.

A figure both distinguished, yet also enigmatic, in the early period of Roman rule in Britain, was Cogidubnus. He probably was of British origins, though nothing certain is known of his descent. Tacitus mentions him in his *Agricola* (14) as an ally who, within his own memory, had remained attached to Rome. This fidelity was rewarded with further grants of land. Such allocations, as Tacitus remarks, conformed with the Roman policy of using kings as the utensils of enslavement. Cogidubnus seems to have emerged as a satellite of the Romans shortly after the Claudian invasion and he remained prominent and successful through three decades. He may have been a member of the ruling house of the Atrebates. It may even be that he was descended from Epillus or Tincommius, Atrebate princes who had been exiles in Rome. The suggestion has been made that he could have had personal experience of Rome through having been reared there (Cunliffe 1973: 22).

The territory of the Atrebates lay between the mutually hostile Durotriges and Dobunni, and kept them apart. It was divided into three administrative districts by the Romans soon after their invasion. The Atrebates proper had their capital at Silchester: Venta, modern Winchester, was the city of the Belgae. Cogidubnus' subjects were called Regni, which possibly was a new or recent cantonal name. Whatever its origin — the Celtic 'Regini', 'proud people', has been suggested — it must have seemed to Romans and others to convey some notion of royalty: these were the people of the 'kingdom' or king's men. The palace at Fishbourne is thought to have been the seat of Cogidubnus' rule. The district could have provided a friendly base for Vespasian's military operations in 43 AD, when he was serving as an officer of some responsibility, but was not yet especially senior.

Nothing is known about the situation of the Regni during Boudicca's revolt in 61–62 AD. Tacitus' comments would lead to the conclusion that he was a firm ally of the Romans. The Roman cause had been beneficial to him and his people. If a widely understood reading of a well-known inscription at Chichester is correct, a distinction extremely rare for a native provincial king came to Cogidubnus at some point in his long career, when he was created *legatus Augusti*. This considerable honour could have been his reward for supporting Vespasian in his contention for imperial power in 68 AD. In 69 AD, Cogidubnus would have been able to deliver, as it were, the British 'vote' of his region in Vespasian's favour (Cunliffe 1973: 27), while exercising a valuable stabilising

217

influence in the province. It has to be said, unfortunately, that the text of the inscription is far from certain.

Yet the great new palace at Fishbourne, one of the largest and most impressive in the Roman world, would certainly harmonise with the status of a *legatus Augusti*. It seems to have been begun about 75 AD. Such a dwelling, pretentious in the basic sense of that word, would be an understandable expression of a Celtic prince's notion of what was suitable to his standing as an honoured friend and ally of the Roman emperor. It would be an expression in Romanised terms of the lavishness of Louernius. The enormous *oppidum* of Camulodunum (Colchester) may indicate similar princely assertion, though military considerations were of overwhelming importance for Cunobelinus, and he was content to live in a simple hut inside the walls. Cogidubnus' ideas of suitable residence for a prince may have been influenced by the ambitious building programme of Nero's Rome. A certain national pride may have impelled him to construct a palace of more than average metropolitan size and dignity.

In contrast, that devoted enemy of Rome, Caractacus, after his escape from the British defeat in 43 AD, gave the Roman authorities trouble for about eight years. He stirred up resistance among the Silures, a hardy and belligerent tribe in Wales. His efforts were nullified here by a defeat at the hands of the Roman commander Ostorius Scapula. He was then sheltered by the queen of the Brigantes, Cartimandua. Caractacus was on the move from one as yet un-Romanised tribe to another. With the exception of the vale of York, the territory of the Brigantes was rough and pastoral, a typical highland zone. It may be that Cartimandua had her centre of government in this favoured valley. A large hill-fort in Barwick-in-Elmet could have been a Brigantian stronghold of importance (Ramm 1978: 28). Although the Brigantes were still independent, they were weakened by the all too prevalent Celtic virus of dissention and schism, which sooner or later admits external interference.

When Cartimandua handed over Caractacus to the Romans in 51 AD, she needed Roman favour and support in an internal Brigantian conflict. Her husband Venutius, an able military commander, had been appointed to power by the Romans in payment for his support in a previous disturbance. He and Cartimandua became estranged and he emerged as leader of an anti-Roman faction of the tribe. Aulus Didius Gallus re-established her authority, but it required certainly one, and perhaps two legions to accomplish this. The betrayal of Caractacus was a minor incident in a war which continued to 58 AD when Didius Gallus came to the end of his period of office as governor. But Roman intervention provided only a temporary relief of the difficulties facing Cartimandua. Rome's own problems in 69 AD during the contest for the emperorship were Venutius' opportunity for launching a fierce attack on Cartimandua. He was encouraged also by a revolt among her own people and he had support from other tribes.

His long-matured resentment originated no doubt in the dishonour of having been divorced by Cartimandua in favour of his former squire Vellocatus. He had much sympathy on this account from parts of the tribe. The quarrel between husband and wife seems to have had some connection with her apparent ambition for power, which her success in the Caractacus affair and her continued collaboration with the Romans stimulated as time passed (Tac. *Hist.* 3.45). Her status and authority in her own kingdom (if that is what it was) lacks definition. Her assertiveness may have resulted from a desire to vindicate rights of which she had been deprived at an earlier stage by some incident in tribal politics.

Cartimandua was rescued with some difficulty by the Romans when her forces were defeated by those on the side of Venutius. In a poem which concerns a certain Bolanus, the son of the Roman governor at the time of this battle, Papinus Statius (40–96 AD) attributes palpable successes to the Romans in their conflict with Venutius (Stat. *Silv.* 5.2). We must remember that Statius was given to exaggeration both by profession as panegyrist and by natural genius. Venutius seems to have been left victorious for a time. He ruled the Brigantes until his defeat by Petilius Cerialis in 71–72 AD, after which the Brigantes and their territory were absorbed into the Roman province.

The Iceni were a tribe who lived in what is now East Anglia. They revolted against the Romans in 48 AD, and as a result, the Romans appointed Praesutagus to rule as a safe client king. When he died, he bequeathed his kingdom to the Emperor as joint heir with his daughters, a typically Roman way of securing a legacy from imperial interference. Ostorius Scapula, the second Roman governor (*legatus*) of Britain, had caused the revolt of 48 AD by his thrusting policy in search of river boundaries for the zone of Roman military control (Syme 1958: 394). His move cut the Iceni off from the Brigantes and the north, and created in them an understandable sense of anxiety for their own future, which no doubt contributed to the violence of their revolt in 60–61 AD.

Praesutagus, and presumably also his wife Boudicca, had hoped that the Iceni would continue after his death in a secure client relationship with Rome. Some Roman local officials could usually be relied upon to behave badly. A disgraceful incident occurred in which Boudicca was beaten and her daughters raped.

While it was never difficult at any time to find Roman officials who were prepared to treat provincials as subhumans and slaves, irrespective of their legal status, there may have been some doubts about the precise standing of the Iceni in relation to Rome after the death of the client king. The revolt of 48 AD would reduce them to the status of a people who were at the arbitrary disposal of the Roman government and it is not known whether this was changed during the years of Praesutagus' rule. He seems to have thought that it was but he may have been relying on some verbal statement or the even more ephemeral Roman sense of honour in relation to provincials. Tacitus' story (*Ann*. 14.31) is that he expected that his kingdom, long prosperous and peaceful, would be allowed to continue. The offenders against Boudicca and her daughters were low-level officials: centurions and the slaves who were agents of Roman procurators. The governor, Suetonius Paulinus, was at the time occupied in killing druids in Wales and was surprised to learn of the revolt which followed the atrocity. His military reputation was excellent but his control over the administration of his province is open to criticism.

Suetonius had a distinguished career behind him before he came to Britain in 58 AD. His best military achievements had been in the Atlas, where he had successfully fought tough tribes of mountaineers. It is not surprising that he should have made it a priority to subdue a dangerous region of Britain which was protected by mountains and in addition was a fertile producer of supplies for the British enemies of Rome. His enthusiasm in this quarter could be regarded at least as a constructive negligence in relation to his important administrative duties elsewhere in an island not yet secured by Rome and certainly chafing at some of the customs of Roman rule.

In purely dramatic terms, his expedition to the island of Mona (Anglesey), the last stronghold of ferocious druids and wild women urging on manic defenders, makes a fitting prologue to the horrors of Boudicca's revolt. The war began on a point of honour, but it was a reaction against other substantial annoyances.

Without the dishonourable assault on the princely women as its detonator, it may be doubted whether it would have been so wide in its effects or so viciously fought. It became a national uprising against a contemptuous and greedy foreign domination. Whether or not Boudicca was herself a native Icenian, she had at this time complete control over the tribe. Tacitus refers to her as a woman of the royal house, which does not precisely define her status or claims. Whether she was an exogamic consort of Praesutagus, or an Icenian princess married to an Icenian client king, or whether she was in fact originally entitled to rule by descent or election, but had been fitted out with a safe consort by the Romans in their own interests, there can be no question about her charismatic influence as a leader in war. Tacitus tells us that the Britons were indifferent whether men or women led them (*Agr.* 14), but he also says that abhorrence of female rule won sympathy for Venutius (*Ann.* 12.40). We may suppose that the Britons were less unwilling to follow the leadership of a woman than some other peoples, but that they were enthusiastically willing to be led by anybody, male or female, who could inspire them with confidence in their cause.

The pent-up fury of the Britons was released in the complete destruction of the hated new colony at Camulodunum. They carried out a scrupulous massacre of all its inhabitants. Petilius Cerialis met the British horde with forces of the Ninth Legion which were not at full strength, and was severely defeated. He sought refuge in Gaul. Suetonius, however, inflicted a decisive defeat on the British. One of the results of this defeat was widespread famine amongst the British tribes, who according to Tacitus, had omitted to sow their crops in the expectation of a plentiful supply of captured Roman grain. Their omission may have another explanation, more pertinent and creditable. If they began their war before the sowing season, they would have the element of surprise on their side. The Romans would not expect them to attack before this necessary ritual of the farming year had been completed. And we have been told that Suetonius was surprised by the revolt. British tribesmen, like the citizen soldiers of pre-Marian Rome, were farmers. Their neglect of their land through their absence on campaign could have terrible consequences, as is amply illustrated by the long-term effects of Hannibal's Italian campaign on the social organisation of the Italian countryside. The enforced absence of the owners of small farms who were serving in the Roman armies, and the consequent disruption of the agricultural calendar of works and days, accomplished more for Hannibal's cause than his military depredations.

Tacitus, in his remarks about the massacre committed by the Iceni during their brief ascendancy, shows a sensitive understanding of the attitude of the archaic warrior. He says that the Celts of Boudicca's army killed promiscuously as if they were taking revenge in advance for the sufferings they knew that they would have to endure when Roman power inevitably reasserted itself. War was a continuing dimension of human experience and could not be expected to end with complete and final victory. Whatever the future might hold, honour must be preserved, and wholesale slaughter would keep the Iceni in credit for a long time. The atrocity with which, as Dio tells us, female prisoners were impaled on stakes after their breasts had been cut off and stuffed into their mouths probably indicates an intrinsic cruelty in the cult of the Celtic goddess of war — here the relevant deity is probably a goddess called Andrasta or Andarta. The prospective desperation mentioned by Tacitus may have exacerbated the fury with which they sought further aid from their goddess by means of these sacrifices. There is no need to introduce the idea of a ceremonial bonding on the part of the participants of such horrors by which they would be irrevocably committed in loyalty to each other by their involvement in atrocious acts. In this context we might adduce the alleged ritual infanticides of secret political societies in Classical Athens, or, as Dudley and Webster say in connection with the rising of Boudicca, the ceremonial atrocities attributed to the administration of the Mau Mau oath in Kenya (1962: 69). We have no reason, however, to suppose that the acts perpetrated by the followers of Boudicca were intrinsically unacceptable to British as distinct from Roman custom.

The Romans had a professional army, even though at this stage of the revolt it was dispersed and disrupted. The sheer energy of the British attack came near to ending Roman rule in the island. Seventy thousand Romans and their adherents were killed in Camulodunum, Verulamium and Londinium. The army of Boudicca was the traditional Celtic hosting, which on its first impact can carry all before it, but which ultimately succumbs when faced by a more organised and disciplined force. One of the last large-scale examples of this ancient mode of warfare was to be seen at Culloden, when the assembled clansmen, eager for the charge and impatient of tactical restraints, called out 'Claidheamh mòr! Claidheamh mòr!' Adherence to this style of warfare points to the persistence in Celtic culture of the theme of heroic pride, a resistance to the submersion of the honour-seeking personality in a drilled group. The consequences of this mode of battle for the Celtic peoples have been disastrous. In the final battle of Boudicca's war, eighty thousand British died. Her tribe was crushed and enslaved. She and her daughters had killed themselves to avoid the destined dishonour of capture and execution. During his period of office as procurator, Julius Classicanus, himself by origin one of the Treveri of Gaul, tried to persuade Nero to be more lenient to the British than Suetonius was inclined to be. In fact, Roman rule was imposed a little less harshly after a war which had shaken Roman confidence so seriously in this part of their Empire.

For a time there was a period of relative quiet which could hardly be called British acquiescence, but it allowed the process of Romanisation to go forward. The north remained a source of anxiety for the Romans as for successive rulers of Britain. In 122 AD the raids from the north became so destructive that a wall was constructed across the country from Wallsend to Bowness. This seemed to be the effective limit of Roman power in the emperorship of Hadrian. He was conscious of Augustus' doctrine that the Empire should be kept within defensible boundaries. In 162 AD, Antoninus Pius moved north from the boundary represented by the wall constructed by Hadrian. A wall was built from the Forth to the Clyde. It was of turf and along its length it was studded with carefully placed stone forts. Neither the Hadrianic nor the Antonine walls proved capable of containing determined uprisings in the Scottish lowland area. The most serious outburst was in 196 AD when the walls were overrun and the security of the south was endangered. In 208 AD Septimius Severus defeated the Caledones and Picti, and rebuilt the walls. He decided to regard the Antonine wall as an outwork rather than a reliable frontier. The lowland tribes of Scotland were left to defend themselves as best they could with its aid. A buffer zone was thereby provided for the south. For most of the third and fourth centuries AD, this defensive system served reasonably well. The Britons of southern Scotland came to regard the Picts and Caledones as a more pressing menace than the Romans.

In 285 AD, a Belgic called Carausius was appointed to a naval and military command in order to rid the North Sea, English Channel and adjacent seaways of pirates. He had campaigned successfully in Gaul against the Bagaudae, an aggregation of deserters and dispossessed peasants who were terrorising the country and who, in various guises, would haunt Europe for centuries. He seized the opportunity offered by his almost unrestricted command and made himself the independent emperor of his sphere of influence. Central government was powerless to dispose of him. He defeated the attempt made to confront him on the sea in 288 AD. Until he was murdered by one of his generals in 293 AD, he remained in possession of his personal empire. But before this time, his power and prestige were already in decline. Constantius had captured his main naval base at Boulogne and was building a fleet with which to attack him. These considerations made him a more likely victim of assassination. His murderer Allectus took over his dead commander's rule, and survived in possession of it for three years. In 286 AD he was defeated by Constantius. He died in battle and a phase of Celtic independence, albeit one which was reliant on Frankish mercenaries, was concluded.

Magnentius' efforts to make himself emperor were substantially dependent on British forces. In 351 AD, he was defeated and he died in 353 AD. Britain remained in bad odour with the Emperor Constantius II (*imp*. 337–361 AD) who suppressed many of the native aristocracy for their support of Magnentius. This further weakened the country and made it more vulnerable to attack from Picts, Scots, Attacots and Saxons. The countship of the 'Saxon Shore', which involved the reinforcement and construction of coastal fortifications in southern and south-eastern Britain, had been established in 342 AD.

The year 367 AD saw a massive conjunction of raids by the tribes mentioned above, with the possible addition of Franks. The country was thrown into chaos for a year. The count of the Saxon Shore was killed and the chief military commander of Britain, the *dux Britannorum*, was taken prisoner. Britain was rescued from protracted pillage and raiding by the Count (*comes*) Theodosius. Hadrian's wall showed its incapacity as a line of defence in a time of crisis. Determined aggression from the tribes of the north was not restrained by it. In 367 AD it was overrun with its garrison still in post and it had to be reconstructed in later years.

The conspicuous success of Maximus as a general in these wars encouraged his soldiers to declare him emperor in 383 AD. Without weakening the watch garrisons of the Saxon Shore, he proceeded to Gaul, where his activities contributed to the chaos of the continental empire at that time. Maximus was not British, but may have been from Spain. He was married to a British princess. His ambition was inflamed by growing British dissatisfaction at the apparent preference on the part of Gratian (*imp.* 367–383 AD) for employing foreign mercenary troops. In fact Gratian was deserted by his Frankish mercenaries and was killed at Lugdunum by Andragathius, an agent of Maximus. Maximus embarked on a brief and brilliant career which did little to discomfit the Suebi, Alani and other barbarians who were preparing to tear the Western Empire asunder. His main achievement was a weakening of the connection between Britain and the Roman continent. He may be said to have debilitated the whole frontier position of the Empire. He had the decency to execute Vallio and Merobaudes, the Frankish commanders who had betrayed his rival, but he did not embark on a wholesale killing of opponents. He attempted to conciliate Theodosius, his present enemy and former patron. His overtures were accepted out of necessity rather than forgiveness. Theodosius was not in a position to attack him. At this time Maximus was the toughest and most wily war-lord at large in the Empire. Theodosius and Valentinian had no option but to recognise him as an Augustus, and the Emperor of Gaul, Spain and Britain. On the pretext of offering Valentinian auxiliaries for his war in Pannonia, Maximus got leave to send his forces through the Alpine passes. Valentinian's advisers had opposed this in vain: soon Maximus was in possession of Italy and Valentinian was in flight to Thessalonica. When Theodosius heard of Valentinian's troubles, he moved forces through half the Roman world from Constantinople to bring him assistance. Maximus was defeated and captured at Aquileia. He was subsequently beheaded.

This chain of extraordinary events, whose effects impinged on the heartland of empire, originated in the marginal island of Britain. Another outgrowth of this province, whose very remoteness made it a credible *seminarium* of rebellions, was the emperorship of Constantine III (*imp.* 407–411 AD) who had nothing in common with Constantine the Great (*imp.* 307–337 AD) but his name. In 407 AD, a rebellion of soldiers in Britain, after an apparently abortive beginning, declared this happily named officer to be emperor. There was no course open to him but acceptance followed by the hazards of unavoidable action on the wider stage of imperial warfare. Accordingly, he took his army to Gaul. The continent was inadequately defended and little stood in his way. The Emperor Honorius (*imp.* 395–423 AD) put the problem into the hands of his Gothic generals, Stilicho and Sarus. The forces of Constantine were badly mauled and two of his best officers, Justinian and Nervigastes, killed. His generals of the second line, Gerontius and Edobincus, retrieved the situation. Honorius found that he could not avoid recognising Constantine as emperor. He no doubt comforted himself with the thought that Constantine might prove to be a useful counterbalance for him in his struggle with the Goths. In the long term, however, he had plans for Constantine which were not at all to his advantage.

Constantine advanced into Italy, in the expectation that he might eliminate Honorius. His progress was checked at Verona by the defection of his general Gerontius, and he had to move quickly back to Gaul. Constans, the son of Constantine, was captured and executed at Vienne, and the forces of Gerontius hemmed Constantine in at Arles (Arelatum). On behalf of Honorius, what might have been a rescue of Constantine was led by Constantius. He drove Gerontius off, but continued to besiege Constantine in the interest of his own emperor, until he persuaded him to surrender on terms, one of which was that he would be allowed to survive. But Constantine and his other son, Julian, were taken to Italy and executed there.

Entwined in this course of events is the career of the British Celt, Gerontius, the disloyal general of Constantine. He turned against his patron, Constans, the son of Constantine, because he was not appointed to accompany him into Spain, where Constantine had sent him to secure the country. He vented his anger when he eventually captured Constans at Vienne. He was a formidable leader. His forces were more than a match for those of Constantine at Arles, but many of them deserted him for the army of Constantius when he arrived to raise the siege of Arles. Gerontius retreated to Spain where he had already installed one of his friends, Maximus, as 'emperor'. His soldiers in Spain thought him a proven failure and plotted to kill him. When the crisis came, he defended himself with fierce courage, but eventually foreseeing the end, he killed first his wife, then a personal servant and at last, himself. His suicide was possibly consummated in much the same spirit as that of earlier Celtic leaders who killed themselves when they realised defeat. His death scene must have been worthy of the sculptors of Pergamum.

From as early as the second century AD, Roman forces in Britain had been subject to being withdrawn in order to fight on frontiers which were thought to be of more importance to the integrity of empire than a remote island. The Roman armies finally left in 407 AD. The British rid themselves of the remnants of Roman officialdom and set about clearing the country of their Germanic enemies. In this they enjoyed some initial success. Not much was to be hoped from Rome: in 410 AD Honorius wrote to the Britons, informing them that in future they would have to be responsible for their own defence. Cities had a new lease of life as centres of administration. For some time previous to this citizens had been constructing walls as a measure of protection in an increasingly insecure country. According to Procopius, from 410 AD 'tyrants' ruled in Britain. This may mean that native kingships were recreated after centuries of burial under the elaborate detritus of Classical culture. One of the most prominent of these kings, Vortigern, brought in a new wave of Germans as mercenaries to cope with the increasing aggressiveness of the Picts and Scots. The fact that the British population had been depleted by plague made this a necessary measure; but the decimation of native manpower itself would be an inducement for such mercenaries to rebel. They did so in 442 AD when they moved out of their allocated zones, and took possession of large tracts of land. In 446 AD, the famous communication known as the 'Laments of the British' was sent to the Roman general Aetius. It complained that the Britons were caught between the foreign invaders and the sea, and would he, please, come to their rescue. No response is recorded. Archaeology reveals that the German intruders settled their squalid huts along the south coast in the territory of the Regni without evident opposition.

In the fifth and sixth centuries AD, it is likely that the highland zones of Britain, in which Celtic customs and society had survived Roman influence, were in a position to assume leadership of the whole country and offer opposition to the invading barbarians. Insecurity brought people together in concentrated settlements and estates. For a person of little or no property the options were desperately simple: either become a *colonus* (a proto-feudal serf) or a robber or starve. In addition to the essentially British core of upland England, there was also Wales, which had been held down by force rather than Romanised. The influence of the highland zone in the twilight period of Roman rule is illustrated by the story of the North British chief Cunedda who took his warriors into Wales as *foederati* at the suggestion of the Romans themselves towards the end of the fourth century AD. His descendants were dynasts of small Welsh kingdoms in later centuries (Jackson 1953: 116).

The Celtic theme was also vigorous in the south. Celtic culture persisted in many urban centres and was by no means overwhelmed by the veteran element in the population. Celtic names appear in Latin dedicatory inscriptions and there is evidence of mixed marriages (Salway 1981: 685). Inscriptions were in Latin, not Celtic, in Roman Britain, but Celtic words can appear in Latin dedications, as in the epithet 'Rigae' applied to Mars in an inscription from Malton (Ramm 1978: 68).

The continuance of Celtic influence after the Roman withdrawal is apparent in the account given by Gildas (*De Excid. Brit.* 25) of Aurelius Ambrosianus, whom he describes as the last of the Romans. Aurelius seems to have waged war against the Saxons in the late fifth century AD: he is said to have tried to recreate Roman tactics and discipline, which may explain the success which he enjoyed. He does not give the impression of the traditional chief of a tribe or *tyrannus*. He did not agree with Vortigern, who certainly came into the latter category. It is not known whether Arthur, the legendary leader of the British resistance, was Romanised as 'Aurelius', or whether he was a *tyrannus* in the native style (Jackson 1953: 115).

Nor was the native religion of Britain eliminated in a Christianised empire. Celtic paganism still survived in the fourth century AD: the Lydney temple was dedicated to Nodens at a date not later than 364 AD. Votive offerings found on the site indicate by their richness that the precinct was used by leading persons of the community, and was not a peasant survival (Chadwick 1963: 35).

In highland districts the Celtic language survived and outlived Latin. Latin was the language of civil affairs, trade, military operations and education. Latin was also the language of the written word in inscriptions and other documents. Celtic seems to have been the native tongue of the greater part of the population. The Latin of Britain was archaic in comparison with that of other Romanised countries. Tacitus says that Agricola first instituted the Roman liberal education amongst the upper classes of Britain (*Agr.* 21). The character of the surviving examples of British Latin suggests that it may have been learned at school rather than in the home (Salway 1981: 506–7). As a 'culture' language, it did not develop a widely used vernacular. Many words, especially those which concern material culture, were borrowed into Celtic from Latin. The Britons seem to have taken over about eight hundred words from Latin. British and Latin seem to have had much in common in their morphologies and in the basic sounds of their respective speeches (Jackson 1953: 77). There was no obvious intellectual difficulty facing the speaker of one of the languages who wanted to learn the other. That Latin did not achieve dominance is a measure of the relatively shallow depth of British Romanisation. We can suppose that there were many bilingual speakers.

Romanised Britain produced an intellectual of international standing in the philosopher Pelagius. Augustine, Orosius, Prosper and Mercadius regard him as a Briton. Jerome thinks that he is Scotic and makes snide remarks about porridge (Ferguson 1956: 40). Another tradition makes him a Welsh Briton, his name the classicised version of something like 'Morigena' or 'Morgan'. There is no reason to suppose that his Greco-Roman name 'Pelagius' means that he was Greek or Roman. His associate Caelestis was said to be from Ireland (Ferguson ibid.). He evidently had a Classical education.

In Rome about 405 AD, he began to put forward views about Christianity which disturbed many of the authorities of the Church. Whether or not he was ever ordained as a priest is open to question: he claims to speak as a layman. One of his teachings was that wealth and the materialism which was rife in his time should be rejected; he did not advocate poverty, but a simple sufficiency. He advocated also a life of purity without masochistic excesses of denial. He emphasised the importance of free will and, consonant with such a view, he deprecated the doctrine of original sin, and argued the possibility of attaining a sinless condition. He taught that no man was by nature a slave and that God did not ordain such a condition.

His ideas about sinlessness obviously ran athwart the Christian view of the crucifixion as the supreme and universal atonement. But this was only one of the problems raised by his philosophy. Though his views, as might be expected, were condemned as heretical, his influence persisted for some time, especially in Celtic countries. The theory that he was influenced by druidic notions of deity is attractive but cannot be proved. His ideas have the distinct flavour of Hellenic critical thinking. The influence of Stoicism cannot be excluded.

Pelagius may very well be claimed as the first known Celtic philosopher to offer a substantial challenge to the assumptions of the intellectual world of his time. Another Briton, Patricius, the son of Calpornus, contributed to the spread of Classical civilisation in his missionary field of Ireland. This was a by-product of his fervid spiritual energy rather than primarily philosophical or literary interests.

We may end by saying that Britain seems to have been partly classicised by the Roman occupation, but was never fully integrated into the cultural order of the Mediterranean *oikoumenē*. Throughout its connection with Rome, Britain was a source of trouble and rebellions disproportionate to its size or its significance as a frontier province. Its disturbances upset the continent: its position in relation to Gaul made such effects inevitable. And this was a factor which provided Julius Caesar with one of his pretexts for landing in Britain in 55 BC and 54 BC. Roman hopes that Britain might prove to be a source of wealth were also disappointed. There is doubt whether the province was ever an economic success. Cicero's disappointment at the lack of silver in the area first touched by Caesar was in the long term justified (*Att.* 4.16).

12

Ausonius and the Civilisation of
Later Roman Gaul

The Gaulish variant of Roman civilisation produced literature of distinction in the fourth and fifth centuries AD. In the fourth century AD especially, a period of peace in Gaul, except for the areas which confronted the territories of the barbarians, enabled literature and literary studies to flourish. Though this interval of civilisation was ended in the fifth century AD by invasions such as had dislocated Roman ways of living in other countries of the West in third century AD, this temporary time of flowering had an individual Gaulish flavour.

Decimus Magnus Ausonius was born in Burdigala (Bordeaux) around 310 AD. When he had completed his legal studies in Burdigala, he took to the profession of grammarian and teacher of rhetoric and worked in this successfully for many years. As his reputation grew, he was in due course invited by the Emperor Valentinian to become the tutor of his son Gratian. From this point his career advanced with rapidity: he was made a *comes* (count) and a *quaestor* under Valentinian. Gratian appointed him *praefectus* of Latium, of Libya, and of Gaul, with the crowning honour of consulship in 379 AD. After Gratian's death, he remained in the capital during the usurpation of Maximus. Nobody seems to have regarded him as a threat. Theodosius wrote to him kindly in his retirement, which suggests that he remained in good standing with the government. Ausonius spent his last years in retirement in Gaul, and he may have written many of his surviving works in this time of peaceful retreat (Fisher 1981 34 ff). He died around the year 390 AD.

In Ausonius' lifetime the period of Gaulish national revival and quasi-imperial status was a vivid memory. This period of Celtic independence, brief though it was, released the vitality of a national self-confidence which had formed under the pressures of Romanisation and, at the same time, had been nurtured and sheltered by Roman power. Gaul had for a time seemed to be a viable political unit. There had been Celtic emperors such as Victorinus and P. Esuvius Tetricus, whose *gentilicium* recalls the Celtic god Esus, just as the names of Victorinus and his mother Victoria must echo some Celtic names of the kind which begin with /Boudo/ (D.E. Evans 1967: 156ff). The rulers were not of the most satisfactory, but they were at least of Gaul.

Within decades of the death of Ausonius, disruptive invasions would once more swamp the basic Celtic culture, but the texture of local identities was too tightly woven ever to be completely unravelled and Celtic Gaul would over the centuries take its captors at least partly captive.

Like others of this time Ausonius moved from the academic life into government. He is of greater interest to us than some others, because his writings have the aroma of locality and a certain national spirit. His work is personal. In some of its idiosyncrasies it seems to have elements in common with the insular Celtic literature of later times as well as with the writings that came from the Latinised world of Gaul in the medieval centuries.

His mother's family seems at one time to have possessed considerable lands, and to have been part of the nobility of the Aedui. His father was a self-made success in his profession as doctor. There is no reason to suppose that the elder Ausonius was of slave origins, but his personality and background are obscure (Fisher 1981: 3). Ausonius himself says (*Dom.* 4.9–10) that his father was not fluent in Latin, but had an adequate knowledge of Greek. This comment does not entail that Greek was the native language of his father. If we accept this, together with the hesitancy of his Latin, and the interesting, but not decisive fact that his son admits to having had difficulty at school with his Greek, we might infer that Ausonius' father was a native speaker of the Celtic of Gaul or perhaps Iberian. Some native language is likely to have survived in this part of Gaul (Sidonius *Ep.* 3.3; Sulpicius Severus *Dial.* 1.27). Given the size and populous nature of Gaul, it would seem difficult to suppose that Celtic speech had been eliminated by the third or fourth century AD in a substantial part of the country. It would be the speech of the ordinary people at large, but the custom of Celtic peoples would tend to preclude its use in literature, for which the international language of the West, Latin, would be the appropriate medium.

Saint Jerome says that the Galatians of Asia Minor speak almost the same language as the Treveri of Gaul. It has been suspected that Jerome (331–420 AD) was using a source as old as Poseidonius for this comment. His words, however, are: 'The Galatae have their own language and it is almost the same as that of the Treveri, nor does it matter if they have subsequently varied it to some extent'. This is not necessarily an antiquarian reference. In fact he lived for a time in Trèves. His remarks occur in his commentary on St Paul's *Epistle to the Galatians* 2.3 (Migne *PL* 26.357). In the third century AD Ulpian had said that Gaulish, along with Latin, Greek and Carthaginian, counted as an acceptable testamentary language (Schmidt 1983: 1010): this would be an interesting exception to the general avoidance of Celtic in written documents. Though few inscriptions from Gaul after the first century AD are in Celtic, it remained for centuries the spoken language of the majority. In the Principate of Tiberius, Latin was beginning to make a little headway in Gallia Narbonensis. In the second century AD, Irenaeus refers to the influence of Celtic on his speaking of Greek (Migne *PG* 7.444). Sulpicius Severus (fourth century AD) refers to speaking *Celtice* or *Gallice* (*Dial.* 1.27). Sometimes it is supposed that the latter is a Gallo-Latin dialect as distinct from Celtic language: the separation of *Celtice* from *Gallice* could be taken as merely an example of stylistic *variatio* for emphasis, so that both words mean the same. We cannot be sure what is meant, apart from the fact that the only acceptable language from the writer's point of view is 'Martinus'. 'Speak either *Celtice* or *Gallice*, but speak of Martinus,' he says. All we can say is that he is conscious of language differences and that the two modes of speech he mentions are less familiar to him than Latin. My guess would be that he refers to Celtic languages. Sidonius Apollinaris says that Ecdicus' urgings turned the upper classes of Gaul away from their native tongue to Latin. Sidonius was writing in the fifth century AD (Haarhoff 1920: 16ff).

Celtic traditions were remembered amongst the intellectual class: Ausonius says that a fellow professor in Burdigala, Attius Patera, came from a druidic family (*Praef.* 4.10; 10.27). The disturbances of the previous century of imperial crisis had in another cultural sphere caused a revival of localism. In pottery style, there was a 'Celtic Revival' (Drinkwater 1983: 216ff). Yet in the increasingly chaotic times of the fifth century AD, Gaul retained longest of all the countries of the Western Empire the vestiges of the old Classical culture. In the case of Sidonius

Apollinaris, composition in a culturally sanctified tongue had taken the place of creative literature. Sidonius records the names of many authors, both in prose and verse, such as Consentius, Lampridius, Leo, Sepaudus, Thaumastus, Tonantius, Secundinus, Ferreolus, Pragmatius, Heronius. Greek was disappearing from Gaul. Germanic dialects were not considered suitable literary vehicles any more than Celtic. Venantius Fortunatius (7.8.3) makes fun of Teutonic 'leudi' (*Lieder*) and the barbarous 'harpa'.

The reputation of barbarity had, of course, pursued Gaul down the centuries, and to the end she was haunted by this product of ancient prejudice and fear. Cato the Elder (3rd–2nd century BC) had said that the greater part of Gaul pursued two objectives with the utmost energy: one of these was military glory; the other was eloquence. According to Julius Caesar, Mercurius, the patron of communication, was the most popular god of Gaul (*BG* 6.17). On the other hand the Emperor Julian (4th century AD) criticises the Celts for their boorishness and insensitivity (*Misopogon* 342). His view of them was that they were completely lacking in cultivation. Martial had passed this same judgement on Burdigala (*Epigr.* 9.32), and St Jerome condemns Celtic incapacity to learn and readiness to believe anything (Commentary on St Paul's *Epistle to the Galatians* 2.3; Migne *PL* 26.357). But Julius Caesar had said that the Celts possessed a natural gift for style and language.

Massilia was preferred as a place for the education of their young by many Roman parents because of its healthy atmosphere and strict way of life. In the south-east part of Gaul, furthest away from the troubled frontier, the city of Burdigala became a most important centre of education. Like Massilia, it preserved elements of an old, strict ethos as well as a high degree of Classical culture. Like some other professors, Ausonius broke through the rigid class structures of the Empire to reach the highest public office (Hopkins 1961). Some exceptions to the rule of caste were made in the case of individuals of marked intellectual distinction. The main argument for their advancement would be the usefulness of intelligence at high levels of bureaucracy. In this they were following the footsteps of those knights and, indeed, freedmen of the early Principates whose abilities were recruited for the management of an increasingly complex empire.

Elevation to high office as the culmination of a literary career was not unprecedented. The opportunity was offered to Horace by Augustus, and refused. Quintilian obtained consular honours. 'If

Fortune is willing,' says Juvenal (7.19ff), 'the rhetorician becomes consul, and the consul, rhetorician'. In one of his letters, Pliny quotes, to the same purpose, Licinianus, a praetor who was exiled and set up as a rhetorician (*Ep.* 4.11.5): 'What games you play, Fortune: you make senators out of professors, and professors out of senators'.

Ausonius' father does not seem to have come of distinguished stock. The name 'Ausonius', 'man of the west', could only too easily be that of an eastern slave or freedman who had come to live in the west. There is no proof of anything of the kind in the case of the elder Ausonius. Nothing in his father's history stood in the way of Ausonius' being advanced in his career. The fact that he was born and bred in Gaul was an advantage to him at a time when his countrymen were coming into prominence in the wider world of imperial administration. His mother's family, as we have seen, was of old respectability. These Arborii had fallen on hard times through being proscribed. Ausonius' maternal grandfather, Arborius, evidently was willing to ally his family with a poor but able physician of humble origins. The family of the Arborii were hereditary priests of Apollo Belenus. This itself could indicate high status in the Celtic community. Whether or not the office meant that they had a druidic background, it is impossible to say (Bachelier 1960). The association of druids with sacred woodland precincts called *nemeta* implies a suggestive connection with the name 'Arborius'.

There may be a connection between the name of the sister of Ausonius who was called Dryadia, and the 'Arborius' of which it is the Greek translation. This sister may have been the only convinced Christian of the family (*Epigr.* 258). While it is possible that these names had a cult significance, on the other hand, they could be merely pretentious. Ausonius' son was called Hesperius, a translation of Ausonius which may dilute any atmosphere of druidism that hangs about the name of Dryadia. His maternal aunt was Veneria; Idalia, his cousin (Bachelier 1960: 96). His colleague Attusius had also the name Delphidius, which again might suggest a cult association. Other such names occur: there was Minervius, an orator of Burdigala, and Jovinus. High-sounding names need not indicate distinguished family or priestly status. Perhaps many of the upper-middle class of the province had hereditary connection with divine functions which encouraged the general use of such personal names, which represent a phase of the *interpretatio Romana* of native cults. We have seen that Belenus was Apollo Belenus. Some references in the poems of Ausonius emphasise the triple character of Diana, Hecate and Mercury. There may be in this a cross-reference to the three-fold nature of certain Celtic deities (Bachelier 1960: 99).

When Ausonius held public office, Gauls had already for some time been replacing Pannonians in the higher responsibilities of the civil service. Gaulish ascendancy was badly shaken when Rufinus fell from favour in 395 AD, carrying some compatriots with him. Lachanius, the father of the poet Rutilius Namatianus, seems to have survived. Irrespective of the social grade that they occupied, the Gauls had that Celtic reverence for old family which we can discern even in the dying notes of seventeenth century AD panegyric poetry in Ireland. The Gallic aristocrats liked to arrogate to themselves ancestors who were distinguished in earlier history (Syme 1958: 796). Sidonius Apollinaris says that Polemius, a man of Gaulish origin, and *praefectus Galliarum* in 471 AD, claimed Cornelius Tacitus amongst his forefathers (14.22). Strings of long names record or pretend to important ancestry. The Gauls brought to imperial administration a sense of aristocratic style which distinguished them from the Pannonians who were professional bureaucrats. The senatorial idea, which for some time had lain in quiet desuetude in Rome, began temporarily to revive.

Ausonius' career was a part of this Gaulish predominance. He seems to have encouraged a tendency which was already in evidence, that of aiding the appointment of friends and relatives to posts in government. Jointly with his son Hesperius, he held the prefectures of Gaul, Italy and Africa in 378 AD. He also favoured his own profession of letters. It is likely that he was responsible for the order issued to the prefect of Gaul, Antonius, that state funds should be used to appoint distinguished men to be professors of rhetoric in the principal cities (Fisher 1981: 34). Valentinian had already established a health service under which doctors in Rome were paid from public monies so that the poor could get medical treatment. Ausonius procured for his father, who at the time was well advanced in his eighties, the post of *praefectus* of Illyricum. Even if the post was mainly honorary, this appointment can hardly have been discouraging to Rome's enemies beyond the Danube. Hesperius' appointment would by our standards also seem undesirable, but he showed himself to be a capable and honest administrator.

Others of Ausonius' Gallic connections found public appointments during his period of influence. His son-in-law Thalassius was *vicarius* of Macedonia in 376–377 AD, and subsequently proconsul in Africa. He also returned eventually to Burdigala. A certain Arborius, the son of Ausonius' cousin, was *comes sacrarum largitionum* in 379 AD, and *praefectus* of Rome. The Cataphronius who was *vicarius* of Italy in 376–377 AD may have been connected with Cataphronia, the aunt of Ausonius (Fisher 1981: 36).

Other notable Gauls had careers which overlapped or included that of Ausonius. Q. Aurelius Symmachus (350–420 AD), was consul in 391 AD. He was an honourable man of Roman patrician instincts and relaxed disposition towards the world. Though we have some specimens of the adulatory speeches he made to Gratian, his most important literary legacy is the collection of letters which his son compiled after his death, and produced after the manner of Pliny's Letters. These are full of information about the times in which he lived and the prominent men who were his friends.

Symmachus was a friend of Ausonius who had come to know him during a period of residence in Gaul. From his letters comes information about several men of Gaulish origins who made successful official careers at this time. There was a medical-rhetorical axis of influence which came from Gallic predominance in the science of medicine as well as in literature. In this connection, we can mention Marcellus, who, after a career which varied in its fortunes, retired to Gaul to compose his textbook on medicine. His work contains Celtic names of plants, healing spells and passages of verse which may be of his own composition. His career antedates that of Ausonius, and he may have been acquainted with the elder Ausonius at Burdigala. Other Gallic worthies were the historian Eutropius, who held his first public appointment in 361 AD; also Flavius Afranius Synagrius, Potitus, Claudius Lachanius and Drepanius. Ambrosius (d. 397 AD) was the son of a *praefectus* of Gaul. He abandoned his work in the public service for a life in the Church and was an able defender of ecclesiastical privilege against the encroachments of secular power.

Sulpicius Severus of Aquitaine wrote a brief history of the world, using very respectable sources. One book of these *Chronica* survives. His life-span was approximately 365–425 AD. He was a priest, the friend of Paulinus and of Martin of Tours, whose biography he wrote. Martin's struggles with the devil, his visions, his hearing of the voices of Christ and the angels belong to a different dimension of the mind than that which emerges in the poems of Ausonius. Another man of Gaul, Quintus Iulius Hilario, who was a contemporary of Sulpicius Severus, also wrote a history of the world. Ausonius addressed his *Technopaegnion*, that curious piece of versifying expertise, to one of his kinsmen and pupils who made a name in literature: Meropius Pontius Anicius Paulinus of Burdigala (353–432 AD). When Theodosius defeated Eugenius, who had been elevated to the imperial throne by the Frank, Arbogast, Paulinus celebrated the occasion with a speech in praise of the new Emperor. In 389 AD he became converted to Christianity. Much of his writing is in favour of the Christian religion. He became bishop of Nola in 409 AD.

Before we consider the literary work of Ausonius, another poet of Gaul, younger than the latter, claims our attention. This is Claudius Rutilius Namatianus. Perhaps the Claudius who presents a letter of introduction from Symmachus to Ausonius was Claudius Lachanius, the father of the poet (Fisher 1981: 99). Rutilius was a member of the second generation of this Gallic establishment. His poetry and the personality revealed in it show more polish and less individual eccentricity than the more innocent and varied talent of Ausonius. There is also less flamboyant rhetoric in his work. He seems to look forward to Sidonius Apollinaris (430–479 AD), who was the last elegant defender of old Latinity, a prisoner of the Goths, against whom he defended his country, a bishop, and eventually, a Christian saint (Fisher 1981: 100).

The literary reputation of Rutilius rests on his poem *De Reditu Suo* (*'On his Return'*), a large portion of which survives to bear witness to his command of the elegaic literary form and metre. It is pure and classical in shape and diction. He says that 'the Gaulish countryside calls him its native,' but he held important office in the Roman court and was *praefectus urbi* of Rome in 413 AD. His journey home was delayed by wartime conditions. The menace of the Goths (Getae) forced him to travel by sea. He probably wrote his poem soon after he had completed his journey home. He saw Rome as having been attacked and injured, but not devastated, by the barbarians. There is no note of despair in the poetry of Rutilius, but rather the calm promise of revival and revenge. Brennus' invasion of Italy and the Roman defeat at the battle of the Allia (390 BC) are adduced as parallels to the latest disaster which carry the assurance of ultimate victory. In this he was mistaken: he misjudged the desperate case of the Empire. He thought its resurgence was inevitable. We can scarcely blame him. It can be difficult, especially for the resilient imagination of the creative mind, accurately to read the entrails of a contemporary catastrophe.

Judged by Classical standards, Rutilius must be considered a better artist than Ausonius, but he is much less individual in his writing, and his work exudes less personality. Like the poem of Ausonius on the river Mosella, Rutilius' *'Return'* describes a journey. Though an obvious generic ancestor is Horace's 'Journey to Brundisium' (*Satires* 1.3), the love of place and natural beauty which we see in such poets as Catullus may also be an influential factor. Though the Irish *Dindshenchas* may have their roots in the intelligence reports memorised by ancient warriors, they reveal an appreciation of nature which seems to be a characteristic of much Celtic poetry. The tendency of Rutilius to engage in digressions and *personalia* calls Ausonius to mind. In addition to Classical influences, we may see in Ausonius, Rutilius and Catullus the inherited genes of an old Celtic oral poetic tradition.

Rutilius was a pagan who had the characteristic Roman dislike of Judaic and Christian beliefs and practices. There is an argument in favour of regarding him as the last truly Roman poet, rather than Sidonius. Ausonius divagated boldly from the Classical tradition which Rutilius observed, but his long poem, the *Mosella*, which traces the course of a famous Gaulish river, is mainly Classical in style. Some of his minor poems also show him capable of accomplished Classicism, but this short epic might have been composed in one of the two or three preceding centuries; to such an extent do the modes and commonplaces of the established literary education prevail in it. Many of his other poems are personal and didactic, recording and presenting information which would be of use to students, friends, or the poet himself. The personal element in some of them could remind us of the individual viewpoint in the neoterics of the first century BC, several of whom were of families of Celtic origin in northern Italy. In the *Mosella*, Ausonius is not slavish or mechanical in his use of phrases and ideas from Classical Roman poets. His reminiscences of Lucan and Virgil are deliberately placed and they increase in number where the intensity of the poem rises (Posani 1962: 517). They are also purposely varied by Ausonius so that they have the same effect as a comic pun, as when *glauca fluentia*, 'green pleasaunces of the river', resonates Virgil's *rauca fluentia*, the cacophony of the rivers of hell in *Aeneid* 6.327. This provides a contrast between the delights of the Mosella and the ugliness of the underworld. Also it discloses a manipulative attitude to the poetry of the past which goes beyond mere imitation reinforced by rhetorical training. It is meta-literary: the creative use of a dominant language by somebody who has become aware that he has forgotten his own native tongue. We may think of James Joyce's creative adaptation of the English language in *Finnegans Wake*, or the works of his less talented precursor, Francis Mahony ('Father Prout'). Sometimes Ausonius imitates the rhythm of another poet and alters only a word or two:

> *lata Caledoniis talis pictura Britannos* — *Mos.* 68
> *unda Caledonios fallet turbata Britannos* — Lucan 6.68

Here the rhythm is the same and two key words are retained.

It is not surprising in the light of such artistic self-consciousness that Ausonius brings into his description of the Mosella references to his own native Burdigala. His poem ends with a mention of the Garonne, the river of his home city. In his *Ordo Urbium Nobilium XX*, we find Burdigala standing last in an exposed but by no means dishonourable position (Fisher 1981: 211f).

The *Mosella* is a poem of indisputable quality, full of delight in the beauty of landscape. His patriotic feelings, like those of Rutilius, are directed not merely to Rome, but to Gaul, indeed to a particular district of Gaul which is home (Fisher, ibid.). Even if they enjoyed great success elsewhere, these Gaulish men of talent did not forget their native place, but returned to it.

Like the Cisalpine poets of an earlier century, Ausonius had an element of fluent gaiety in his temperament which is essentially alien to the Roman spirit of literature, even in those works which are intended to be funny. Ausonius is certainly conscious of Catullus: at the beginning of his *Griphus* or '*Puzzle*', he parodies the first line of the first poem of Catullus' collection of poems, the *Libellus*. For Catullus' 'To whom shall I present this charming, new, small book?' he substitutes 'To whom shall I present this repellent, rude, small book?' He is fully aware of the playful component in the talent of his predecessor. Ausonius also shares with the north Italian 'neoteric' poets a certain naïvety, combined with subtle and perceptive intelligence. The neoterics were attracted to the studied ironies, emotion and personalism of the poets of Alexandria because they appealed to some assumptions about the nature and texture of poetry which were part of their own inheritance. Ausonius' approach to poetry had some of this formalism and some of this sense of play. While we are saying this, we may as well add that in medieval and modern Celtic poetry the strand of satire and learning persists. The best of Ausonius is his personal poetry in which he addresses his comments, ideas and feelings to his friends in a way which can remind us of Catullus in his most humane and sympathetic mood. Ausonius' verses about Bissula, the little German slave girl who was his mistress and consoled his widowed years, are tender, affectionate and also shy.

He has a genuine and innocent love of words. In the *'grammaticomastix'*, 'whip of letters', which he invented after the fashion of the *Homeromastix*, 'Homer-whip', in his *Technopaegnion*, he gives a humorous personality to verbal monstrosities, as Joyce does in *Finnegans Wake*. Coinage was a game which he happily and irreverently played. Bold fusions such as *'Dionysopoietes'*, and *'memigmenobarbaron'*, 'mixed barbarism' (it does not translate well), remind Fisher of Rabelais (1981: 91). Lists of towns: the *Ordo Urbium Nobilium*; lists of the professors at Burdigala; riddles; the word-games of the *Technopaegnion*: lists of epitaphs of Greek heroes; the *Parentalia*, a store of information about his family — perhaps these are the products of his teaching method, but they are of a distinct literary genus which looks forward to the Middle Ages.

These riddles and cryptograms may possibly be related to a specifically Celtic attitude to language and they may have their roots in druidic secrecy. It is possible that the druids had a secret version of the native language for their own initiate use (MacAlister 1937). Such games are not exclusively Celtic: the Egyptian Tryphiodorus (4th century AD) wrote a version of the *Odyssey* (it is said) which did not contain the letter *s*. There was also the 'hissless' ode of Lasus of Cumae (6th century BC) and even the great Simonides (6th century BC) indulged in frivolities of this kind. Nevertheless, this tendency remained in the Celtic tradition of poetry throughout the centuries. Ausonius uses cryptograms and acrostics as vehicles of obscene insult addressed to enemies. He puts lubricious interpretations on the shapes of Greek letters inserted in his Latin text. In *Epigram* 85, he employs a code of initial letters: *'Lais Eros et Itys, Chiron et Eros Itys alter'*, and says, 'If you take the first letters of these names, when you write them down, you make a word which means what you do, Schoolmaster Eunus: I would be ashamed to say it in Latin.' The word is *'leichei'*, a Greek verb which can bear the meaning 'fellate'.

The *Cento Nuptialis* (*'Marriage anthology'*) was made up by Ausonius from lines plucked out of the text of the *Aeneid* of Virgil. It is an amusing deployment of scholarly expertise for the purpose of traditional congratulatory obscenity at a marriage celebration. Almost in the fashion of an oral poet of earlier times he manipulates received formulae of poetry to suit his own compositional intention. His repertoire of formulae happens to be the highly respected epic of Virgil, which he happily puts to undignified use. The texture and method of the *Cento* again foreshadows the sportive and irreverent strand in the literature of the Middle Ages. In the late fourth century AD, Proba made a *Cento* from Virgilian lines which told a Biblical tale. She may have been the wife of one of Ausonius' colleagues. There were a number of *Homerocentones* in Byzantine times. And in a more serious vein, the *Christus Patiens* was made up from lines pillaged from Greek tragedies. This tragedy of the Passion was attributed to Gregory of Nazianzus (4th century AD), but it probably dates from the twelfth century AD.

In *Epistle* 20, Ausonius is responsible for a notable early example of macaronic verse (verse in two languages). Cicero commits a macaronic word, *'facteon'*, in which he puts a Greek ending on to the stem of a Latin verb (*Att.* 1.16.13; Sedgwick 1930). He may show a certain embarrassment about his literary devices in his preface to *Cupido Cruciatus* (*'Cupid Crucified'*), in which he says that he was inspired by a painting: in this he was following an old tradition in Roman poetry, which maintained a close relationship with painting. Pathos was well within his range in addition to humour and the absurd. Many of his *Epitaphs* express a deep sense of family attachment and affection. This is evident in many of his shorter poems, but especially in the *Parentalia*.

'Rhopalic' verses of prayer come closest of all his work to the Christian spirit. (Rhopalic verse was written in varied lengths of line which gave the completed poem the shape of a club — *rhopalon* in Greek.) There was no particular incongruity in using this shape of poem for the expression of Christian sentiments. Ausonius' intellectual training and background were so strongly Classical that it is the pagan idea which predominates in his work. In the poems in which he poignantly commemorates the deaths of members of his family, there is no evidence of Christian consolation. We know nothing about this aspect of his life: he may have embraced Christianity for the purposes of his career, but there is no indication that he embraced it warmly. No interest in any religion appears in his work as a whole. He speaks with a merely polite approval of the Christian theme. His speech of thanks to Gratian (*Gratiarum Actio* may be a pun in honour of his patron's name) has more references to Christianity than elsewhere in his work, because Gratian was a pious Christian.

The interest in astrology which we find in the poetry of Ausonius need not be druidic in origin. The elder Pliny speaks of Crinas of Massilia who wrote an *Iatromathematica* in which he introduced astrological factors into medicine. We need not discern traces of possible druidism in this. The fact that the druids are regarded as a species of 'Pythagorean' in their belief in the immortality of the soul should not lead us to impute to them a special interest in astrology (De la Ville Mirmont 1902). There was plenty of astrology available from other sources.

Two of the teachers whom Ausonius mentions in his poem about the *professores* of Burdigala were supposed to be of druidic family. The transition from druid to rhetorician was likely enough in the process by which Gaul was Romanised. We may consider the analogy offered by the Christianisation of Ireland. The druidic order (or orders) divided into two branches: one was to become a powerful type of learned poet (no mere bard); and the other, Christian clergy.

We have commented that Ausonius' use of poetry as a medium of instruction and play looks forward to the Middle Ages. It also harks back to the didactic poetry of Hesiod, Nicander and Aratus; to Virgil in his *Georgics* and to Manilius, who wrote on the movements of the stars. Perhaps it also bears some imprint of the druidic use of verse as record — with the difference that the ancient Celtic ethos did not accept that such material should be put in writing. The lists of fish in the *Mosella* and other catalogic elements in his work may be of ultimately Celtic inspiration (Fisher 1981: 24). The strain of primitivism in Ausonius is genuinely alien to the Classical tradition and has more in common with the archaic spirit of Hesiod or the 'Catalogue of Ships' in the *Iliad*. His descriptions of people from head to foot in detail may be at least in part a Celtic feature in his work. It certainly becomes a well known commonplace of medieval literature. Fisher (1981: 216–17) adduces instances from Geoffroi de Vinsauf (13th century AD), from Sidonius, whose work Geoffroi knew, and from the description of the Édain in the *Togail Bruidne Dá Derga* ('*The destruction of the hostel of Da Derga*'). He suggests that all three are specimens of a Celtic literary genus. We might add that women are spoken of as being of considerable importance and authority in the family in the poems of Ausonius. Of course this may not indicate anything more than Romanised middle-class civility, and it is perhaps better not to suppose that has the flavour of a Celtic social trait. Yet the women he mentions seem to have a more than Roman importance (Jullian 1891: 248).

Most of the hexameter lines of Ausonius are carved out in an impeccable Classicism of metre. In writing the Sapphic metre he closely observes Horace's adaptation of the measure created by the great poetess of the seventh century BC. He does not, however, entirely comprehend iambic, the most conversational of all metrical forms, and he is sometimes arbitrary in his treatment of the quantities of the syllables. It would appear that he wrote quickly and we could easily suppose that the heavy impetus and sound of his spoken Latin had its effect when he was composing in a metre that resembled actual talk. The only prose work we have from him is his speech thanking the Emperor Gratian. He delivered this at Trèves. There are also summaries of the *Iliad* and *Odyssey*, which can scarcely be classified as serious prose. These *Periochae* are accompanied by translations in Latin verse of the first lines of the constituent books of both epic poems. He may have intended to develop this into a full translation of Homer. If so, we can only guess what we have lost by his failure to continue the work.

Ausonius was not a major poet by any standards, but he was often a genuine one, and there is an impressive variety and individualism about his work, even when he is apparently in his most conventional and donnish mood. He was a learned and scholarly man who had great technical command of the Classical languages, and it may be significant that he does speak of himself as a poet. Symmachus was right when he praised him for his seriousness of manner and his old-fashioned scholarship. His seriousness took nothing away from the humour and civility of his mind and in this he was an admirable forerunner of the great Frenchmen of later centuries.

13

Celtic Women in the Classical World

Aristotle thought that the Celts were exceptional among barbarian warrior-nations in that they were not ruled by their women (*gynaikokratoumenoi: Pol.* 1269b 27), but preferred masculine attachments. Pausanias refers to the notable courage of Celtic women: his theme probably goes back to Phylarchus, or Duris of Samos (10. 23.7–8; *Sot.* 36). In Classical literature there are examples of Celtic women outstanding in character and bravery. Greek authors who record these instances of female individuality were particularly struck by the contrast they presented with the repressed attitudes of most Greek women. So the descriptions of Celtic women in Classical writings are supported in point of general likelihood by information which is available about insular Celtic customs. The Romans also noted the vigour and independence of some of the women of the Celtic peoples, though they themselves were not without their own ethnic paradigms of female strength of character.

Roman women enjoyed high familial and social status (Nepos *Vit. Pr.* 6ff): Volumnia, the wife of Coriolanus, and his mother, Veturia, give evidence of the importance of wife and mother in society as well as family in their leading of a great delegation of women to appeal to Coriolanus not to destroy his native city of Rome (Livy 2.40). Volumnia added to the strength of her appeal by taking her children along with her. In the period of the Civil War which brought the Roman Republic to its collapse, a certain Q. Lucretius Vespillo went to war on the side of Pompey in 49 BC. This was almost immediately after his marriage to a lady called Turia. She was a Roman woman in the heroic mould: in the absence of her husband she vigorously pursued those who had suddenly and savagely murdered her parents: she kept her husband supplied with necessities; she defended her villa against a siege by irregular troops of Julius Caesar; she successfully protected her inheritance against relatives who contested the will of her dead parents. When the war was over and Lucretius found himself proscribed, she assiduously helped him in hiding. She braved the insults of the triumvir Lepidus, in order to intercede for him. She was more successful in petitioning Octavian, and eventually was reunited with Lucretius. When she died, her husband commemorated her steadfast heroism in a funerary laudation which was carved on her monument (*CIL* 6.1527). This is the source of our information about her. Her loyalty went so far as to prompt her to offer to release Lucretius from the marriage when they found that they could not have children. To his everlasting credit, he indignantly rejected this suggestion.

The fidelity of Turia is paralleled by that of the Celtic Eponina. Her name would seem to have some connection with that of the Celtic horse-goddess Epona, and may be an indicator of the status of her family in relation to a cult. She was married to a Celtic grandee, Sabinus, who had been implicated in the revolt of Civilis in 69 AD. When the revolt failed, Sabinus became a fugitive. Our sources of information about Eponina are Tacitus (*Hist.* 4.67) and Plutarch (*De Amore* 770d): both praise her highly. The latter author had met and conversed with one of her sons.

In order to evade his hunters, Sabinus pretended to have taken poison, and set fire to his house. This act of suicide on the part of a Celtic prince in defeat was entirely understandable to the Roman mind. We might note once more that the sacrificial element involved in the apparent self-destruction by burning is not unlike the Irish traditions about heroes being burned in a *bruiden*. In fact, Sabinus had hidden himself in a dug-out under the building. He had also taken the precaution of burying some of his wealth. When he heard that Eponina was about to die of grief, he sent word to her that he was still alive. For years she kept him supplied with food and clothes. She took him to Rome in disguise to see whether a pardon could be negotiated, but this project failed. She managed, however, to conceal her pregnancy and gave birth in the wilderness 'like a lioness'. Eventually Eponina and Sabinus were arrested, and Vespasian had them both executed, but it is said that no luck came to him or his family from this time on.

These instances of feminine heroism are distinct from questions of matriarchy and matriliny which themselves fascinated the

Greeks and Romans as manifestations of the primitive way of life. Among the Germans of antiquity the authoritative position of the mother's brother (Tac. *Germ.* 20.4) may indicate a matrilineal or matriarchal element in their custom. This seems to be reflected in early Germanic saga (Weisweiler 1953: 208). The Greeks were unaccustomed in their society to women as independent as Turia or Eponina. The heroines of *epos*, however, gave them models of outstanding courage and initiative in women within a convention which they could understand as archaic and no longer applicable. These atavistic women appeared in Attic tragedy, but were not to be imitated by the Hellenic wife and mother.

Yet the Greeks did not withhold their admiration of outstanding qualities of mind and spirit in women when they encountered them. In his essay on the courage of women (22), Plutarch reports that Polybius met and talked to an impressive Galatian woman in Sardis. This was Chiomara, whose story Plutarch relates (Dinan 1911: 275). When the Romans defeated the Galatians at Olympus in Asia Minor in 189 AD, Chiomara, the wife of a Celtic chief of the Tolistobogii, was captured. She fell into the possession of a Roman centurion, who not only raped her, but demanded a large sum of money for her ransom. The price was accepted and the place agreed for the payment to take place was near a certain river. The clansmen of Chiomara were to cross the river with the gold. They did so and paid over the money. The centurion was confident enough and sufficiently deceived by Chiomara to make his farewells to her in a friendly and polite fashion. While he was performing these amiable duties, one of the Celts was given a nod by Chiomara and, with commendable presence of mind, he cut off the centurion's head. She wrapped it up and brought it home to her husband, following the Celtic custom of taking and keeping the heads of enemies.

Plutarch gives us a snatch of conversation between the couple, which for its brevity and directness could easily come from the *Taín Bó Cúalgne* or some other Irish saga. When the head of the Roman was placed at the feet of her husband, Ortagion, he is reported to have said:

'Woman, a fine thing (is) good faith.' (*Gynai, kalon hē pistis.*)
'A better thing only one man should be alive who had intercourse with me,' she answered.

We might almost suppose that this verbal exchange preserved

genuine, gnomic, Celtic idiom. The nominal predicate coming first in the sentence, with or without a part of the verb 'to be', is an idiom of both kinds of Celtic (Evans 1976: 140), though it is also a satisfactory Greek construction. At the beginning of *TBC*, there is a pillow-talk between Medb and Ailill which has an unmistakably similar tone:

> '(It is) a true word, girl, it is well off a woman (is) (who is) wife of a nobleman.' ('Firbrathar, a ingen, is maith ben, ben dagfir')
> 'Well off she is,' said the woman, 'why do you think that?'
> 'I think that,' said Ailill, 'because you are richer today than when I got you.' (*TBC* 5).

There is an echo of Chiomara's attitude in the rule mentioned in the *Penitentia Vinniani* 21,45.46 (Davies 1983: 158). This prescribes that a woman who has been sent away by her husband must not mate with another man while her former husband is 'in the body'. Such a rule could be a Christianised version of an older taboo.

Although there may have been differences in the latitude of behaviour allowed to queens and aristocratic women in Celtic society from that permitted to ordinary people, we may suppose that both men and women were regulated in their personal relationships by a complex of rules now substantially lost. The parallel between the various kinds of marriage observed in ancient India and among the Celts suggests the opposite of primitive simplicity. Romance and tragedy attending it were not impossibilities. In the same essay, Plutarch tells the story of another Celtic heroine, also of Galatia. This was Kamma, a priestess of Artemis, and she was conspicuously faithful to the memory of her spouse after his death (Dottin 1915: 183ff). We have described (Chapter 9) how her husband, Sinatus, was killed by a kinsman, Sinorix, who was in love with Kamma. When she was forced to marry Sinorix, she used a trick to persuade him to drink poison from a cup from which she had previously drunk, and declared to the goddess before dying that her act was a sacrificial one and that she had outlived her husband only for this day of revenge.

As a converse to this reputation of unswerving fidelity in the marriage bond, Greek and Roman writers have commented on the apparent promiscuity of the Celts in sexual relationships. Caesar (*BG* 5.14) and Cassius Dio (62.6) refer to the prevalence of communal marriage among the Celts and say that polyandry is practised by the British and the Caledonians. Both reports depend to a degree on the anthropological discourses of such writers as Poseidonius. This applies also to Strabo (4.5.4) who says that Britons not only cohabit with the wives of others, but with their own sisters and mothers: he admits, however, that he has no reliable evidence for these assertions. Certainly we know that both Irish and Welsh systems of marriage recognised various marital categories. Also categorised were unions not of marital status, but which also were taken into account from the point of view of compensatory payments, as were the more permanent bonds. It would be easy for foreign observers to remain unaware of the vaious ramifications of a system which recognised, say, eight or nine categories of union, and in the case of Old Irish Law, three classes of legitimate wife. In the sixteenth century AD, an Anglo-Irish lady from Dublin, Mabel Bagenal, married the great Hugh O'Neill who gave the generals of Elizabeth I such trouble. When she arrived in Tyrone, she was astonished to find several of the Earl her husband's concubines calmly in residence.

It is not easy to accept that a writer as astute as Julius Caesar would fall into the vulgar fallacy of interpreting alien marital customs in terms of libertinism. He may have thought that this version made useful propaganda for his cause, and no doubt he would be well aware that the philosophic idea of natural man was prevalent enough in the educated mind to make his comments convincing. It could also be the case, however, that Caesar, in spite of his long residence in Gaul, did not care to inform himself about the details of Celtic custom, except where these had a political or military relevance. He mentions that Dumnorix, the leader of the Aedui (*BG* 3.5), married off his female relatives to men of power and by this means increased his own influence (Syme 1939: 455). He also records (*BG* 6.19) that Celtic women were provided with dowries in kind rather than cash and that the man had to put up an equal amount of property. There is an allusion to this, perhaps, in the passage we have quoted from *TBC*. We may cautiously suppose that a wife of sufficient status in Gaul, like her insular counterpart, could have rights over the joint property. In the Old Irish situation, we find that the woman's capacity to make contracts as freely as her husband is part of a later law code, the *Cáin Lánamna* ('Law of the married pair'). The '*Díre*' ('Law') system allowed women fewer rights, but no doubt the original status of the woman counted for much (MacCall 1980: 11ff).

Tests of legitimacy applied to the new-born and strictness of enquiries into the deaths of husbands do not in themselves assert that female fidelity was enforced by restrictions on freedom of movement or association. Caesar mentions these tests (*BG* 6.19.3). So do others: Julian refers to them (*Or.* 2); so also does a poem in the *Anthology* (*AP* 9.125): the new-born infant is floated in the Rhine before it is accepted as legitimate.

Heroic permissiveness was not acceptable to St Jerome, who, when he says that the Irish are given to promiscuity and incest, may be continuing the tradition we read in Strabo (4.5.4.). On the other hand, some female patterns of behaviour in the Celtic tribes must have been strange and striking. In the seige of Gergovia (*BG* 7.47), the Celtic matrons let down jewels and other property from the walls to bribe the Romans not to injure them if the town should fall. They also bared their breasts and stretched out their arms in supplication. Some of them even came down from the walls in person and handed themselves over to the soldiers in a final desperate act of entreaty, which we might imagine was intended to place a burden of shame on the soldiers if they should mistreat them. The baring of bodies may be compared with an incident in *TBC*: Cu Chulain is on his way back from the borders of Ulaid where he has been fighting savagely, and he is still in such a state of fury that he is liable to be dangerous to anybody, friend or enemy. In order to defuse his wrath, one hundred and fifty naked women are sent out to meet him (*TBC* 1185ff). This is an act which operates within a social context in which individual honour and shame are respected by all parties. With little enough justification, the women of Gergovia were assuming a sense of heroic honour in the Romans.

Similar concepts of honour and shame may explain such extreme examples of female independence, verging on the apparently promiscuous, as Medb's offer of herself and Finnabhair for sexual intercourse in return for political and military support (Davies 1983: 155). Possibly a queen and a princess were subject to different rules of living from other Celtic women and were in a position to dispose of their sexual favours as a deliberate act of diplomacy. Such women are not the chattels of their menfolk. They are making use of the men to whom they make the offer which confers prestige and honour on its recipient. In *Fled Bricrend* (11.63) Medb goes to spend the night with Cu Chulain as an act of friendship and political insurance, not as an act of passion. We might wonder to what extent the insults inflicted on Boudicca's daughters may have resulted from Roman misunderstanding of princely Celtic custom.

In both Goidelic and Brythonic traditions, the law places a high value on honour or 'face'. The word for 'face' is actually used: Welsh *wyneb*, Breton *eneb*, and Irish *enech* are legal terms. The Old Welsh legal term *wynebwerth* means 'face'-price, which is 'honour'-price. It is the fine paid for insult to some person's honour. Apart from *galanas*, an imposition for physical injury, the Welsh law recognised *sarhaed* (from *sarhau*, vb 'insult'). It is reasonable to infer that these rules applied also to the Celts of antiquity, both insular and continental. Poets and satirists were feared for the injury they could do to the actual fleshly face, not merely to the public image. The great paid their poets to maintain their public image by means of lavish praise, so that the person praised retained general respect. The core of the honour code resides in other peoples' opinion of one's standing in relation to accepted assumptions about behaviour and achievement (Owen 1980: 40–68).

We might be inclined to conjecture that Medb's *démarche* in the *Tain* indicated a matriarchal or matrilineal system, but there is no need to explain a warrior-queen in terms of matriarchy. Patriarchal societies have often been content to be led by queens, without any thought of the possibility of gynaecocracy at the domestic level. The city states of Greece and Rome had highly organised political structures which allowed no place for women in power. Greeks and Romans were all the more astonished at the relative freedom and individuality of Celtic women.

Tacitus comments that the Celts have no objection to being led by women (*Ann.* 14.35); he also makes this point in *Agricola* 16, specifically about women 'in commands' (*in imperiis*). He does not suggest equality of the sexes in Celtic society. There are contrasts in descriptions of the war-queen which have survived. In *TBC* (Henderson 136) Medb is beautiful, pale, long in countenance and with long fair hair. She wears a crimson cloak fastened with a good brooch, and she carries a spear in her hand. The description of Boudicca in Cassius Dio tells us that she is great in bulk and intimidating to look at; her expression is fierce, her voice harsh; her gold hair cascades down to her hips. She also has a cloak and gold torque, and she carries a spear (62.2.3).

The ancient Irish, or at least the Goidelic element of them, found the matrilineal succession of Pictish society sufficiently remarkable to require an explanatory myth. The myth is Goidelic in origin, for it assumes that the Goidels were in Ireland before the Picts. According to its version of events, the Picts had no women when they arrived in Ireland. The Goidelic founding hero, Eremon, gave them three wives of men killed in battle on condition that their kingdom in Britain should be inherited by the female line. They swore by the sun and the moon that their kingdom would be ruled by the female line of descent to the end of the world (*FF* 2.114). The oath is typical of the early Celts in its cosmic references. Not only did this myth explain the strange customs of the Picts (Ir. *Cruithni*), it had the advantage of supporting Goidelic claims to rule over Cruithnic territories, as in the case of Ulster and, perhaps later, western Scotland.

There may have been a considerable non-IE admixture in Pictish culture. Inscriptions from Pictland in an apparently non-IE language appear to support this. But we cannot point to a Celtic or any other society which is not some kind of blend with others. Legendary sources claim that the Picts came from Thrace or Scythia. Those kings of Pictland (*Cruithentuath*) whose fathers' names are mentioned in extant lists of kings are many of them of non-Pictish paternity (H.M. Chadwick 1949: 91). There is no evidence that this matrilineal custom was specifically non-Celtic or non-IE. Variety in such matters is always possible. The Picts were matrilineal in their kingship custom, but women did not rule them. The king of Ulster, Conchobhar Mac Nesa, whose name is a matronymic, not a patronymic, may represent a matrilineal and 'Pictish' predominance in the province. Nes, the daughter of Eochaid Salbuide, was told by the druid Cathbad that the day was an auspicious one for begetting a king on a queen. There was no other man about, so Nes took the druid into the house with her and allowed him to proceed with the begetting. The product, after three years' pregnancy, was Conchobar (*Compert Conchobuir*).

The influence of Medb on the course of events in *TBC* is crucial, and not invariably constructive. Emer, the wife of Cu Chulain, in the Ulster cycle of saga, has many points of resemblance to Medb. The demeanour of Medb is not dissimilar to descriptions of Celtic queens such as Cartimandua and Boudicca in Tacitus (Gwynn 1924: 366; Thurneysen 1921: 585, 680; Tac. *Ann.* 12.36–40; 14. 31ff; *Hist.* 3.45; *Agr.* 16. 31). Onomaris was the woman leader of the Celts in their wanderings into south-eastern Europe (Weisweiler 1953: 208). Women and children accompanied the warriors to the battlefield just as they followed them in the wagon-train in a long journey of speculative brigandry and conquest. They were clearly influential in the Celtic sections of Hannibal's army and were not an element which intelligent military management could neglect. An arrangement had to be made for the rectification of offences between Carthaginians and Celts in the joint army: it was agreed that Carthaginian generals should judge offences against Carthaginians, but that Celtic women should judge in cases where Celtic men had been injured by Carthaginians (Plut. *De Virt. Mul.* 6).

To the inhabitants of the Greco-Roman world, the Celtic woman could be terrifying. She could provoke reactions not unlike those felt by Odysseus in his interview with the Laestrygonian queen. Ammianus Marcellinus (4th century AD) paints a truly awesome picture of a Celtic woman enraged and joining in a fight in support of her spouse (15.12.1). As he waited for Ursicinus to be relieved after the fall of Silvanus, Ammianus spent some time studying the history and way of life of the Celts of Gaul (Thompson 1949: 4). He even examined some inscriptions which he thought would throw some light on the origins of the Celts (15.9.6). He noted the loud voices and heavy drinking of the Celts, as well as the formidable character of their women (15.12). His observations have the merit of being first hand. Also they confirm the persistence of certain Celtic characteristics in the behaviour and customs of the Gauls at this time. The comments he makes about women do not necessarily apply to female soldiers of the kind whose miseries were relieved by the reforms procured by St Adomnan in Ireland. Ammianus describes women who have more in common with the ferocious fishwives of eighteenth century AD Dublin and Edinburgh.

Classical references to women accompanying armies, to warlike and dangerous queens, and the belligerence of the average woman of Gaul testify not so much to a species of sexual equality, as to a more equitable balance of the functions of men and women in society. The range of roles possible for women in ancient Celtic societies was wider than that permitted in Greece or Rome. The Irish tradition, which presents us with a picture of an archaic Iron Age society, speaks not only of women warriors, but women prophets, druids, bards, doctors, and even satirists. The warrior heroine Estiu plays an important part in the tragic and romantic story of Snámh Dá Én (Swim-two-birds) (Gwynn 1906: 44). The lady Gaine was outstanding among women: she was learned, a prophetess and a chief druid. Fedelm, a woman of striking beauty, was prophetess of the magic hill of Cruachan (*TBC* 211 Windisch). She was one of Medb's following and was of British origins.

In the struggle to take the island of Mona (Angelsey), the Romans had to contend with the fury of women devotees as well as that of the embattled druids (Tac. *Ann.* 14.30). There is no suggestion that these women had themselves the status of druids. An inscription from La Prugnon des Antibes describes a woman as *flaminica sacerdos*: she was evidently the priestess of the goddess Thucolis. Boudicca acted as the priestess of the goddess Adrasta (possibly the Celtic 'Andarta') (Dio Cassius 62.6). Again there is no evidence that these were druids. If there were female druids in the Celtic tribes which they encountered, the Greeks and Romans have not seen fit to mention them. It is possible that they were an Irish institution but we cannot be certain.

The conservatism of ancient Irish society preserved in Christian times a notable barbarity in its treatment of certain grades of women soldiers. For women of humble status, war was not a theatre of glory. We are not speaking now of Medb or Scathach or Nes, but of women slaves who were made to fight in battles, either as front-line soldiers or as servants of warriors, according to status (Ryan 1936: 273, 279). The law tract *Cáin Adomnáin* which is attributed to St Adomnan may be connected with his visit to Ireland in 697 AD. According to the *Annals of Ulster*, the visit was inspired by an angel and its purpose was to institute more humane legislation. His proposals forbade the killing of women in almost every circumstance and certainly banned their use in warfare. This *lex innocentium* was much needed. There are many examples in literature of women being killed in feuds between families and also when they were captured in battle (Ryan 1936: 273; Weisweiler 1953: 228).

Adomnan was responsible for the emancipation of women from this savage hardship. He did not succeed in enacting his laws until he had threatened the chiefs with bell and curse (Meyer 1905: 27ff). The chiefs were made to guarantee the laws by the surrender of sureties. Before his reforms, many ordinary women were treated as *cumalach*, 'of slave status'. A woman who was in the position of being a *cumal* was an item of currency, being worth three cows. His work ensured that no longer would women be flogged into battle by their husbands. It had been customary to equip women with long poles which had hooks fitted to the end to attack other women.

His prohibition of the use of women in war is said to have been in response to an appeal from his mother Ronnat. When he was carrying her over a battlefield, they saw the most pitiful sight of a beheaded woman with her child still suckling at her breasts: 'a stream of milk on one of its cheeks, and a stream of blood on the other' ('sruth lomna for in dara n-óil dó agus sruth folae forsinn óil ailiu': Meyer 1905: 71).

There is no evidence for this kind of practice in any Classical author, and none of them was so enthusiastic an admirer of Celtic society to have been likely to omit so sensational a piece of information had it been known to him. It is possible that it was a local insular custom, or that it had been superseded in the Celtic peoples with whom the Greeks and Romans came into contact. Yet we must bear in mind that Celtic reputation for indiscriminate slaughter which was so deeply imprinted on the mind of the Greeks and Romans. Even if the general service of women in war remained a cultural fossil on the outer margins of the Celtic province, something akin to the atrocities suppressed by Adomnan is recorded in the account of Boudicca's uprising. This was the wholesale impalement of captured women. The act was sacrificial, but it can scarcely be excused of its cruelty on those grounds. Adomnan's reforms were part of a Christianising process, and Christianity carried with it in Ireland a strong second-order Classical influence from the Continental world.

I can see no means within the available evidence of evaluating closely the status of women in the ancient Celtic world in relation to their status in Greco-Roman society. The Greek and Roman writers express little more than a prejudiced and impressionistic notion of the roles of women in the Celtic societies that they discuss. The complexity of women's functions in Celtic society is well illustrated by a post-Classical example, that of St Brigit. Although her life was passed in a time of change, that time saw a confluence of pagan Iron Age and Christian-Classical cultures.

Brigit was the daughter of a slave woman, Broicseth, and a noble called Dubthach. While Broicseth was pregnant and driving with Dubthach in a chariot, a druid prophesied from the noise that the vehicle was making that the child to be born would be no ordinary person. Dubthach's more senior and legitimate wife was jealous of Broicseth, and forced her husband to sell her. He sold her to a poet of the Uí Néill, though he took care to sell only the woman and not the child she was carrying, which would remain his property.

What is probably the earliest version of the life of Brigit, the sixth-century AD version in Latin by Cogitosus (O hAodha 1978: *Bethu Brigte*) says nothing about the slave status of the mother. The household was, however, very likely to have been polygamous, and the wife who compelled the husband to sell Broicseth no doubt belonged to the Cétmuinter class of wife, who had considerable legal rights and financial authority in the family. According to the version of the *BB*, Broicseth seems to have been merely *cumaltach*.

The poet who had bought Broicseth sold her to a druid, and the child was born in his house. The druid had a vision in his sleep of three clergy, one of whom said, 'Let Brigit be the name of the girl for you'. This suggests that the druid was divinely inspired by a Christian apparition to give her the name of a most prestigious Celtic goddess. The name itself by its ancient authority could do much to advance the Christian cause in Ireland. The maternal uncle of the druid was a Christian. We have an account here of a family with elements of druidism and Christianity coexisting within it in a period of cultural transition. Both the druid and his uncle saw a mystic fire rising from the house where mother and child were asleep. It is the uncle who declares that Brigit is a holy child.

After a period of residence in Connacht where the mother of the druid lived, Brigit was brought back to Dubthach. She had already foretold that the part of Connacht in which she had been living would some day belong to her. During her childhood years she performed many wonders, and was identified by Bishop Ibor of Cell Dara in Leinster as the 'Maria' he had seen in a dream.

When she was older a certain Dubthach moccu Lugair wanted to marry her, and was refused by her. Her half-brothers tried to compel her in the direction of marriage, and one of them became so tedious on the subject that she was obliged to curse him. They were angry at her refusal to marry, because this deprived them of the bride-price. She made certain of her celibacy by putting out one of her eyes, thereby ruining her value in the marriage market (*BB* 15).

Her conversation with males, father, brothers and those outside the family suggest that her subordinate position as a woman born of a slave mother did not inhibit her liberty of speech or independence of action. We must make some allowance for the fact that she was recognised as a magical person, but nevertheless her freedom is notable. She is not shown as behaving like a mere appendage to male society.

Her father was irritated at her habit of giving away his property to poor people and even to hungry dogs. She was such an unconscionable nuisance about this, that he decided to sell her as a slave to Dunlang the king of the Lagin (*BB* 13). Her uncontrollable generosity was not only in accord with Christian precepts, but also followed the 'potlatch' custom of Celtic chiefs such as Louernius. Her father's decision to leave her with the king was reinforced when he came out of the king's house where he had been negotiating the deal to find that Brigit, whom he had left in the chariot, had given away a sword worth ten cows to a begging leper. When her father was on his way home, he found that she had been miraculously replaced in his chariot. The king was so impressed by this that he gave her a valuable sword and sent her home with her father. He may well have felt that her departure was well worth the cost of a sword.

At last her father gave her leave to take the veil and her consecration was performed by Bishop Mel. She gathered a group of pious virgins about her and the miracles which she performed have become part of a hagiographic tradition. The *Bethu Brigte* places her as a contemporary of St Patrick. The tradition of the lives of Brigit gives her an importance which is comparable to his in the missionary conversion of an Ireland which had already in part accepted Christianity into its native culture.

Some points of interest emerge from Brigit's life and career. First, there is the mixture of druidism and Christianity, indicating a druidism which is liberal and mild, probably because it is in the decline of its power in face of the advance of Classical Christian culture. We remember the professors at Burdigala whom Ausonius describes as being from druidic families. Secondly, we note that polygamic custom does not preclude from respect on the part of druids the offspring of a slave woman who was a consort of very minor standing. Next, we notice the device by which an apparently Christian inspiration suggests that the child will have a distinguished pagan name. The prophecies and dreams which precede the birth of Brigit may be similar to supernatural communications which precede the arrival of a prospective druid or *ban-drui* into the world. But we can only guess at this. Also, in spite of her humble birth, Brigit is eligible for purchase by brideprice like any other woman. Her father pays her considerable attention. She drives with him in the chariot — which is not the position we might expect if she were treated as a mere chattel. He thinks she is remarkable enough to be offered in sale to an important, but non-Goidelic king. Yet the society in which she lives is decidedly patriarchal.

Brigit is depicted as a character not to be intimidated readily by males. As a destined priestess, she might be expected to treat the male sex with a certain briskness. The 'Bacchanalian' priestesses on the island of Sena in northern Gaul were hostile to men, and would allow no man to land on the island (Str. 4.4.3).

With comparative impunity, Brigit was able to take on herself the redistributive functions of a Celtic chieftain. She may be suspected of exaggerating this custom of giving to the point of reckless prodigality in order to put pressure on her menfolk to allow her to do what she really wanted to do: namely, make her vows as a Christian virgin.

Obviously there are discounts which we must make in considering how far the biography of this remarkable person can inform us about the women of Celtic peoples in the Classical world. Perhaps it is reassuring that the relationships between men and women, and owners and slaves, are more reminiscent of the society depicted in the Homeric epic than that of Archaic or Classical periods of Greek history. One of the striking facts about Celtic society is its archaism in relation to that of the classical civilisation of the Mediterranean. The account of Brigit can only reinforce the view that Celtic women in antiquity lived in a confluence of varied themes and pressures, and were not mechanically placed in a rigid social scale. The classifications of society seemed to be rigid but were not: if women were bound by a multiplicity of customs, so also were men in relation to them. Classical literature simplifies their position. The reality was too complex to fit neatly under a romantic template of primitivism with its ideas about the equality and communism of women in wilder and more remote nations. Occasionally, as in the example of Chiomara, clearer evidence filters through.

14

Religion and the Druids

Julius Caesar remarked that the whole Gallic nation was devoted to religion and superstition (*BG* 6.16). I do not propose to illustrate this statement with a catalogue of Celtic deities or of divine names which interact and interlock with each other and with those of Rome. As in the blending of parts of the Greek pantheon with that of Rome, the meeting of the Greco-Roman gods and goddesses with those of the Celts was the contact of polytheisms of IE origin which were broadly similar in character. The Romans drew correspondences between the deities and those of the Celts with whom they came in contact. Their procedure, the *interpretatio Romana*, identified the gods of the two peoples in order to weld the loyalty of Celtic worshippers to Rome. Where possible, in the early Principates, Augustan cults were grafted on to native custom: Augustus had no objection to being worshipped as a god outside Italy. The connection of the druids with the religious cults and practices of the Celtic countries is beyond dispute, but the precise nature of the connection remains unclear. It seems that the Romans did little to encourage the continuance of whatever religious influence the druids possessed. They were a dangerous elite. It was safer to entrust the new Augustan graftings to the priestly care of more humble members of the Celtic community. All these topics are related to each other, and I hope to discuss aspects of them which bear upon the theme of this book.

We have mentioned the Celt who supposed that the statue of Minerva which he saw in Massilia was one of his native goddesses. It was not likely that he was guilty of a naïve misapprehension. He was more likely of the view that this was one more manifestation of the multiplex personality of his goddess of war. We know also that some goddesses were personifications of the tribe: Brigantia

259

may be an example (Salway 1981: 666). Caesar reports that the Gauls particularly worship Mercury, and after him, Mars, Apollo, Jupiter, Minerva. The Gauls regard themselves as descendants of Dis pater, and this is apparently one of the doctrines of the druids. The array of gods in Celtic countries was varied, and personalities overlapped. This made for a situation which was hospitable to new deities, who could be assimilated with the native gods and goddesses. In Roman Britain, for instance, there was eventually a miscellany of native Celtic deities, some imported from other parts of the European Celtic domain, together with Sol Invictus and Astarte from the East, and also Mithraism and Christianity (Salway 1981: 667–9). According to Macrobius (2nd century AD) an ancient Celtic god called Neton left memories of his worship at Acci on the Baetis in Spain (1.19). This town of veterans seems to have equated him with Mars. He may be connected with the Irish Néit. Netus and Neton were worshipped also in Celtic and Celtiberian parts of Spain (Strabo 3.4.6).

A tradition in the Classical world held that the Celts worshipped forces of nature and that they had no defined notion of the gods like that which was realised in the Greco-Roman pantheon. It is said that when Brennus entered the precinct of Delphi and saw no gold and silver dedications, but only stone and wooden statues, he laughed at the Greeks for setting up figures of the gods whom they regarded as being endowed with human shape (*anthrōpomorphas*: Diod. 22.11). I think it likely that it was the naturalistic character of the images which struck him as especially strange. At this time (*c.* 278 BC) the branch of the Celtic peoples that were the invaders of Greece may have been as yet unfamiliar with statues of this kind. In the insular Celtic tradition which long preserved archaic ways, cult statues of an abstract and primitive style survive into late pre-Christian centuries. Celtic art tended towards abstraction in earlier times before it was influenced by Greco-Roman styles. The impact of these styles was never universally predominant.

Celtic attitudes to deity seemed no less strange to the Greek and Roman mind. Strabo (3.4.16) says that the Celtiberians worshipped an unnamed god at the full moon. They perform their devotions in company with all their families in front of the gates of their townships and hold dances lasting throughout the night. The Callaeci he describes as *atheoi*. This word usually implies the worship of gods unrecognisable to the Greeks and probably without determined physical characteristics or not represented in anthropomorphic statues. In this, the Spanish deities resemble the minor gods and *numina* of the early Roman religion before they were shaped by Hellenic influences.

The religious beliefs of the continental Gauls seem in many respects to resemble those of the ancient British and Irish (Van Hamel 1934: 203). We have no grounds for thinking that the Celts had gods with whom they stood in a lasting spiritual relationship, or who were consistently benevolent to them. This is largely true of Greco-Roman religion, execept that in its wide and varied tradition we can quote persistent interest on the part of certain deities in certain human beings — for example, Athene's constant protection of Odysseus in the *Odyssey*. Fate played an important part in Celtic religious thinking. This accords with the tendency of some Greek observers to see the druids as Stoicising students of a universal cosmic mechanism. Germanic peoples seem to have thought that only death is fated.

If the Homeric *epos* had not so concentrated the minds of the Greeks and ourselves on the principal Olympians, we should, if we approached the evidence for Classical Greek religion, face a comparably baffling multiplicity of divine names and the same problem of separating apparent identicals as we have in considering the Celtic religion. The Romans, with their immense population of 'smaller gods' (*di minores*), would be no easier to understand in this area. The more Roman deities, humanised and Hellenised though they may be, are not capable of being completely identified with apparent Hellenic counterparts, any more than Celtic gods can be made to correspond accurately with those of Greece and Rome. Names of four hundred gods and goddesses occur only once in inscriptions throughout the Celtic domain (N. Chadwick 1984: 152).

There is literary evidence, as we have seen, for the Celts swearing by the main forces of nature. An eclipse of the moon brought a Galatian army to a halt in 218 (Polyb. 5.78). This was not necessarily a sign that they particularly worshipped the moon (DeVries 1963: 141). It is reasonable, however, to suppose that as a principal feature of nature, it enjoyed their abiding awe. Caesar mentions that the Germans worship forces of nature only (*BG* 6.21). St Patrick inveighs against the worship of the sun in Ireland. A pre-IE element in Celtic worship of the sun may possibly be seen in the fact that the sun could be regarded as a female entity. As in German, the Celtic languages gave it a feminine grammatical gender. Perhaps, as DeVries suggests (1963: 141), the insular god Mog Ruith, a supernatural solar being, was introduced to represent a masculine element in the cult. He is an adventurous hero, capable of successful opposition to druidic magical powers. Also he is able to fly through the air. His name means 'servant of the wheel', which is very probably the sun-disc.

In addition to being assiduous worshippers of Mercury, the Celts revered Apollo, Mars, Jupiter and Minerva (*BG* 6.17). There was a deliberate assimilative policy in the first Principate: the Celtic Grannus became an attribute of Apollo: Grannus was probably connected with the word for 'sun' (cf. Ir. *grian*). Belesina was changed into Minerva Belesina. Some of the Gaulish gods were nominated household gods of the *princeps: Lares Augusti*. Eastern gods such as Cybele and Mithras were introduced into Gaul. We have pointed out that assimilated Celtic gods were not invariably attended by a priesthood drawn from the well-born of Gaul. This was not the case with the priests of Roman gods proper who were introduced into the Celtic environment. Even freed slaves could be in charge of the cult of *Lares Augusti*. These officials were in Roman terms called *Severi Augusti*. The policy of Rome was to break up old complexes of religious and aristocratic influence which could develop into centres of resistance, and at the same time to create bonds between Rome and the various social classes of the conquered country.

There are themes in Celtic religion which we should now note, and which seemed characteristic of the Celts to ancient observers. These are the cult of the severed head, dedication of offerings in water and human sacrifice. Tacitus relates that the Germans set up the skulls of Roman prisoners whose heads they had severed after the *Clades Variana* (*Ann.* 1.61). He does not mention severed heads in his description of the last stand of the druids at Anglesey. The cult of the severed head was noted by Poseidonius in his travels in southern Gaul. It must be regarded as of very ancient origins. Some form of it may have been practised in the early Stone Age, when cave 'dedications' or 'burials' of skull and long bones were laid down. Add to this the apparent severed heads which are part of the sculptural adornment of the cathedral at Clonfert in Ireland, and we are presented with a long preoccupation with the human head in separation from the body. It is a preoccupation which transcends several strata of religious ideology. Anne Ross refers to the story in the *Dindschenchas*

(Gwynn XI 258) by which Loch Cend ('Lake of the Heads') got its name: after an ancient battle, Caipre threw into it nine hundred heads of the men he had killed. Hence its name (Ross 1968: 144ff). Before the battle, Cath Cumair, a druid, prophesies new names of places: one will be Drum Cró ('Bloodyridge') and the other Tiobrend na gCeann ('Headswell') because of the beheadings which will take place there (Ross 1968: 169). We cannot deduce from this story that druids were intimately connected with the cult of heads. The story looks like a prophecy after the event devised to explain the names, the latter of which must surely have some connection with the ritual of the severed head. The druid may be simply a formal spokesman. At the same time, we must bear in mind that druids were, as a matter of course, in attendance at all sacrifices, and their association with the head-cult cannot be excluded.

The dedication of heads and other prestigious and precious objects in wells and other watery places is exemplified in the case of the famous treasure from Tolosa which Caepio tried to divert for his own purposes. This came from a sacred pond which the greed and engineering skill of the Romans enabled them to drain. Also in Wales, Llyn Cerrig has yielded many objects of beauty and interest which were undoubtedly dedicated there. The opinion that they were thrown into the water as a last desperate plea for aid by the druids under the threat of attack by the forces of Suetonius Paulinus, can neither be confirmed nor refuted. The worship of wells continues: well-dressing ceremonies take place under the patronage of the Anglican church in several parts of Britain even at the present time. There is also a by no means implausible opinion that the votive pits in which dedicated objects have been found are dried-out or filled-in wells (Salway 1981: 669). Several British gods are associated with water and springs: the most obvious example is that of Sul Minerva at Bath (Salway ibid.). In Spain, the water deities Ataecina and Endovellius were worshipped. Ataecina was a goddess of the Underworld. Her cult seems to have been strong in Turobriga of Celtic Baeturia (Bouchier 1914: 115). There is no definite evidence of druidism in Spain, though it would be rash to exclude its presence on the testimony of silence. Nor, incidentally, is there evidence for a distinctively Celtic moon-goddess in Spain. There is however *Luna Augusta*.

Cauldrons are important in Irish literature as symbols of sustenance and noble hospitality. Such cauldrons never go empty.

The Gundestrupp cauldron's relief illustrates a scene in which a man is being sacrificed by drowning in a cauldron. The officiating personage could be a druid or perhaps a deity. A tree carried by a group of warriors is a prominent feature of the scene. This might be the great tree of the cosmos. The cauldron may signify the recreation of plenteous livelihood by a powerful god of the Under-world. The god in question (who is depicted on the Gundestrupp vessel) could be the Dis pater whom Caesar speaks of as the chief god of the Celtic people and their common ancestor. Medea's cauldron of regeneration is called to mind by the scene. Also, cauldrons in the form of tripods are highly valued possessions in the Bronze Age culture which is the background of much of the *Iliad* and *Odyssey*. The ancient, magical discovery of cooked flesh, reinforced much later by the almost incredible and possibly super-natural skill of the bronze smith, may well form the core of the mystery of the cauldron, itself an everlasting vessel in comparison with its earthen predecessors. In the Celtic world, apart from its possible regenerative symbolism, it has the glory of being the instrument of kingly generosity (see Chapter 2 above).

The *lorica* or 'breastplate' of St Patrick is a hymn intended to generate a spiritual force-field against the powers of paganism. It contains an invocation against the three-fold death of burning, drowning and slaying. Hanging, burning and drowning are the more usual triad of sacrificial deaths among the Celts: the iron of 'slaying' is more characteristic of the Germanic tribes. No doubt the customs of sacrifice were varied in different areas of the Celtic domain. Burning is attributed to the Gauls; also divination by observing the dying twitches of a victim who has been stabbed. The threefold death is probably of IE origin. It may refer to three kinds of death respectively associated with three social divisions: kings, warriors and ordinary people in relation to the cults particularly associated with these groups. Its meaning has not been entirely explained. The triadic form of some Celtic deities, which is sometimes represented in tricephalous statues, may be connected with some early triplication of deities and rites. The three mythical culture *daemones* of Ireland, Mac Cuill, Mac Cecht, and Mac Greine, who refer to the hazel-tree, the plough and the sun, may preserve a trace of this ancient theme.

In the *Pharsalia*, an epic which has as its subject the Civil War which ended the Roman Republic, the poet Lucan mentions a trio of Celtic gods, Teutates, Esus and Taranis, without attempting to relate them to Roman equivalents. According to him (7.445ff), all three are recipients of human sacrifice. An ancient commentator on the poem says that Taranis is Jupiter, the god of thunder; Teutates is Mars, and Esus is Mercury. Another commentator identifies Teutates differently as the 'tribal god'; an etymological explanation of the name. N. Chadwick connects him with a familiar oath by the god of the tribe (*tuath*) in Irish sagas (1984: 144, 193). The oath is: 'tongaim do dia tonges mo thuath': 'I swear by the god my tribe swears by'. The identity of this unnamed god, who may remind us of the anonymous Ibero-Celtic god whom Strabo mentions, could have been forgotten at the time when the saga was written down. The formula has the flavour of the genuinely archaic. We need not doubt that this form of address to a tribal god was originally a means of avoiding divine anger through misidentification of the addressee. The commentator on Lucan is inclined to identify Teutates with Mercury: he says that the god is worshipped by human sacrifice. The identification with Mercury is not easy to sustain, because he is widely represented by inscriptions throughout the Celtic realm which would seem to suggest that he has characteristics more like those of Mars. Nor is the commentator certain whether Esus is Mercury or Mars. The rite of human sacrifice associated with Esus is, according to his account, executed by means of hanging and blood-letting, which might suggest a warrior's god. The name of this god may be cognate with the Latin *herus* or *erus*, meaning 'master'. Another suggestion is that it means 'good' as in Greek *eus* (known in Greek from its adverbial form '*eu*', 'well'). A case could be made out from Roman iconography that Esus was Mercury: this would not necessarily indicate that the Celts everywhere made this identification.

We have heard more than once of the importance of Dis pater, as god and ethnic ancestor. Dis may be the Roman version of a Celtic word similar to OIr. *díth* ('death', 'destruction'). He may be connected with Sucellus, the god who wields the hammer (DeVries 1963: 89). In the insular tradition, Vulcan's equivalent may be Goibniu, or Govannon, but strict parallels are impossible to substantiate. We should bear this in mind with regard to the interesting suggestion that the prominence of the horned god Cernunnos in the Celtic domain may mean that he is to be identified with Dis pater (Ross 1968: 212). Certainly it is notable that a horned figure appears in an animal motif on the Gundestrupp cauldron. He may be lord of living things because he is also lord of death. The cult of Cernunnos was possibly promoted by the druids (Ross 1968: 212): an Underworld god of death and rebirth would be likely to have a persuasive appeal at a time of general crisis for the Celts. The refutation of the fear of death would be expedient propaganda for the defence of the Celtic world against the encroachments of Rome and the Germanic tribes.

Caesar (*BG* 6.17.2) speaks of a Celtic Mars: Romanised inscriptions show him with a multiplicity of attributive surnames. The Celtiberian Aernus may be a species of Mars. Hercules (Herakles) also has many different Celtic epithets. In this variety of names, male and female couples emerge: Mars Loucetius and Nemetona; Mars Visucius and Visucia, Mars Cicolus and Rosmerta; Apollo Grannus and Sirona (DeVries 1963: 150). Rosmerta seems also to be a feminine doublet of Mercurius (DeVries 1963: 127). Her name may be connected with the same roots as those of the Greek *meros, Moira*, 'portion' or 'fate'. If it is related to /smer/, it would have the meaning of plentitude or prosperity. We might be tempted to think that this doubling may be the result of early contacts between the Celts and people who had similar gods whom they took over. Perhaps a more likely view is that there could be uncertainty in earlier times about the sex of deities, and the best way to avoid misundertanding with the supernatural realm on this point was to suppose that there were both male and female aspects of any given divine functionary. This caution is enshrined in the Roman formula of prayer: *sive deus sive dea*: 'whether you be god or goddess'.

Various Celtic deities were thought to correspond with Apollo. These were such as Belenus, Bormo, Grannus (DeVries 1963: 82). Sirona or Dirona often appears as his companion. We have seen that Grannus may have been a sun-god: Belenus may also have the meaning of 'bright god'. The Celtic 'Apollo' is the god of healing. Another attribute of Apollo is Maponos (Goidelic: *Mac Óc*). The name would seem to be connected with /maqos/, /mapos/, 'male child'. He could be the patron of children not yet strong enough to bear arms and on that account excluded from the company of their fathers (DeVries 1963: 84). The Brythonic Mabon passes through a testing period of dangers in the legends associated with him: these are no doubt rites of passage towards the attainment of maturity.

The sky-god, mentioned but not named by Caesar, is to be related to the supreme day-god of the IE peoples. He is known in Gaul from various inscriptions and his surnames are varied — for example, Accionis, Poeninus, Taranus, and Uxellinus 'highest' may indicate a supremacy which he enjoyed or used in the past to enjoy. He could be seen as the equivalent of the father-god of the Irish pantheon, the Dagda, or Eochu Ollathir Ruadrofessa. The correspondences are more plausible than assured. 'Ollathir' which actually means 'all-father' is suggestive enough, but the names Eochu, which is from /ek^{w}o/, 'horse', and Ruadrofessa, which means the 'red very wise one', might lead us to suppose that the mobile sun-god was meant.

Lugh (Lugos) seems to be the Celtic god whose worship is most widespread. He was originally a raven-god, as his name suggests, but this aspect of him does not seem to be prominent either in Gaul or in the insular tradition (Ross 1968: 319). In Britain, his name occurs only in placenames, not in inscriptions (N. Chadwick 1984: 152). His importance in Ireland might suggest that he was also a popular subject of worship in Britain. Many towns and settlements were named after him — for instance Lyons and Leiden were originally 'Lugdunum'; Carlisle was 'Luguvallum'. In Celtiberian and Gallaecian inscriptions, Lugeres and Lucares correspond to Lugus in Gaul. He has been equated with Jupiter, Apollo and Hercules, but his most frequent Roman equivalent is Mercury. His association with birds might suggest shamanistic origins or influences in his early cult. The Celtic goddesses of war had avian connections, and Lugus or Loucetius of Lugdunum has characteristics which in some ways suggest a type of Mars. As apparent chief of the Celtic pantheon, magician, warrior, poet, ancestor of heroic families, he has points of resemblance to the Germanic Wotan and Indic Varuna (DeVries 1963: 62).

In Irish mythology, Lugh is a god of great skill and brilliance, who in some texts also appears as king of the Underworld. He is described as a *scál*, an underworld spirit, giant, or ghost (MacNeill 1962: 5ff). His festival 'Lughnásad' (the *násad* or 'games' of Lugh) is still celebrated in Ireland under a Christian guise in August. In this month, a festival in honour of Augustus was held in Lugdunum in Gaul. Lugh was so important a god in Ireland that St Columcille found it expedient to allow his festival to continue under Christian auspices. It was a celebration of the maturity of the year's crops. The Coligny Calendar indicates a festival in the month Rivros, which is August. Anglo-Saxon Lammas is probably another survival of this great European rejoicing (MacNeill 1962: 1–11).

Of the many goddesses worshipped by the Celts, the majority were associated with earth and war and Minerva-like skills. It would be hard to identify a goddess among them who corresponded to Venus or Aphrodite. The importance of mother-goddesses amongst the Celts need have no bearing on the status of women in Celtic society (Weisweiler 1953: 217). Many Latin inscriptions in Celtic countries honour the Matres, Matrae, Matronae, Proxumae, Suleviae, and Iunones. They are represented as three, and in Christian times they possibly became the Three Maries in some places. They occur in Spain as Matres Gallaecae (*CIL* 2764, 2766: Bouchier 1914: 117). In Ireland the three aspects of the goddess Macha may suggest comparison: in Wales y Mamau remain in tradition as fairies, spirits of the earth (DeVries 1963: 131). Of this genus also may have been Epona, the horse-goddess, who is mentioned by Juvenal in his *Satires* (8.158ff). She also occurs in the *Octavius* of Minucius Felix (27.7). Many inscriptions from France to Hungary preserve her name. She was clearly of much greater significance as a chthonic goddess than as a patroness of horses. It has been suggested that she might be identified with the Cymric Rhiannon or 'queen'. Her cult was popular along the European *limes* of the Empire, where cavalry units were a substantial component of the Roman garrison (DeVries 1963: 134). She was still worshipped in the third century AD.

Morrigan ('great queen'), Macha and Badb ('Raven') are one set of names for the Irish version of this triad: Fodla, Banba and Eire are another, and they are probably manifestations of the chthonic Macha, the ancient mother-goddess of the island. One of these Machas was capable of transformation from a sinister crone to a beautiful queen and as such has become the theme of centuries of poetry. The frequency of these goddesses in Ireland has led to the speculation that in that country they may have been derived from, or grafted on to, pre-Celtic deities.

The theme of the transformation of these goddesses survives in the folk tradition of Celtic countries: witches are supposed to be able to change themselves into hares, and the hare which runs out of the last uncut piece of a harvest field is called 'cailleach' ('old woman') in some parts of Ireland. Boudicca is said to have taken omens from the running of a hare before she went to war with the Romans (Rhys 1898: 200).

We have already discussed the incident in which the raven perched on the helmet of M. Valerius when he was fighting his duel with the Celtic chieftain. The Romans took it as a good omen and prayed to it, 'whether god or goddess', to help him. It attacked the Celt with beak and claws (Livy 7.26ff). He was thrown into such confusion of mind that Valerius (afterwards 'Corvinus' in honour of the occasion) easily killed him. We have supposed that the Celt's confidence failed him because he interpreted the bird as a manifestation of the goddesses of war and believed that his defeat was fated. On a naturalistic level, aggressiveness of this kind is well within the range of a raven's pattern of behaviour.

The black-clad women in war in the battle for Anglesey's *nemeton* could be representatives of the raven-black goddesses who move among the warriors in battle spreading dismay with their curses. A raven sits on the shoulder of the terrifying Medb and ravens roost on the dying Cu Chulain. The Gaulish goddess Nantosuelta sometimes has this raven guise (Ross 1968: 314). And Gallo-Roman grave monuments sometimes show the dead holding a raven (Ross 1968: 312). It has been suggested that the goddess called Andrasta in the texts and whom Boudicca held in high regard was Andarta, a Vocontian goddess; further, that she may have been a goddess of war, one of several identities, like the Morrigan, or Badb Catha, 'battle-raven' (Cathubodua) (Ross in Dudley and Webster 1962: 151).

Caesar reports that the Gauls worship a goddess like Minerva (*BG* 6.17). Celtic goddesses, like Sul Minerva, were associated with her. In some places she is Belisaima, which seems to connect with Belenus, a name of the Celtic Apollo, whom she sometimes accompanies. The Gallo-Roman Minerva is in charge of preparations for war and the making of armour. Her identity seems to flow into those of the goddesses whom we have been discussing: the goddesses of war.

The Irish goddess Brigit, like the great tribe of the Brigantes, has a name which suggests authority and power (Ir. *bríg*; Bryth. *bri*). Irish tradition makes her the daughter of the Dagda ('the good god'). Poets, craftsmen and doctors are under her special protection. In this manifestation, as patroness of craftsmen ('be Goibne') she presents a comparison with the Minerva described by Caesar as having originated skills among mankind (*BG* 6.17). Correlatively, Mercury is the inventor of skills, and Apollo is the god of medicine (*BG* ibid.; Weisweiler 1953: 251). As daughter of the Dagda, Brigit is a goddess of the Tuatha Dé Danann, an ancient, probably Bronze Age layer of the Irish population. She may possibly have several identities, each concerned with a particular area of patronage: arts, medicine and the craft of smiths. There is also the hypothesis that 'Brigit' may have been a general word for goddess in Ireland (Weisweiler 1953: 247).

The Irish saint called Brigit is supposed to have had supernatural powers and she also had druidic associations. This could lead to the supposition that there may be some overlap in the traditions relating to the goddess and the saint. They may indeed be the same personality viewed from different angles. At an age before she could speak in ordinary life, the child Brigit is said by the tradition to have murmured in her sleep and in Latin, that the land where she was living would be hers.

The owner of the land where she was at this time living with her mother was a Christian. When she utters the fateful words, *'meum erit hoc'*, the owner's nephew, a druid, understands the import of her utterance. He refuses to go near her because he is not a Christian and he knows from a dream that she is to become a Christian. We note that her infantine prophecy before she could speak her own language was in the sacral and cultural language of the new religion; also that the druid could understand it. 'You're not going to be happy about this' ('Nípu failtiu de em'), the druid says to his uncle: 'she is going to own this land to the crack of doom.'

Christian or not, the uncle is not keen that even a Christian wonderchild should own his estate. But the druid insists that she will be the owner of the land. He has been asked to interpret the child's words, because he not only has learning, but powers of insight which extend even to Christian affairs and he is more able to comprehend them than a Christian layman. This situation seemed reasonable to the writer or writers of the Old Irish life of Brigit in the ninth century AD (or in the eighth century AD, if we suppose that a Latin original was translated into Old Irish). The assimilation of druidism to Christianity was accepted as a historical fact by the authorship of *BB*, and the possibility was conceivable that the two could coexist within one family.

Celtic religion in the ancient world cannot be considered in isolation from the question posed by druidism. This order (if that is an appropriate word) had vigorous powers of survival. In the Gaul of Ausonius, it was remembered with respect in certain families, and evidently it blended gradually with Christianity in some parts, at least, of Christianised Ireland. Roman emperors and governors had in earlier centuries thought it necessary to attack it vigorously, though no Roman proscription seems to have eradicated it entirely from Celtic lands under Roman control.

What was it? No answer can be definitive. It was a learned body of men, which did not completely exclude women. One of its functions was that of intermediary between gods and mankind. It was an intellectual class, artistocratic in composition and tendency. It educated the noble classes in the accumulated learning of the race by means of oral instruction.

There seems to be a pale shadow of evidence in Diogenes Laertius (1.1) that Aristotle or some Peripatetic follower of his spoke of them. The treatise *Magikos* which Diogenes mentions may well originate in the Peripatetic tradition. It would be difficult to suppose that it actually came from the pen of Aristotle himself, though there is no reason why he should not have known about the druids. The reference can hardly be earlier than the third century BC. Diogenes also mentions Sotion of Alexandria as a source, and he may probably be attributed to the second century BC. The passage from Diogenes runs as follows:

> Some say that philosophy began among the barbarians; that the Persians had Magi; the Babylonians or Assyrians had Chaldaeans; the Indians, *gymnosophistai*; and amongst Celts and Galatai, those who were called Druidai and *semnotheoi*, as Aristotle says in his *Magikos*, and Sotion in the third book of his *Succession of Philosophers*.

The *semnotheoi* may have been a class of priest with some druidic learning (Tierney 1960: 170; Ross 1968: 93), or seers, like the *ouateis* (Latin: *vates*) whom Strabo mentions as having sacral functions. I do not think it advisable to make much of the occurrence of Galatai as well as Celts in this passage of Diogenes. Even if the source were of the second century BC, the word 'Galatai' need not specifically refer to Asiatic Galatia, whose inhabitants, however, probably did have the services of druids. The antiquity of the reference is to some modest degree supported by the fact that three authors, Diogenes Laertius, Cyril of Alexandria (*PG* 9.705 Migne), and Clement of Alexandria (*PG* 8.775 Migne) all make similar reports. The Egyptians have philosophical prophets; the Persians, Magi; the Assyrians, Chaldaei; the Indians, gymnosophists; the Celts, in Cyril and Clement, *philosophati*. As we see, Diogenes says that the Celts and Galatai have druids. Cyril and Clement say that the Celts have druids. These two references are, claim the authors, based on the work of Alexander Polyhistor (end of 2nd century BC) whom Diogenes also mentions as having written on Pythagoreanism (8.24). It is impossible to determine whether druids and *philosophati* represent more than one intellectual class or are a verbal doublet. It may be that the *philosophati* can be identified with the *ouateis* whom Strabo mentions and who are versed in the study of nature as well as being priests. It has been suggested that these sources have their origins in an authentic but dispersed and varied tradition about the Pythagoreans (N. Chadwick 1966: 67).

The druids seemed to the Greeks to be a species of philosopher and to resemble the Pythagoreans in their combination of philosophy with superstition. Diodorus, possibly following Poseidonius, says that a druid has to be present when a human sacrifice by stabbing takes place (5.28). There is no information that the druid handles the knife himself. No ancient author applies the word for 'priest' to druids (N. Chadwick 1966: 21). Hippolytus (3rd century AD) claims that the druids learned Pythagorean philosophy from Zalmoxis, the Thracian seer (*Philosophoumena* 1.22). Herodotus tells us that Zalmoxis was the slave of Pythagoras (4.94). Hippolytus also says that Zalmoxis imparted the Pythagorean doctrine to the Getai of Thrace. The flow of information, if it took place, is likely to have been in the opposite direction to that indicated by Hippolytus and his sources. The view that Pythagoreanism was inspired by religious and quasi-philosophical ideas from zones to the north and east of the Mediterranean can be more plausibly argued (Dodds 1951: 141, 146).

Diodorus describes the druids as *philosophoi* and *theologoi*: that is 'philosophers' and 'those who study the gods'. He mentions two other intellectual classes: *bardoi*, 'lyric poets', and *manteis*, 'seers'. No sacrifice is made, he says, without the presence of a *philosophos*, that is, a druid who, as intermediary, can interpret the sacrificial requirements of the gods. The philosophers and poets are obeyed in matters of peace and war by friend and enemy alike, and both classes have the capacity to bring conflicts to an end by rushing into the field of battle and, as it were, singing calming spells over the combatants, just as people might soothe wild beasts. The context, perhaps misleadingly, gives the poets equal importance with the druids in this particular function.

Strabo mentions the druids together with two other classes, the *ouateis*, and the *bardoi* (4.197). As in the account of Diodorus, the *bardoi* are poets; the *ouateis* are priests and also students of nature (*physiologoi*). The name and function of the *ouatis* may correspond to the Irish *fáith* or 'seer' (Ross 1968: 80). The druids study *physiologia* ('physics') and ethical philosophy, and they also have a juridicial function, especially in cases of homicide. When there are many such cases, it is predicted that the harvest will be good. Strabo attributes to druids the doctrine of the immortality of the soul and the universe; and also the view that in the universe, sometimes fire prevails and sometimes flood. It has been suggested that Strabo has omitted some sentences about human sacrifice just before the reference to harvests (N. Chadwick 1966: 20ff). Following the point about harvests in Strabo's account comes his well-known passage about the embalming of the severed heads of worthy enemies, and divination from the writhings of stabbed human sacrificial victims. There is no direct link in our information which associates druids with headhunting. We may accept the view (N. Chadwick, ibid.) that Strabo's compilation from his source, which was probably Poseidonius, is confused. The picture emerges clearly enough, however, of the druids as the most senior and influential of the intellectual classes. The account was not designed to be friendly to Celts or druids.

It would not be unreasonable to suppose that the study of the natural universe was not the exclusive domain of the druids, though they were chief practitioners of this research. Strabo suggests that the *hieropoioi* or 'priests' were also educated in this subject. It is possible that the *hieropoioi* correspond to the *manteis* in Diodorus' account.

Caesar refers to only one intellectual class in the Celtic community, the druids, whom he describes as the educators of the Gaulish nobles (*BG* 6.13). In Lucan's *Pharsalia* (1.451ff), bards and *druidae* occur. His description of sinister rites held in the secrecy of the forests conveys an atmosphere of human sacrifice as well as explicitly mentioning it:

> . . . these also by whom cruel
> Teutates is placated by dreadful blood, and Esus,
> horrid on his ferocious altars, no more kindly
> than the cult of Scythian Diana.   (7.445ff)

The allusion is to the alleged Thracian practice of sacrificing strangers, which informs the plot of Euripides' tragedy *Iphigeneia in Tauris*. In ancient Ireland there were a number of learned classes: a bard was a lyric poet, a *fili* was a more elevated species of poet whose work had a certain sacral atmosphere; the *drui* was

273

the druid (N. Chadwick 1966: 18ff). Their functions cannot be paralleled exactly with their earlier continental counterparts. It would be fair to suppose only a broad correspondence between them.

The accounts of the druids in Strabo, Diodorus and Caesar overlap noticeably. They seem to be based mainly on Poseidonius (N. Chadwick 1966: 9; Tierney 1960: 203). Diodorus cites the work of Timagenes, who came to Rome as a prisoner in the middle of the first century BC, was freed and lived to make a career as a historian, specialising in research on the Celts. Referring to Timagenes, Ammianus Marcellinus (4th century AD) says that there were *bardi, euhages* and *drasidai* amongst the Celts; the last two names of learned classes are obvious mutants of *ouateis* and *druidai* (N. Chadwick 1966: 19).

The Irish myth of Mide, the eponymous hero of Meath, may symbolise quarrels between learned brotherhoods and the secular power (*Dindshenchas* vol. 9.2.44). Not only was Mide a man of power, he was also a poet and prophet; thus the question of rivalry and hostility between learned groups is involved.

When Mide had called the 'great and noble druids' to an assembly, he cut out their tongues. 'Then he sat down, that great seer and poet, over the place where they were buried.' There seems to have been some element of sympathetic magic in this act. Mide's nurse — a foster-mother rather than servant — the druidess Gaine, uttered a kenning in the form of a prescriptive pun, in order to formalise his action. It is 'over something' she said: 'ós neod' — and the place was called 'Usneid' afterwards. She was careful, we may observe, to be vague and not to rehearse Mide's treatment of the druids in precise, referential detail. The poet Aed Ua Carthaig (12th century AD) was careful to include this piece of characterisation. He also cautiously asks God and the king of Meath for protection, since he has told the story. This is, of course, a polite formula, but it shows in addition that he thought it prudent to enlist the aid not only of the Christian God, but the pagan daemon, in case the latter should still have some residual and malignant power. The story shows that the druids could seem to be an obstacle to a primitive war-lord (and poet) who might find that he was able to cut off their magic at source, namely their tongues. More sophisticated rulers, like Augustus and Tiberius, could place them under ban or, if an occasion offered, have them massacred, as happened in Anglesey in the reign of Claudius.

Julius Caesar concentrates upon the role of the druids as a politically influential class like the nobles. He neglects or does not know of the other learned classes of Celtic society. His purpose always is to generate publicity in support of his own record of conquest in Gaul. He takes from Poseidonius only what he needs for this purpose. The 'Golden Age' and 'Noble Savage' themes have no interest for him as a writer with a practical aim in view within the confines of an unheroic political environment. In contrast to Caesar, the primitive hero and the Stoic philosopher have in common a devotion to the cult of the honourable life: the former through physical courage that brings glory in battle; the latter through the purposeful integration of his life's activities with the intentions and movements of an animated cosmos. Both see death as a pathway to some other condition of existence. Both regard suicide as far from inglorious. Neither would have much time for Julius Caesar.

Caesar interposes a brief note on the Celtic aristocratic class between his account of the druids and his comments on the Celtic religion. He describes druids as philosophers who are interested in the structure of the natural universe and who exercise a political influence almost on a national level (*BG* 6.15). Their power, however it may be defined, was based on a religious authority which they were able to invoke forcefully. Druids could ban a person from sacrifices, a most painful sanction, which involved a public boycott of the individual under their interdict. They were present at sacrificial executions, which not infrequently took the form of burning the victim alive. Nor had the druids, according to Caesar, any inhibitions about choosing as sacrificial victims individuals who were neither criminals nor prisoners of war, if no members of these classes were available (*BG* 6.16.4). Caesar is happy to present these physiologers as having more than a tincture of cruel irrationality. The practice of human sacrifice was an excellent utensil for his propaganda campaign. The more barbarous the Celts seem, the better pretext he has for treating them as he does. Cicero uses the prejudice against human sacrifice in his speech, delivered in 69 BC, in defence of Fonteius whom the Gauls were accusing of maladministration.

Pliny (*NH* 16.95) connects the word 'druid' with the Greek word 'drys' which means an 'oak'. This could simply be a calque from the Greek. 'Dru' may be a Celtic intensive prefix added to the root /wid/, 'know'; or again, the 'id' of druid could be a Celtic dental noun-stem ending: *drui/ druid* : *fili/filid* (N. Chadwick

1966: 12; Ross 1968: 89). By the former analysis, druid 'wise person' could be translated directly as Greek *'philosophos'*. The druids were the teachers of young nobles. So were they also in insular Celtic tradition. Cathbad taught Cu Chulain. He is represented in *TBC* 922ff as teaching the Ulster hero to-be about god and bad omens in a class of several pupils. We hear of the god of the druid cult, *dé druidechta*, but his name is not mentioned. There is a suggestion that since the druids, as students of the natural universe, have an interest in meteorological phenomena with which many of their wonderful feats are connected, the god in question might be the god of the sky. Maximus of Tyre (2nd century AD) says that the Celts believed Jupiter to be an oak (8.8). The mistletoe is sacred because it grows on the oak (Pliny *NH* 16.95). The god of the druids could be the Brythonic Math Hen (Rhys 1898: 222–5). A Jupiter figure or Dis pater are possible candidates. There is no evidence that the god or gods of the druids were those of the population at large (Ross 1968: 29).

In her invaluable study, Dr Anne Ross asks whether the popularity of such gods as Esus, Teutates, Lugos and Cernunnos could have been due to their pre-eminence in the druidic cult. Her argument is that an intensification of druidic activity as a nationalistic movement in response to the threat from Rome might have promoted an ecumenism under these gods in order to give coherence to the defence of the national culture and territory. Further, she wonders whether Cernunnos may not be the Dis pater mentioned by Caesar as the ancestor god of the Celts (Ross 1968: 80, 212).

On this argument, since Lugos and other gods supposed to be of special interest to the druids occur in the British Isles, it might be possible to infer that this particular form of their worship was brought into Britain from Gaul, where Roman pressure was being particularly applied, and the new phases of their cult had their strongest motivation (Ross 1968: 457). There would be no need to assume that their cults did not antedate this new movement in Britain and Ireland, nor would there be any obligation to contest Caesar's opinion that the druids originated in Britain (*BG* 6.13). Britain would be a secure base from which to manage a national and religious revival. The activity of British druids could easily give rise to the impression, or the fabrication, that Britain was the home of druidism. We have no reason to believe that it was. We do not know where it came into being.

Caesar does not draw attention to the fact that the Aeduan

prince Divitiacus was a druid, even though he had some negotiations with him. The omission may be deliberate. Cicero claims that Divitiacus was a friend of his and that he was an expert in *physiologia* (*De Div.* I. 90). Their friendship must have been modified by the fact that neither could speak the other's language. Cicero's remark about the scientific interests in Divitiacus may have been taken from Poseidonius' comments about druids (Tierney 1960: 224). Divitiacus seems to have been a civilised man and it would have been of interest to hear his opinions about human sacrifice. We bear in mind that civilised Roman individuals could tolerate the gladiatorial games.

The cult of the druids has been thought to be of pre-Celtic origin. This does not necessarily mean pre-IE, though the inevitable blending of tribes and the assimilation of ideas and speech in the ancient world would indicate that some pre-IE themes were adopted, as they were in ancient Greek religion. There seems to have been an awareness of this possibility in antiquity: Ammianus reports that the druids believed that the Celts were composed of an element of population which was aboriginal in Gaul and another which had come in from the regions beyond the Rhine (15.9.4). He cites Timagenes as his authority for this. It is by no means an unreasonable view.

Certain aspects of the druids suggest the influence of that ancient complex of ideas and customs which has been called 'shamanism'. Not only the doctrine of the survival of the soul after death, but the importance of birds in Celtic religion may point to such a component. Augury by the flight of birds was practised by Celts, Greeks and Romans (Diod. 5.31), but in shamanism the bird is more immediately significant. We have noted the significance of the raven-goddesses in the Celtic world. The cock was also revered amongst the Gauls (*BG* 5.12). In a cult statue, the goose is the companion of a god who is similar to Mars. The archaism of the Irish tradition presents us with the druid Mag Ruith (who may well be a god) dressed in bird-costume like a Eurasian shaman (Ross 1968: 333). In his *Lorica*, St Columba, who himself has an avian name, makes a connection between druids and birds:

I do not care for the language of birds:
My druid is Jesus Christ, the Son of God   (Ross 1968: 329)

There may be a trace of shamanism in the story of Suibhne

Geilt, 'Mad Sweeny', the anti-hero of a Middle Irish romance, who became or thought he became a bird as the result of a curse. At all events he spent several miserable years roosting in the trees (Beneš 1960). These are slight traces, but not, I suggest, negligible; they may be aboriginal in the parts of Europe in which the IE-speaking Celts settled, or the Celts themselves may have brought them from some other place. In either case, there seem to be elements in the Celtic religion which have an origin in the foreworld of European and Eurasian life. Comparable traces have been discerned in the Greek world. Zalmoxis, the Thracian seer, who taught Epimenides of Crete, may have been a carrier of shamanistic ideas. Some of the ceremonies and teachings of the Pythagoreans, as far as the slight evidence about them allows us to judge, could be considered shamanistic (Dodds 1951: 144ff). If the doctrine of the immortality, or at least the survival, of the soul was prevalent in the Celtic domain, as Strabo, following Poseidonius and other authorities, maintains, then it is hard to accept that it was not propounded by the druids. There is no evidence to connect this Celtic belief with the Pythagorean doctrine of immortality, but the connection could be there all the same. Pomponius (*De Sit. Orb.* 3.19), and Ammianus (15.9.8) regard the burial of grave-goods with the deceased in Celtic lands as proof that the Celts believed in the immortality of the soul. To judge by the articles which have been found, the warrior-class expected to do some fighting in the next world. The cult of the dead may also imply a reverence for ancestors, characteristic of a warrior-aristocracy. Possibly some family lines were traced back to Dis pater (Ross 1968: 85ff). We should not assume that the ancient Celtic notion of survival after death was like the transmigration of the Pythagoreans, of which we perhaps have an adorned version in Plato's *Phaedo* and *Republic* 10, or that it was like the doctrines of Indic religion. Lucan, in his *Pharsalia* (1.458), brilliantly intuits that for the Celts, 'death is the middle of a long life'. This may be closer to the feelings of a Celtic warrior than a more developed code of transmigration. Lucan is convinced that this teaching is druidic and that it is their exclusive function to understand the nature of the universe. He is impressed by the absence from Celtic eschatological teaching of any idea of punishment or retribution after death. This differs from Pythagorean notions of death and rebirth. In the Irish tradition, the Celtic notion of a happy other world was translated early into Christian terms in the *Echtra Conlai* ('The Expedition of Conla') and *Imram*

Bráin ('Voyage of Bran') (MacCana 1972: 100). Lucan also takes the view that the Celts are released by this doctrine from the fear of death, and consequently are bolder in battle (1.441). The same view had already been been expressed by Caesar, who no doubt took it from an earlier source (*BG* 6.14). Pomponius takes the view that this was the only one of their secret doctrines that the druids allowed to be published among the people at large, because it would be conducive to an intensification of courage in battle (3.2.19). Valerius Maximus recalls that Celts would lend money on the understanding that it would be repaid in the next world. He clearly regards this as an absurd notion but is constrained to point out that the Pythagoreans held similar opinions to the barbarians (2.6.10). It is an exaggeration on the part of ancient authors to attribute the doctrine of immortality to a deliberate policy on the part of the druids in order to increase the bravery of warriors in the field and, of course, their own public influence (N. Chadwick 1966: 54). But we can have no doubt that the doctrine had the practical effect of relieving warriors of much of their fear.

Caesar is suspected of exaggerating the power and influence of the druids as part of his broad propagandist effort (Tierney 1960: 203, 223). And following this comes the further implication that the druids need not have been very different from the priests of the Germanic tribes (Tierney 1960: 224). These opinions do not lack plausibility. There is, however, too much evidence that the druids were a special class of religious intermediary, with a distinctly intellectual side to their functions in society, for us to be able to accept this more elementary view of them. Caesar is only one of our witnesses. And it is admitted that some ancient authorities tended to emphasise their intellectuality in a way that arouses suspicion: Poseidonius (Str. 4.4.97) sees druids as philosophers, and they are frequently referred to in Greek sources by that designation. The teaching attributed to them that the universe is subject to periodic conflagrations and floods (Str., ibid.) adds to the impression that they were thought of as some species of wild Stoic. If they were no more remarkable than the priests of the Germans, we may ask why the ancients did not give us a similarly dramatic description of these Germanic priests. We need not distrust Caesar when he says that the druids had a *disciplina*, a 'philosophy' (*BG* 6.13). They were an intellectual force in Celtic society, and a force to be taken seriously. Dio Chrysostom (2nd century AD) is less convincing when he asserts, with more rhetoric than conviction, that, as a political element, they were superior in authority to the kings (*Or.* 49).

Caesar gives us the interesting information that druids had to spend twenty years in learning the traditional knowledge of their order (*BG* 6.14). In Gaelic Ireland, the higher grade of poets, the *filid*, took twenty years to learn their art. These poets seem to have inherited some of the functions and prestige of the druids. Since the mode of ancient Celtic learning and record was oral, it is highly likely that the druids, who had much legal, religious and 'philosophical' material to assimilate, took a very long time to qualify for membership of their order. Twenty years would seem to be a reasonable period for their studies.

Were these ruthless presidents at the rite of human sacrifice really comparable with Stoic gentlemen? We may say immediately that there was no shortage of ruthlessness among the Stoics of Rome, though there was also humane good feeling and sympathy. Poseidonius sees druids through Stoicising spectacles. It may be true that the Pythagoreans and druids drank from the same ancient well of superstitious wisdom. In one part of the ancient Celtic world, the druids certainly were a caste of revered educators, religious leaders and political advisers: this situation in second- and first-century BC Gaul may at that time have had its analogies elsewhere in the Celtic domain. In less prosperous and advanced parts of this domain, however, the druids could have been more like shamanistic witch-doctors than Greek philosophers. Also, it is by no means unknown for the practitioners of cruelty and unreason to be at the same time subtle intellectuals.

There is no literary evidence for druidism in Spain or Galatia. In Galatia, the name of their sacred precinct 'Drunemeton' suggests that there was druidism in the country. It was the custom of druids to teach their students in remote glades of the forest (Pomponius 2.6.10; *Actas* 136). Since we have a reasonable amount of information about the Galatians, we might suppose that druids would have been mentioned in literature if they had been a significant factor in Galatian national life. They may have played a part less influential than that attributed to them in Gaul. We cannot tell: in Spanish Galicia, the placename 'Nemetobriga' suggests a tree-cult and possibly the presence of druids.

Lucan thought that the druids performed their rites in dark and remote woodland areas. He uses the related Latin word *nemus* to describe the locations of their ceremonies. This seems to be the common opinion of the time when he lived (1st century AD), and it very probably came from Poseidonius. *Nemus* can also bear this kind of sacral meaning: the sacred grove of Diana at Aricia was guarded by a priest called the *rex nemorensis*, who ruled until some challenger came to fight him and succeed in killing him. In Celtic lands, the *nemet* element occurs in the names of places as separate as Medionemeton in southern Scotland and the Drunemeton of Galatia (Salway 1981: 673, 713). Old Irish *nemed* ('sanctuary') which is glossed in the texts by Latin *sacellum*, is related to *nemeton*. The word may be connected with /nem/ 'share out, divide'.

Within the confines of our evidence we may cautiously infer some connection between the druids and the *nemeta*, the tree-cult and the great World Tree. The Gundestrupp cauldron shows a tree being carried on the tips of the spears of warriors in a ceremonial act. We have asked whether the officiating priest in the picture is a druid or the god of druids — he may, for all that we have of certain evidence, simply be a *hieropoios* — some ordinary priest, though that might seem to be inherently unlikely. Nor are we in a position to say that all *nemeta* are associated with the druidic cult, though if important sacrifices are to take place in them, we are assured that a druid will be present. Druids were in some sense the administrators, but not necessarily always the executives of religious ceremonies (*BG* 6.13).

Traces of the tree-cult are widely encountered in the Celtic domain. Erriapus, an apparent form of the Roman Mercury in the Garonne district, is depicted as a head projecting from leafage (Ross 1968: 62). Trees represented the many-branching vitality of the world itself, and they would be of importance to druids in their role as philosophers of nature (Ross 1968: 63ff). Nemetona and Arnemetia are names of goddesses which also suggest the cult. Tacitus mentions the sacred groves of Anglesey; also Boudicca made her sacrifices to 'Andrasta' in a grove. In Irish placenames the word 'bile' for 'tree' is a frequent component — for example, Movilla is *magh bile*, 'tree-plain', and no doubt it preserves the memory of the pagan worship of trees in County Down. There is an ancient Christian foundation in this place, which may have been put there to keep the spiritual energy associated with the old worship under firm Christian control. The precise Gaulish equivalent is *Biliomagus* (Dottin 1920: 234). Silvanus or Colturius at Colchester may be cognate with the Irish god of the *Tuatha Dé Danann*, Mac Cuill, who is named after the hazel-tree (Ross 1968: 64).

Later Celtic temples were not generally impressive in architectural terms. There was little of the imposing in most Celtic buildings. In many instances an element of impermanency seemed to be in the very premiss of their construction. We tend to assume that the generality of Greco-Roman religious buildings were elegant. This was not the case: many shrines and cult objects in the Greek and Roman world were simple and primitive, and were not altered from that condition throughout long centuries (Salway 1981: 672). For example, the influential oracular shrine of Dodona retained its rural atmosphere and surroundings, though Delphi was equipped with lavish temples and treasuries. Classical influences under the Empire, together with the assimilative process of the *interpretatio Romana*, led to examples of more robust building-construction. At Lydney, a substantial Romano-British temple was dedicated to the Celtic god Nodens, who is possibly the Irish god Nuadu argatlám, 'silver-handed Nuada' (N. Chadwick 1966: 84).

Our lack of knowledge about the precise contents and direction of the druids' teaching on the great topics of their concern originates in their institutional secrecy and their reluctance to set down their doctrines in writing. In this point at least they accurately resemble the early Pythagoreans, about whose philosophy we have similar difficulties. The druids only used the Greek alphabetic system for the record of unimportant matters (*BG* 6.14). The only barbarian people of Europe who used writing in a more general way were the Turditani of Spain, who are reputed to have had their own system of writing and to have written down six thousand verses of their own laws (Str. 3.16). As far as we know, the Turditani were not a Celtic people. Numerous inscriptions from Spain in a number of scripts and from various tribes prove the use of writing from early times for a variety of purposes.

Our oldest extensive document from Gaul is the Coligny Calendar, which was inscribed on brass. Since the druids were interested in astronomical matters, it may have some connection with their teaching and thought. Since it is available in writing, it no doubt had, as we might expect of a calendar, a secular as well as a sacral significance and use. In the names of its months, it embodies with 'q' forms instead of the expected 'p', namely, *equos*, and *quimon* and *qut* (Dottin 1920: 175ff). We have mentioned that this could suggest the admixture of q-Celtic speakers in the district, or the preservation for ceremonial purposes of dialect forms (Chapter 1 above).

Later generations of druids had fewer inhibitions about writing. Muirchu's *Life of Patrick* (8th century AD) mentions a suggested ordeal by water in which a druidic and a Christian book were tested to see which would float and which would sink. If this is anything more than an anecdote, it suggests that, in the time of Patrick's ministry (5th century AD), it was not unthinkable for druidic wisdom to be recorded in a book.

The oral system of recording and imparting knowledge leaves its traces in the older layers of Irish law tracts. Some laws are expressed in verse (like those of the Turditani and the ancient Japanese), and these verses may be derived from the typical IE 'short line' (Watkins 1963). The legal consultant would speak his answer to questions of law in verse. The text of such law tracts follows the question and answer procedure which strongly suggests the memorising discipline of oral learning. The introductory phrase preceding the answer to a point of law is often the formulaic phrase: 'Ara chen fenechas': 'the law tradition sings'. The responses themselves sometimes have the rhythm and alliterative character of very early Irish verse (Thurneysen 1928: 20).

The importance of spoken language in the Celtic world is illustrated by the striking artistic motif of the head from which chains stretch to attach to other heads. A picture of this, in a more or less Classical form, is described by Lucian (2nd century AD). He claims that he saw the picture of an old man in a lion-skin, armed with a club and followed by people who were attached by gold and amber chains of great delicacy to his tongue. An educated Celtic bystander informed the narrator that the Celts identify the god of communication, not with the Greek Hermes, but with Heracles. This god is Ogmios. The likening of this god to Heracles is indicative of the power which is attributed to eloquence, and he is old in the picture, because age and experience contribute to the growth of the power of eloquence, which is infinitely more strong than brute force. One noteworthy point about the picture was that the followers were willing to be led (Lucian 5.1–6).

Poseidonius, through the agency of Strabo (5.31), refers to the ability of bards to stop battles and notes that in this ferocious Celtic race the Muses are treated with deference by the god of war. This was the tendency of the message conveyed to Lucian. There may be a reflex of this picture in one of the versions of *TBC* (DeVries 1963: 74). Here, there is a scene in which a figure advances over the plain of Meath dragging a veritable multitude of people attached to him by chains in much the same way as is described in Lucian's essay, except that they are being dragged unwillingly, with their faces to the ground and, as they proceed, they utter recriminations against their leader, who contradicts their abuse. Possibly both versions are derived from something much more primitive: perhaps the magical distortion that is sometimes said to affect heroic and semi-divine personages — the *riastrad*. For instance, Cu Chulain is described as having some species of ectoplasmic projection emanating from the top of his head to the height of a ship's mast (DeVries 1963: 75). If we take this view, the Irish version, which we might be tempted to see as a mere trace of a forgotten function of Ogmios, could be closer to an original and more cruel notion of divine intervention in human life than the civilised Hellenising allegory narrated by Lucian. In the Leinster *TBC* (4081), Ogma is given the attribute *grianainech*, which must mean 'bright' or 'sunny' (rather than 'one who possesses a grÍanan or *solarium*'). The solar allusion might help to explain the chains as rays of the sun. DeVries refers to the occurrence on Celtic coins of an eye with projections — rays, most likely, coming from it (1963: 75). These images could have iconic significances which need not be uniform at all times and places in the ancient Celtic world.

According to the story of Lucian, the Celts regarded language as the strongest power in the universe and Heracles, rather than Hermes or Mercurius, seemed to the Classically influenced Celt to be its appropriate patron. But we may suppose that originally it was the magical power of the word rather than its rhetorical persuasiveness which was the basis of its power. Eloquence grew out of magic; persuasion, from spells.

The Ogam script of the insular Celtic world may carry the name of its divine discoverer, Ogmios. Nennius (*Hist. Brit.* 13) says that Ogma was a brother of the Dagda; he was inventor of the 'Scotic', that is, Goidelic alphabet. He was also, as his relationship to the Dagda indicates, one of the gods of the Tuatha Dé Danann. In the battle of Magh Tured, Ogma appears as a heroic fighter. We have already noted him in a list of warriors in *TBC*.

We must at least mention the possibility that this linear script, Ogam, was used or perhaps invented by the druids, but we have no evidence about its precise origins. It seems to be a mutant offspring of the Greek alphabet, which was used, Caesar tells us, by the druids of Gaul. It consists of lines incised in various sizes and shapes — on either side of an edge or line. This kind of writing is particularly useful for inscriptional purposes. Usually its name is associated with Ogmios. J.F. Killeen has ingeniously derived the word 'Ogam' from the Greek word *'ogmos'*, meaning 'a furrow' (1965). His theory can be supported by many examples from Greek literature which compare writing to ploughing. His view carries with it the implication that this form of writing, which in Celtic, by epenthesis, would probably have been pronounced 'ogamos', originated in the Greco-Celtic culture of southern France. This is the zone in which we might expect old prejudices about writing to have been subjected to their earliest modification. The abstract shapes of Ogam signs would sympathetically meet the druids' traditional distrust of writing, and it would have the merit of secrecy in being so different from the current Greek alphabets.

We shall now turn our attention to the question of human sacrifice, which was regarded in the ancient Classical world as characteristic of the Celt religion — and consequently associated with the druids. Poseidonius' information about human sacrifice is detailed enough to suggest, though not beyond reasonable doubt, that he had personal acquaintance with societies which practised it. His account of holocausts of victims imprisoned in gigantic anthropomorphic crates of wicker is transmitted to us by Strabo (4.4.198) and Julius Caesar (*BG* 6.16). This was one method of sacrifice: stabbing and drowning were others. In her revolt, Boudicca is said to have impaled prisoners, whom she sacrificed to a deity, and to her resentment.

The *Dindshenchas* record apparent examples of human sacrifice in their topographical poems about Tailten and Magh Slecht (Joyce 1913: I. 281). These entries, which suggest comparison with continental Celtic practices, may perhaps on these very grounds be regarded with suspicion, since the *Dindshenchas* cannot be free of the prejudices of Latinate Christians who could be attracted by material derogatory to the old religion. In the *Tripartite Life* of St Patrick, where his overthrow of Cromm Cruach, the principal 'idol' of pagan Ireland, is described, there is no allusion to human sacrifice. The precinct of Cromm Cruach at Magh Slecht was famous for human as well as animal sacrifice. According to the *Dindshenchas*, the god was entitled to the first-born of every family. Perhaps this practice had fallen into desuetude in Patrician times.

Stories concerning *bruidne*, hostels of an apparently other-world character, sometimes involve the conflagration of the building with heroes trapped inside. These stories may be part of a tradition, fossilised in this form in Irish literature, which reflects the kind of enactment described by Poseidonius and Caesar (Ross 1968: 82). In the mythological history of Ireland, a number of kings are said to have been killed by their successors. This tradition, which reminds us of the *rex nemorensis*, indicates a sacral or sacrificial aspect of Celtic kingship which is consistent with a king's killing himself when he suffers a defeat which must in itself blemish him and render him unfit for rule (Binchy 1970: 11). In these terms, the suicide of Brennus in 278 BC becomes easier to understand.

In the *Iliad* we are told that Achilles sacrificed twelve noble Trojan prisoners in honour of the dead Patroclus. This act is extraordinary within the context of the epic. In the Classical Mediterranean world, the Arcadians, notoriously a race of rough and primitive mountaineers, are supposed to have engaged in human sacrifice. The pseudo-Platonic *Minos* (315c) refers to the sacrifice of human beings as a contemporary practice in certain festivals of Greece (Burkert 1983: 89). This little dialogue can hardly be later than the third century BC.

Nor were the Romans incapable of human sacrifice. The effigies of the mysterious Argei which were bound hand and foot and thrown into the Tiber are clearly vestiges of original human sacrifices, though it has been suggested with little plausibility that these mere models were used from the beginning of the custom in earliest antiquity. In 228 BC, an imminent attack from the Insubres may have helped to motivate the sacrifice of a Gaulish man and woman, and a Greek man and woman. This may have been an act of apotropaic magic against threatening nations. The custom was reinstated in a time of extreme crisis during the Second Punic War (Latte 1960: 156). Sacrifices were made to placate these victims in Plutarch's lifetime (1st–2nd centuries AD) (Dumézil 1970: 447). This may indicate a continuing guilty fear about the consequences of a sacrifice which, even at the time of anxiety which prompted it, was seen to be archaic and desperate. Livy records that after the terrible defeat of Cannae in 216 BC, the Romans modified the sacrifice of the Argei and began to use real people instead of effigies. Their authority for this change was the Sibylline Books. Livy castigates it as a most un-Roman ceremony (*minime Romano sacro*: 22.57).

The Etruscans held contests at burials, and these contests involved the shedding of blood (Ath. 153f). Prisoners and criminals were used for this purpose. The Etruscan terminology of Roman gladiatorial games suggests an element of Etruscan inspiration in their origin and development. Gladiators were customarily regarded as the dregs of society, fit only for combat and death. Roman citizens of sufficient prominence and wealth held gladiatorial games in honour of the funerals of members of their own families. Livy mentions several instances of private games from 215 BC to 183 BC (Latte 1960: 155). The earliest recorded example of such games being instituted by private individuals is in 264 BC, when two brothers of the *gens Iunia* decided to honour their dead father by this means (Val. Max. 2.47).

The Romans seemed to be able to make a distinction in their minds between these gladiatorial sacrifices and the human sacrifice practised by the Celts. Perhaps they reassured themselves by means of the element of fighting chance which gladiatorial contests afforded their victims. In the late Republic and early Principate, the custom of human sacrifice survived unofficially on a 'lower-culture' level (to use Margaret Murray's phrase, 1970): children were sacrificed in rites to conjure up the spirits of the dead (Cic. *In Vat.* 14). The fifth *Epode* of Horace is a curiously horrifying and pathetic description of a sacrifice in which a child is sadistically killed for the making of a love-potion.

According to the elder Pliny, the custom of human sacrifice was not accepted as civilised (*HN* 30.12). Yet the practice was not so obsolete in Rome of middle to late first century AD, as so advanced a person might wish to be the case (*HN* 29.12). During the Principate of Claudius, and probably at the instigation of his antiquarian cruelty, foreigners were buried alive at Rome, as Gaulish and Greek victims had been in the past. Syme thinks that they may have been Britons, who were specially active enemies of Rome at the time (1958: 456–9).

Christian authors, such as Tertullian (2nd and 3rd centuries AD) (*Apol.* 9), Minucius Felix (*Octavius* 304) and Tatian (2nd century AD) (29), report that human sacrifices were carried out at the festival of the Latini. This may be a reference to gladiatorial games, though it is not certain that such games formed part of the celebration of this festival (Latte 1960: 256). These writers regard human sacrifice as typically pagan, just as Greeks and Romans looked on it as characteristically Celtic. In the first century AD, Pomponius Mela seemed to think that human sacrifice among the Celts was a thing of the past. According to him, the druids were teachers of eloquence and students of the nature of the universe (3.2). He does not seem to connect the reputation of human sacrifice with the druids, but with the Celts in general. He admits, however, that some individuals commit suicide at the funeral pyres of those with whom they hope to live in the other world. Roman expressions of distaste for human sacrifice were more vociferous than sincere. Their professed disgust for it was a useful pretext for dismantling the authority of the druids and thus making way for the operation of the *interpretatio Romana* upon the native cults (Ross 1968: 462). The influence of the druids did not succumb even in the closer embrace in which Gaul was held by Rome in the Julio-Claudian Principates. But to what extent were they a power in their own land in these early imperial times? The principal Celtic families took to Classical education, the rational basis of which would tend to argue down the religious component of druidic teaching. We need not assume that many druids did not adopt the new learning. The testimony of later centuries suggests that many did. Syme conjectures that the distinctive culture and learning of the upper class of druids died out in Gaul, and that all that were left were village witch-doctors. Julius Caesar had granted citizenship to many of the Gaulish chiefs in order to secure their alliance in the Civil War. Gallia Comata had become similar to provinces like Asia or Galatia in that the landowners, as the chiefs had become, were firmly joined to the imperial power of which they were effectively clients (Syme 1939: 474). This served to stabilise volatile communities, but it also tended to institution-alise the already marked social differentiations of Celtic society. There was no special role in this political script for druids.

Roman conquest may have suppressed Celtic human sacrifice (Str. 198), but the custom is likely to have persisted in remoter areas. Pliny (*NH* 30.13) says that in the Principate of Tiberius, the druids and other learned orders were abolished; we note that, like Poseido-nian sources other than Julius Caesar, Pliny speaks of them in the plural. According to Suetonius (*Claudius* 25), Claudius was respons-ible for this abolition, but the process was initiated by Augustus. From the very nature of the case, the policy could only be inter-mittently applied. Except when druids were in congregation in a place such as Anglesey, it would not be easy, at one blow, to get rid of a large number of a class accustomed to the ways of secrecy.

The Romans had an inherited dislike of religious exclusiveness, which they associated almost unconsciously with political sub-version — witness their repeated suppression of *sodalicia* and *collegia* in Rome itself and their persecution of the Neo-Pythagoreans. They professed to dislike cults which involved the cruelty of human sacrifice, though their hands were not spotless at any time of the Republic's history, and there was the perpetual bloodiness of the gladiatorial sacrifices. We should also mention their revolting custom of ritually strangling important prisoners as part of the celebration of the triumph of a victorious general.

Their fear of secret and exclusive religions is amply illustrated by the long and sanguinary conflicts between the Jews and the Roman imperial power, which resulted in the dispersal of the Jewish people. A consequence was that certain emperors — Nero and Titus are the most obvious instances — became synonymous with evil and cruelty in the Talmudic tradition. In the Celtic lands, it seemed in the Roman interest to find familiar and suitable names as quickly as possible for the multifarious deities. The sheer number and variety of function of Celtic gods and goddesses, though their sum cannot be proved to be equal to that of Roman major and minor deities and *numina*, provided generous scope for cross-reference in nomenclature between the two traditions. Gallia Comata and Galatia were introduced to the worship of Rome and Augustus. In the former instance the purpose was to give the war against the German tribes the flavour of a crusade. Drusus established a temple to Rome and Augustus at Lugdunum. In this he was encouraged by his scholarly brother, Claudius.

The decline of Italy after the Civil War was implicitly recognised by the increase in the number of senators from Gaul. The upper classes of Gaul had at least this measure of redress for their sufferings. Though Claudius in particular was active in adding Gauls to the roll of senators, he not only kept druids at arm's length, but vigorously suppressed them. It is impossible that we should simply fall back on the familiar argument of Claudian whimsicality to explain this attitude. He saw them as a real danger to the process of Romanisation, which was essential both to the security of Roman rule in Gaul and to the safety of Italy. No historian could forget the traditional menace of an unconstrained Gaul. Potential centres of ideological opposition to Rome had to be eliminated. The druids were not warrior princes, though they were of their kindred. As Caesar tells us, they were immune from military service. Since their influence was capable of rivalling that of the kings and chieftains, these latter perhaps did not take too unkindly to a policy which kept the druids down.

In the early Empire, Bibracte, the chief town of the Aedui and a notable druidic school, was replaced by Augustodunum in 12 BC. When the Aedui and Treveri rebelled in 21 BC, they made it their chief object to take Augustodunum, so that they could get control of the noble Celtic young who were being educated there. This would have provided them with hostages to persuade the alliance of other tribes and families throughout Gaul (Tac. *Ann.* 3.43). Tiberius' acts of suppression followed the revolt of Sacrovir (21 AD). It was then, as Pliny tells us, that Tiberius suppressed the learned classes of Gaul. The druids and the others continued to practise in caves and glades, like the hedge-schoolmasters of Ireland. In 54 AD, Claudius abolished the whole order, as Suetonius reports, along with its religion of cruelty. Augustus had merely forbidden druids to become Roman citizens. Yet in 71 AD, in the revolt of Civilis, we find druids prophesying the destruction of Roman power, as portended by a fire which broke out on the Capitol (Tac. *Hist.* 4.54.2). Clearly the suppressions were not entirely effective (N. Chadwick 1966: 77). Their survival to this point and beyond was of comparatively little importance: they were doomed to decline when they ceased to be the teachers of the Celtic upper class.

Yet they could fan some sources of discontent among the rich, who were proud, aggressive, and still retained some of the marks of the old heroic ethos. Lowly though many druids had become, they could still be used by the rich, and might yet inspire the poor, who were ripe for revolution under the Empire, since they associated their hardships with the domination of Rome rather than with the system under which they lived. Both the chiefs, who were now landlords, and the poor were aggrieved at the burden of taxation and the perpetual annoyance of foreign rule. Druids could have a hand in rousing the people by appealing to the imperatives of the old religion (Syme 1958: 457). Whatever their private views about the druids, the chiefs would be prepared to reap the benefits of druidic influence on the people. Tacitus describes how the druids, by their spells (*canebant*), urged their countrymen to revolt in the period after the death of Vitellius in 69 AD (Tac. *Hist.* 4.54).

The gods whom the druids possibly tried to promote as national deities, such as Taranis, Esus, Teutates and Lugos (Ross 1968: 80), were not suppressed by the Romans, who sought where possible to integrate Celtic gods into their own religious system. Individual instances of druidic attachment were nevertheless punished severely. A chief of the Vocontii, a man with the status of Roman *eques*, was found during the course of a lawsuit in Rome to be in possession of a druidic talisman. He was put to death (Pliny *HN* 29.12). His punishment was intended to be exemplary. Pliny praises Rome for its destruction of a religion which placed such a high value on human sacrifice and cannibalism (*HN* 30.4). He had been procurator in Gallia Narbonensis and Gallia Belgica, and may be thought to have acquired some personal acquaintance with druidism. His personal hostility is clear enough. The druids can scarcely have eased his administrative burden as financial officer. He emphasises the magical aspects of the druids: perhaps during his time of duty in Gaul there was no other. Pliny and Lucan do not stress the high status of druids, but speak of them as savages. A similar attitude is adopted by Tacitus in relation to the druids and wild women on Anglesey. Making an appropriate discount for Roman prejudice, we may properly conclude that the mighty had fallen on harder times. But they were still there. Pliny attributes a healing as well as a magical function to them (*HN* 16.95; 24.62).

There is little mention of druidic influence in Britain before the revolt of Boudicca. It is true that Caesar regarded Britain as the home of druidism, and we cannot doubt the presence and influence of druids in Britain at the time of his expedition or imagine that they were passive members of British society between that time and 61 AD. But druids may not always or in all places have been the fanatical ideologues and exponents of ethnic tradition that the Romans describe. They may have been more aggressive when alien pressure was strongest and they were forced into such positions as we find described in Tacitus' account of the final terrible scenes on Anglesey. The Romans may have been surprised by the furious desperation of the druids and women on this occasion. We could argue that if this ecstasy of anger were the usual druidic reaction, it would have seemed less worthy of so strong a passage of prose in Tacitus. Tacitus uses the word *fanaticus* to describe their wild irrationality (*Ann.* 14.30.2). He applies the same word to an Aeduan religious and subversive leader in 69 AD, who claimed to be divine (*Hist.* 2.61). Tacitus is concerned to point out the contrast between the wild superstition of the Celts and the dignified religious ceremonies of the Romans (Salway 1981: 681). He has a rhetorical need to keep up the flow of antitheses and paradoxes in his narrative. In his view, the Celts of Britain are talented children of nature, in many ways less corrupt than the decadent and avaricious elements of the superior Roman civilisation which constantly confronts them. At the same time, the Celts were capable of extreme cruelty, as befits their character as children of nature. Unlike the best type of Roman, they are capable of a Bacchic savagery which stands in sharp contrast with the rational deliberation and Stoical constancy of the Roman mind. It is thus very difficult to find out anything reliable about the druids from Tacitus' account. We may be reasonably assured, however, that he is not describing British druids at the peak of their power and prestige. Suetonius Paulinus' treatment of them in Anglesey is in accordance with imperial policy towards them and their cult.

The maenadic women who assisted at the battle of Anglesey were not described as female druids. The virgin acolytes of Sena in Gaul are said to be prophetesses, but are not described as druidesses (Pomponius Mela 3.6). In other areas, prophetic women occur, as in the case of Veleda, who practised amongst the German Bructeri (69 AD). Of the writers who contribute to that late and contested work, the *Historia Augusta* (4th–5th centuries AD), Lampridius relates that a *mulier dryas*, which surely means a woman druid, foretold to Alexander Severus that he would be defeated. She spoke to him *Gallico sermone*, which probably means in Celtic. Another writer in *HA*, Vopiscus, tells us that Diocletian consulted a *dryadas*, a woman druid of the Belgic Tongri, and she foresaw an imperial crown for him. We recall that Ausonius had an aunt called Dryadia. These apparent female druids may indeed be what they seem to be; on the other hand, it is not impossible that in these later times in Gaul (as distinct from un-Romanised Ireland), women seers could simply be called druids, without being a participant in the genuine tradition. Their standing may have been no higher than that of the 'wise woman' of later British centuries.

The decline and death of druidism proper is related to the fact that it was an upper-class religion with little depth of affection in the minds of ordinary people, Celtic or subjects to the Celts. Its esoteric teachings, which were the substantial core of druidic prestige, had little popular appeal, for the simple reason that they were, in the first place, too complex; and secondly, were in no respect designed for popularisation. The magical and sacrificial aspects of druidism, which survived in various forms for centuries, inspired wider respect and fear. In Ireland, druids remained reputable longer. According to the Brehon law, there were three classes of people in pre-Patrician Ireland who were entitled to address the people: the historian, the *brehon* ('judge') and the poet. The first two of these are functions of the druid. Irish literary traditions agrees with Pliny that healing was a function of the druid and attributes great importance to druids in pagan times: Cathbad, the teacher of Cu Chulain, was a druid and he was also an influential adviser of the king of Ulaid. St Patrick found that druids were a force which was by no means trivial, but they were not dauntingly formidable, unless their power is understated by the Christian prejudice of later writers. This seems unlikely, since the more powerful the druid, the more glorious the achievement of the saint who gets the better of him.

Patrick's *Lorica* has some of the traits of a druidic spell. Like other ancient Irish Christian hymns, it requests comprehensive protection against the powers of pagan darkness. This comprehensiveness suggests an obsessive and almost pagan fear of attracting the hostility of some daemon by failing to mention all the points at which such a spirit might attack. The introduction to the *Lorica* in the Irish *Liber Hymnorum* makes this point unequivocally:

> Patrick composed this hymn. It was made in the time of Loegaire son of Niall. The reason for making it was of course that it should be protection [for him] along with his monks against the enemy agents of death that are in ambush against the clergy . . .   (Stokes and Strachan 1901: 354)

In the roster of enemies against whom he seeks divine protection, Patrick mentions the incantation of prophets (druidic spells?); the black judgements of heathens (the residual pagan rulers of Ireland); false judgements of heresy; other carriers of supernatural evil such as 'spells of women and of smiths and druids'; also every knowledge that overthrows the body and soul of man (Stokes and Strachan 1901: 357).

On the Continent, druids may have been at the height of their political influence in 121 BC, when the tribes of Gaul were in a state of greater unity than they were found to be by Julius Caesar. If we accept this, then we can say that from this point Continental druidism began to be a declining force in Celtic society. Even if it retained its prestige in Britain and Ireland for a longer time, it was ultimately to succumb, in these countries also, at the hands of Roman rulers in the former case; and of Christian in the latter. Druidism was defeated by Christianity in Ireland without the prodigious and protracted struggle that would be expected if it were a comprehensive religious ideology deeply rooted in the whole social fabric. In opposing the Roman Empire, the druids were fighting a civilisation rather than a set of doctrines. As Classical education spread in Celtic countries, it undercut and supplanted the intellectual prestige of the druids. In Christianity, the druids faced the hostile encroachments of Classical civilisation sharpened into a purposeful missionary ideology. They had neither the intellectual nor the spiritual resources to resist such an intruder.

Popular tradition in Celtic countries came to present the druids as sinister and undignified conjurors. The Romantic movement brought them a popularity in intellectual circles which was based on a conception of them that ancient evidence (such as it is) does not support (Ross 1968: 79). Our contemporary, benign and respectable druidic order is derived from such Romanticism. It is some tribute to the hold of druidism on the British imagination, that it should survive even in this metamorphosis.

15

Concluding Speculations

With the discussion of the religion of the Celts in Antiquity we come to the end of our review of the complex relationship over many centuries between the civilisation of the Mediterranean basin and the great aggregate of Celtic peoples which stretched across Europe and which, from the fourth century BC onwards, began to decline in power. In the centuries through which our discussion has ranged, there was scarcely any time when the Celts were not in some place seen as a menace, real or imagined, to the Mediterranean way of life represented by the Greek city-states and Rome with her allies and provinces. The intelligence and vigour of the Celts made them close in potential to the more settled societies of Greece and Rome. It was their primary physical energy in battle and their devotion to raiding that posed a special threat to the Classical world.

When the Celts invaded Greece in 278 BC, the likelihood is that Greece would have been wrecked, but not destroyed, by a Celtic victory. Greece was difficult in terrain and essentially out of range of Celtic capacities to overrun and colonise it. The Galatians of Asia Minor founded a powerful and lasting nation in the lands into which they were eventually thrust by the Hellenistic kingdoms, but their impact on the history of this sizeable continent was disproportionately small. A lateral federation of tribes made it difficult here, as elsewhere, for strong leadership to develop which could give effect to national policies. Consequently these Celts were used by others for the furtherance of alien policies.

The Celtic armies made a greater impact on Italy, part of which they made into a Celtic country. They helped to destroy, but could not replace, the advanced civilisation of Etruria. It was the misfortune of the Celts that they came into contact with Rome at a time when her energies were increasing. They managed to take most of Rome in 390 BC, but they were unable to destroy its identity. They implanted in the Roman mind a lasting fear of themselves, which had no trivial effects in moulding the attitude of Roman governments towards the Celtic tribes of Spain, Gaul and Britain.

Their own culture, unlike that of Rome, did not imbibe sufficient Hellenic and Helleno-Etrurian technical and theoretical knowledge in time for them to be able to withstand the expansive hostility of Rome, which had, in its highly organised army, the most efficient military machine yet devised. Also, the Celts were too late in beginning to form cities to benefit substantially from the increase in political and military efficiency that follows civic development. In spite of what ancient commentators said about such tribes as the Hispanic Vaccaei, the Celts remained politically at an undeveloped stage. They moved beyond the level of primitive monarchy in Gaul, but they never came close to evolving *dēmokratia*, or a functional mixed constitution like that of the Roman Republic. Nor did they ever have an overall monarchy which would have given them some of the benefits of centralisation. They preserved almost intact the aristocratic IE system of social classes. In spite of enjoying a relatively advanced culture and possessing a marked degree of inventive and imaginative talent in their society, they did not apply their natural gifts to the evolution of a political scheme which would have enabled them to enlarge their influence and territory on a permanent basis or even defend themselves effectively when they were invaded. In allowing the individual of warrior status free outlet for his heroic ambition, they made it difficult for society as a whole to coagulate into a resistant political tissue. Individuals amongst them had political acumen, but there was little or no political life as such, any more than there was amongst the Achaeans before the walls of Troy. Making every allowance, it must be said that the Celtic peoples of Antiquity showed the same tendency to schismatic infighting, the same delight in opposing each other, the same tragic tendency to call in the aid of rapacious foreigners, that have bedevilled their descendants and successors in Scotland and Ireland in the medieval and modern centuries. This attitude does credit to their lack of sense of racial exclusiveness, but it has helped to make the Celtic people of today dwellers on the margin, people whose main contribution to the political thought of Europe has been a sense of inspirational and dedicated resistance to alien government with a concomitant preservation of the idea of the heroic individual.

We may see in the Celts of the Ancient World an intense respect for tradition which could at times prove tactically crippling in the face of more organised enemies. Nothing suggests that they were able to criticise the assumptions upon which their lives were based. Their philosophies were sacral, not Socratic, and it is not easy to see that the druidic order (orders) would ever have allowed radical theorising to play a part in their teaching. Writing was little used, and certainly not for recording the historical experience of the tribe. History was oral and therefore had little chance of developing an analytical facility. The past could not easily be consulted. The tradition of knowledge was ceremonial rather than critical.

Though they are mostly assimilated with other ethnic and cultural groups, some identifiably Celtic patterns of living still survive on the edges of the European world. Even there, the inherited culture is being constantly eroded by the modern technological society which is a descendant of that Mediterranean civilisation with which the ancient Celts came into conflict. France is still in many ways Romanised Gaul, but not Celtic Gaul, though many of her inhabitants may physically be descended from the population of Caesar's time. The only independent modern nation which is largely descended from an earlier Celtic society is the Republic of Ireland. Even it is almost completely Anglicised. The fate of the contemporary Gael, that is, the native speaker of Irish with little or no English, at the hands of an essential Anglo-Saxon system of administration and law is admirably described by 'Flann O'Brien' (Brian O'Nolan) in his satirical novel *An Béal Bocht* ('The Poor Mouth'). Much of what he says could be applied to Gaelic-speaking Highlanders until comparatively recent times and also to native speakers of Welsh.

To say that the Celtic retreat to the margins of Europe began with the failure of Brennus to crush Rome in 390 BC may seem to be an extravagant proposition. It is indeed; but it is not entirely implausible. Contact with the Roman version of Hellenic civilisation destroyed what might have developed into a brilliant and creative Celtic-Hellenic society — if Greek ideas had been gradually filtered into the Celtic world through civilised points of contact such as Massalia. The German tribes occupied lands which lay beyond Rome's effective sphere of influence. Their independence remained largely unimpaired by Roman interference. While I understand that counterfactuals have no right to subsist in the bloodstream of historiography, I think we can nevertheless feel free to speculate about the possible development of Celtic society had it not been enmeshed in the greedy, socially inflexible and militaristic reticulations of Roman overlordship. We need not suppose that a typical Hellenistic monarchy would have emerged, since such a state did not evolve from the aggregation of Celtic tribes in Galatia. Admittedly, these Celtic tribes who settled in Asia Minor cannot be said to have added much of significance to the sum of human intellectual or artistic achievement.

I do not think that the heroic ideal of the warrior which predominated in the ancient Celtic societies, and which has to some degree survived in modern Celtic descended peoples, would have been an obstacle to a creative fusion of Celts and Hellenes. It was an ideal which they respected in common. The Greeks of the Classical period were heroically proud, and their education in the poems of Homer gave to the citizens of the most advanced democracy as yet achieved, fifth-century BC Athens, Achilles as their model. Heroic ideas did not impede the political development of the Greek city-state: they were the engine of the city's growth. Modern Greek *philótimo* is of the same tissue as Achilles' sense of the honour that was due to him.

We have seen that individuals from Celtic regions made important contributions to the literature of the Roman Empire. Britain was imperfectly Latinised, and contributed less; but it remained as a base of Classical and Celtic civilisation for some time after the Roman armies left. Latin became for a time the literary language of Ireland, a country never conquered by Rome. The Latin version of Christianity was implanted in Ireland and it carried with it many of the ideas of the Greco-Roman world, as well as the teachings of the Church. Latin was the main literary language of Ireland until 900 AD. Greek was scarcely known in Ireland at this time. In spite of optimistic traditions about its presence, there is no sure testimony to it.

If the *Confessio S. Patricii* is correct in its information, there was a native of Britain called Patricius in the fifth century AD, the son of Calpornus, who was taken prisoner by Irish pirates and lived for a time as a slave in Ireland. He later returned to the island as a Christian missionary. The place in which he had been held captive was called Fochut, and the women of Fochut appeared to him in a dream, beseeching him to return. He was by no means the first preacher of Christianity in Ireland, and other men with the same name as himself have been associated with the process of Christianising the country. The son of Calpornus is usually associated with the most successful missionary effort, which in its whole effect included the introduction of many aspects of Greco-Roman civilisation.

The Iron Age culture of Ireland embraced these Classical influences, and they were absorbed in native literary tradition of the Irish language. As time passed, Irish became an acceptable medium for literature. It is doubtful whether this would have happened without the inspiration of Latin examples. Reminiscences of Virgil's *Aeneid* break the stormy surface of the *Táin Bó Cúalgne* from time to time, and this saga would never have been written down without the influence of the book tradition of the Latin Christians. Yet like Homeric poetry, the *Táin* uses formulaic phrases which come from the earlier, oral tradition of composition (O'Nolan 1968). These features are evidence of an archaic origin for at least a portion of the material rather than of the actual influence of the *Iliad* or *Odyssey*. The *Aeneid* is a more likely literary influence upon the formation of the saga as we have it, which may well have been put into its first Irish-language version as early as the eighth century AD. Precise correlations of characters between the *Táin* and the *Aeneid*, such as the equation of the fearful goddess Alecto in the Latin poem with the Morrigan in the *Táin*, can hardly be sustained (MacCana 1972: 86–7). The *Táin* is very much itself and is unlike most other epic tales; but its identity could not have crystallised, even in its splintered surviving shape, without the influence of Latinity.

Just as some of the atmosphere of the pagan Iron Age is hermetically preserved in the *Táin*, so the rhetorical traditions of the Roman world, blended with the oral poetic and literary education of the Irish Celtic civilisation, have persisted through the centuries, in no respect less eloquently voiced because of the growing parallel tradition of written literature. In the nineteenth century AD Anthony Raftery, being blind, had of necessity to be a poet in the oral tradition. He was the product of the mainly oral education of a Hedge School, and his work is full of Classical allusions. We might argue that he belongs in an oral tradition stretching unbroken from the schools of Britain and of Gaul. The statement of this hypothesis can bring this book to an end. An attempt to sustain it would occupy the whole of another.

Abbreviations

Actas	*Actas del 'I' colloquio sobre lenguas y culturas preromanas de la peninsula iberica* (ed. Jordá, da Hoz and Michelena, Salamanca, 1974)
ANRW	*Aufstieg und Niedergang der Römischen Welt* (eds. Temperini and Haase, Berlin, 1972–)
AP	*Anthologia Palatina*
BB	*Bethu Brigte* (O hAodha)
CIG	*Corpus Inscriptiones Graecae*
CIL	*Corpus Inscriptionum Latinarum*
EIHM	*Early Irish history and mythology* (O'Rahilly)
Etym. Mag.	*Etymologicum Magnum*
FB	*Fled Bricrend* (ed. Henderson)
FF	*Foras Feasa ar Éirinn*
FGH	*Fragmente der Griechischen Historiker* (ed. Jacoby)
FHG	*Fragmenta Historicorum Graecorum* (ed. Müller)
Ha.	Hallstatt
HA	*Historia Augusta*
IE	Indo-European
imp.	*imperavit*
LB	*Leabar Breathnach: the Irish version of the Historia Britonum of Nennius* (ed. Todd, Dublin 1848)
LGE	*Lebor Gabála Érenn*
LT	La Tène
LU	*Lebor Uidre*
OGIS	*Orientis Graeci Inscriptiones Selecrtae* (ed. Dittenberger)
OIr.	Old Irish
PCB	*Pagan Celtic Britain* (Ross)
PG	*Patrologia Graeca* (Migne)
PIE	Proto-Indo-European
PL	*Patrologia Latina* (Migne)
reg.	*regnavit*
Skt.	Sanskrit
Sot.	*Soteria* (Nachtergael)
TBC	*Taín Bó Cúalgne*
YBL	*Yellow Book of Lecan*

Bibliography

Alföldi, G. (1974) *Noricum*, translated by A. Birley, Routledge and Kegan Paul, London

Anderson, J.G.C. (ed.) (1938) *Tacitus. De origine et situ Germanorum*, Oxford University Press, Oxford

Anderson, R.D., Parsons, P.J. and Nisbet, R.G.M. (1979) 'Elegiacs by Gallus from Qaṣr Ibrim', *Journal of Roman Studies*, 69, 125–55

Arribas, A. (1981) *The Iberians*, Thames and Hudson, London

Bachelier, E. (1960) 'Les Druides en Gaule', *Ogam*, 12, 91–100

Bachellery, É. (1972) 'Le Celtique continental', *Études Celtiques*, 13, 29–60

Beneš, B. (1960) 'Spuren von Schamanismus in der Saga *Buile Suibhne*', *Zeitschrift für Celtische Philologie*, 28, 309–332

Benveniste, E. (1973) *Indo-European language and society*, London

Berciu, D. (1967) *Romania before Bourebista*, Thames and Hudson, London

Betham, W. (1842) *Etruria Celtica*, Hardy, Dublin

Bicknell, P.J. (1962) 'Gaius and the sea-shells', *Acta Classica*, 5, 72–4

Bienkowski, P.R. von (1908) *Die Darstellungen der Gallier in der hellenistischen Kunst*, A. Hölder, Vienna

Binchy, D.A. (1970) 'Celtic and Ango-Saxon kingship', *The O'Donnell Lectures for 1967–8*, Oxford University Press, Oxford

Bjersby, B. (1951) 'The interpretation of the Cu Chulain legend in the works of W.B. Yeats', *Irish Studies*, I

Bonfante, G. (1946) 'Indo-Hittite and Areal linguistics', *American Journal of Philology*, 268, 289–310

Bouchier, E.S. (1914) *Spain under the Roman Empire*, Oxford University Press, Oxford

Burkert, W. (1983) *Homo necans, the anthropology of ancient Greek sacrificial ritual and myth*, California University Press, California

Cáin Adamnáin: see Meyer, K.

Cary, M. (1949) *The geographical background to Greek history*, Oxford University Press, Oxford

Chadwick, H.M. (1949) *Early Scotland. The Picts, the Scots, and the Welsh of southern Scotland*, Oxford University Press, Oxford

Chadwick, N. (1963) *Celtic Britain*, Thames and Hudson, London

—— (1966) *The Druids*, University of Wales, Cardiff

—— (1984) *The Celts*, Penguin, Harmondsworth

Champion, T. (1975) 'Britain in the European Iron Age', *Archaeologia Atlantica*, I. 2, 127–45

—— (1980) 'Mass migration in later prehistoric Europe' in P. Sörbom (ed.) *Transport Technology and Social Change*, Stockholm, 33–42

Chevallier, R. (1962) 'La Celtique du Pô, position des problèmes', *Eranos*, 21, 356–370

Chilver, G.E.F. (1941) *Cisalpine Gaul, A social and economic history from 49 BC to the death of Trajan*, Oxford University Press, Oxford

Cichorius, C. (1922) 'Petronius und Massilia' in his *Römische Studien*, Berlin

Clerc, M. (1929) *Histoire de Marseille dans l'antiquité*, Marseilles
Comrie, B. (1981) *The languages of the Soviet Union*, Cambridge University Press, Cambridge
Cunliffe, B. (1973) *The Regni*, Duckworth, London
Curtin, J. (1890) *Myths and folklore of Ireland*, Little, Brown and Co., Boston
Davies, W. (1983) 'Celtic women in the Early Middle Ages' in A. Kuhrt and A. Cameron (eds.) *Images of women in antiquity*, Croom Helm, London, 145–66
De La Ville Mirmont, H. (1902) 'L'Astrologie chez les Gallo-Romaines', *Revue des Études Anciennes*, 4, 115–41
DeVries, J. (1960) *Kelten und Germanen*, Francke, Bern and Munich
———— (1963) *La Religion des Celts*, Payot, Paris
Dillon, M. (1944) 'Italic and Celtic', *American Journal of Philology*, 258, 124–34
———— (1947) 'The Hindu act of truth in Celtic tradition', *Modern Philology*, 44.3, 137–40
———— (1975) *Celts and Aryans*, Indian Institute of Advanced Study, Simla
Dinan, W. (1911) *Monumenta Historica Celtica*, vol. 1, D. Nutt, London
Dodds, E.R. (1951) *The Greeks and the irrational*, California University Press, California
Dottin, G. (1915) *Manuel pour servir à l'étude d l'antiquité celtique*, H. Champion, Paris
———— (1920) *La Langue gauloise*, Paris
Drinkwater, J.F. (1983) *Roman Gaul*, Croom Helm, London
Dudley, D.R. and Webster, G. (1962) *The rebellion of Boudicca*, Routledge and Kegan Paul, London
Dudley Edwards, R. (1977) *Padraig Pearse, the triumph of failure*, Faber, London
Dumézil, G. (1970) *Archaic Roman religion* translated by P. Krapp, University of Chicago Press, Chicago and London
Dunbabin, T.J. (1948) *The western Greeks*, Oxford University Pres, Oxford
Dunnett, R. (1975) *The Trinovantes*, Duckworth, London
Ebel, C. (1976) Transalpine Gaul, Brill, Leiden
Elliott, R.C. (1960) *The power of satire*, Princeton University Press, Princeton
Evans, D.E. (1967) *Gaulish personal names*, Oxford University Press, Oxford
Evans, D.S. (1976) *A grammar of Middle Welsh*, Institute for Advanced Studies, Dublin
Evans, E. (1983) 'Language contact in pre-Roman and Roman Britain', *ANRW*, II.29.2, 949–87
Ferguson, J. (1956) *Pelagius, a historical and theological study*, Cambridge University Press, Cambridge
Fisher, G.J. (1981) 'Studies in fourth and fifth-century literature with particular reference to Ausonius' (PhD Diss. University of Southampton)
Friedrich, P. (1966) 'Proto-Indo-European kinship', *Ethnology*, 5.1, 1–36
Gimbutas, M. (1963) 'The Indo-Europeans: Archaeological problems', *American Anthropologist*, 65, 815–36

Gordon, M.L. (1934) 'The family of Vergil', *Journal of Roman Studies*, 24, 1–12

Gregory, A. (1902) *Cu Chulain of Muirthemne*, John Murray, London

Greene, D. (1967) 'The Celtic languages', in J. Raftery (ed.) *The Celts*, Radio Teilifís Éireann, Cork

Gwynn, E. (1900–35) *The metrical Dindshenchas*, Todd Lecture Series, pt 1 (1900), pt 2 (1906), pt 3 (1913), pt 4 (1924), pt 5 (1935), Royal Irish Academy, Dublin

Haarhoff, T.J. (1920) *The schools of Gaul: a study of pagan and Christian education in the last century of the Western Empire*, Oxford University Press, Oxford

Hamp, E. (1962) 'Consonant allophones in Proto-Celtic', *Lochlainn*, I, 207–17

Henderson, G. (1899) *Fled Bricrend: the feast of Bricriu: an early Gaelic saga transcribed from older manuscripts into the book of the dun cow by Moelmuri Mac Mic Cuinn na m-Bocht*, Irish Texts Society, London

Hind, J. (1972) 'Pyrene and the date of the Massiliot sailing manual', *Rivista Storica dell' Antichità*, 2, 39–52

Hoddinott, R.F. (1981) *The Thracians*, Thames and Hudson, London

Holland, L.A. (1979) *Lucretius and the Transpadanes*, Princeton University Press, Princeton

Hopkins, K. (1961) 'Social mobility in the later Roman Empire', *Classical Quarterly*, n.s. II, 239–48

Hornblower, J. (1981) *Hieronymus of Cardia*, Oxford University Press, Oxford

Hubert, H. (1934) *The greatness and decline of the Celts*, Routledge and Kegan Paul, London

Jackson, K.H. (1953) *Language and history in early Britain*, University of Edinburgh, Edinburgh

Jazdzewski, K. (1965) *Poland*, Thames and Hudson, London

Jenkins, D. and Owen, M.E. (1980) (eds) *The Welsh law of women*, Cardiff University Press, Cardiff

Joffroy, R. (1954) *Le Trésor de Vix*, Presses Universitaires de France, Paris

Joyce, P.W. (1913) *A social history of ancient Ireland*, 2 vols., Longmans, Green and Co., Dublin

Jullian, C. (1891) 'Ausone et son temps', *Revue Historique*, 241–66

—— (1906) 'La Chute du ciel sur les Gaulois', *Revue des Études Anciennes*, 8, 259

Keating, G. (ed.) and Comyn, D. (trans.) (1901) *Foras Feasa ar Éirinn*, Irish Texts Society, London

Keller, R.E. (1978) *The German language*, Faber, London

Kendrick, T.D. (1927) *The Druids*, Methuen, London

Killeen, J.F. (1965) 'The word *Ogam*', *Lochlainn*, 3, 415–9

Latte, K. (1960) 'Römische Religionsgeschichte', *Handbücher der Altertums-wissenschaft*, 5, 4

Lazenby, J.F. (1978) *A military history of the Second Punic War*, Aris and Phillips, Warminster

Lejeune, M. (1955) 'Celtiberica', *Acta Salamantica*, 7.4

Lévi-Strauss, C. (1972) *Structural Anthropology* translated by C. Jacobson and B. Grundfest Schoepf, Penguin, Harmondsworth

Lloyd, S. (1967) *Early highland peoples of Anatolia*, Thames and Hudson, London

Lovejoy, A.O. and Boas, G. (1935) *Primitivism and related ideas in Antiquity*, Johns Hopkins University, Baltimore

Lockwood, W.B. (1972) *A panorama of Indo-European languages*, Hutchinson, London

MacAlister R.A.S. (1937) *The secret languages of Ireland*, Cambridge University Press, Cambridge

MacCall, C. (1980) 'The moral paradigms of a woman's life' in D. Jenkins and M.E. Owen (eds.), *The Welsh law of women*, Cardiff University Press, Cardiff, 7–22

MacCana, P. (1972) 'Conservation and Innovation in Early Celtic Literature' *Études Celtiques*, 13, 61–119

——— (1979) *'Regnum* and *Sacerdotium*: Notes on Irish tradition', *Proceedings of the British Academy*, LXV, 443–79

MacNeill, M. (1962) *The festival of Lugnasa: a study of the survival of the Celtic festival of the beginning of the harvest*, Irish Folklore Commission, Oxford University Press, Oxford

MacWhite, E. (1957) 'Problems of Irish archaeology and Celtic philology', *Zeitschrift für Celtische Philologie*, 25, 1–29

Marx, F. (1899) 'Der Dichter Lucretius', *Neue Jahrbücher für das Klassische Altertum*, 8, 532–48

Meid, W. (1972) 'Old Celtic Languages', *Current Trends in Linguistics*, 9, 1190–1201

Mette, H.J. (1952) *Pytheas von Massilia*, De Gruyter, Berlin

Meyer, K. (1904) 'The death of Connla (*YBL*)', *Ériu*, 1, 113–21

——— (ed.) (1905) *Cáin Adomnáin. An Old Irish Treatise on the law of Adomnan*, Oxford University Press, Oxford

Minns, E.H. (1913) *Scythians and Greeks*, Cambridge University Press, Cambridge

Momigliano, A. (1975) *Alien wisdom: the limits of Hellenisation*, Cambridge University Press, Cambridge

Morel, J.-P. (1966) 'Les Phocéens en occident: certitudes et hypothèses', *Parola del Passato*, 21, 370–420

Murray, M. (1970) *The god of the witches*, Oxford University Press, Oxford

Nachtergael, G. (1977) 'Les Galates en Grèce et les Sôteries de Delphes'. Recherches d'histoire et d'épigraphie hellénistiques', *Academie Royale de Belgique: Memoires de la Classe de Lettres*, 63, 1

Neustupny, E. and Neustupny, J. (1961) *Czechoslovakia before the Slavs*, Thames and Hudson, London

O hAodha, D. (1978) *Bethu Brigte*, Institute of Advanced Studies, Dublin

O'Donovan, J. (1845) *A grammar of the Irish language*, Hodges and Smith, Dublin

O'Nolan, K. (1968) 'Homer and the Irish hero tale', *Studia Hibernica*, 8, 7–20

——— (1975) 'The use of formula in story telling', *Béaloideas*, 39–41, 233–56

O'Rahilly, Cecile (1970) *Taín Bó Cúalgne from the Book of Leinster*, Institute of Advanced Studies, Dublin

O'Rahilly, T.F. (1946) *Early Irish history and mythology*, Institute of

Advanced Studies, Dublin

Owen, M. (1980) 'Shame and reparation: women's place in the kin' in D. Jenkins and M.E. Owen (eds), *The Welsh law of women*, Cardiff University Press, Cardiff, 48–68

Page, D.L. (1962) *Select papyri*, Heinemann, London

Parke, H.W. and Wormell, D.E.W. (1956) *The Delphic Oracle*, Blackwell, Oxford

Peter, H. (ed.) (1906–14) *Historicorum Romanorum Reliquiae*, 2 vols., Teubner, Leipzig

Phillips, E.D. (1965) *The royal hordes*, Thames and Hudson, London

Piggott, S. (1962) *The Druids*, Thames and Hudson, London

—— (1983) *The earliest wheeled transport from the Atlantic coast to the Caspian sea*, Thames and Hudson, London

Pokorny, J. (1938) *Zur Urgeschichte der Kelten und Illyrier*, Halle

Pollitt, J.J. (1986) *Art in the Hellenistic age*, Cambridge University Press, Cambridge

Polomé, E.C. (1983) 'The linguistic situation in the western Provinces of the Roman Empire', *ANRW*, II.29.2, 509–53

Posani, M.R. (1962) 'Reminiscenze di poeti latini nella *Mosella* di Ausonio', *Studi Italiani di Filologia Classica* ' 34, 31–69

Powell, J.U. (1925) *Collectanea Alexandrina*, Oxford University Press, Oxford

Powell, T.G.E. (1958) *The Celts*, Thames and Hudson, London

Puhvel, J. (ed.) (1970a) *Myth and law amongst the Indo-Europeans. Studies in Indo-European comparative mythology*, California University Press, California

—— (1970b) 'Aspects of equine functionality' in J. Puhvel, *Myth and law amongst the Indo-Europeans. Studies in Indo-European comparative mythology*, California University Press, California, 159–72

Ramm, H. (1978) *The Parisi*, Duckworth, London

Ramsay, W.M. (1895–7) *The cities and bishoprics of Phrygia*, Arno, New York

—— (1900) *A historical commentary on St Paul's Epistle to the Galatians*, Hodder and Stoughton, London

Rankin, H.D. (1964) *Plato and the individual*, Methuen, London

—— (1971) *Petronius the artist*, Nijhoff, The Hague

Rhys, J. (1898) *Lectures on the origin and growth of religion as illustrated by Celtic heathendom*, Hibbert Lectures of 1886, London and Edinburgh

—— (1905–6) 'Celtae and Galli', *Proceedings of the British Academy*, 71–133

—— (1913) 'The Celtic inscriptions of Cisalpine Gaul', *Proceedings of the British Academy*, 6, 1–112

Robertson, M. (1975) *A history of Greek art*, Cambridge University Press, Cambridge

Ross, A. (1968) *Pagan Celtic Britain: studies in iconography and tradition*, Routledge and Kegan Paul, London

Ryan, J. (1936) 'The *Cáin Adomnáin* studies', *Studies in early Irish law*

Salway, P. (1981) *Roman Britain, The Oxford history of England*, Vol. 1 (Oxford University Press, London)

Savory, H.N. (1968) *Spain and Portugal: the prehistory of the Iberian peninsula*, Thames and Hudson, London

Schmidt, K.H. (1983) 'Keltisch-lateinische Sprachkontakte im römischen

Bibliography

Gallien der Kaiserzeit', *ANRW*, II.29.2, 988–1018
——— 'The contribution of Celt-Iberian to the reconstruction of Common Celtic' *Actas*, 329–342
Schmoll, U. (1958) *Die Sprachen der vorkeltischen Indogermanen Hispaniens und das Keltiberische*, Wiesbaden
Scott, T. (1966) *Dunbar, a critical exposition of the poems*, Oliver and Boyd, Edinburgh
Scott Littleton, C. (1970) 'The "Kingship in Heaven Theme"', in J. Puhvel (ed.), *Myth and law amongst the Indo-Europeans. Studies in Indo-European comparative mythology*, California University Press, California, 83–121
Sedgwick, W.B. (1930) 'Anient *jeux d'esprit* and poetical eccentricities', *Classical Weekly*, 24, 153–7
Sherwin White, A.N. (1967) *Racial prejudice in Imperial Rome*, Cambridge University Press, Cambridge
Schröder, A. (1921) 'De ethnographiae antiquae locis quibusdam communibus observationes', Dissertation, Halle
Stähelin, F. (1907) *Geschichte der kleinasiatischen Galater*, 2nd edn, Leipzig
Stokes, W. (1894) 'Urkeltischer Sprachschatz' in A. Fick (ed.) *Vergleichendes Wörterbuch der Indogermanischen Sprachen 2*, Vanderhoek und Rupprecht, Göttingen
——— and Strachan, J. (1901) *Thesaurus Palaeohibernicus*, Cambridge University Press, Cambridge
Sullivan, J.P. (1976) *The genesis of Hiberno-English*, Dissertation, Yeshiva University
Syme, R. (1939) *The Roman revolution*, Oxford University Press, Oxford
——— (1958) *Tacitus*, 2 vols., Oxford University Press, Oxford
Szabo, M. (1971) *The Celtic heritage in Hungary*, Budapest
Thompson, E.A. (1949) *The historical works of Ammianus Marcellinus*, Cambridge University Press, Cambridge
Thurneysen, R. (1921) *Die irische Helden- und Königsage bis zum siebzehnten Jahrhundert* (Halle)
——— (1928) 'Die Bürgschaft im Irischen Recht', *Preussische Akademie der Wissenschaften. Phil.-Hist. Klasse, 2*
Tierney, J.J. (1960) 'The Celtic ethnography of Poseidonius', *Proceedings of the Royal Irish Academy*, 60, 189–246
Tovar, A. (1958) 'Das Keltiberische, ein neuer Zweig des Festlandkeltischen', *Kratylos*, 3, 1–13
——— (1961) *The ancient languages of Spain and Portugal*, S.F. Vanni, New York
——— (1973) *Sprachen und Inschriften: Studien zum Mykenischen Lateinischen und Hispanokeltischen*, Amsterdam
Toynbee, A. (1965) *Hannibal's legacy: the Hannibalic War's effects on Roman life*, 2 vols., Oxford University Press, Oxford
Van Hamel, A.G. (1934) 'Aspects of Celtic mythology', Rhys Memorial Lecture, *Proceedings of the British Academy*, 20, 207–48
Vendryes, J. 'Les Correspondences de vacabulaire entre L'indo-iranien et l'italo-celtique', *Mémoires de la Société de Linguistique*, 20.6, 265–85
Wagner, H. (1971) *Studies in the origins of the Celts and of early Celtic civilisation*, The Queen's University, Belfast

Wainwright, F.T. (1958) *The Problem of the Picts*, Edinburgh University Press, Edinburgh

Walbank, F.W. (1957–79) *A historical commentary on Polybius*, 3 vols., Oxford University Press, Oxford

Watkins, C. (1963) 'Indo-European metres and archaic Irish verse', *Celtica*, 6, 194–249

―――― (1966) 'Ancient Indo-European dialects' in H. Birnbaum and J. Puhvel (eds), *Proceedings of the Conference on Indo-European Linguistics*, California University Press, California, 29–57

Weisweiler, J. (1953) 'Die Stellung der Frau bei den Kelten und das Problem des "Keltischen Mutterrechts"', *Zeitschrift für Celtische Philologie*, 21.2, 205–79

Wells, C.M. (1972) *The German policy of Augustus*, Oxford University Press, Oxford

Wennig, R. (1978) *Die Galateranatheme Attalus I* (Berlin)

Whatmough, J. (1970) *A study of the dialects of Ancient Gaul* (Ann Arbor)

Windisch, E. (1880) *Irische Texte*, Leipzig

Wiseman, F.J. (1956) *Roman Spain*, Bell, London

Index